AF348392

Lise Herzog

365 DAYS OF DRAWING PEOPLE

FIREFLY BOOKS

When starting to draw figures, we often forget to add depth and movement
to the volumes, that is, the spaces occupied by the figures.

The body is made up of the same simple shapes that make up everything
else around us: circles, ovals, straight lines, angles… The only differences are
the number of shapes used and the ratios created by their different sizes.

It's therefore important to carefully observe a figure's different volumes —
and to look past and through them — before getting started.

In fact, when a figure is not in a simple pose, such as standing straight
and viewed head-on or in profile, the articulated lines that make it up are
affected by perspective, which changes the proportions.

To differentiate a female figure from a more masculine one, for example,
you can adjust the width of the volumes in proportion to each other, even if
this means exaggerating a little, although in real life a body is almost never
so cartoonish.

Each drawing is an essential step, easy or difficult, on the road to progress.
The best way to improve your skills is therefore to draw regularly, so why not
draw every day for an entire year?

Date of first drawing:

....

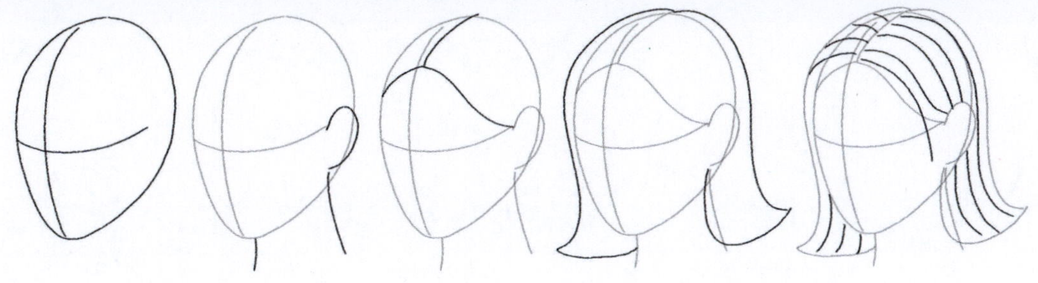

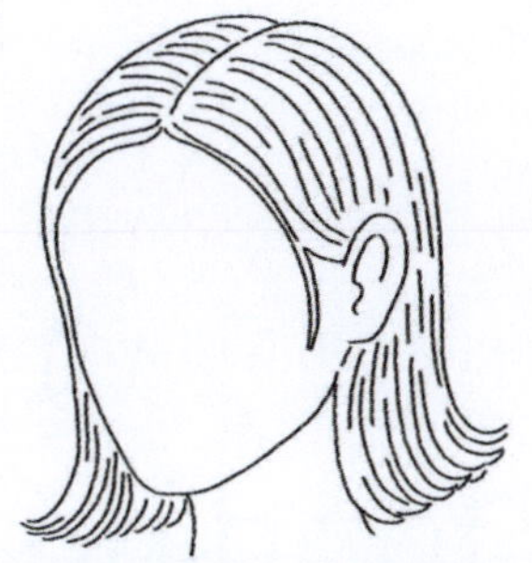

Straight Hair

To draw straight hair, keep the lines relatively straight and space them out a bit.

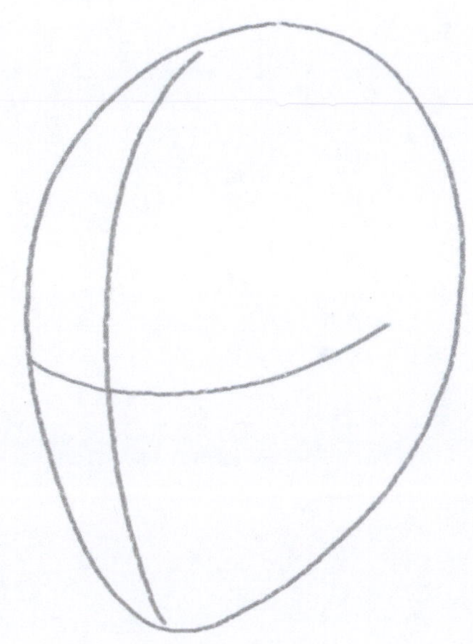

1st **day**

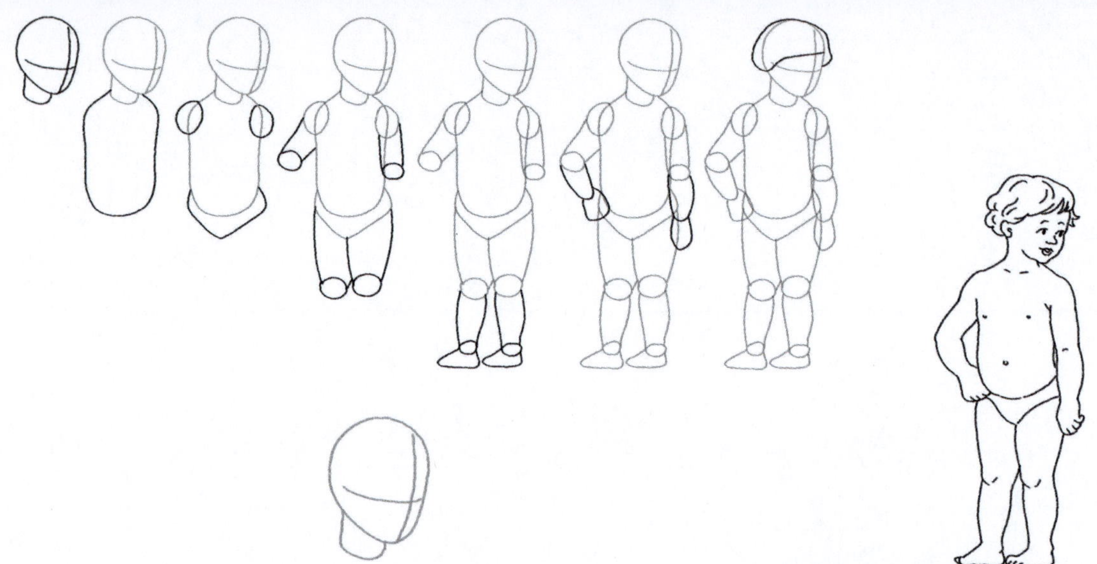

Standing Toddler

A young child's proportions are fairly compact and rounded. You don't actually need to accentuate the height.

2nd day

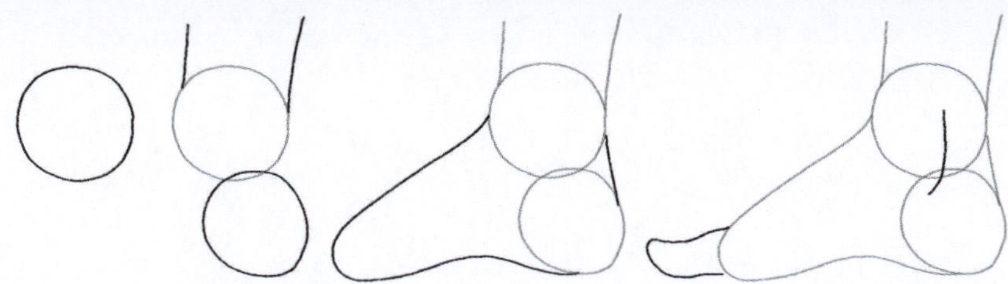

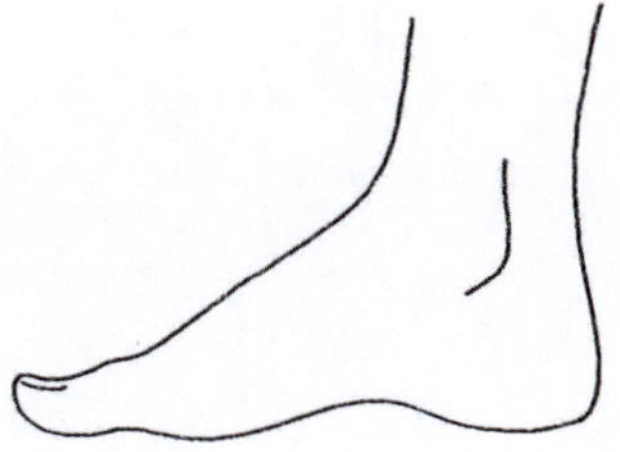

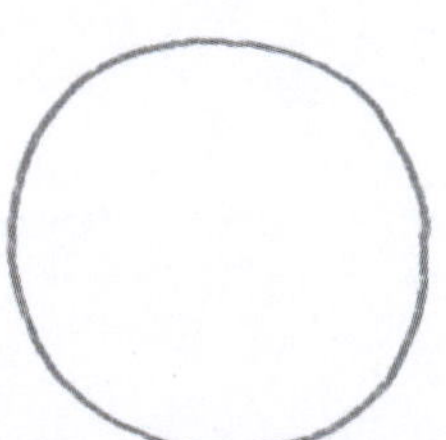

Foot

When a foot is viewed in profile, the inward curves under the toes and along the arch are visible. The top of the foot is slightly convex, while the ankle is more concave.

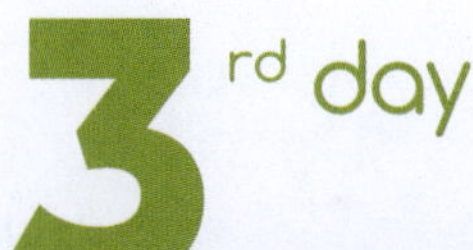

3 rd day

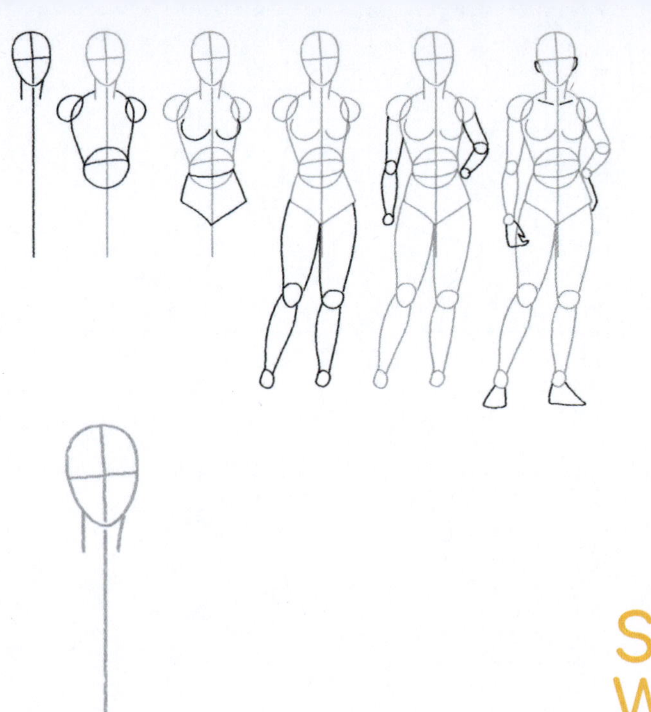

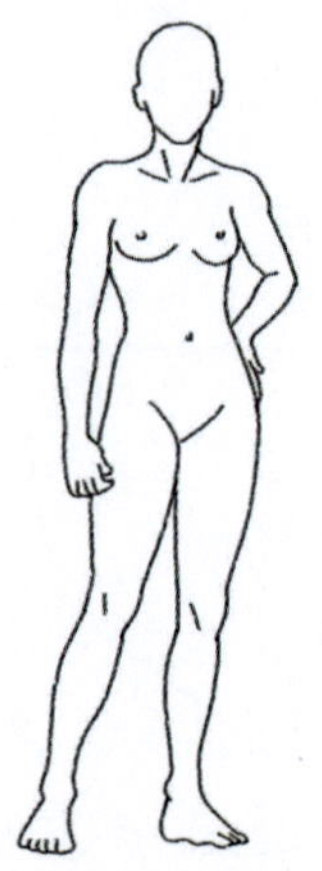

Standing
Woman

In this pose, there is a slight swing to the hips, which is emphasized by the placement of the arms and the slightly bent leg.

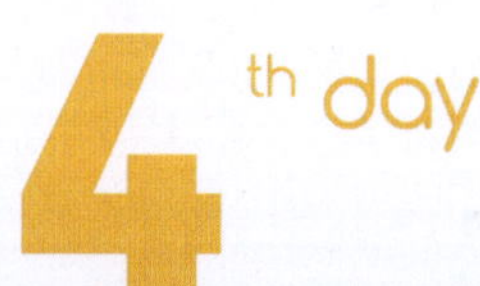

4th day

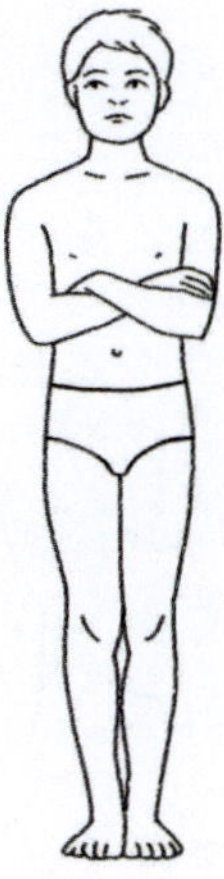

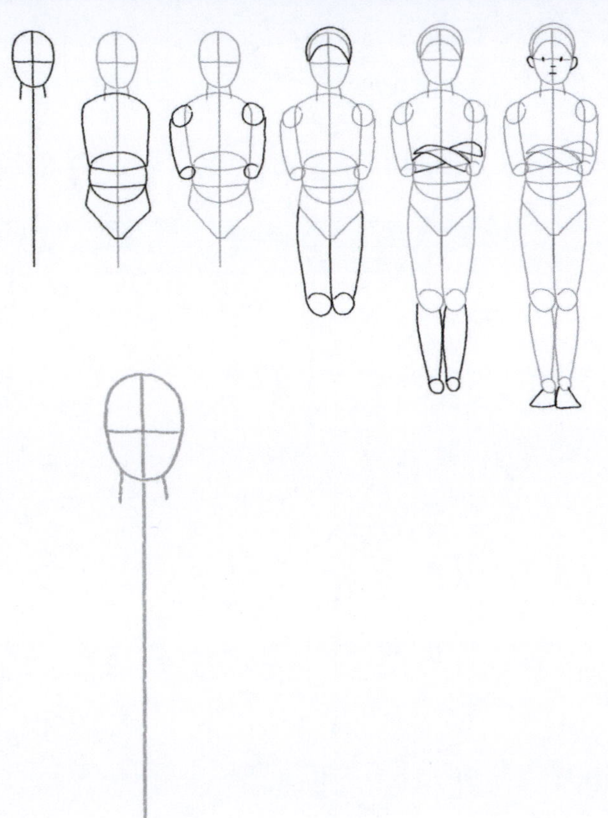

Young Boy

When a boy between the ages of 8 and 12 years is viewed head-on, you can see the shoulders starting to develop and become a bit broader. The waist is slimmer, but the head remains a little large compared to the rest of the body.

5th day

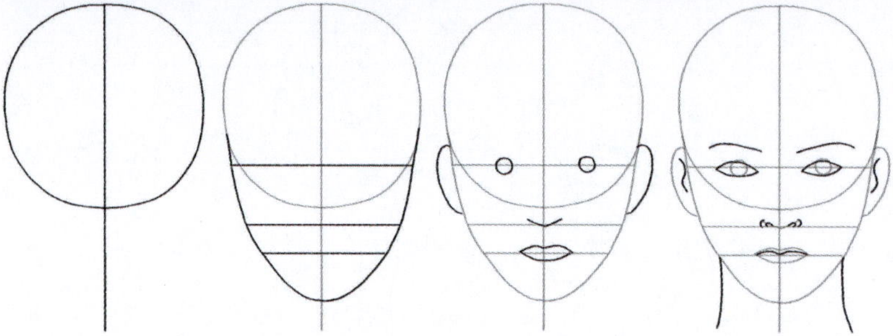

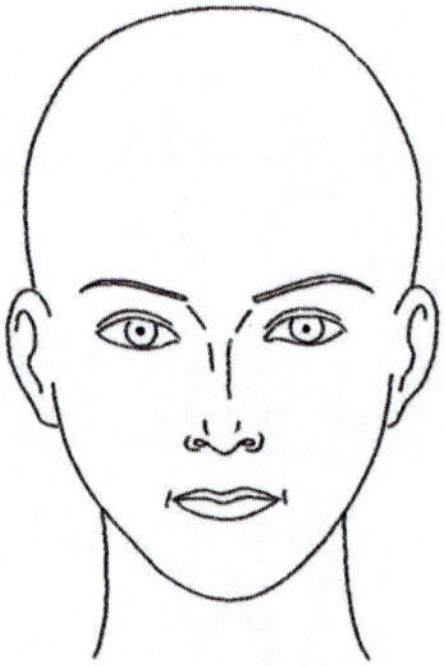

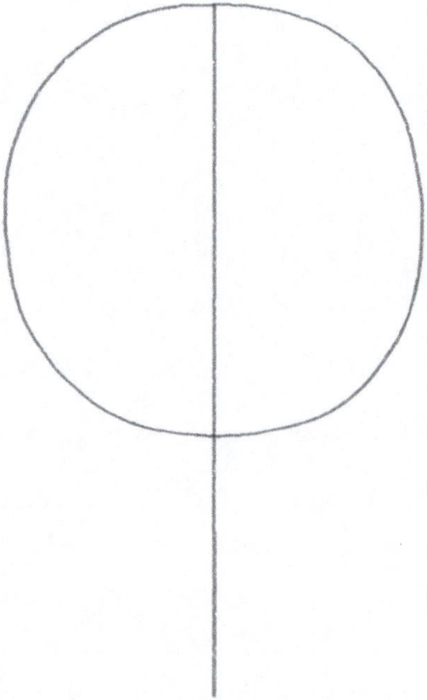

Woman's Head

To draw a woman's face from the front, trace a central axis and lay out the various elements in symmetry, following the rules of proportion.

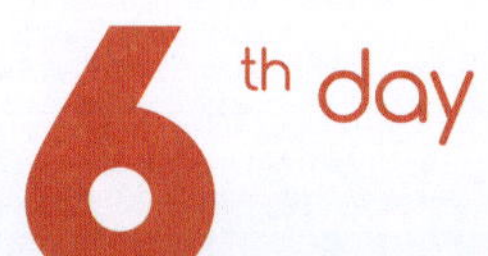

6th day

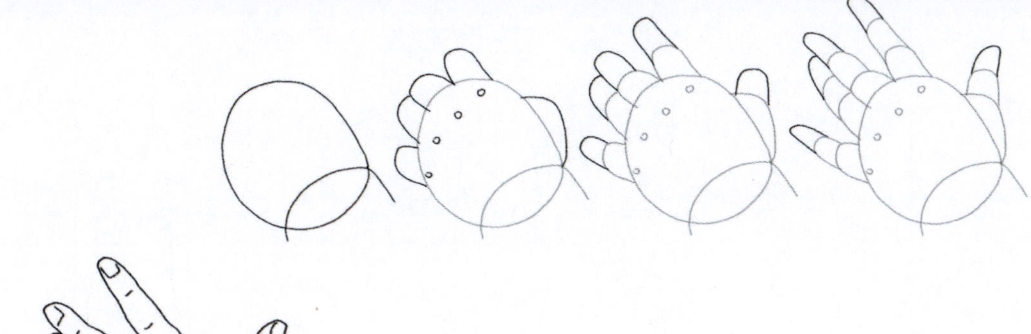

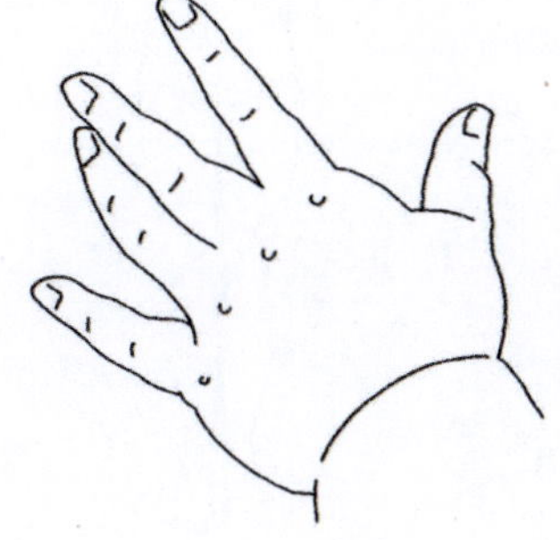

Baby's Hand

A baby's hand has a rounded palm and very short, chubby fingers with pointed tips.

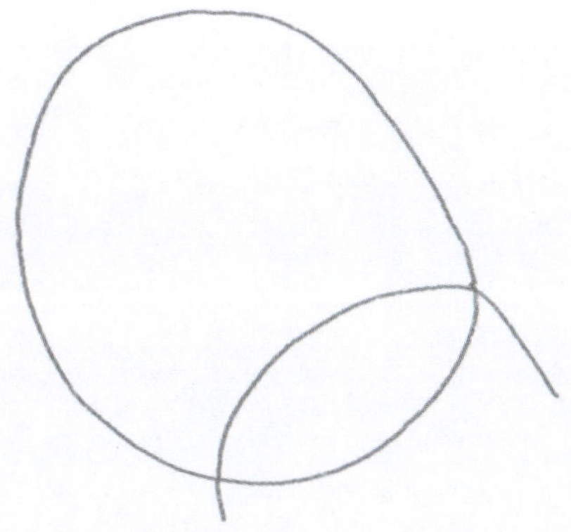

7th day

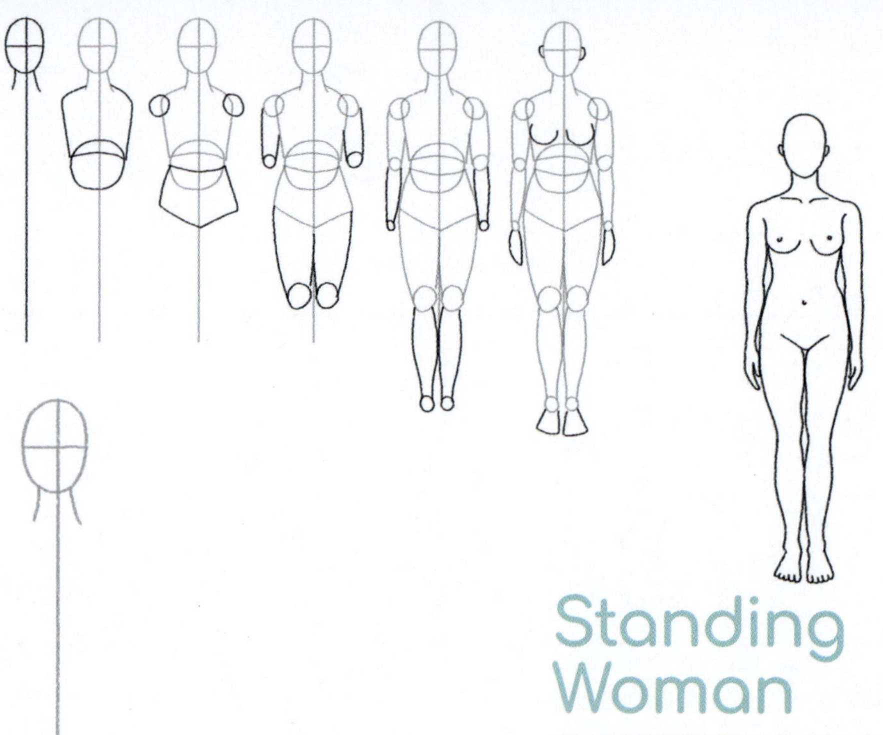

Standing Woman

It's relatively easy to represent a woman's shape from the front: slightly wider hips, narrower shoulders, a slim torso and slim ankles, knees, elbows and other joints.

8 th day

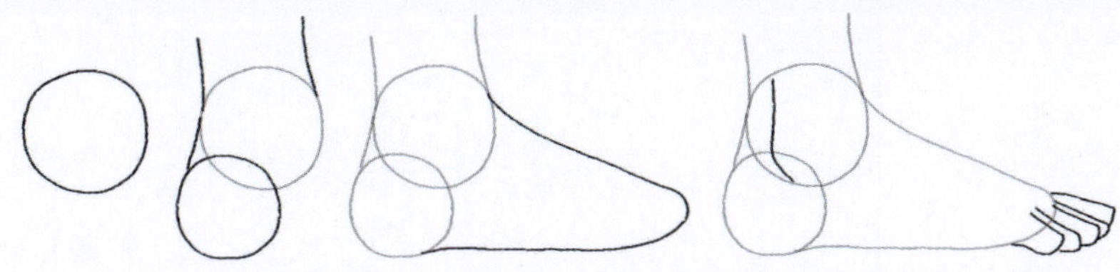

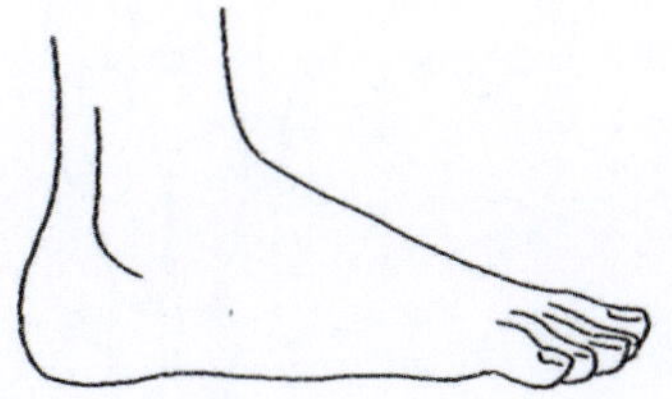

Foot

When the outer side of a foot is viewed in profile, you can see the alignment of the toes. The sole is relatively flat.

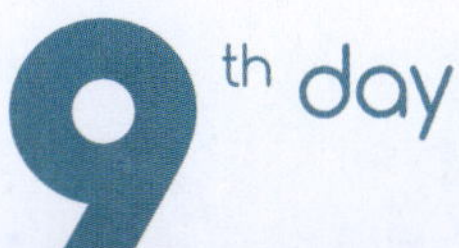

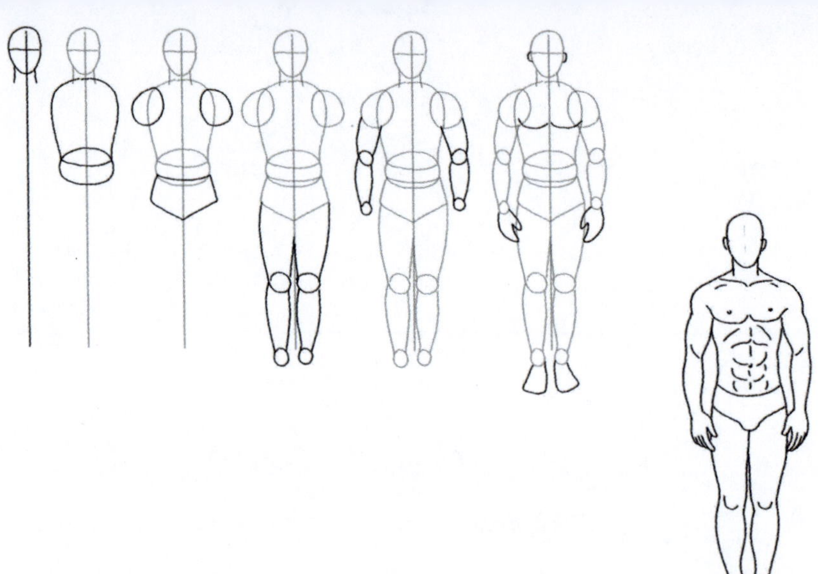

Standing Man

The more lines you add, the more muscles you create. A very muscular torso is fairly broad and well developed.

10th day

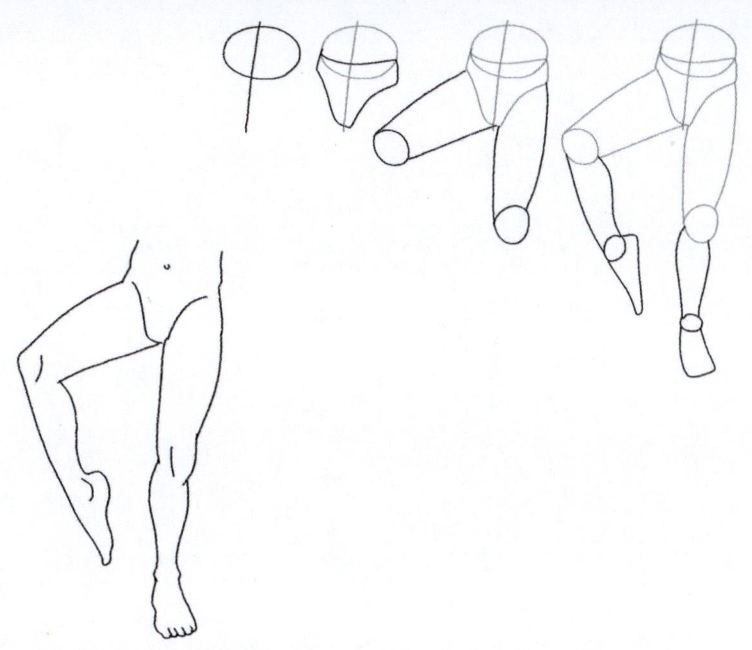

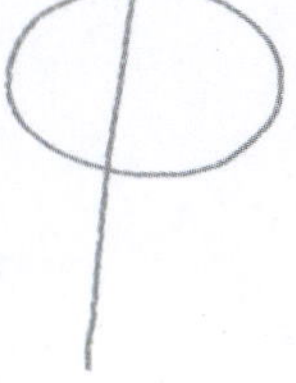

Man's Legs

A close-up of a man's legs shows the contours of the muscles and the lines along the knees and ankles.

11th day

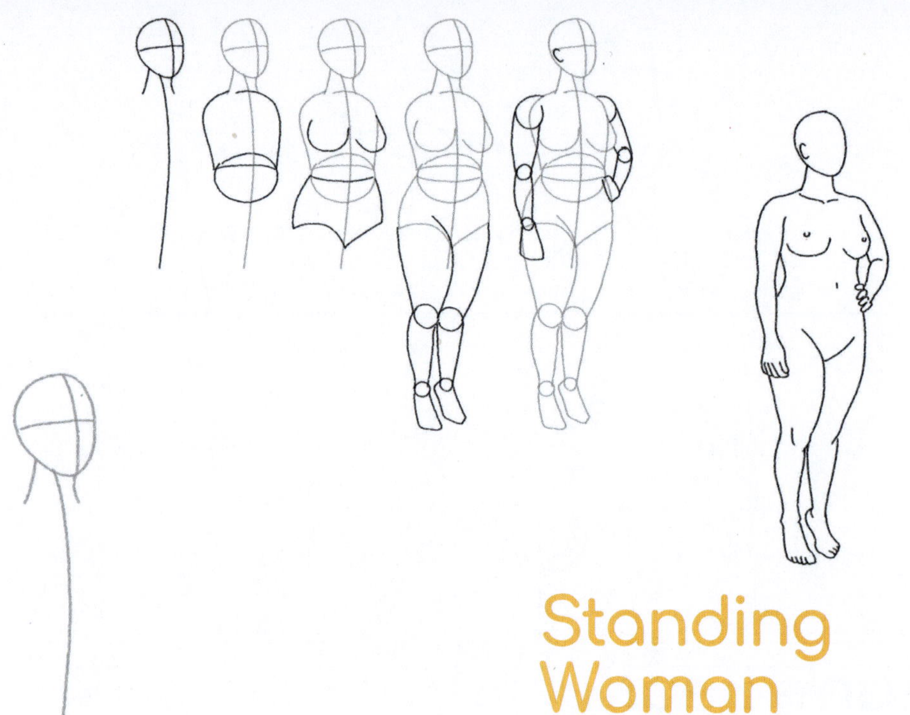

Standing Woman

A more voluptuous woman still has fairly slim joints. The section between the knees and shoulders is a bit thicker.

12th day

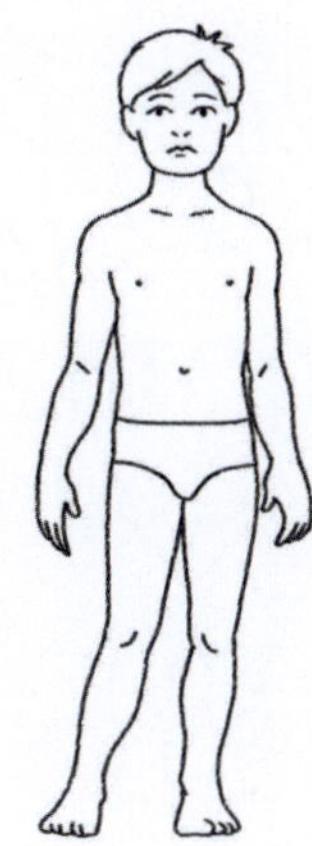

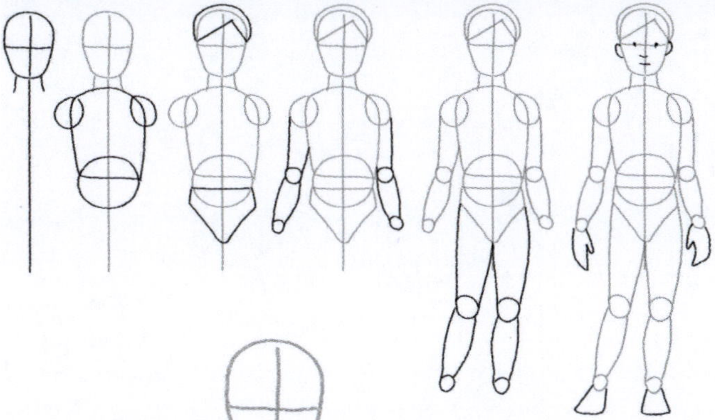

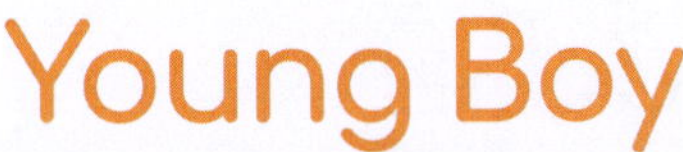

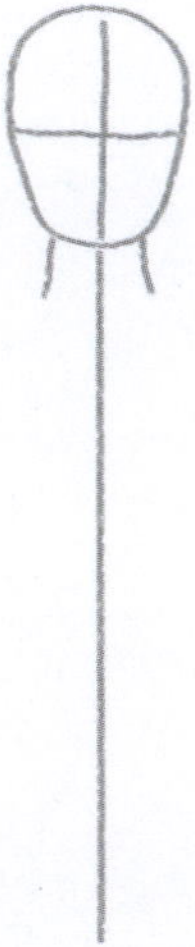

Young Boy

When a boy younger than eight years old is viewed from the front, the torso appears to be fairly broad in relation to the length of the arms and legs, and the head is quite large in relation to the rest of the body.

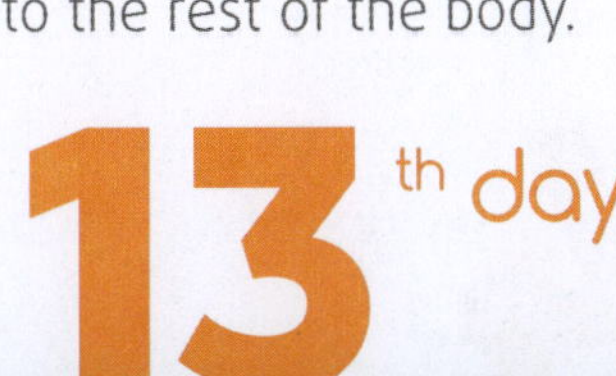

13 **th day**

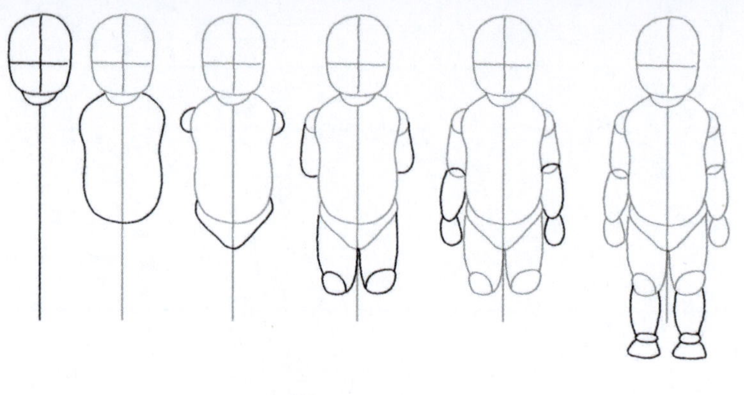

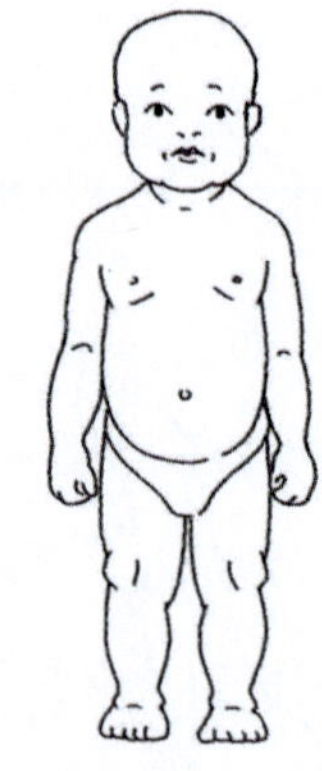

Toddler

Viewed from the front, a toddler's torso is a large oval with a slight depression in the middle. The head is large, and the legs are very short.

14 14 th day

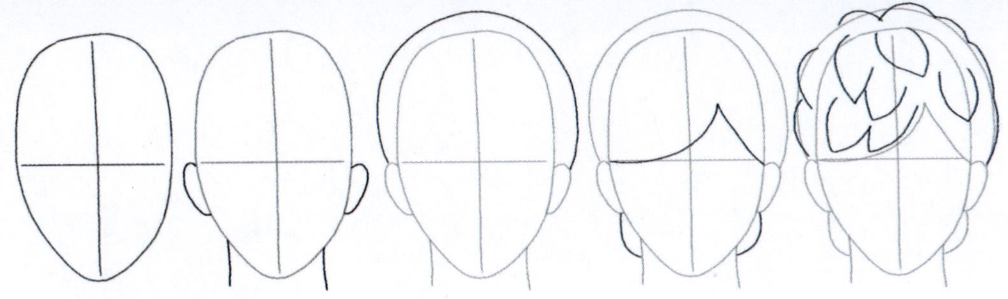

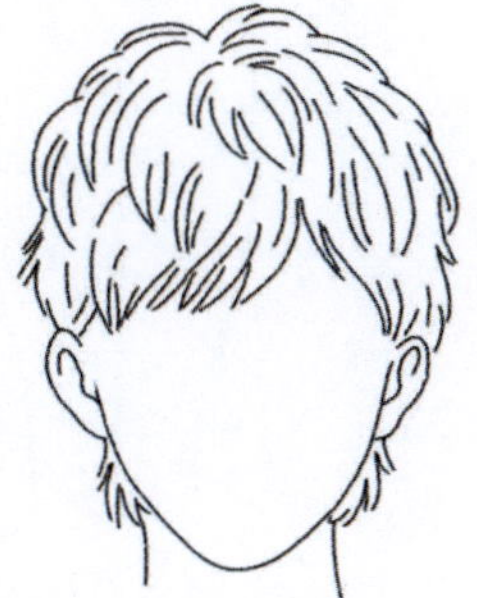

Short Hair

For shorter hairstyles, you can draw lines that curve into each other to distinguish the strands of hair.

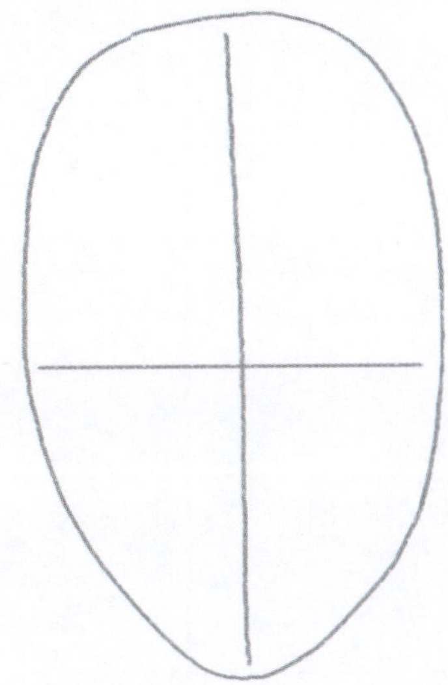

15th day

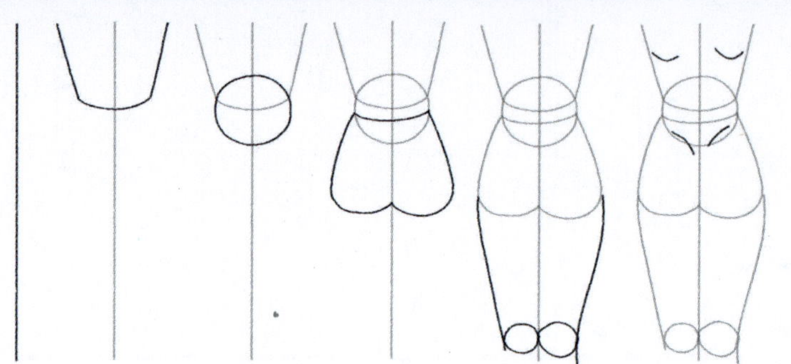

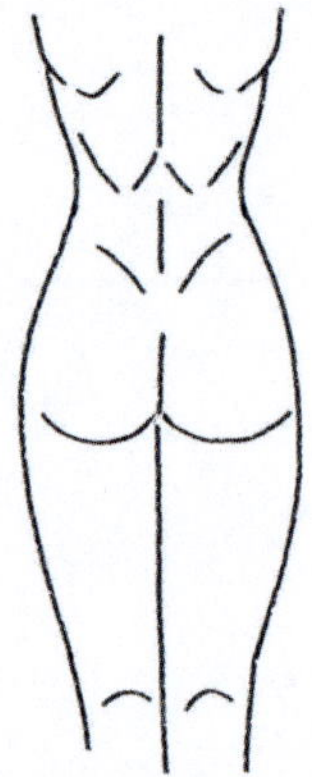

Woman from the Back

Drawing a close-up of a woman's back allows you to trace the creases and projections of the ribs, spine, kidneys and knees.

16 th day

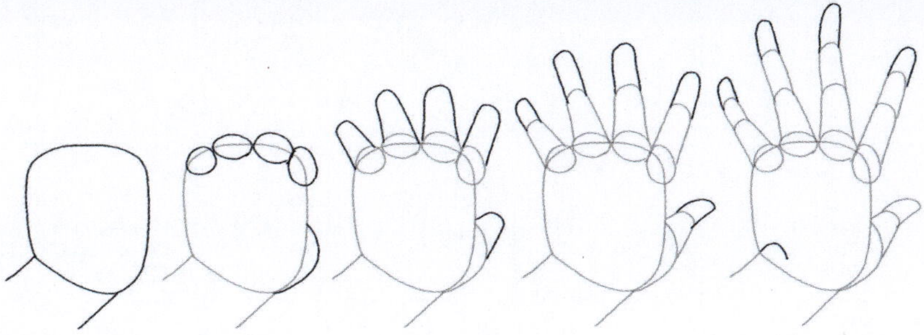

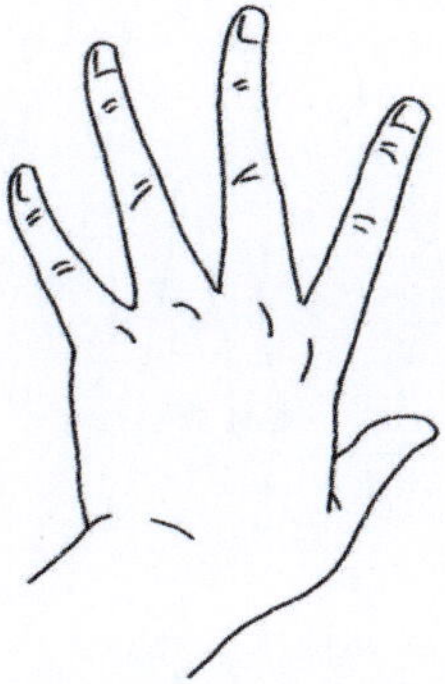

Hand

The fingers of this hand are so
tense and spread out that they
are curling up at the tips.

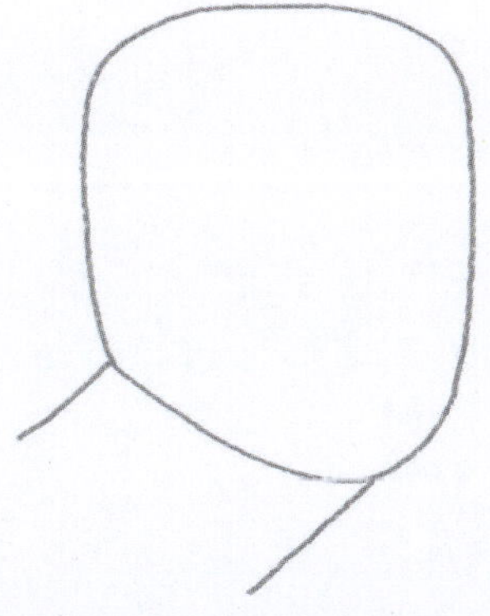

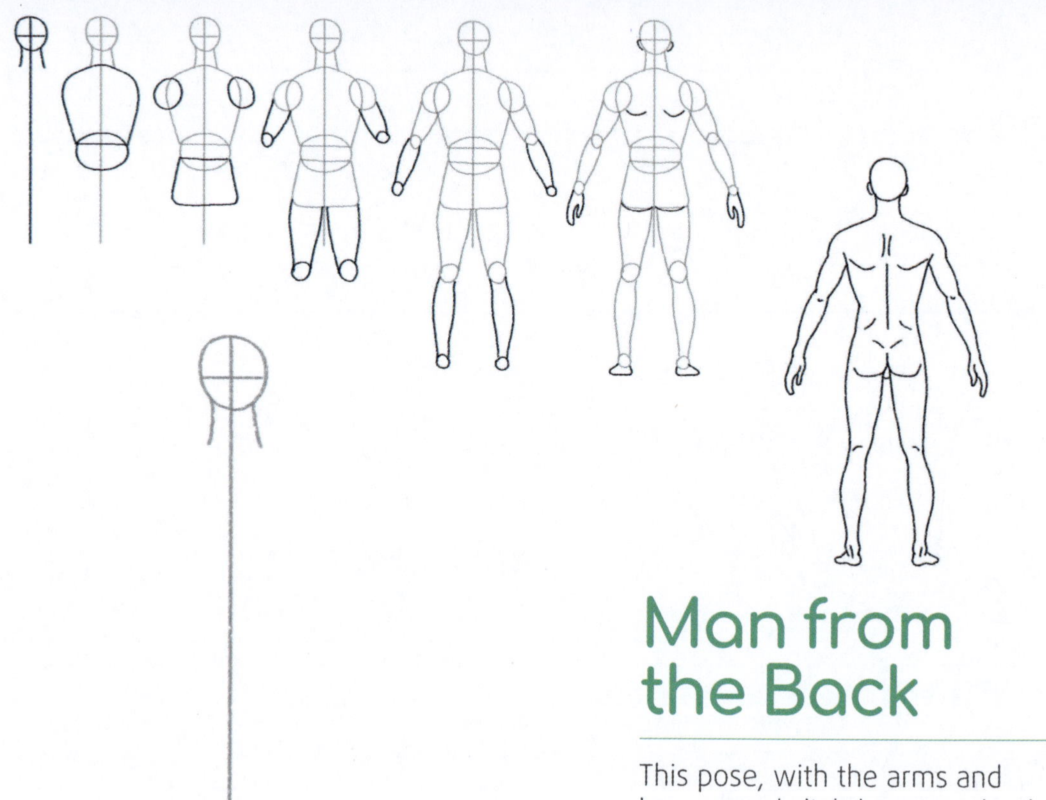

Man from
the Back

This pose, with the arms and legs spread slightly apart, clearly shows the triangular shape of the torso.

18th day

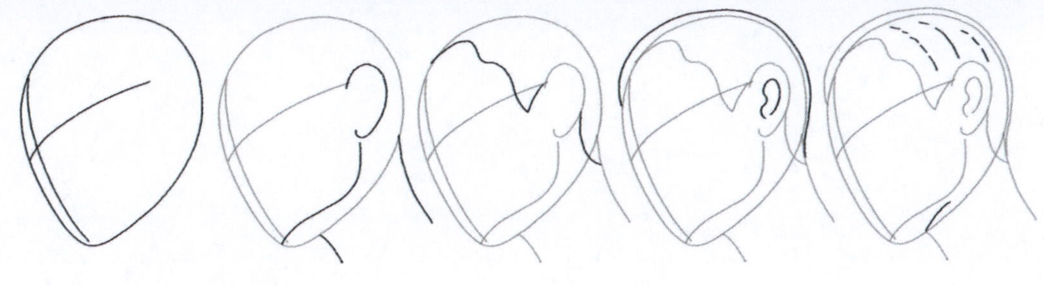

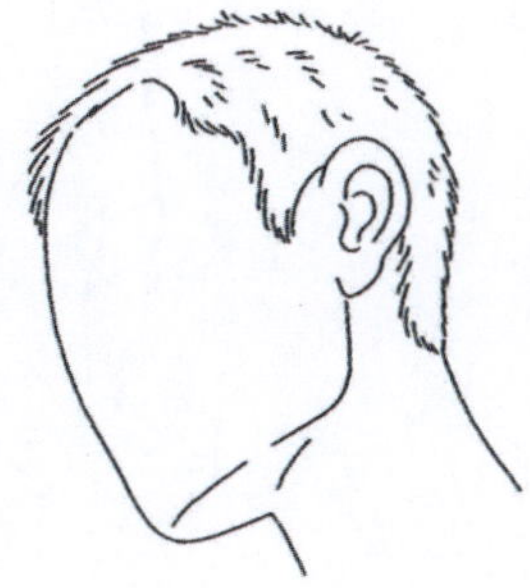

Buzz Cut

For a nearly shaved head, draw small strokes that follow the hairs' movements.

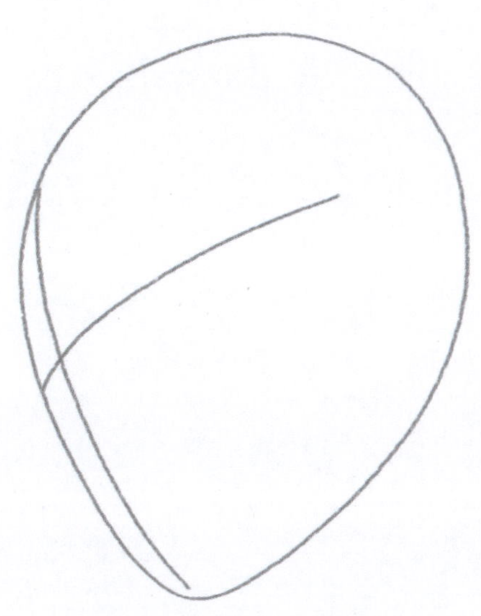

19th day

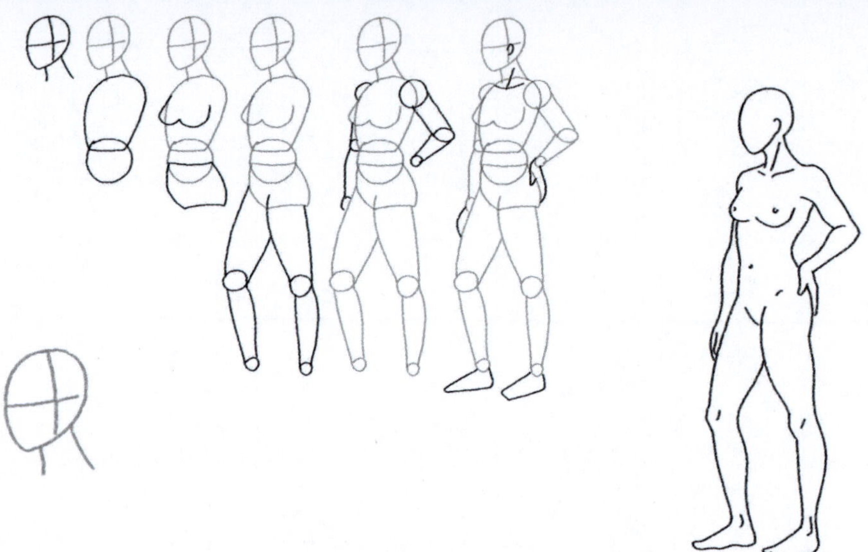

Standing Woman

In this three-quarter perspective, the position of the figure's arms and bent legs create a slight swing to the hips.

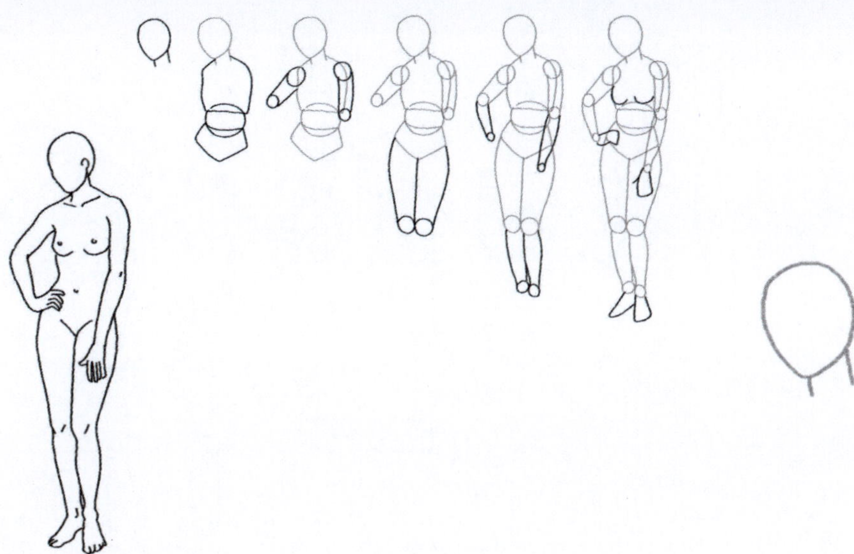

Standing Woman

This pose is also drawn from a three-quarter view and slightly in perspective. The rear shoulder and foot extend ever so slightly toward the vanishing point.

21st day

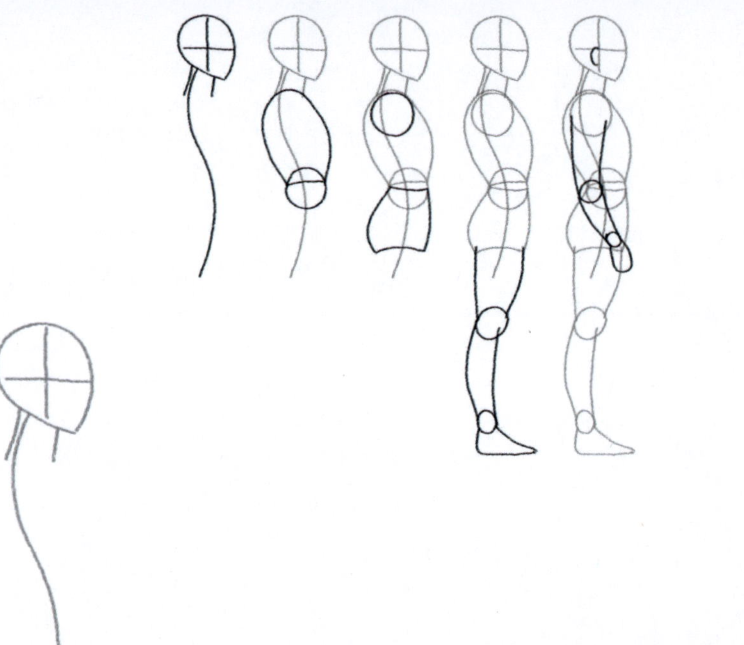

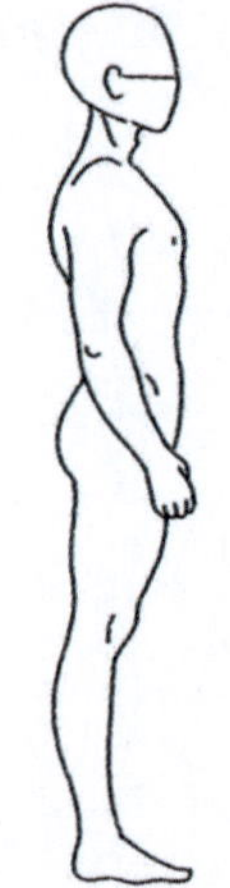

Man in Profile

When viewed in profile, a man
will appear to have a rather flat
stomach and a rounded chest.
The spine is S shaped.

22nd day

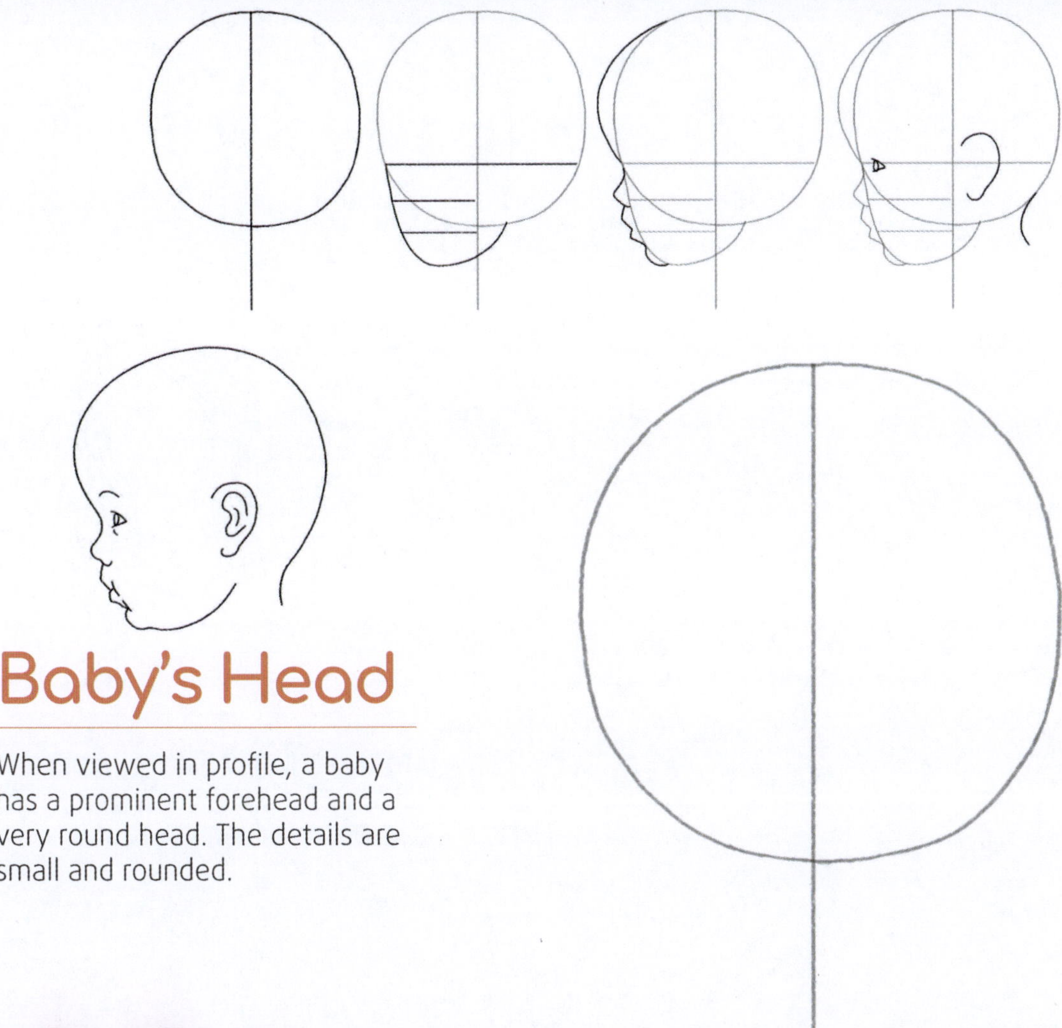

Baby's Head

When viewed in profile, a baby has a prominent forehead and a very round head. The details are small and rounded.

23rd day

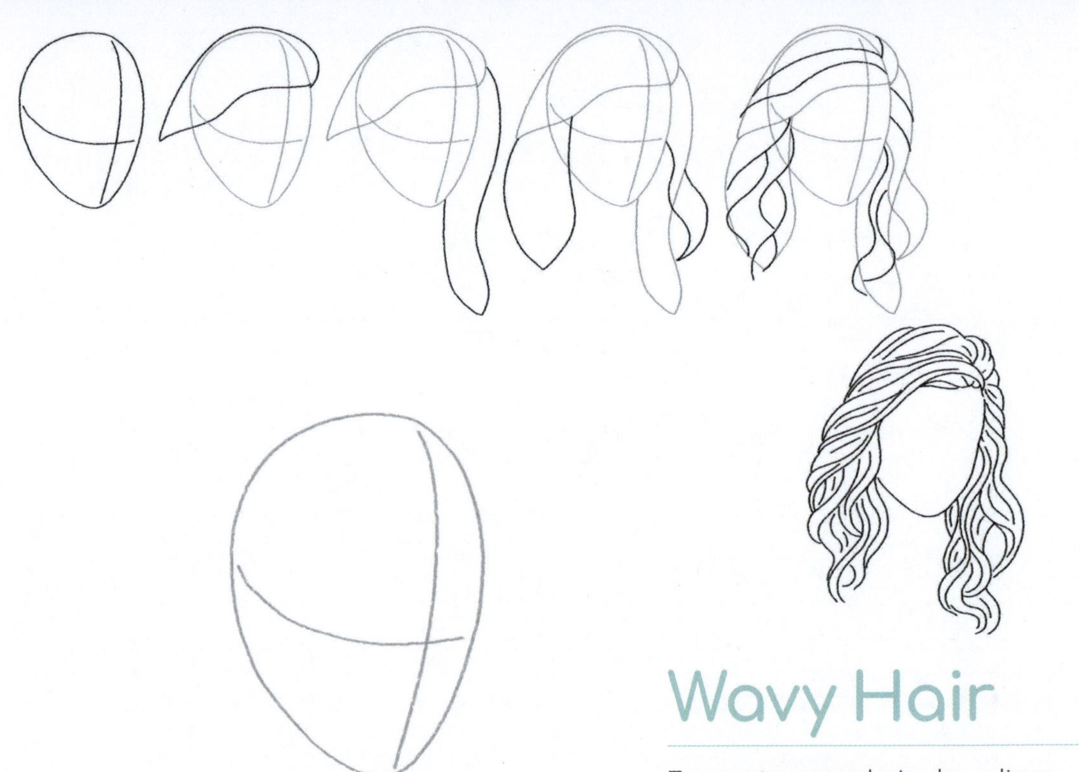

Wavy Hair

To create wavy hair, draw lines in long, relaxed spirals that wrap around the head.

24th day

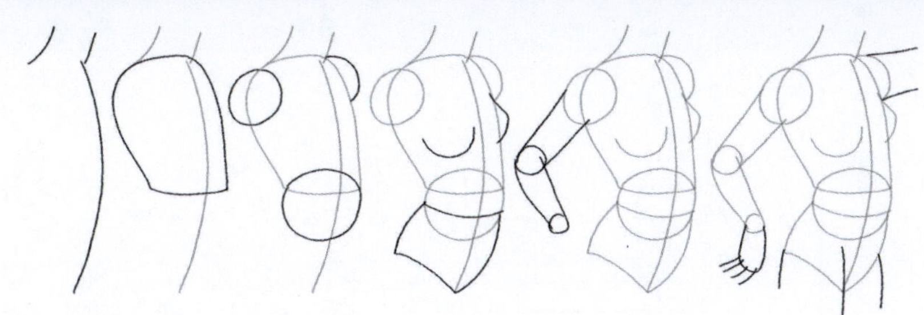

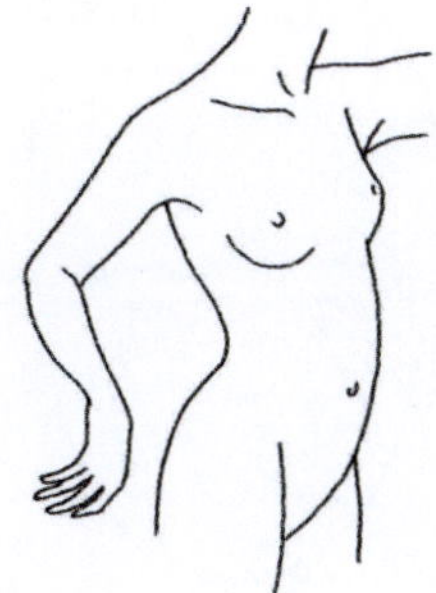

Woman's Torso

This pose is very arched and curved. You can see the lines of a collarbone and the neck.

25th **day**

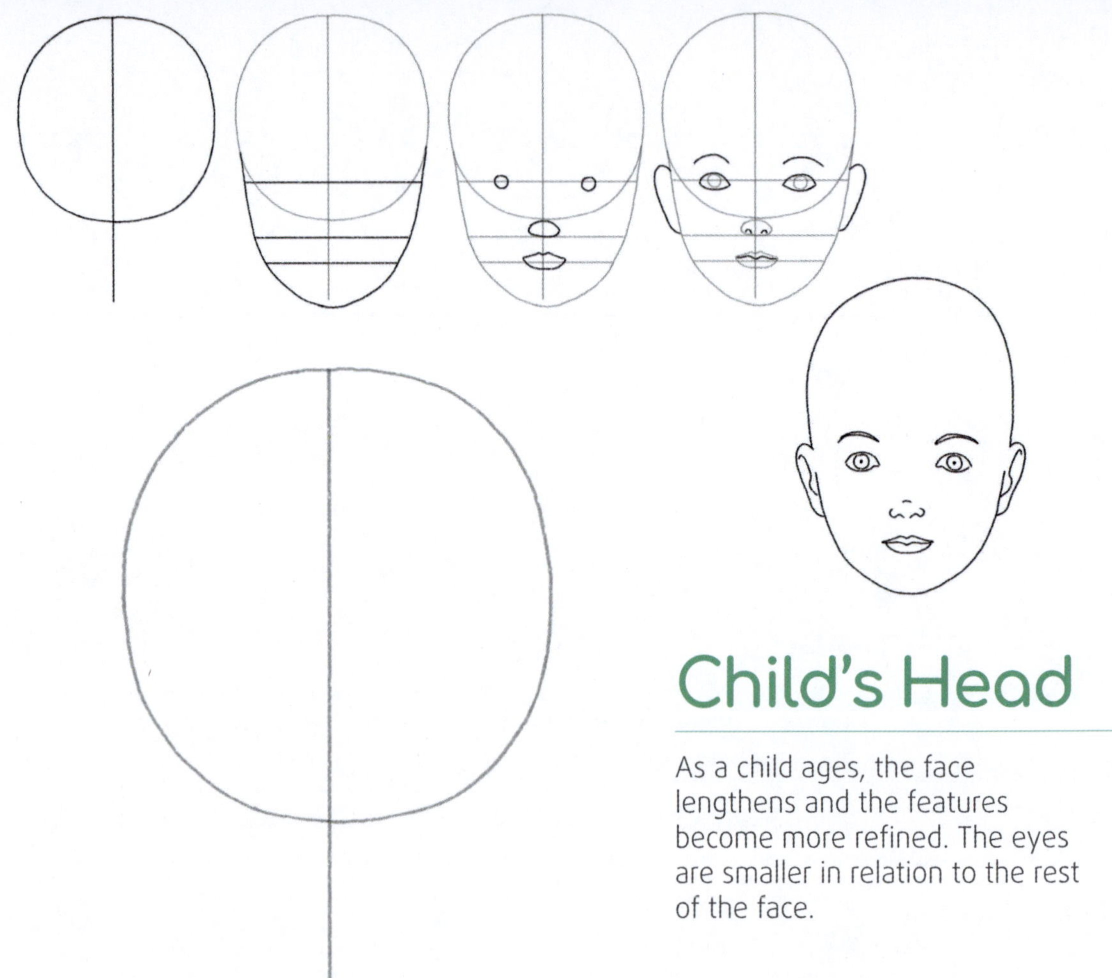

Child's Head

As a child ages, the face lengthens and the features become more refined. The eyes are smaller in relation to the rest of the face.

26 th day

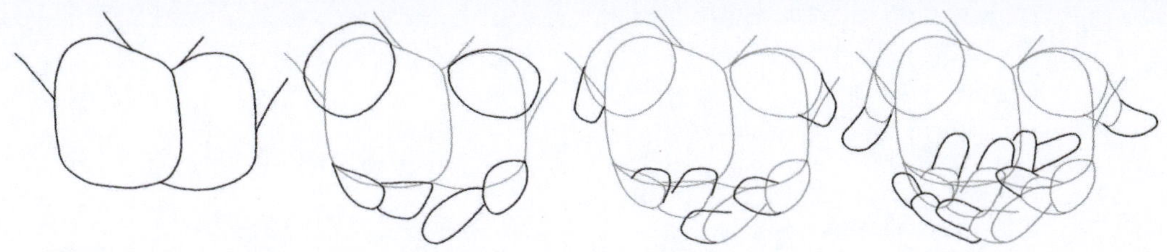

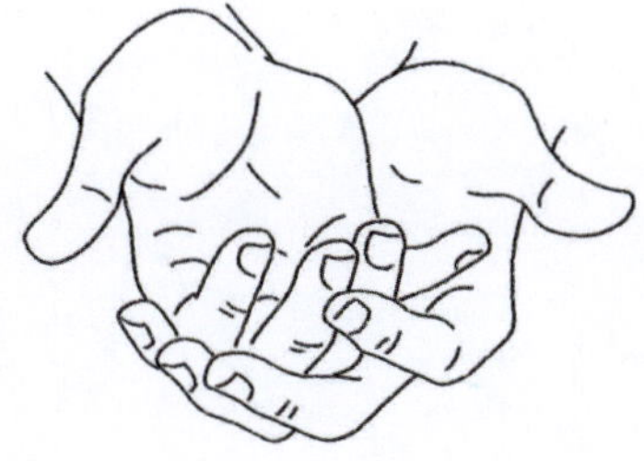

Cupped Hands

These two hands are in the same position and stacked one on top of the other. The top hand partially covers the one underneath.

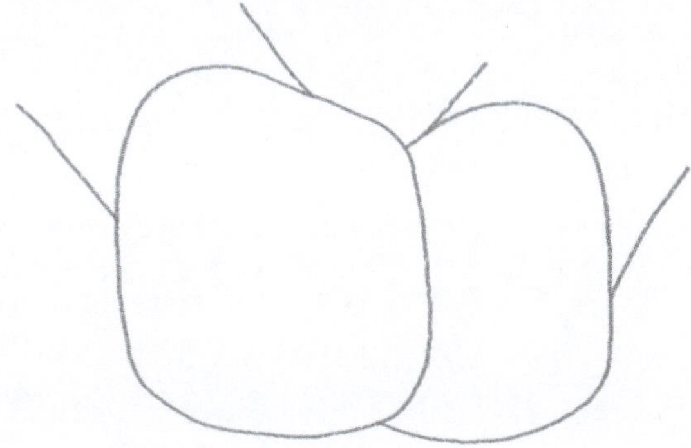

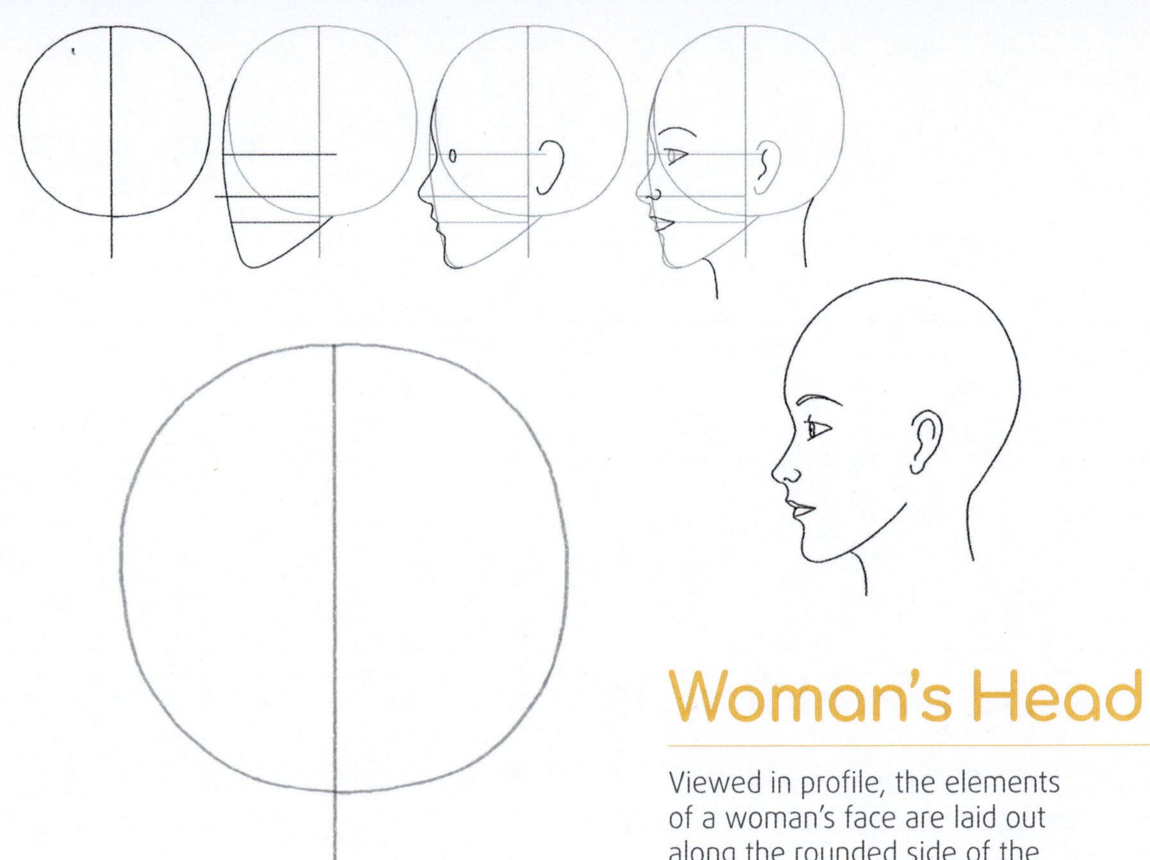

Woman's Head

Viewed in profile, the elements of a woman's face are laid out along the rounded side of the skull, but the distances between them are the same as on a face viewed head-on.

28th **day**

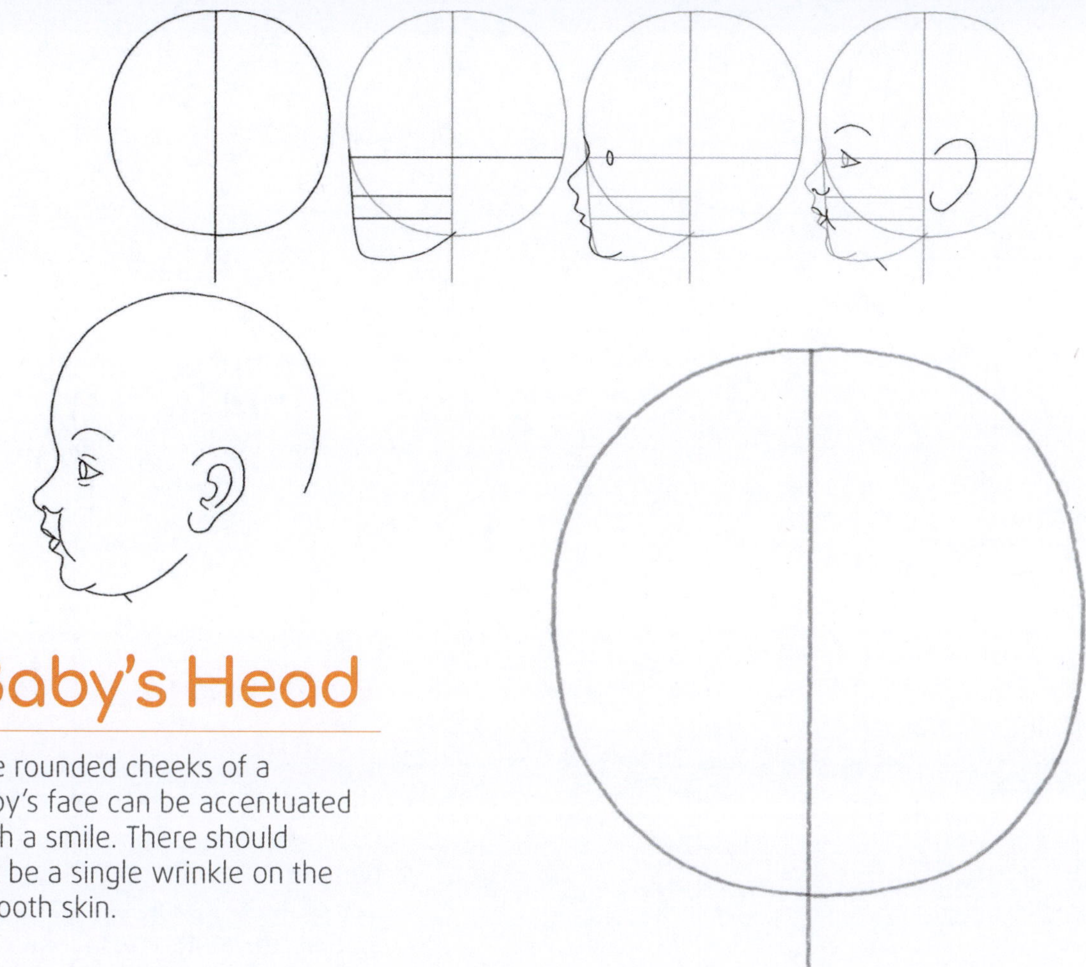

Baby's Head

The rounded cheeks of a
baby's face can be accentuated
with a smile. There should
not be a single wrinkle on the
smooth skin.

29th day

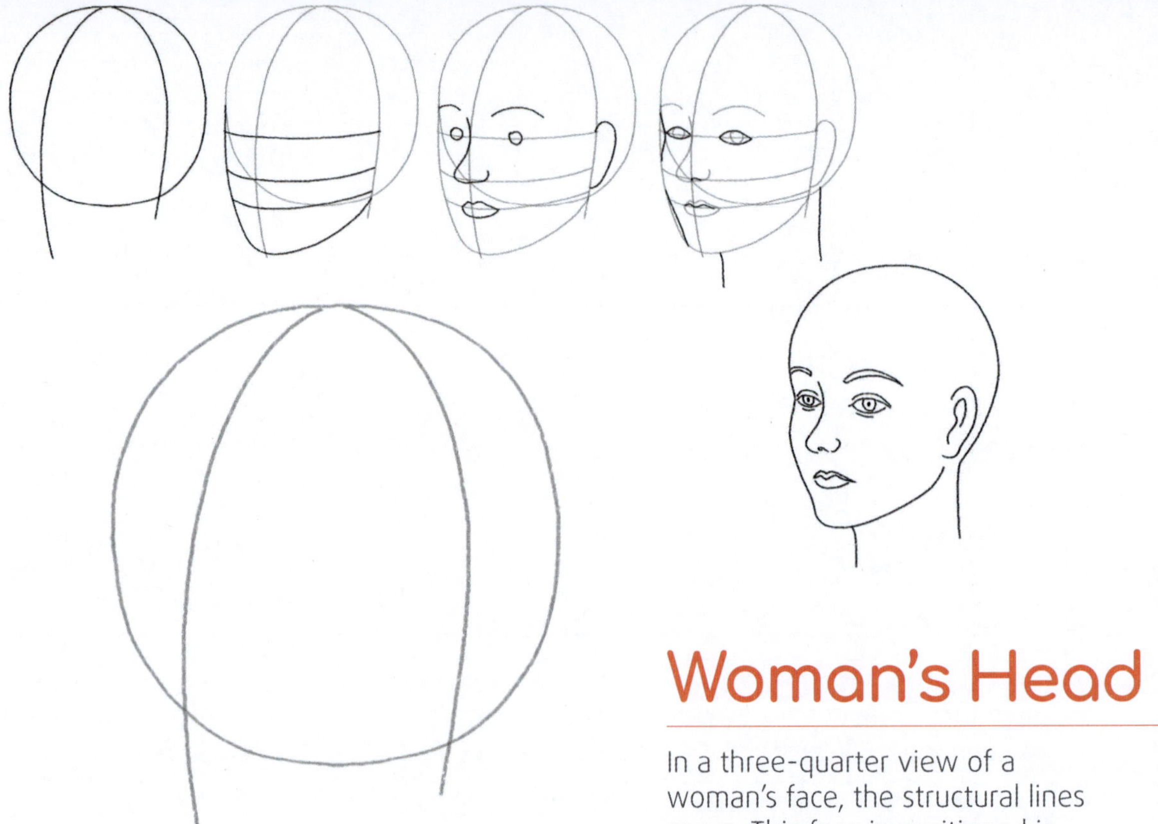

Woman's Head

In a three-quarter view of a woman's face, the structural lines curve. This face is positioned in perspective, which changes the size of the elements placed on one side of the centerline in relation to the elements on the other side.

30th day

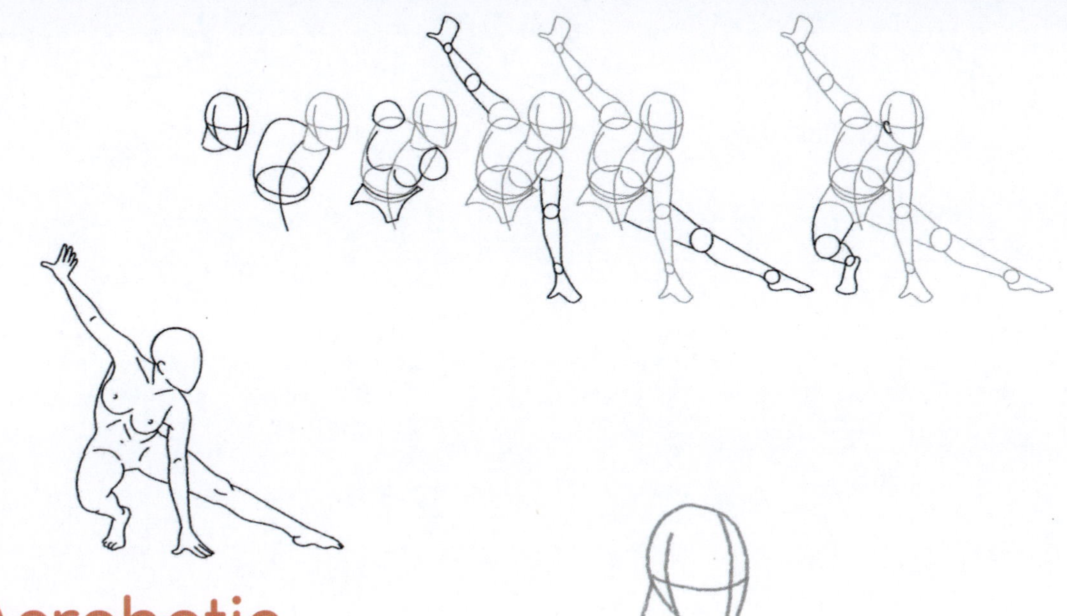

Acrobatic Woman

The leg bent toward us
is in perspective, so it is
differently proportioned and
partially hidden.

31st day

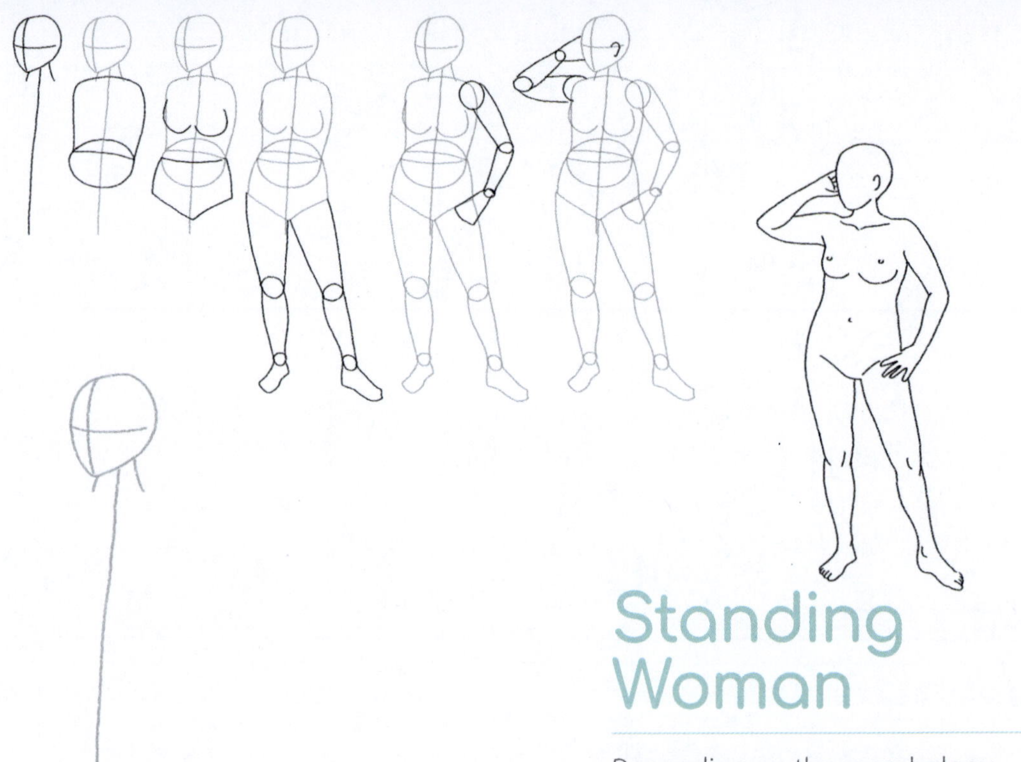

Standing Woman

Depending on the morphology,
the body may look stocky and
the waist barely defined.

32nd **day**

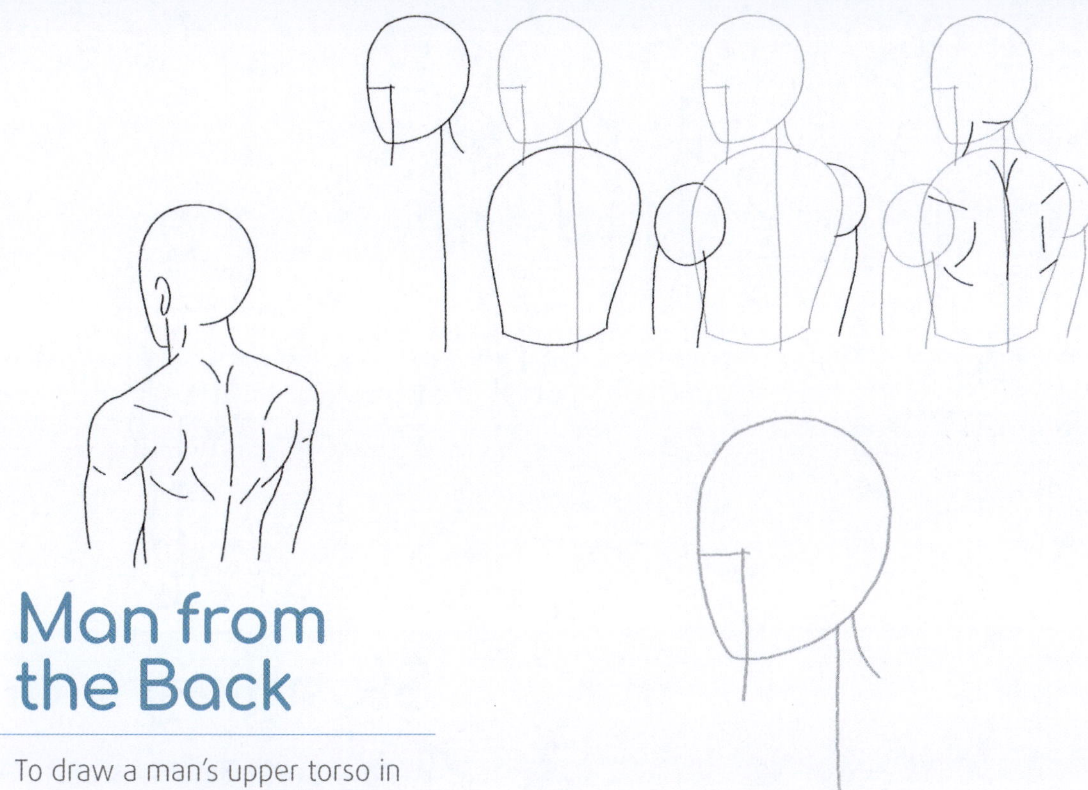

Man from
the Back

To draw a man's upper torso in close-up, you can add lines to emphasize the muscles and the contractions created by the pose.

33rd day

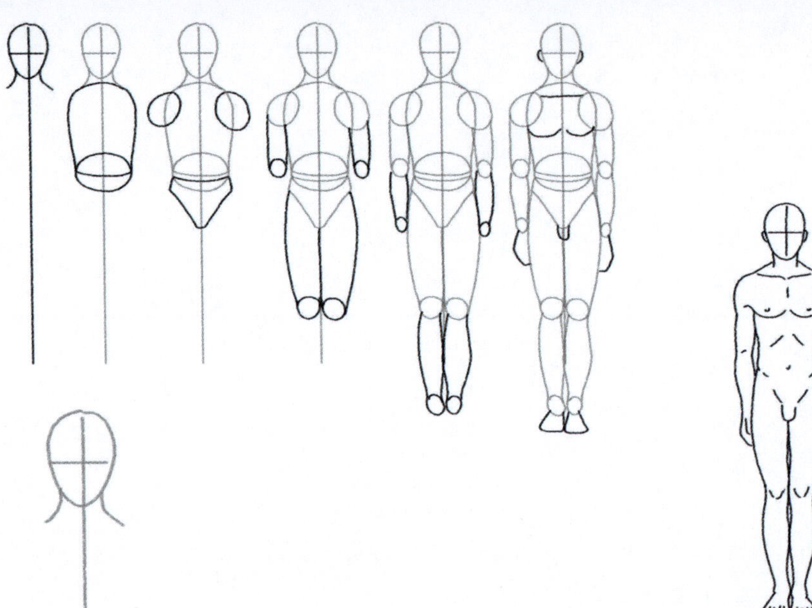

Standing Man

When viewed head-on,
a man has smaller volumes.
The shoulders are broad and the
hips narrow, and the joints, such
as the knees and elbows, are
thicker than in a woman.

34 th day

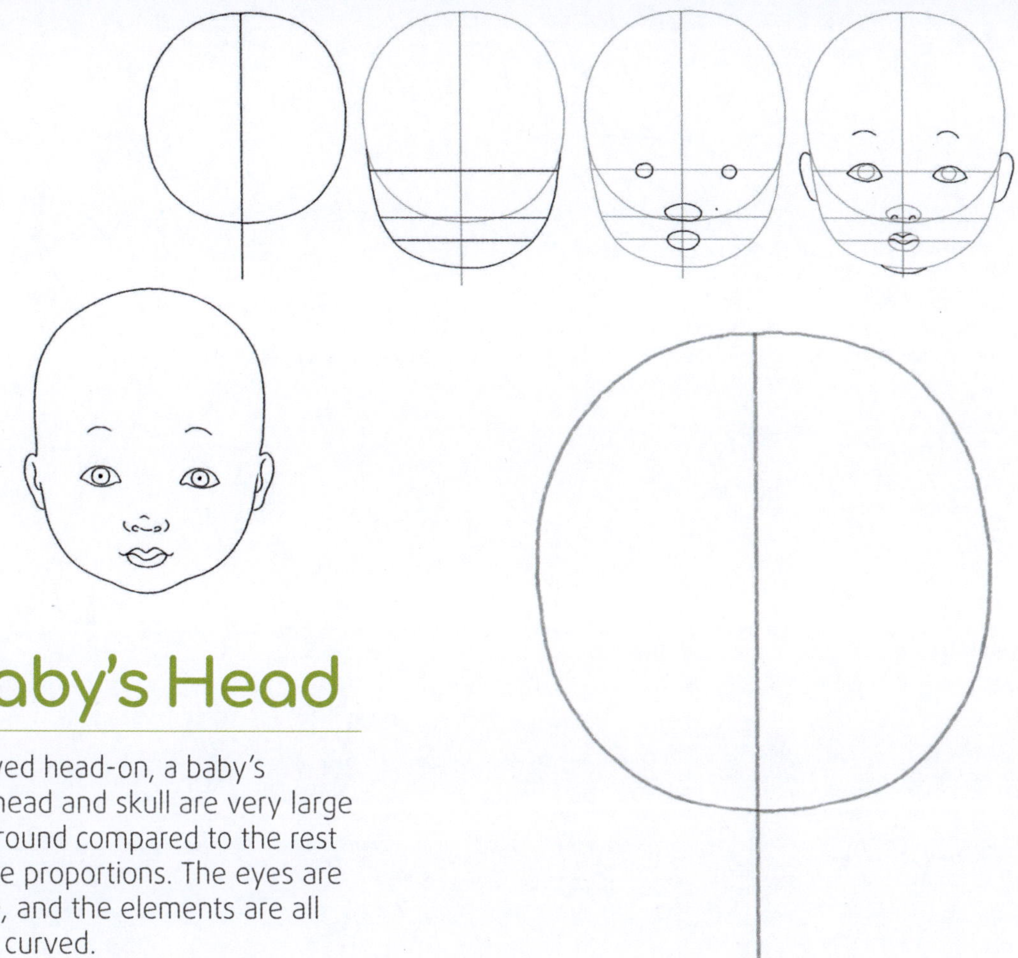

Baby's Head

Viewed head-on, a baby's forehead and skull are very large and round compared to the rest of the proportions. The eyes are wide, and the elements are all very curved.

35th day

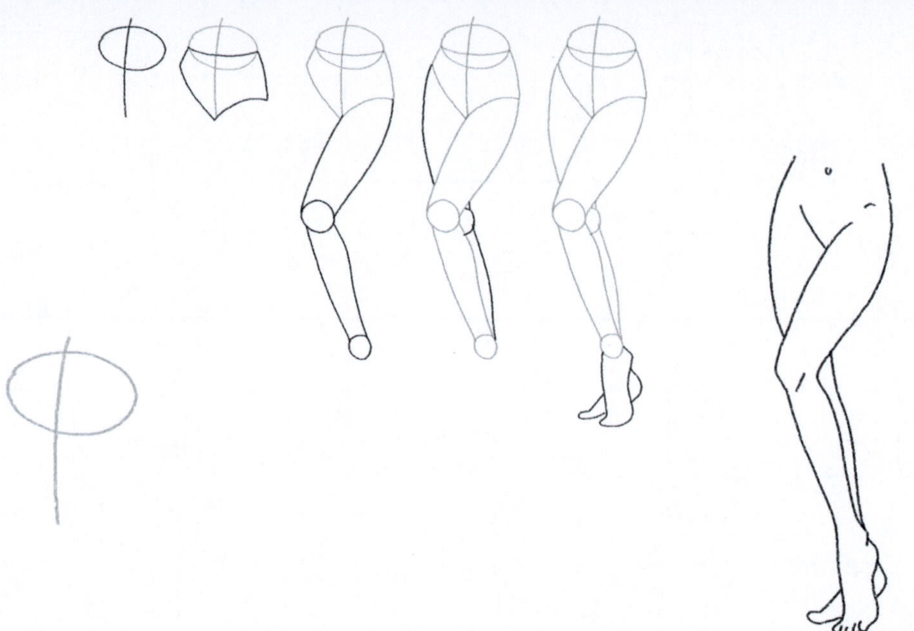

Woman's Legs

Bending one leg creates a sway to the hips. The other foot remains flat on the ground.

36th day

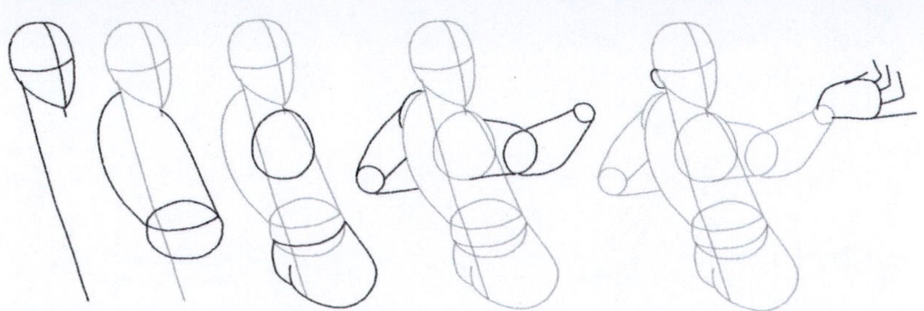

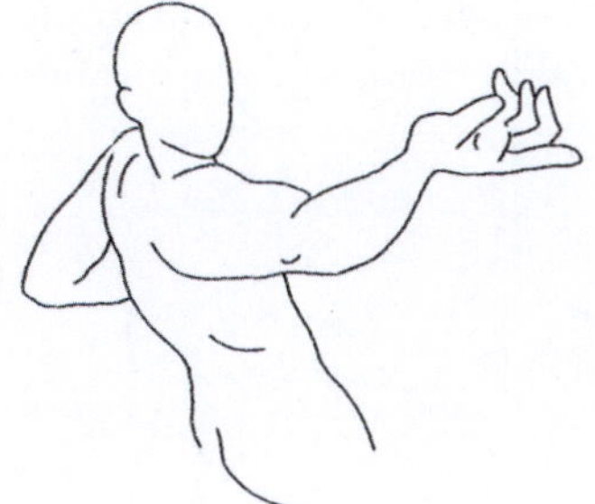

Man's Torso

This pose shows the front arm in perspective, making it look rather imposing. The hand in the foreground seems very large in relation to the rest of the arm and the torso.

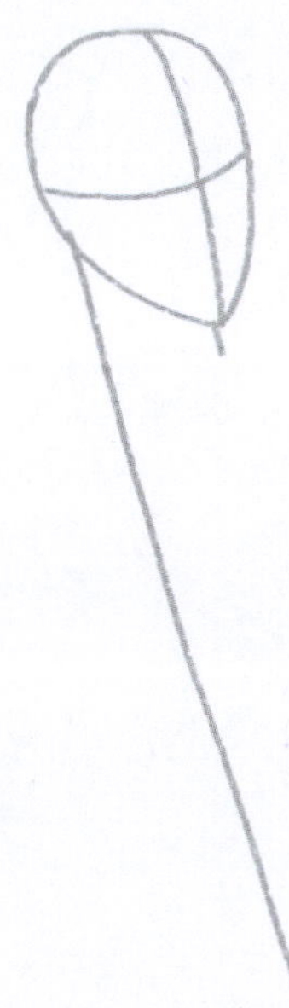

37th **day**

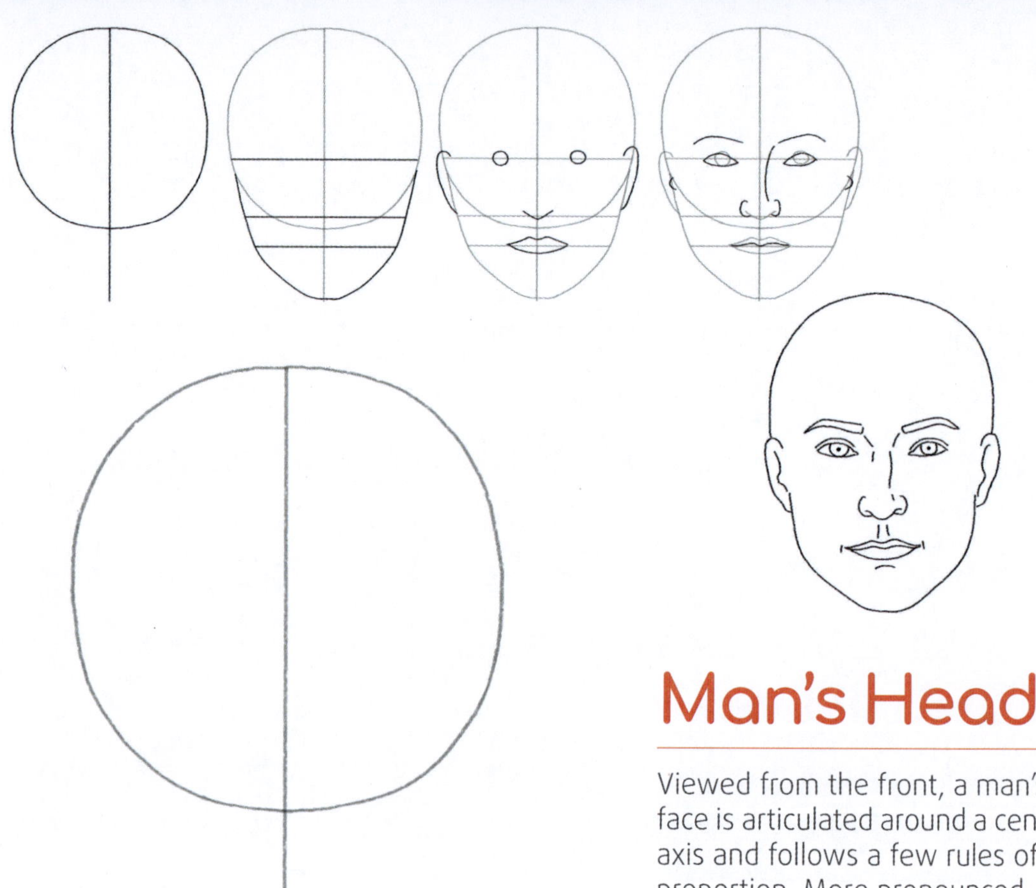

Man's Head

Viewed from the front, a man's face is articulated around a central axis and follows a few rules of proportion. More pronounced features and wider, more angular contours make the face look more masculine.

38th day

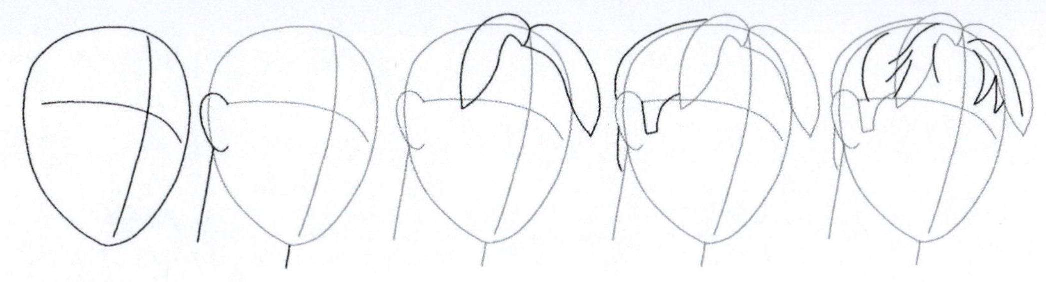

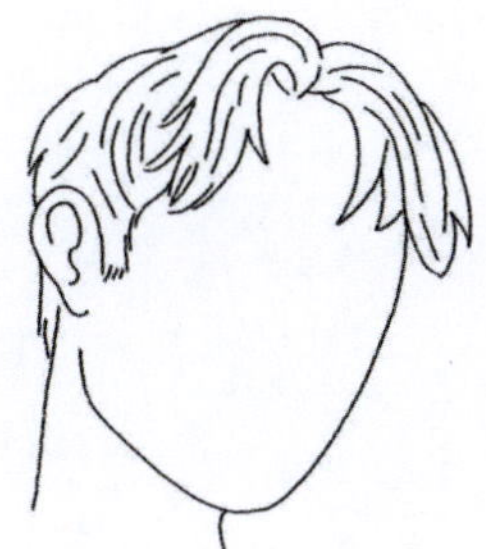

Short Hair

The front of the hair frames the face in long, soft, curved strands that meet near the middle of the top of the forehead.

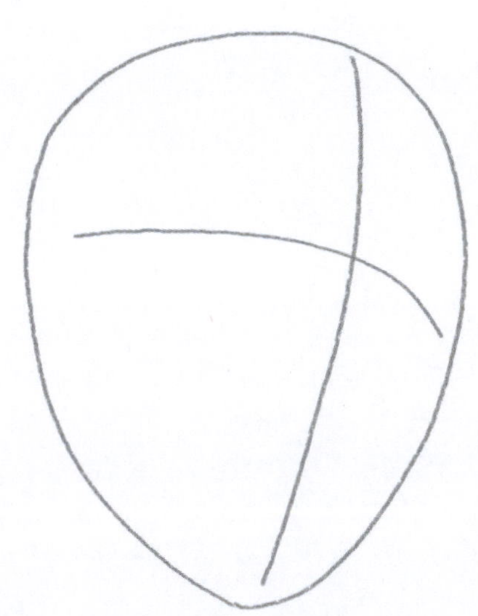

39th day

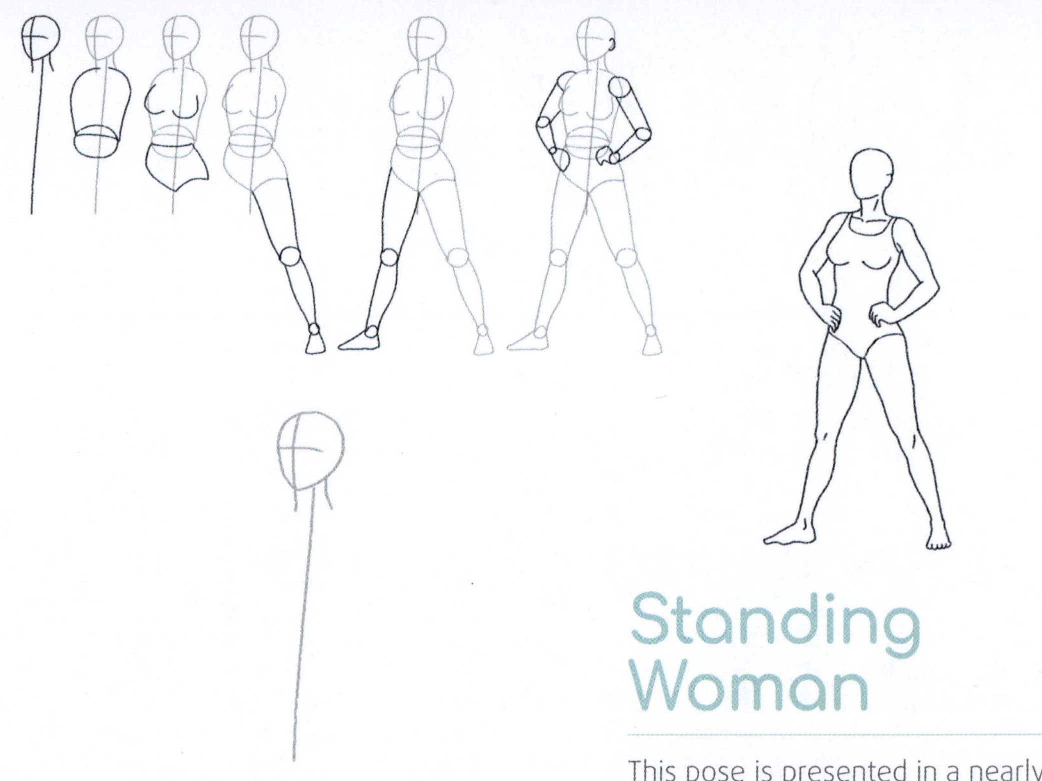

Standing Woman

This pose is presented in a nearly head-on perspective. One leg is facing the front, and the other is shown in profile.

40th day

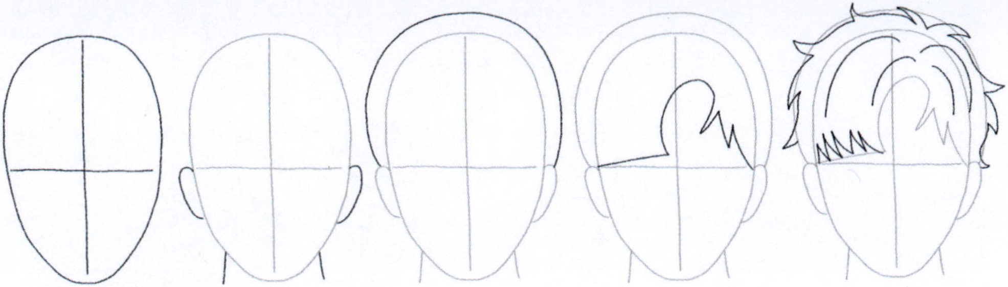

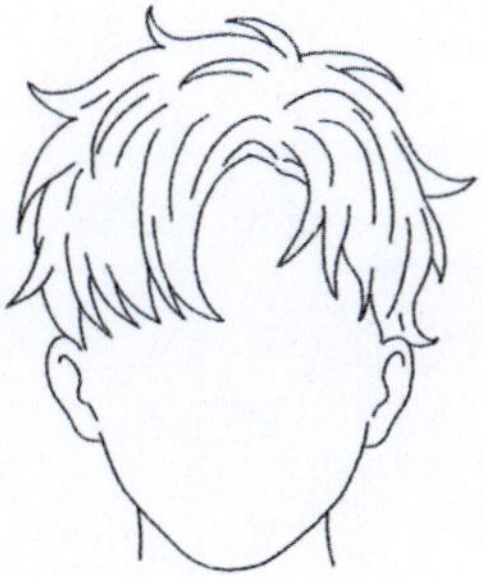

Tousled Hair

For short, wispy strands of hair,
add small spiky strokes all over
the head.

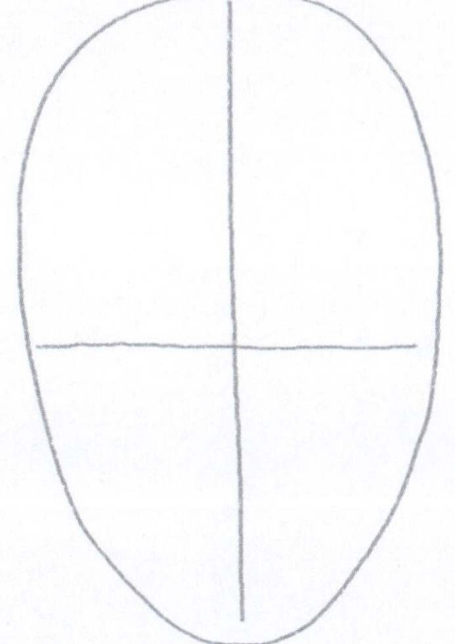

41st day

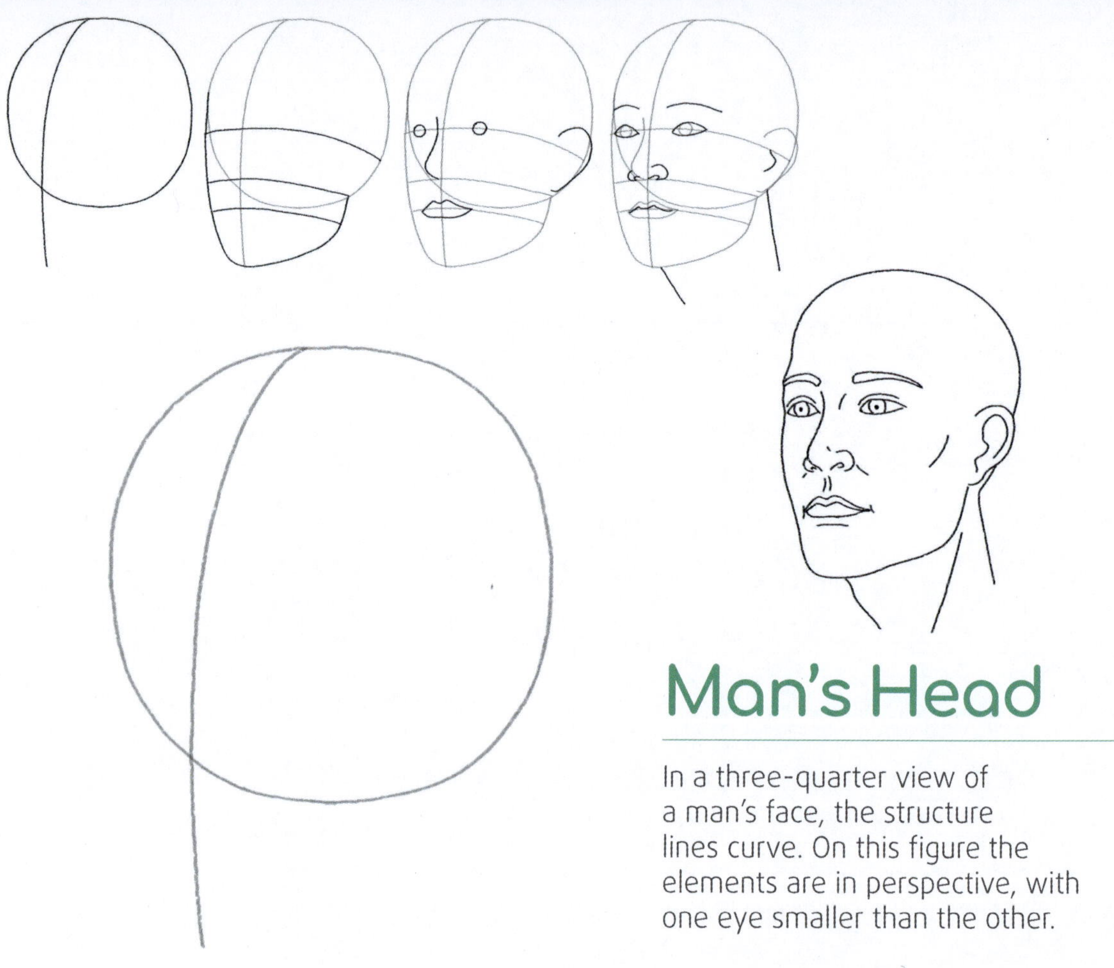

Man's Head

In a three-quarter view of
a man's face, the structure
lines curve. On this figure the
elements are in perspective, with
one eye smaller than the other.

42nd day

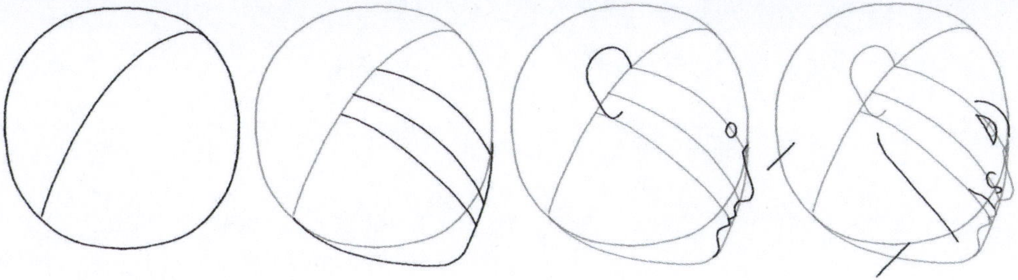

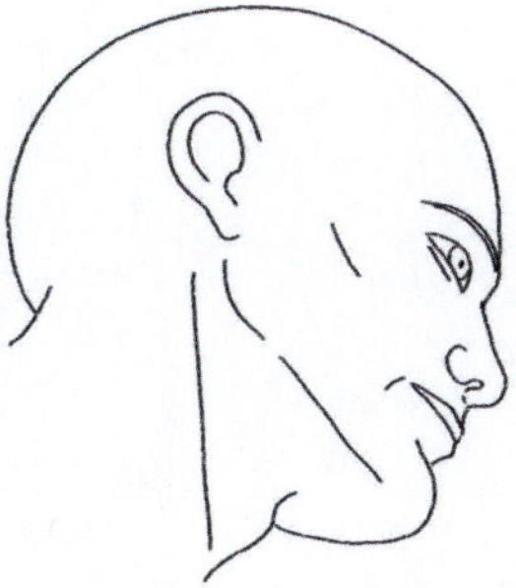

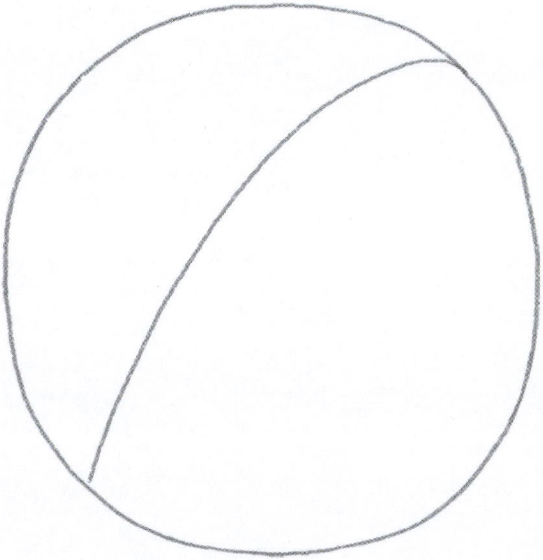

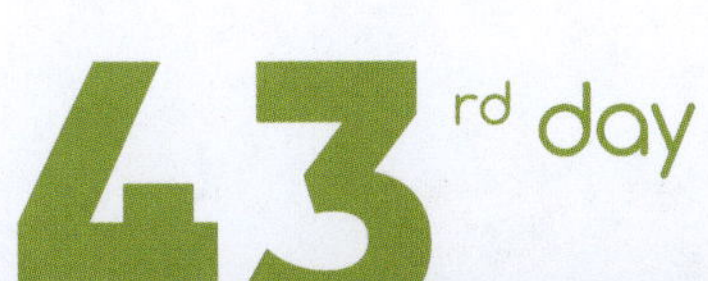

Head in Profile

The side angle of this head in profile makes much of the face disappear and highlights the underside of the chin.

43rd day

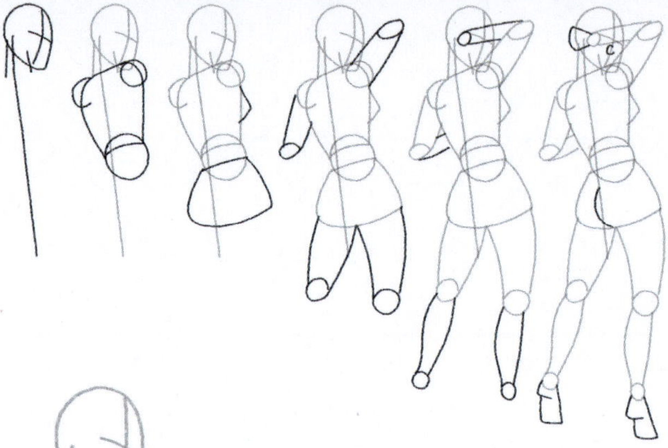

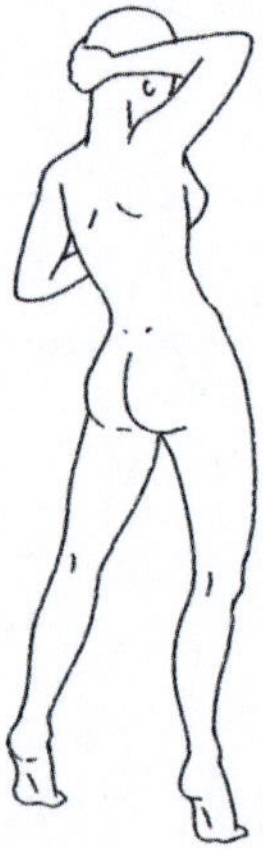

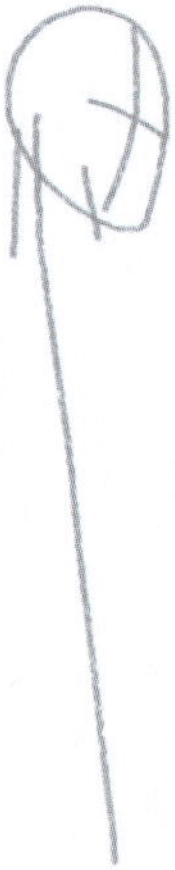

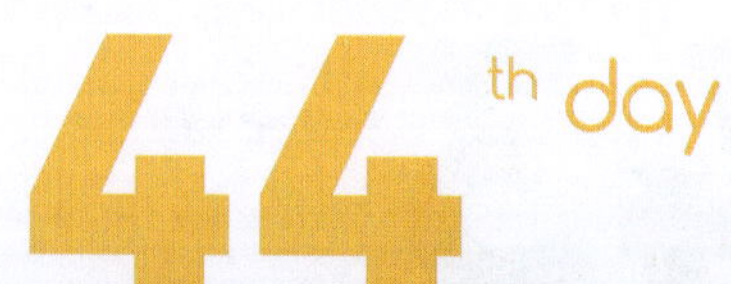

Woman from the Back

This pose is slightly tilted and extends upward. Depicting the figure on tiptoes creates movement.

44 th day

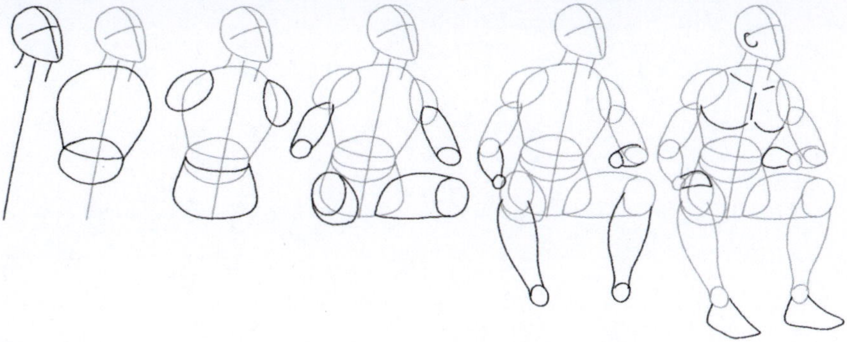

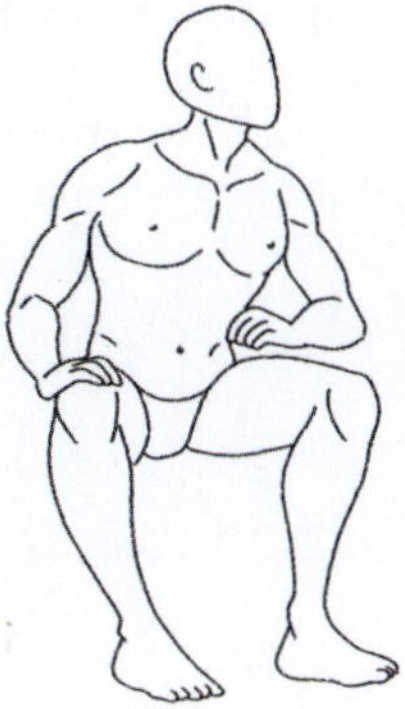

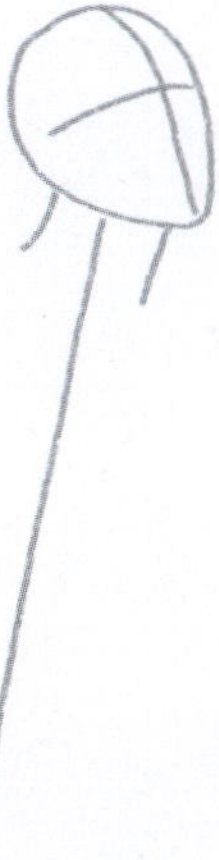

Seated Man

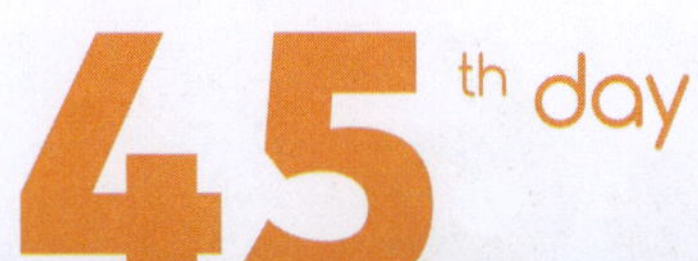

This slightly rotated seated pose puts the front thigh in perspective. The figure's torso is very well developed and muscular.

45th **day**

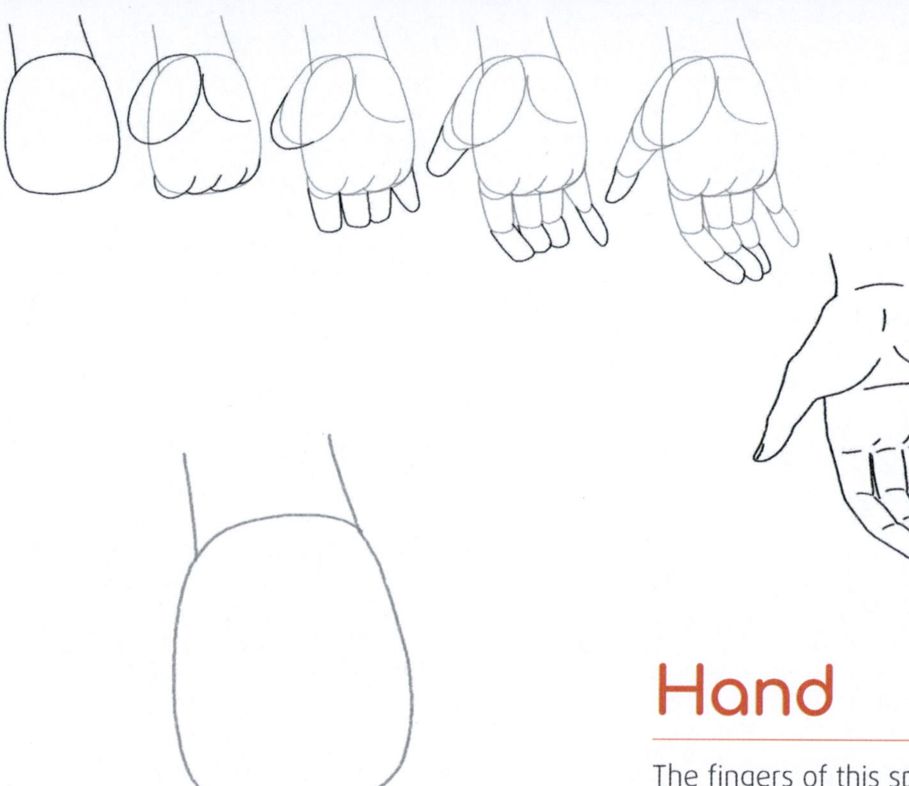

Hand

The fingers of this spoon-shaped
hand are cradled together
and curved as if ready to pick
something up.

46 th day

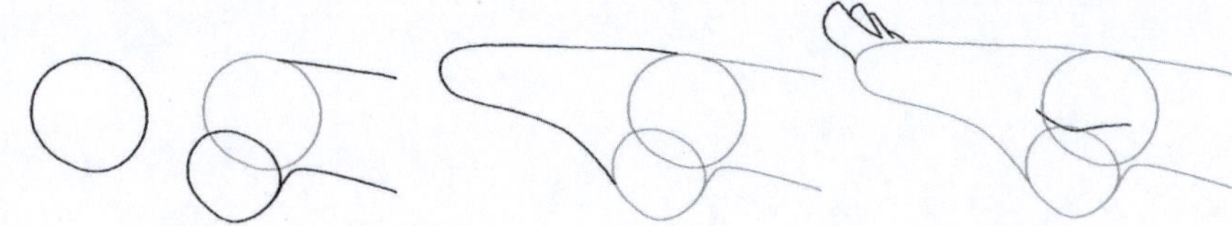

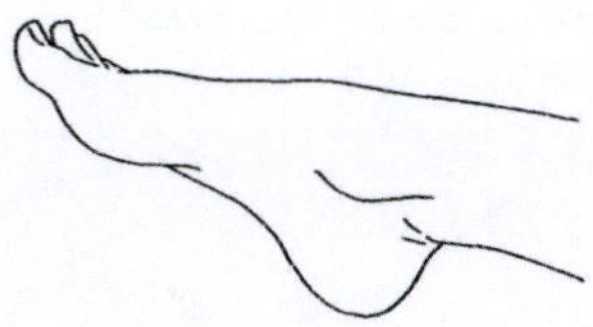

Foot

When the legs and feet are
stretched out, the bump on top
of the foot and the indentation
underneath it are accentuated.

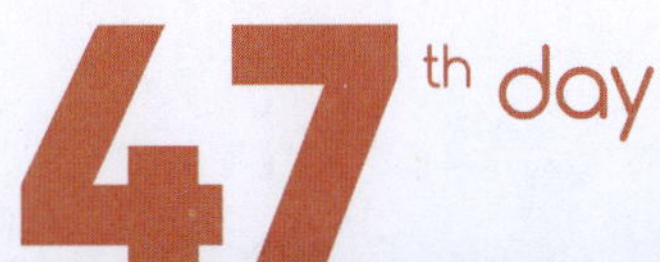

47

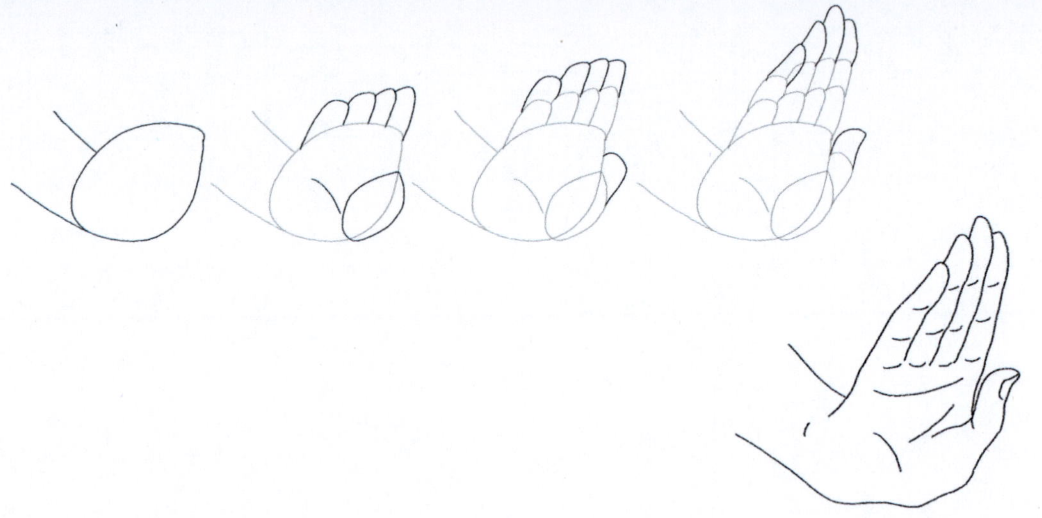

Hand

For this pose, the hand is held straight up, completely perpendicular to the arm.

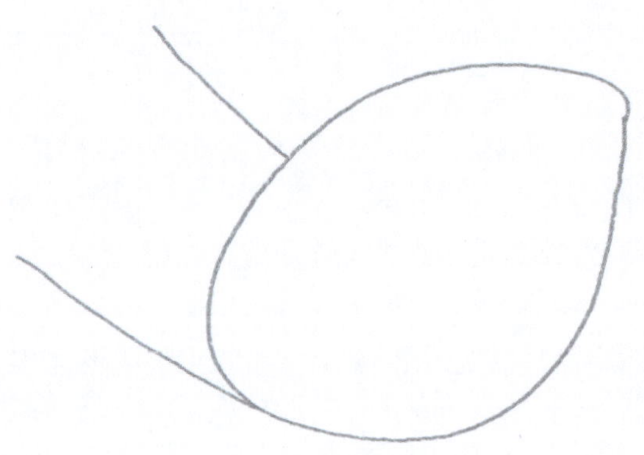

48 th day

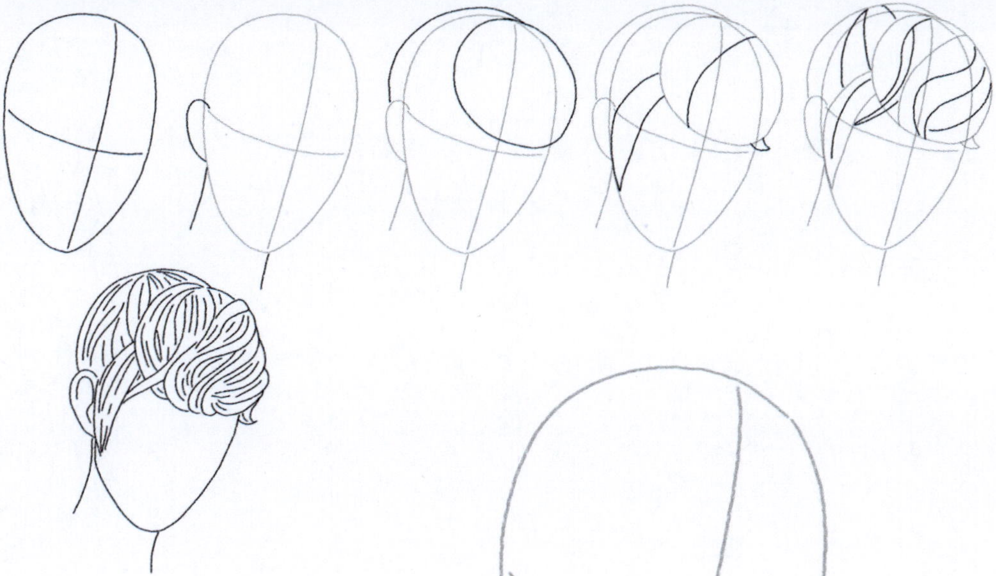

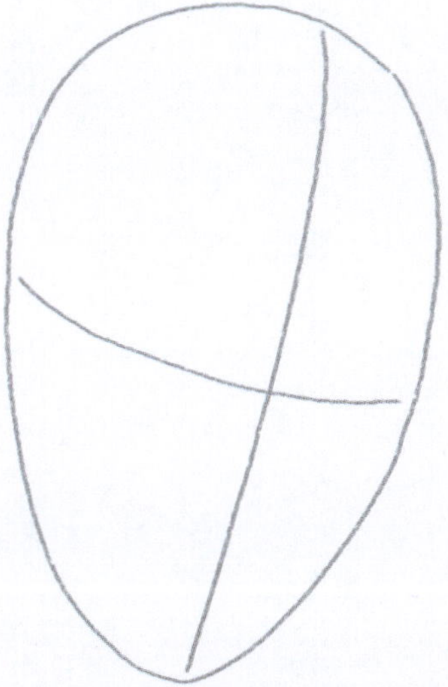

Short Hair

To give texture and movement to a hairstyle, draw short, curved strands in many different directions.

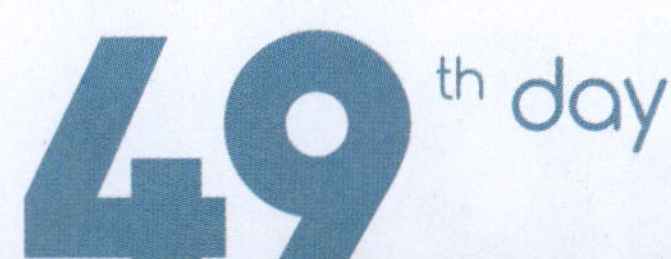

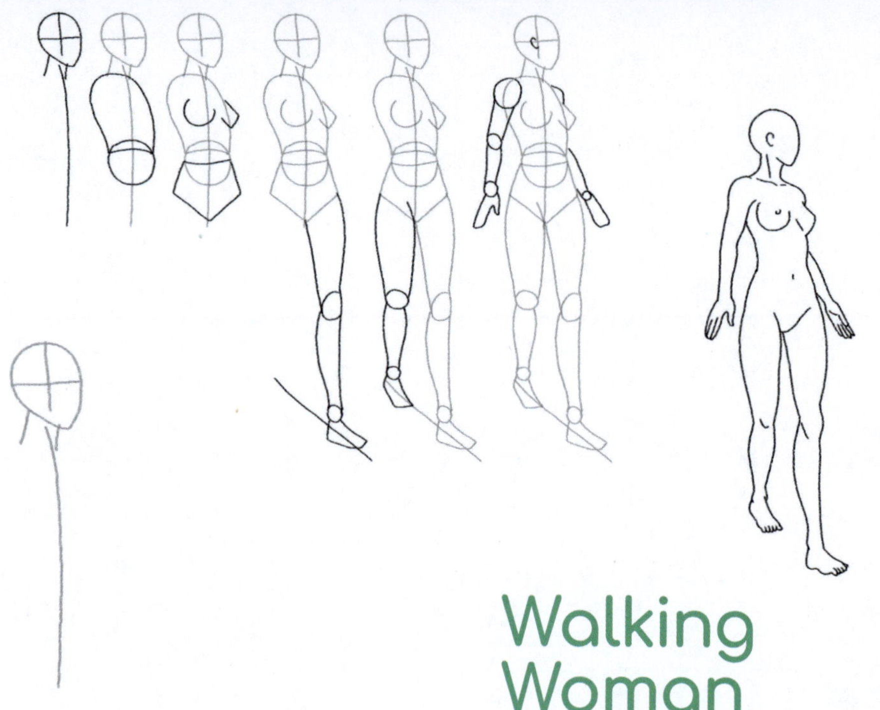

Walking Woman

This walking pose puts one leg sharply in perspective. You can sketch a line along the ground toward the vanishing point to help you keep the elements in proportion.

50th day

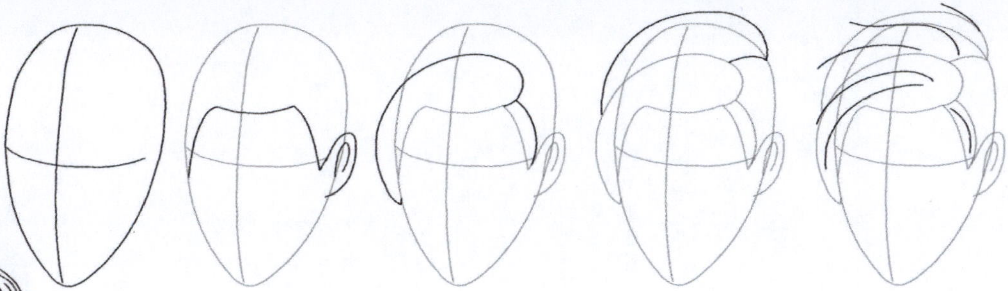

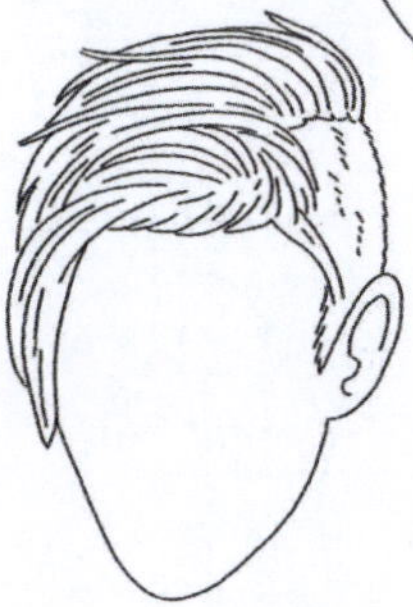

Shaved Hairstyle

The shaved portion of this hairstyle is created with only a few very short lines. On the other side, the strands of hair are long and follow the shape of the head.

51st day

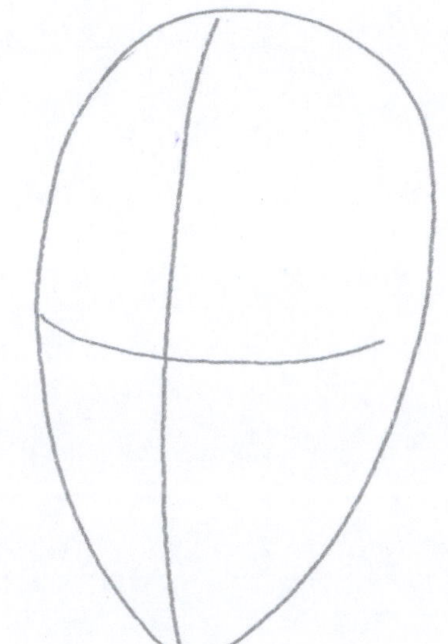

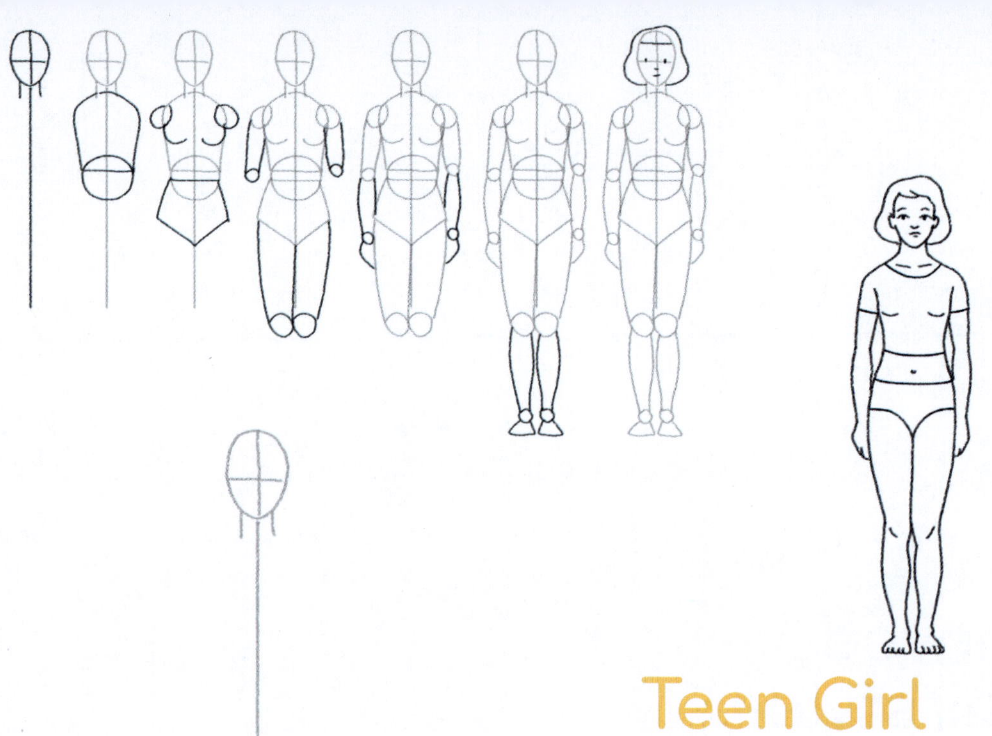

Teen Girl

Viewed from the front, the more feminine forms of a teenage girl begin to become perceptible.

52nd day

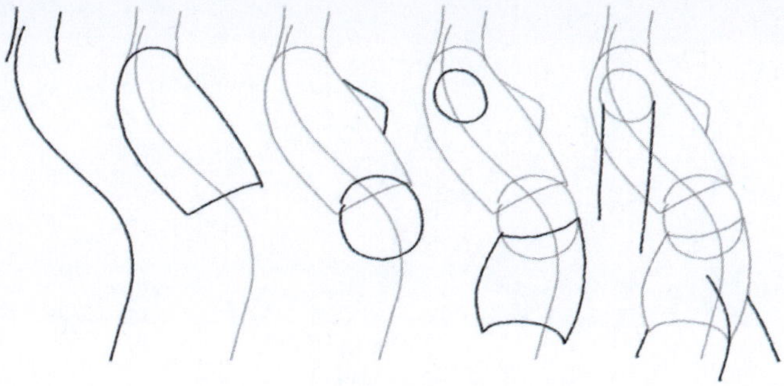

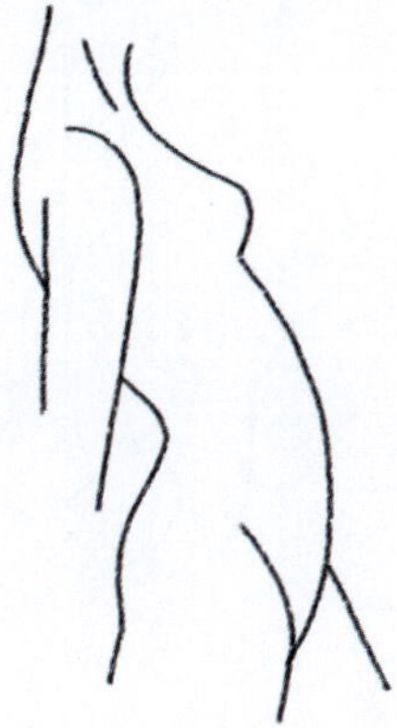

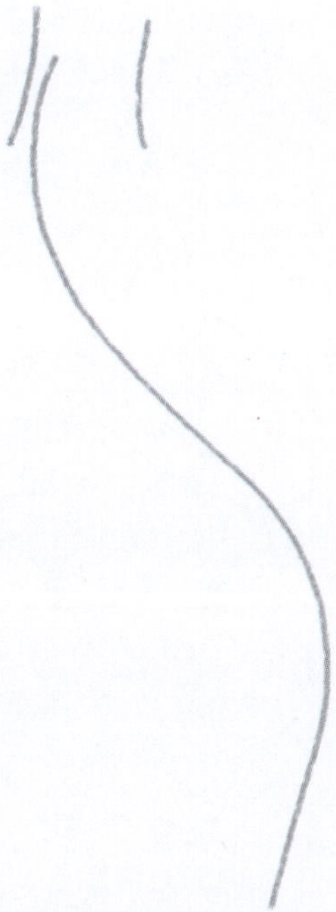

Woman's Torso

This very arched pose creates an
S shape along the torso.

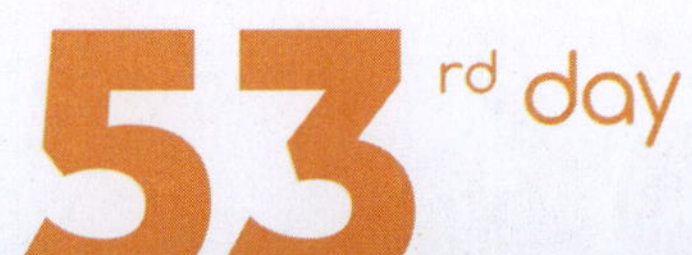

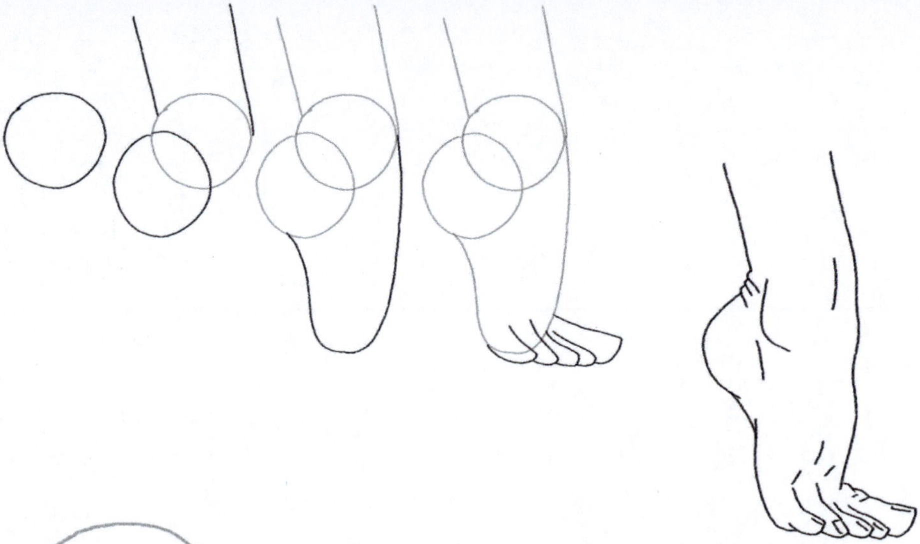

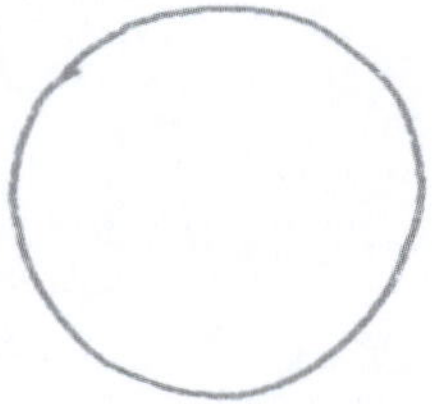

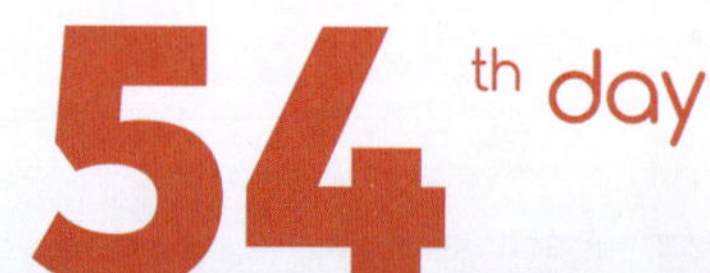

Foot on Tiptoes

The toes of this foot are very flexed, as is the ankle. In a pose such as this, you can emphasize elements by drawing lines to outline the resulting creases.

54 th day

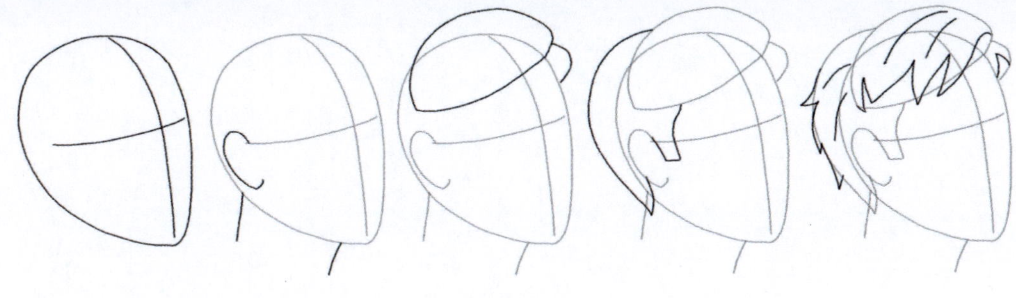

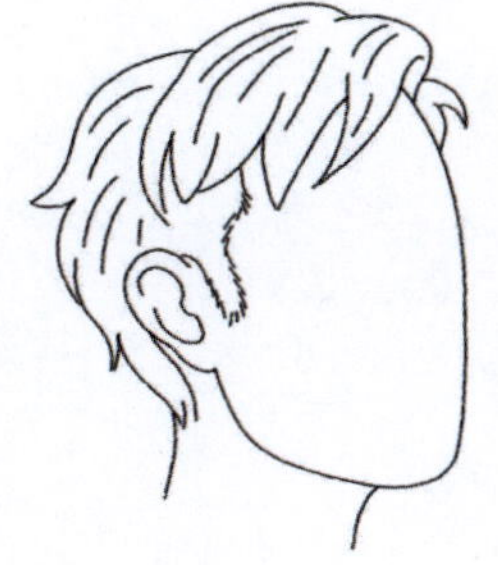

Short Hair

The contour of the ear is short,
so it's finished with small strokes.
The long, thick strands of hair
are created with a few lines, just
enough to indicate movement.

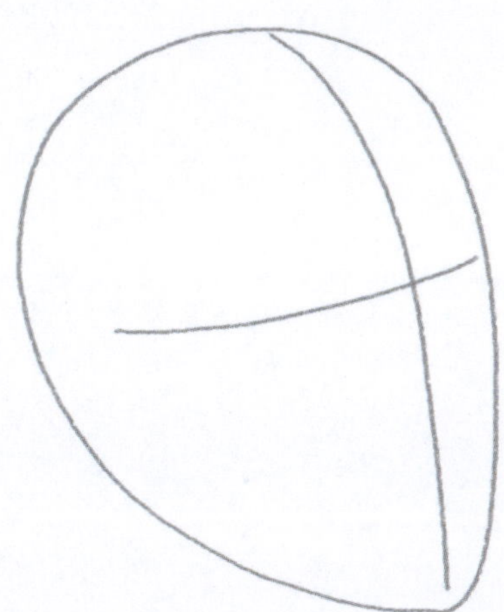

55th **day**

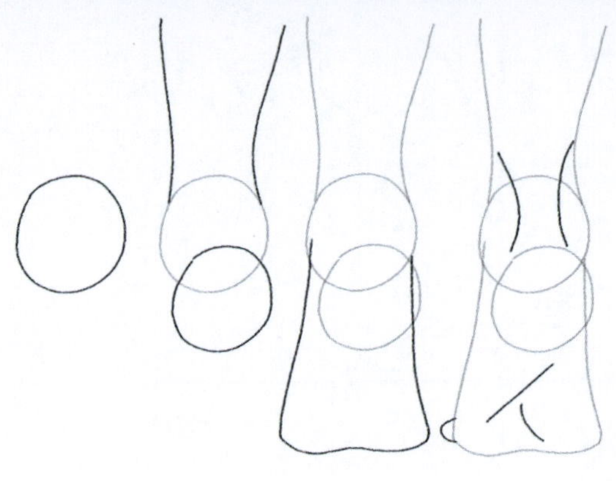

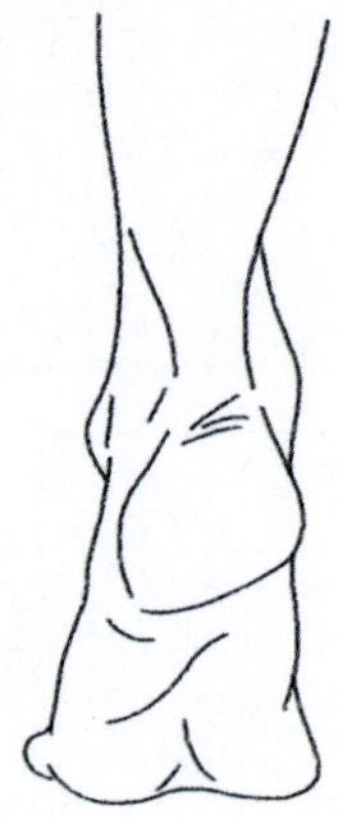

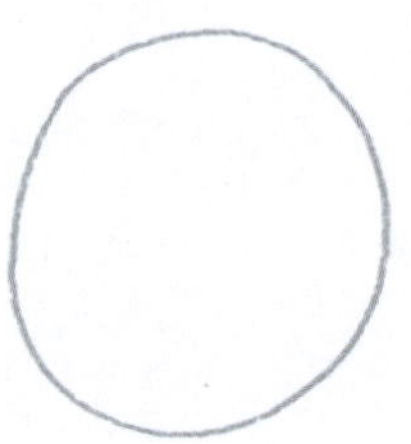

Foot

The heel and the skin folds along the sole are the main features of this foot. We can't see the toes.

56th day

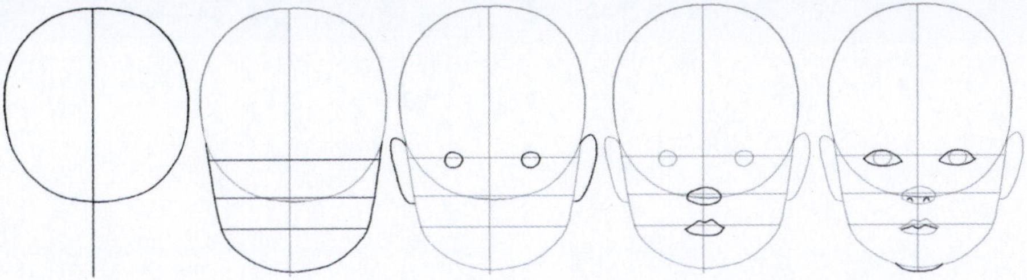

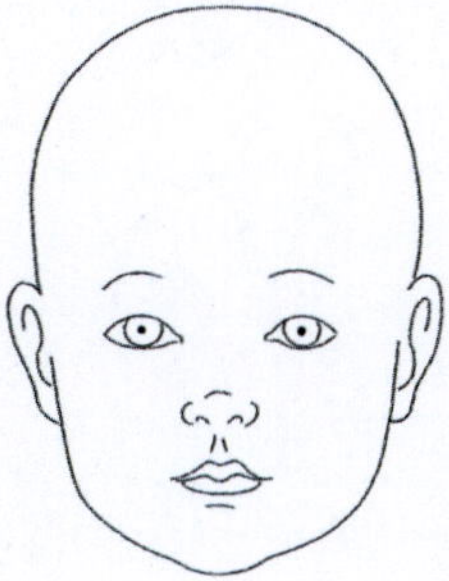

Toddler's Head

Viewed from the front, a toddler's face is still rounded like a baby's face, but it is becoming longer. The forehead is more compact than in an older child.

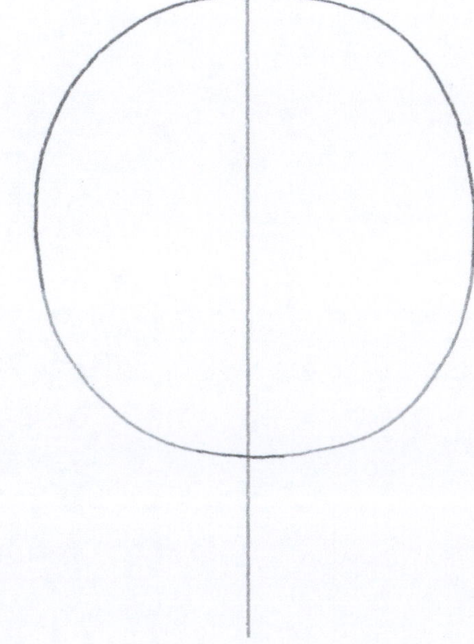

57th day

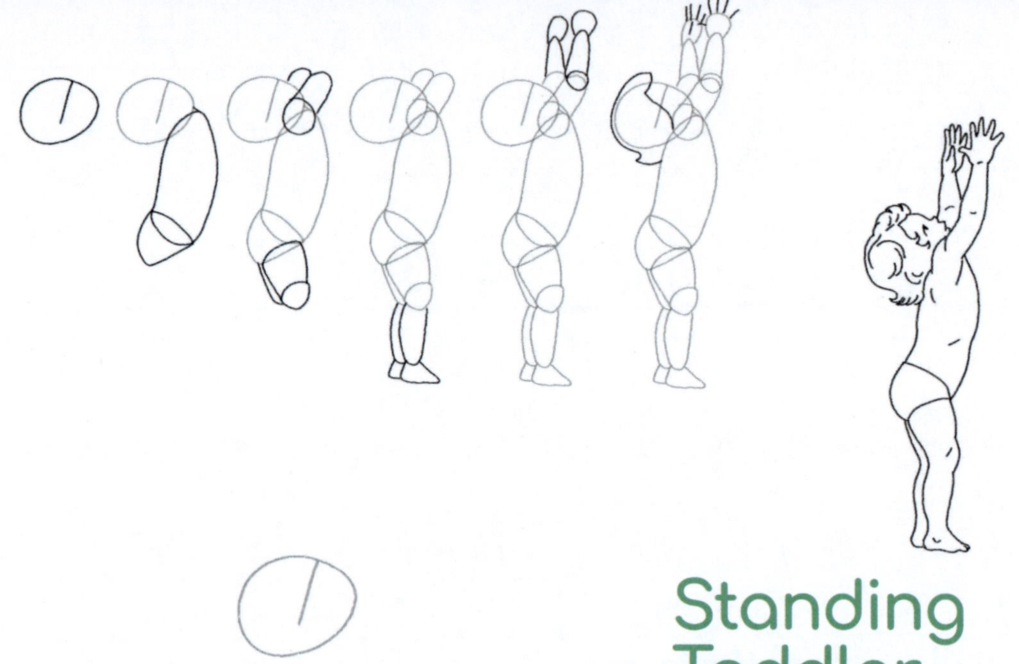

Standing Toddler

This child's raised arms stretch
and narrow the torso. We can't
see the neck.

58 th day

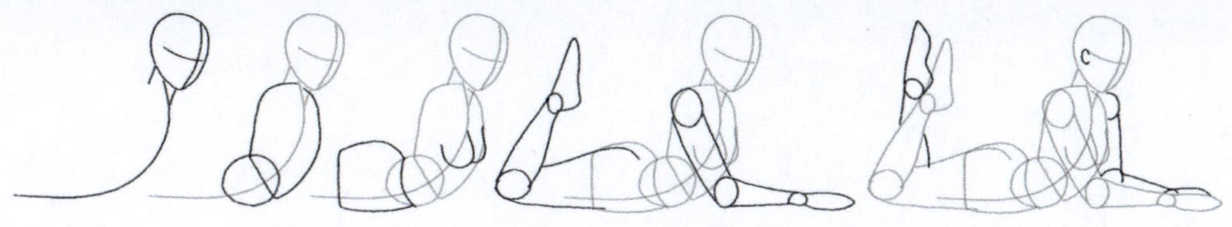

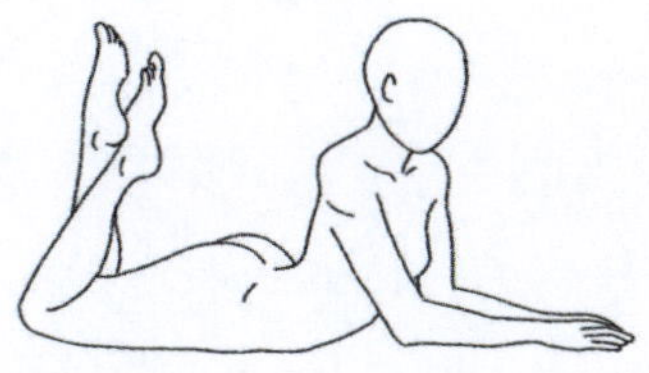

Woman Lying on Stomach

This woman's reclining pose, viewed in profile, hides one side of the body. The entire body is articulated in a U shape.

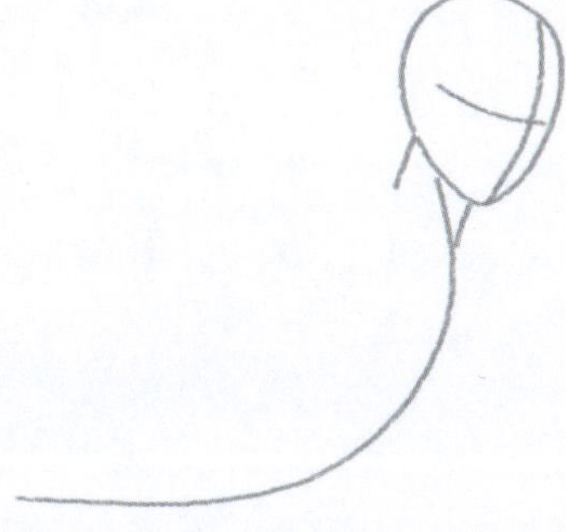

59 th day

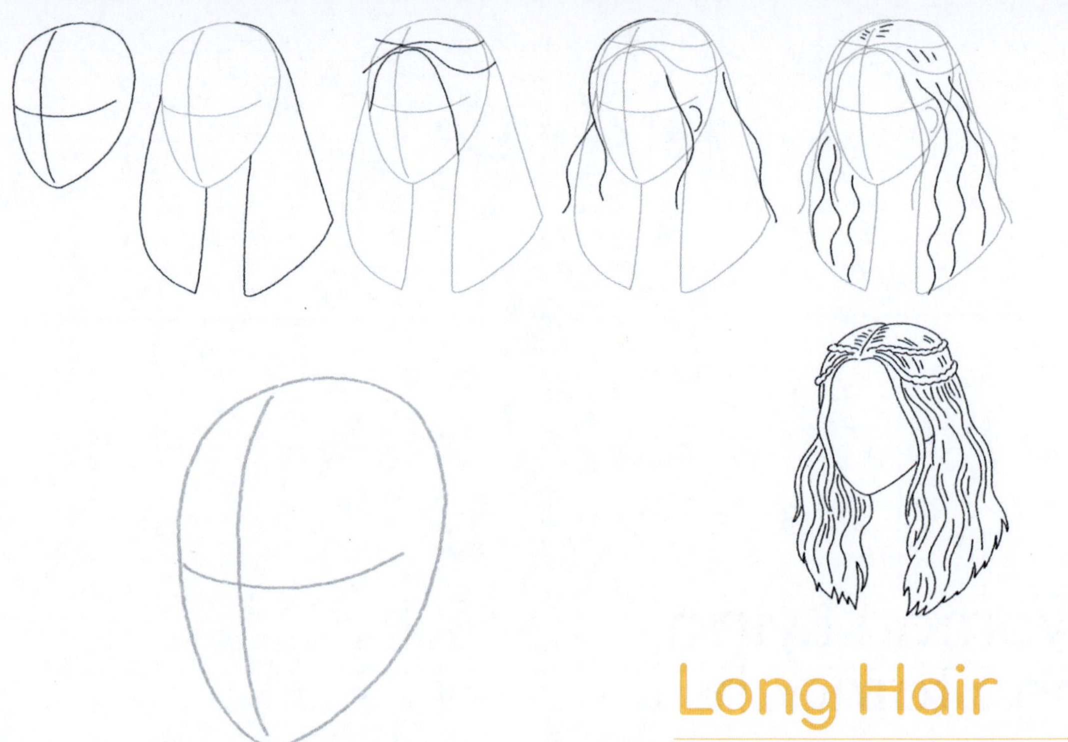

Long Hair

The lines creating the strands
of hair are tighter in the shaded
areas and around the part.

60th day

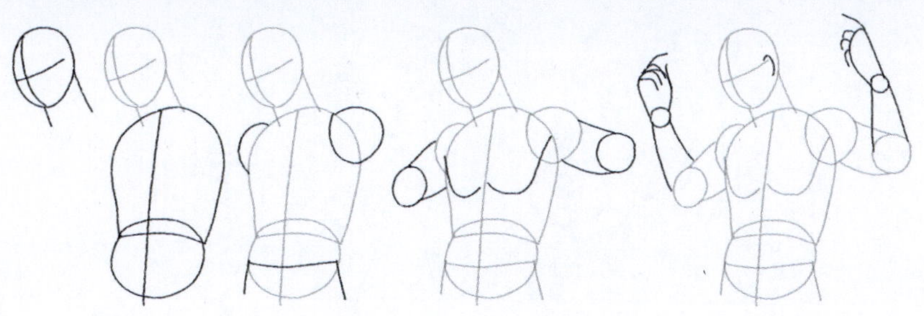

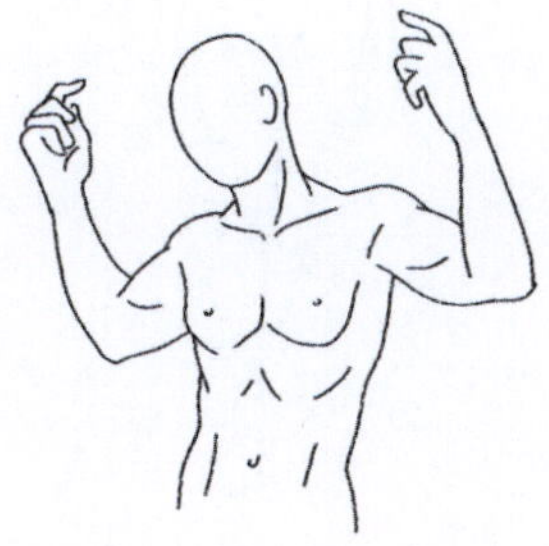

Man's Torso

This figure's raised arms emphasize the creases and bulges of the torso and tuck in the stomach.

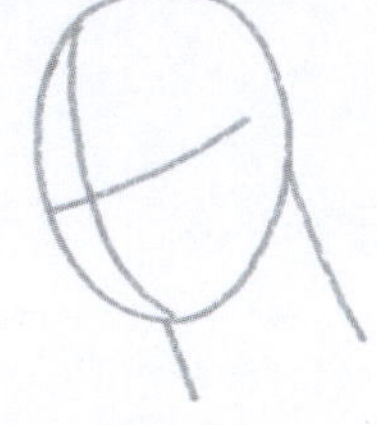

61st day

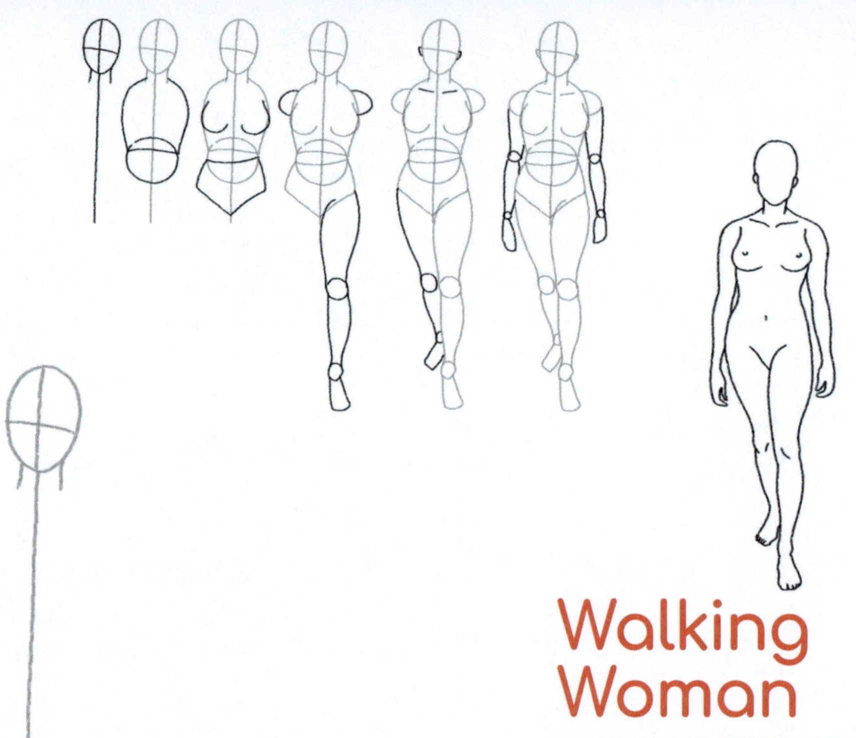

Walking Woman

Viewed from the front, this walking figure has a slight sway to the hips. The size of the back leg is reduced by the perspective.

62nd day

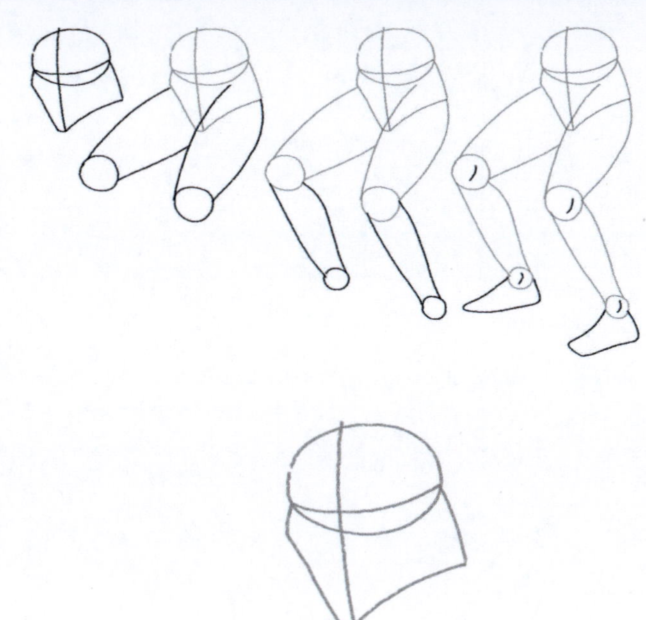

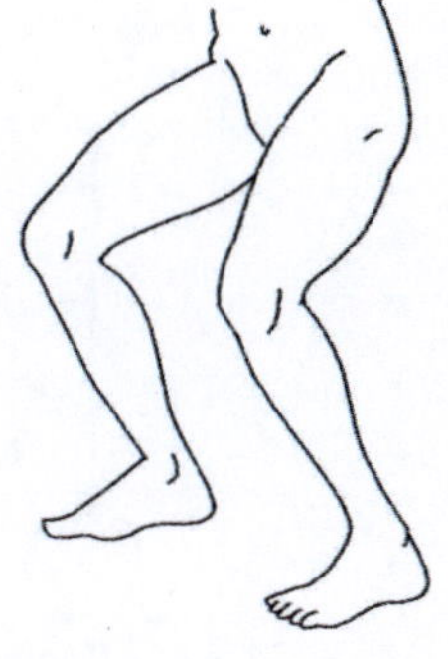

Man's Legs

When drawing legs in close-up, you can emphasize the lines of the knees and ankles and the crease of the buttocks.

63rd day

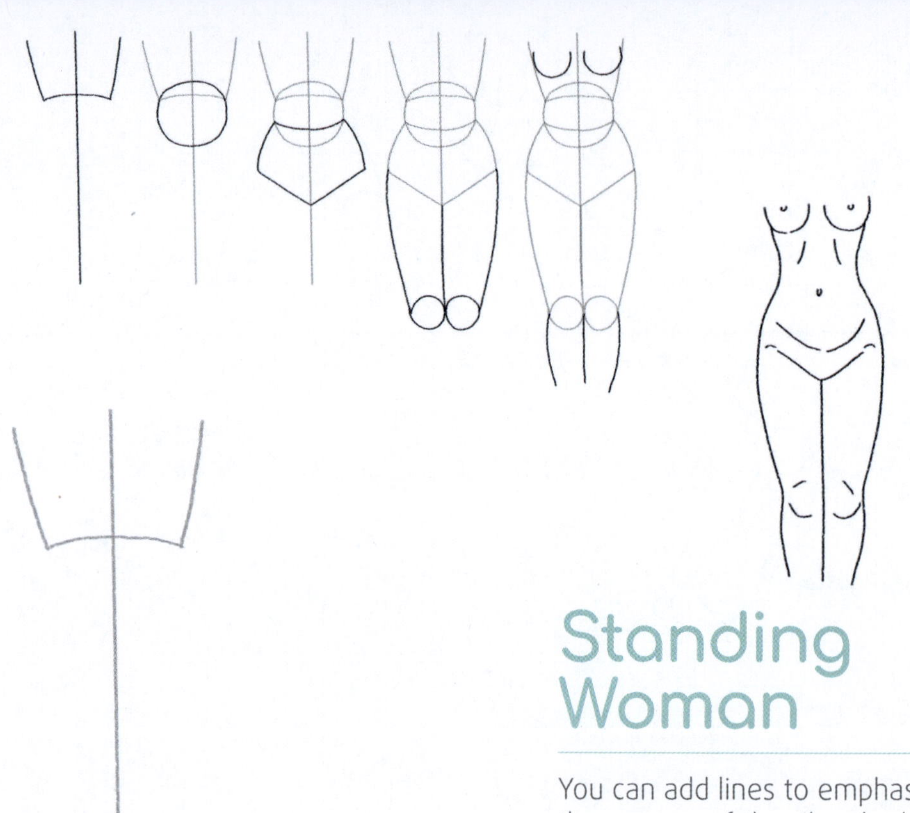

Standing Woman

You can add lines to emphasize the creases of the ribs, the lower abdomen and the knees.

64th day

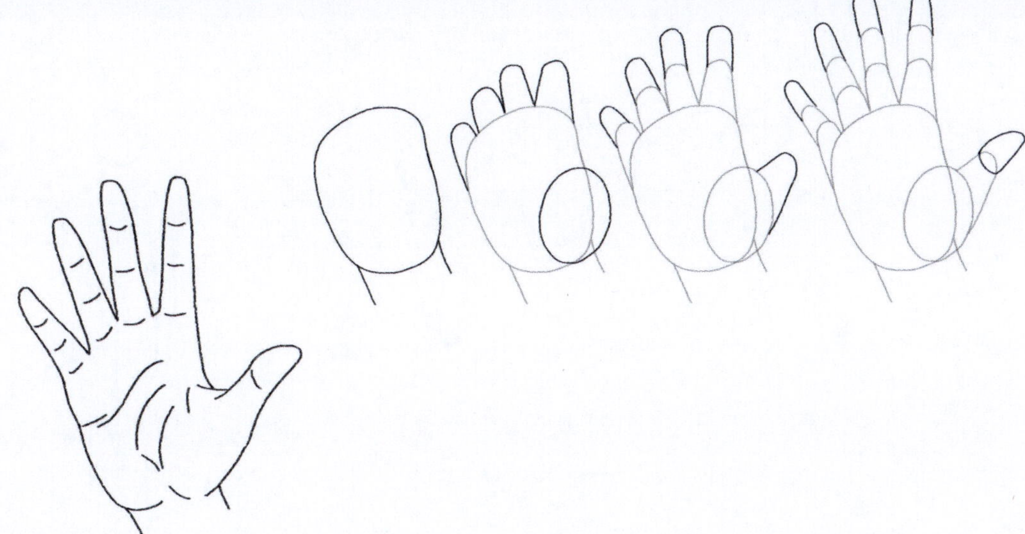

Hand

The fingers of this hand are spread apart, and the folds on the inside of the palm emphasize the tension of the pose.

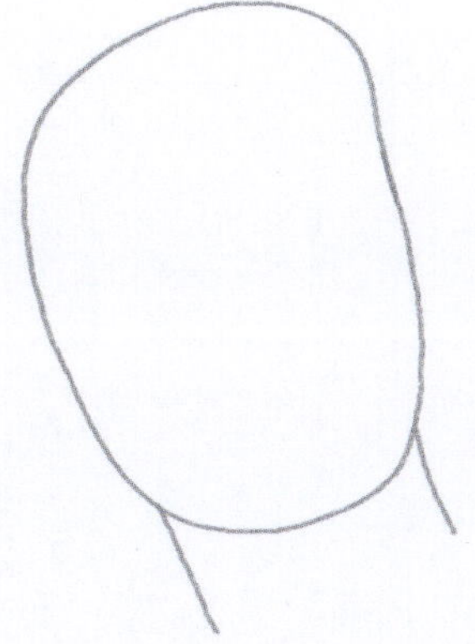

65th **day**

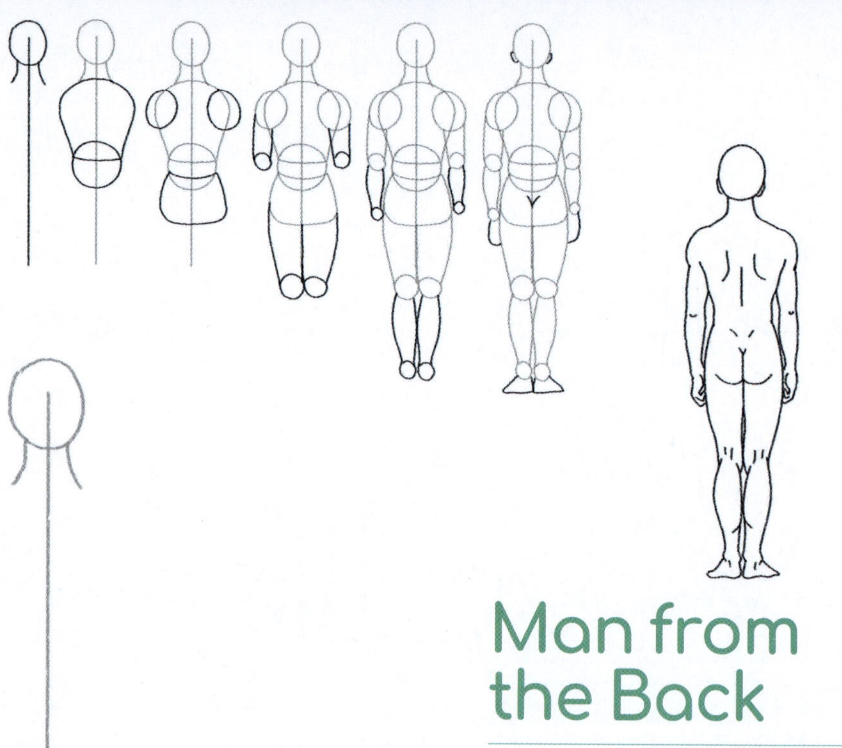

Man from
the Back

This figure's broad shoulders are emphasized by the narrowness of the hips.

66th day

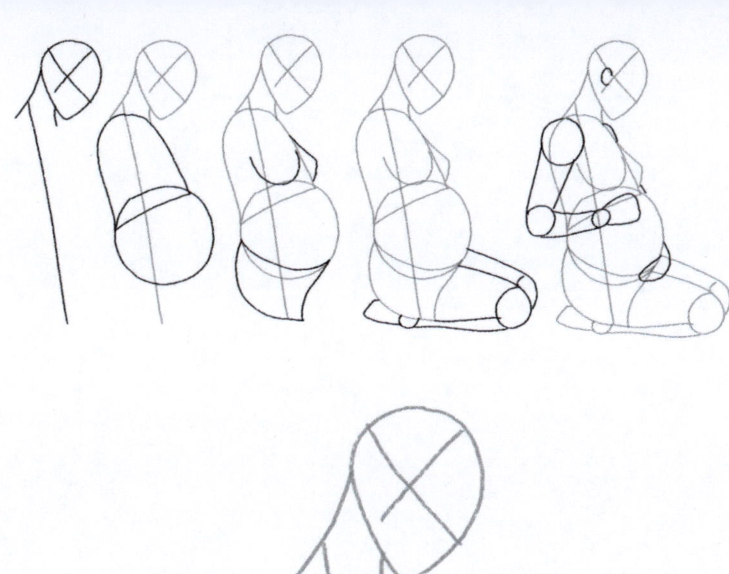

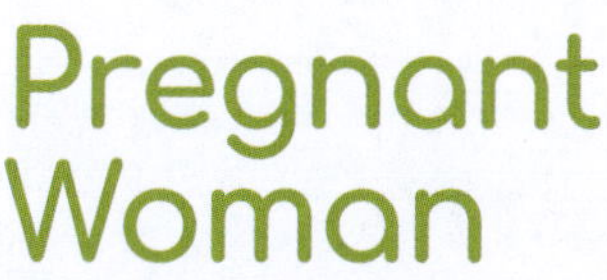

Pregnant
Woman

To draw a pregnant woman, you transform the volumes of the torso and tilt the body's weight backward, to act as a counterweight.

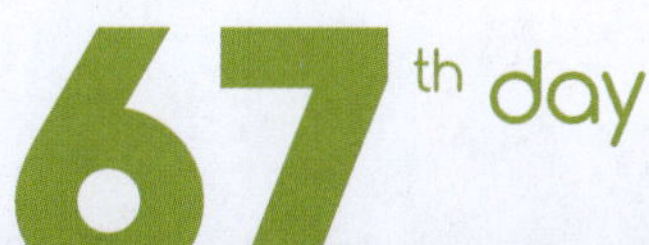

67th day

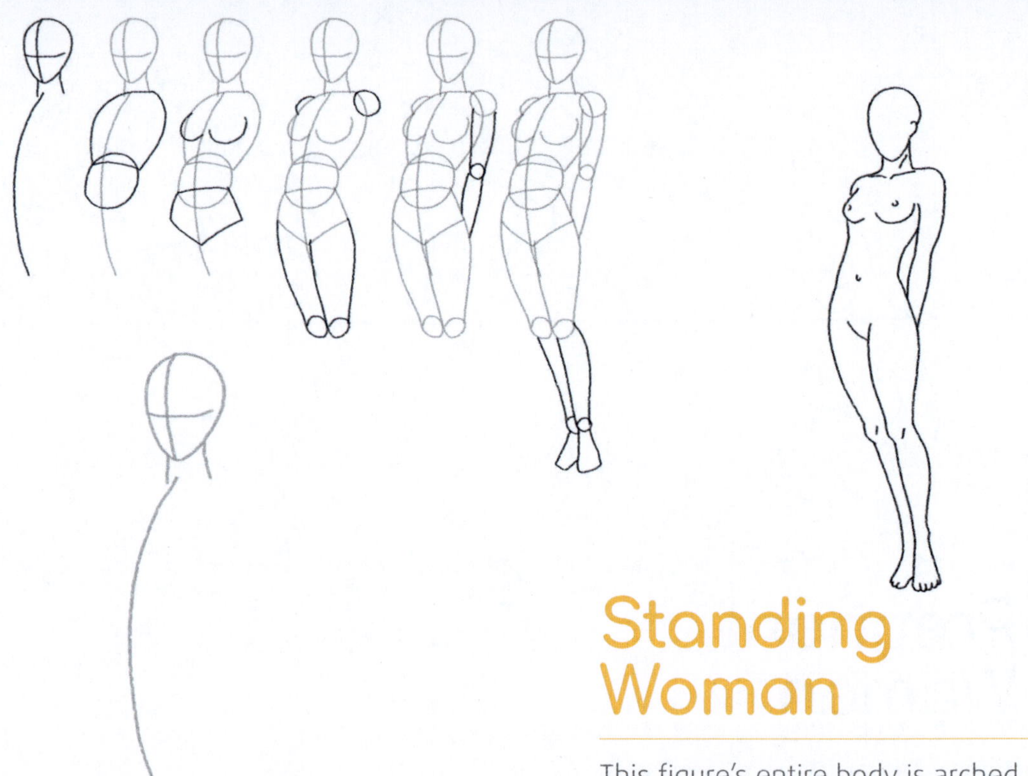

Standing Woman

This figure's entire body is arched forward, and the shoulders are pulled back by the arms, which are stretched down.

68th day

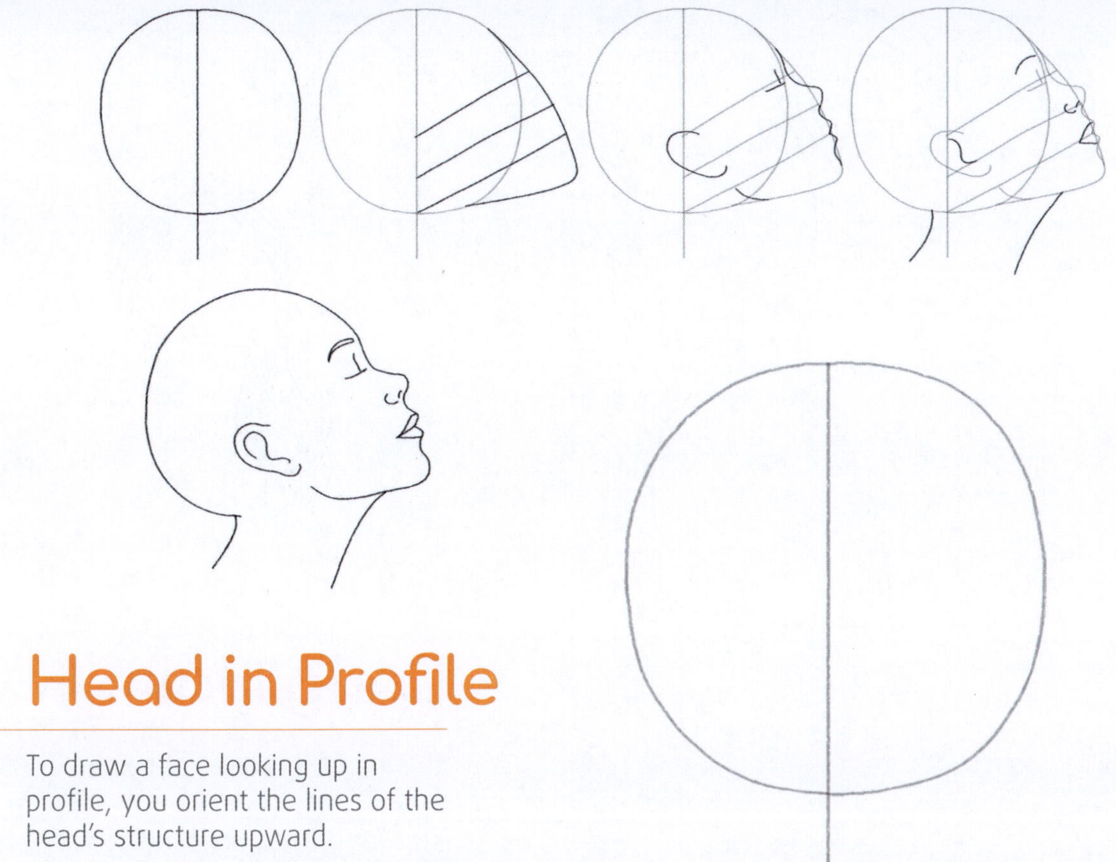

Head in Profile

To draw a face looking up in
profile, you orient the lines of the
head's structure upward.

69th day

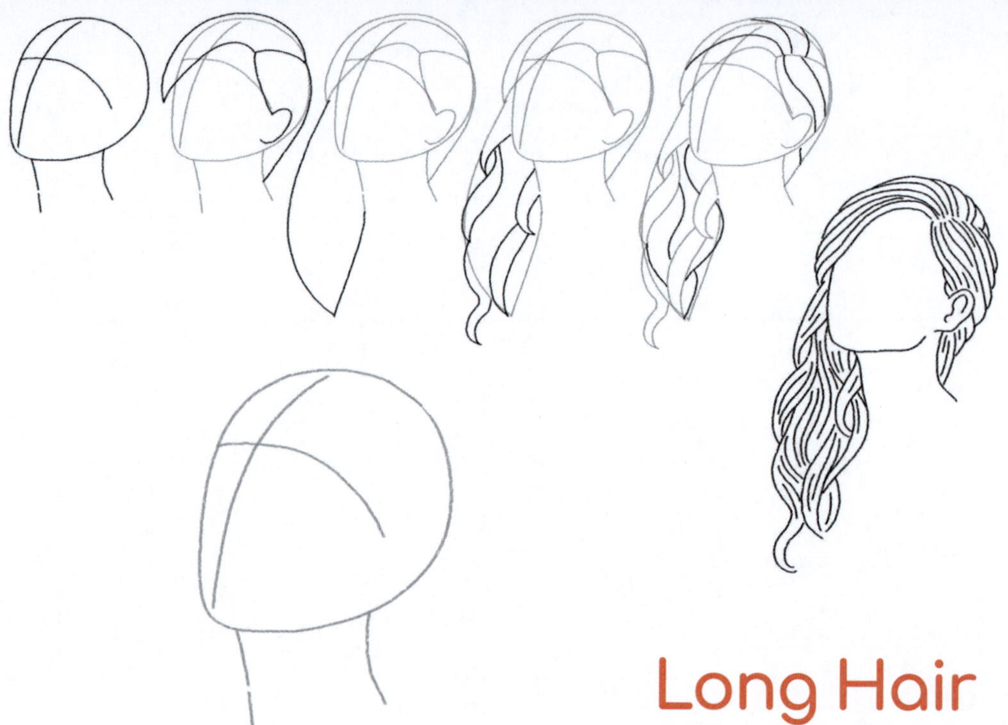

Long Hair

The top of this head of hair is
smooth and follows the shape of
the head. The strands are wavy
along their length and thin out
near the bottom.

70th day

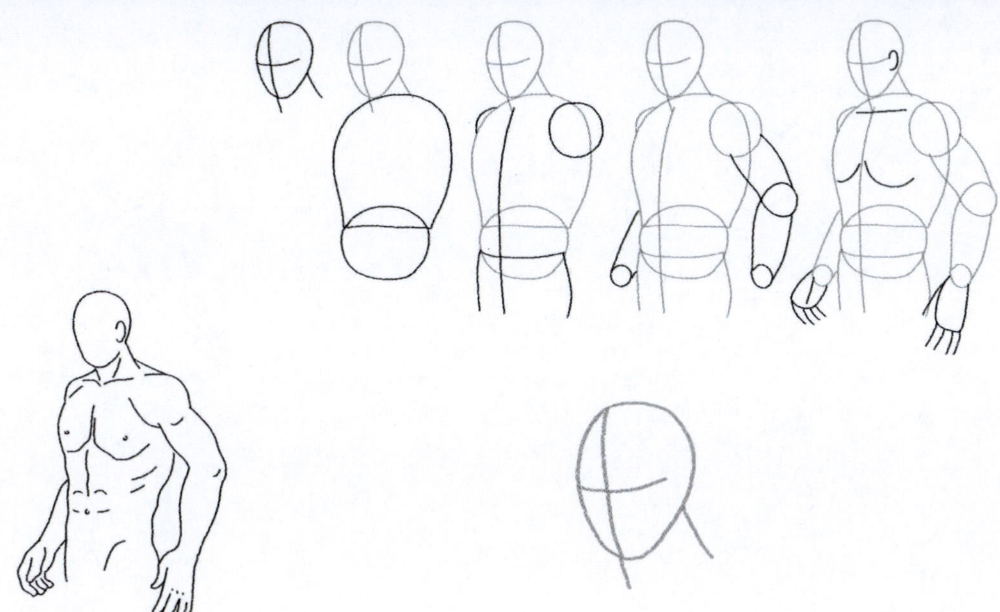

Man's Torso

The three-quarter view of this figure obscures part of an arm. Up close, small lines outline the muscles of the chest and of the arm that's closest to us.

71st day

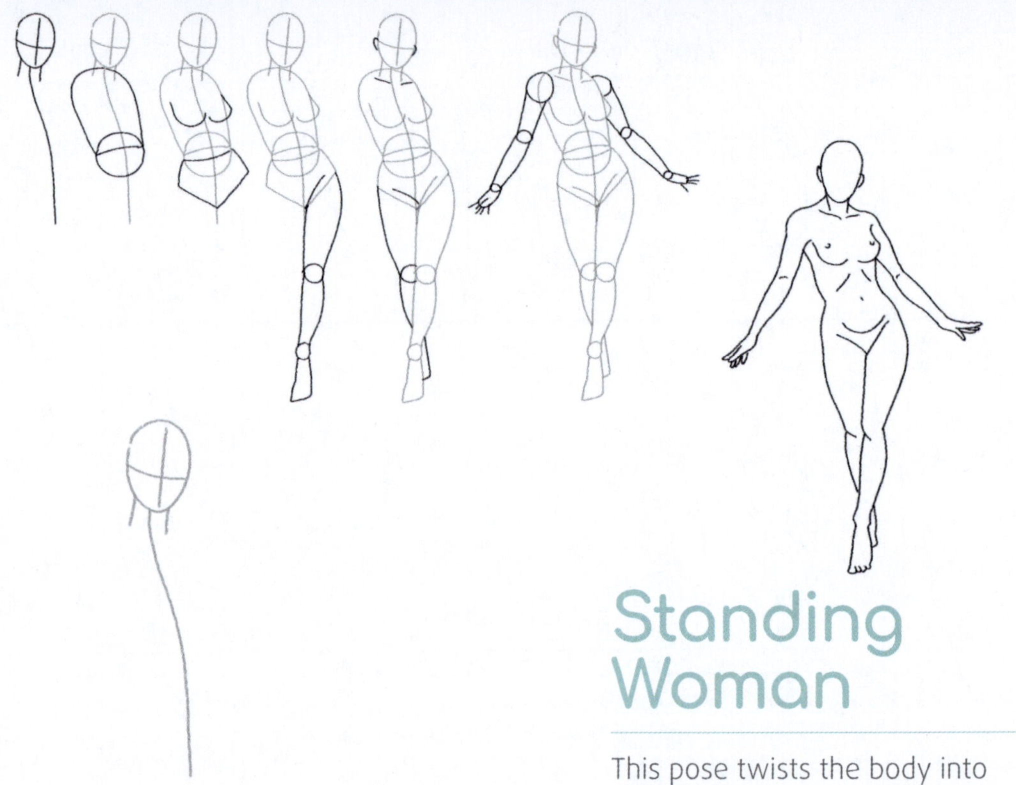

Standing Woman

This pose twists the body into a swaying stance. One shoulder and the opposite foot push the body forward.

72nd day

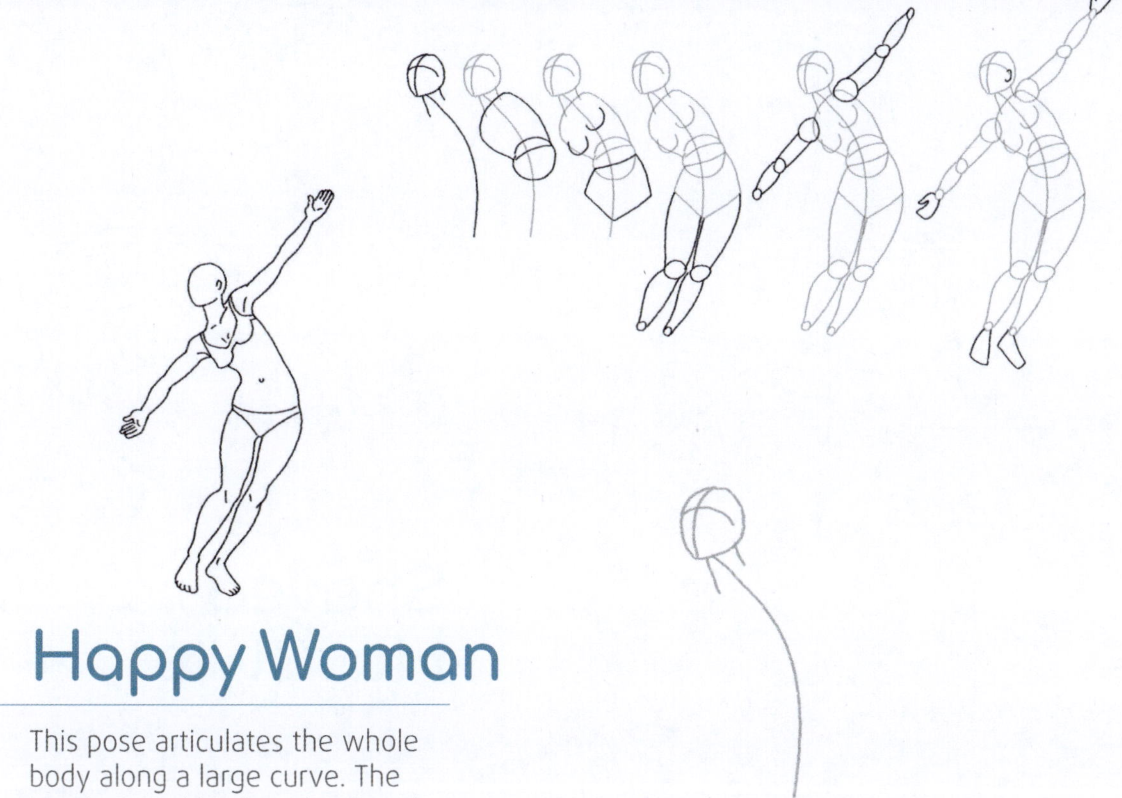

Happy Woman

This pose articulates the whole body along a large curve. The head is tilted back and reduced by the perspective.

73rd day

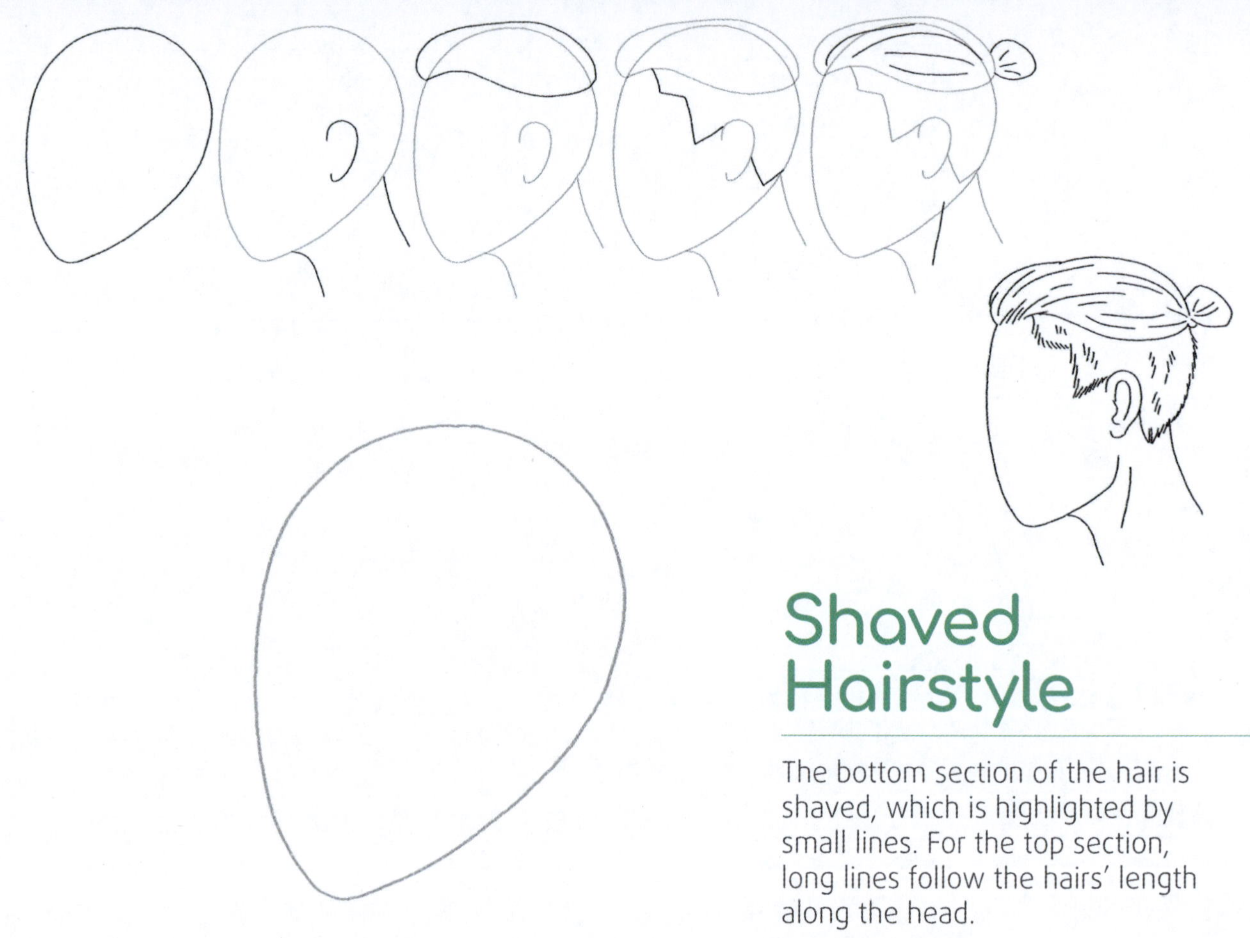

Shaved
Hairstyle

The bottom section of the hair is shaved, which is highlighted by small lines. For the top section, long lines follow the hairs' length along the head.

74th day

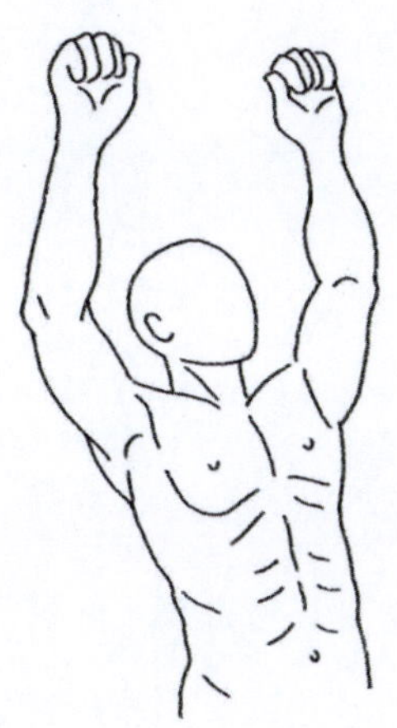

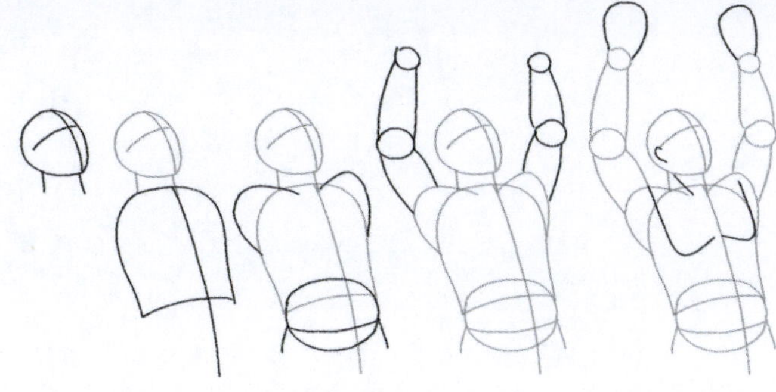

Cheering Man

This figure's raised arms stretch
the torso and emphasize
the lines along the ribs and
abdominal muscles.

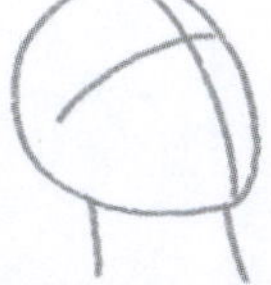

75th day

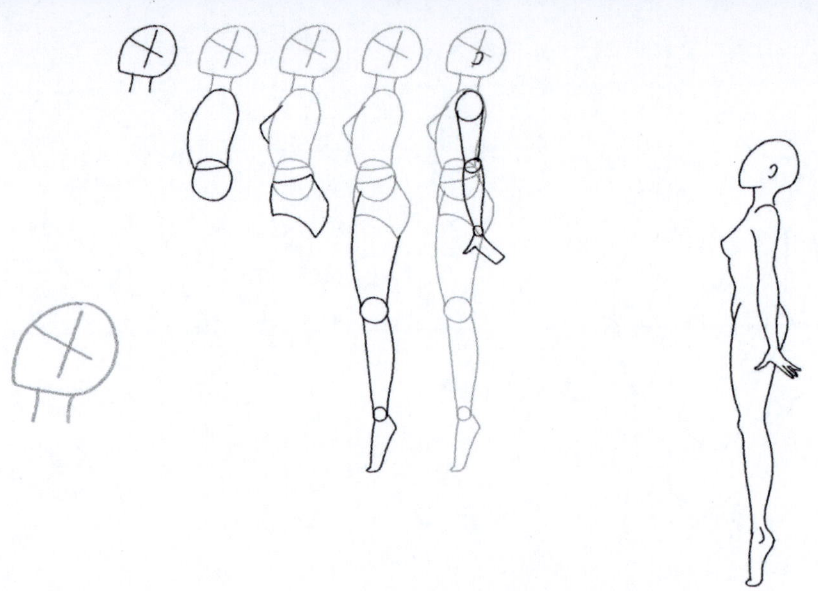

Woman in Profile

This stretched profile perfectly obscures half the body. The pointed toes lengthen the legs.

76th day

Head in Profile

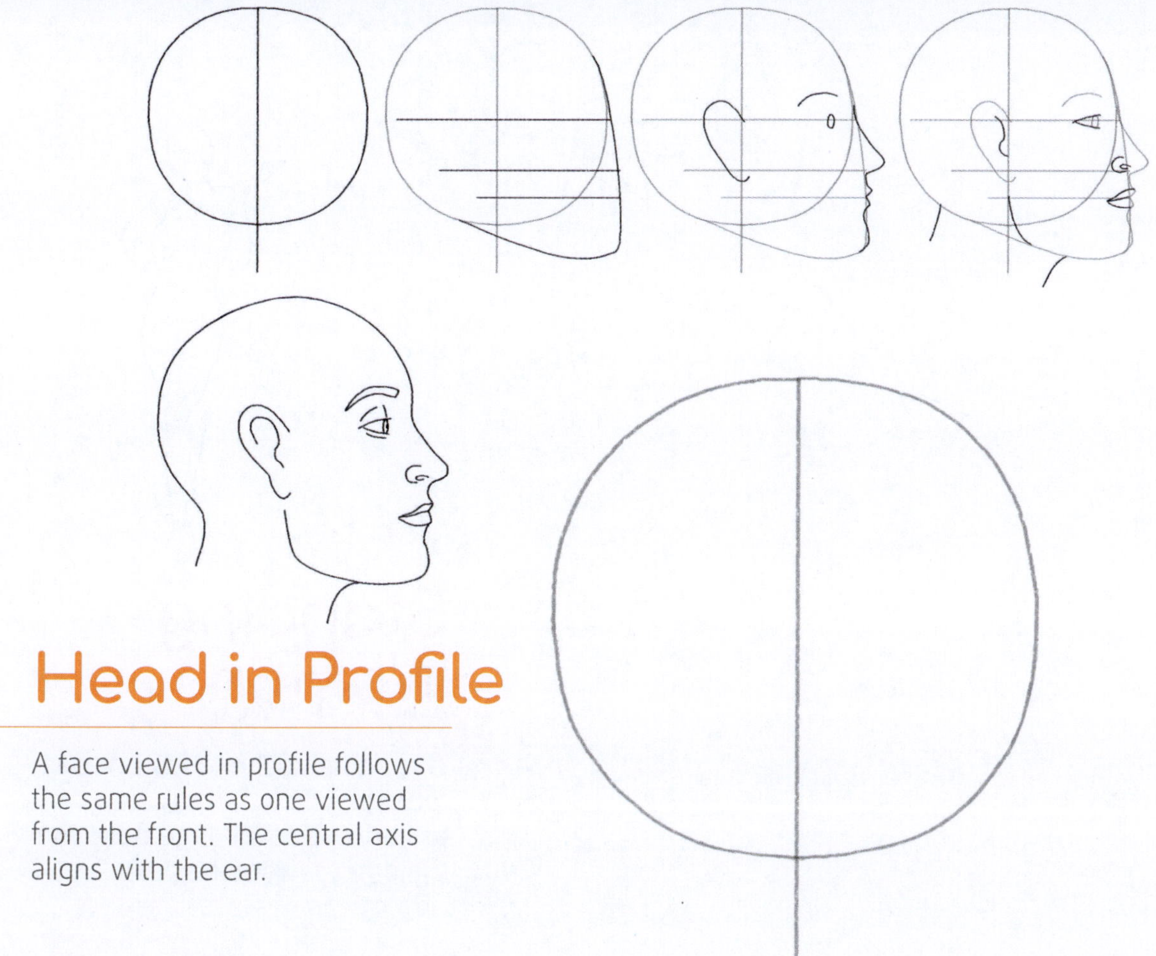

A face viewed in profile follows the same rules as one viewed from the front. The central axis aligns with the ear.

77th day

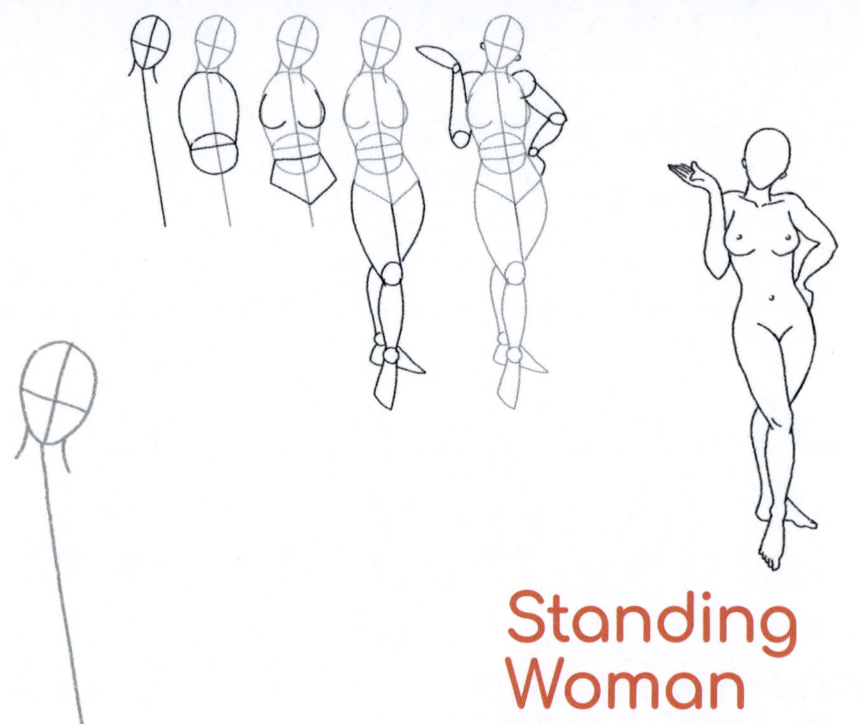

Standing
Woman

This figure's upper body is facing forward, while the legs are turned, one toward the front and the other toward the back.

78th day

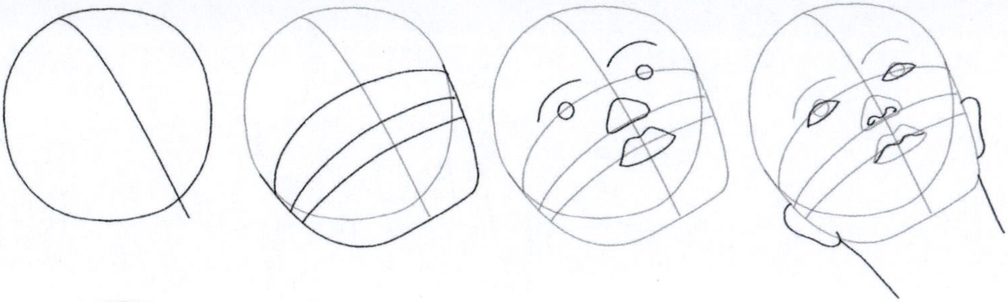

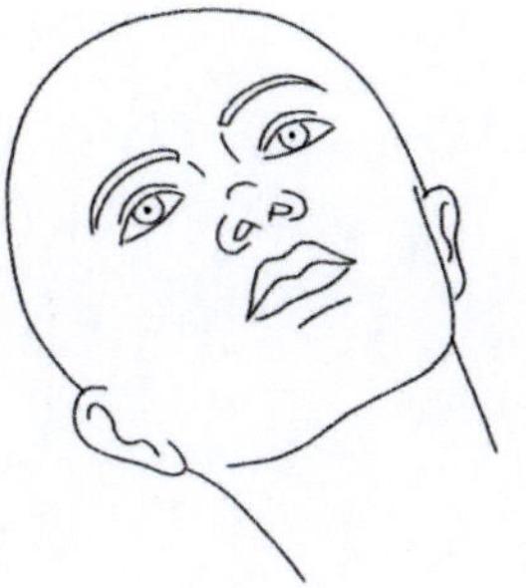

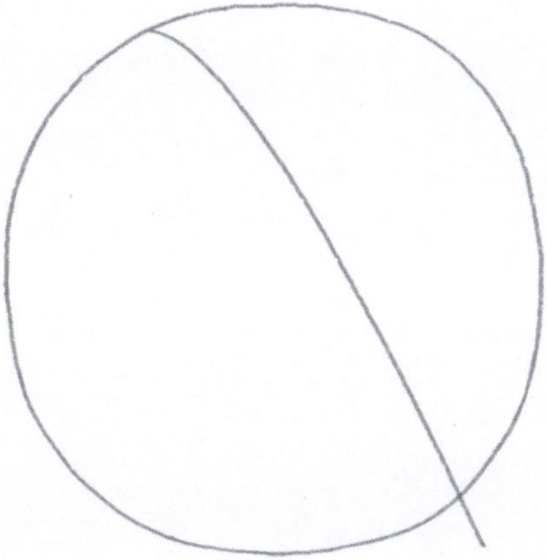

Woman's Head

The upturned face of this figure has soft features. The perspective slightly alters the position of the central axis and thus the shape of the eyes, nose and mouth.

79th day

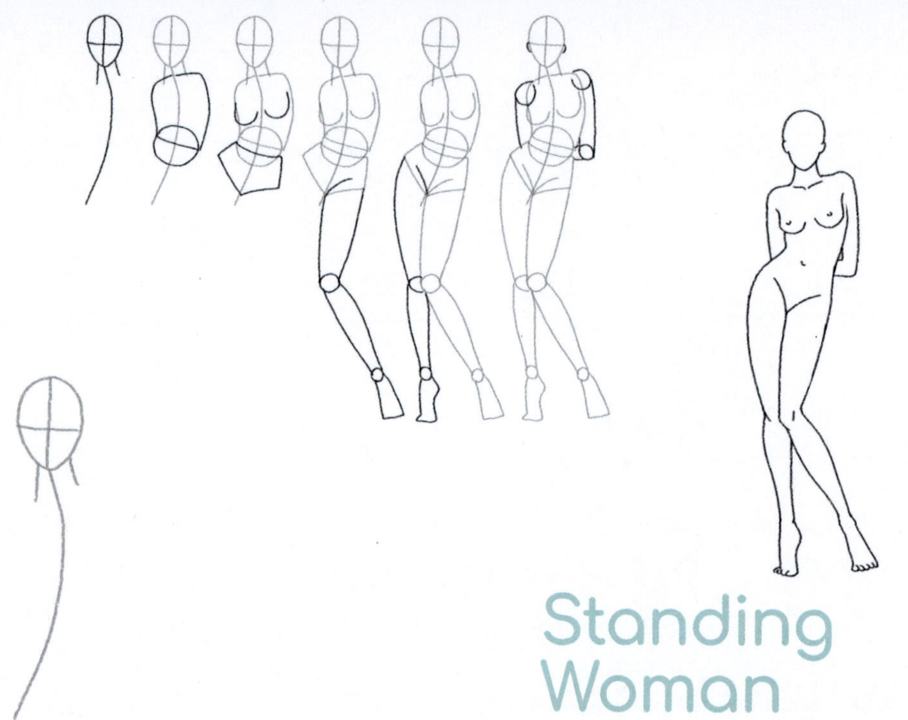

Standing Woman

This figure has a graceful swaying movement. The torso is slightly twisted, and the knees are touching.

80 th day

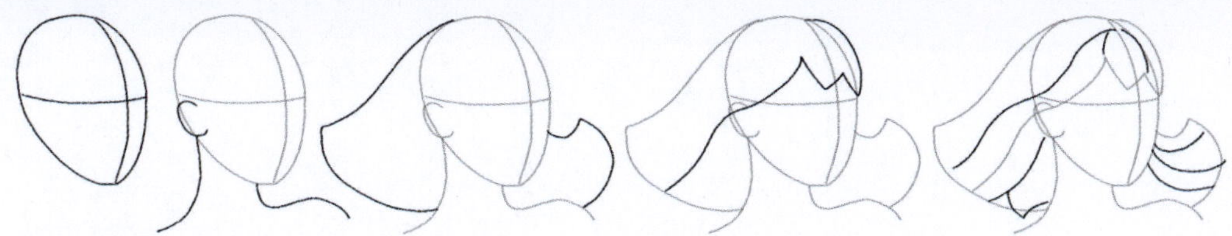

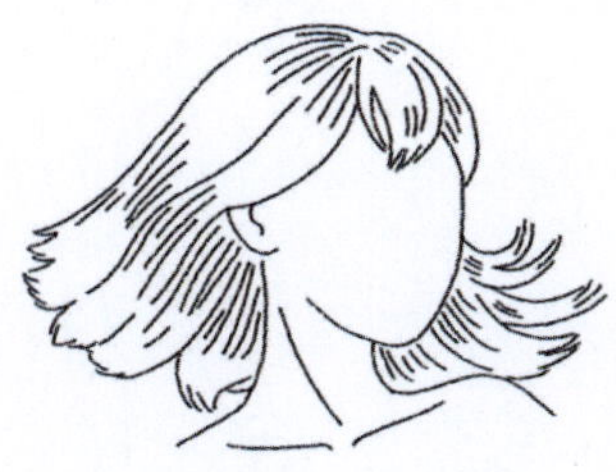

Wind-Blown Hair

As hair moves, the lines become tighter the closer they get to the part.

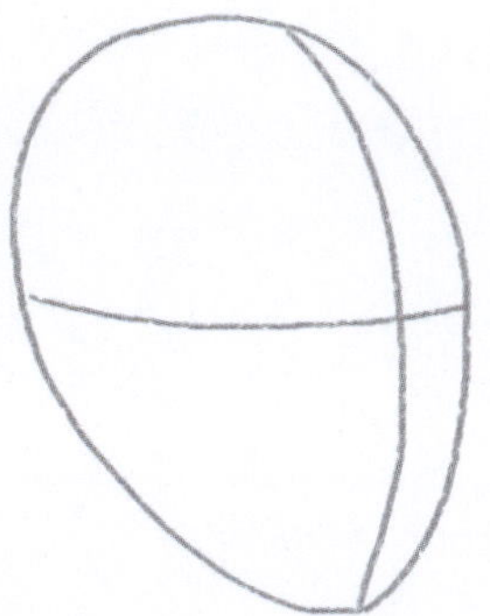

81st day

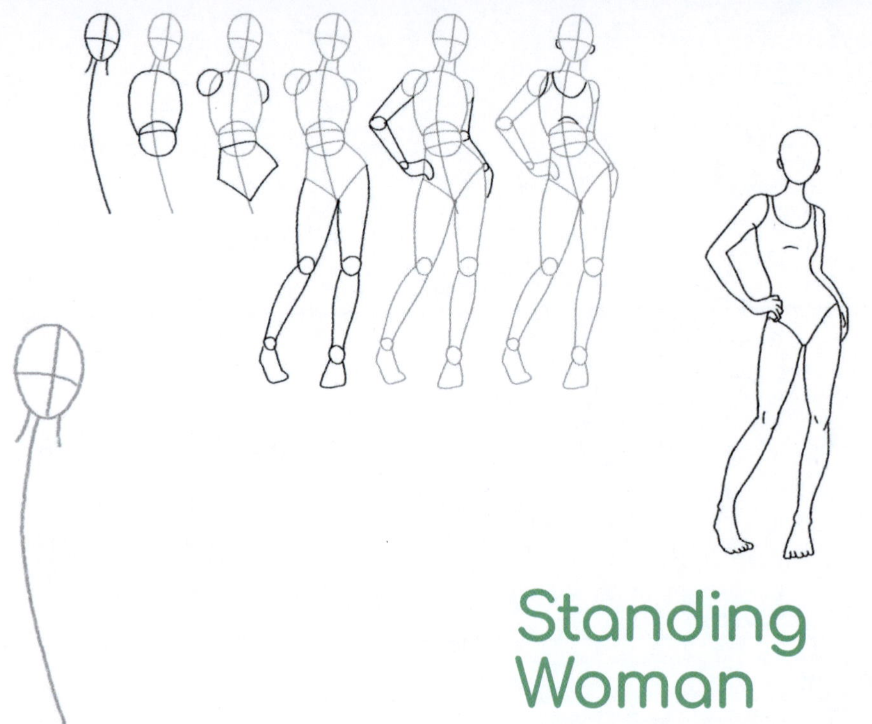

Standing Woman

A fluid sway of the hips articulates this figure's torso in a curve that is very wide on one side and tighter on the other.

82nd day

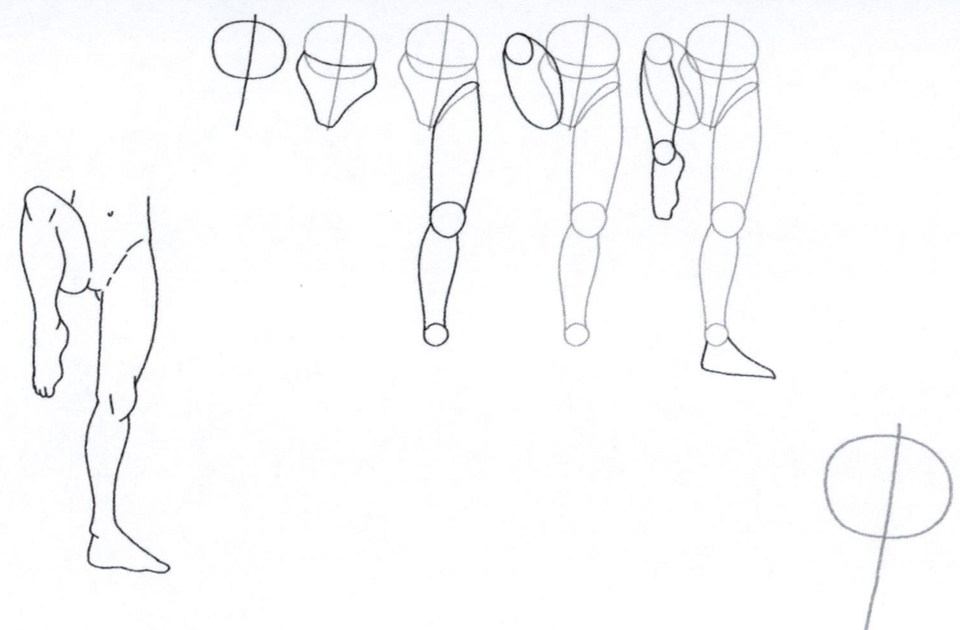

Man's Legs

The grounded leg looks quite
shapely and tense from
the effort of the pose. The
perspective created by the raised
leg obscures a bit of that thigh.

83rd day

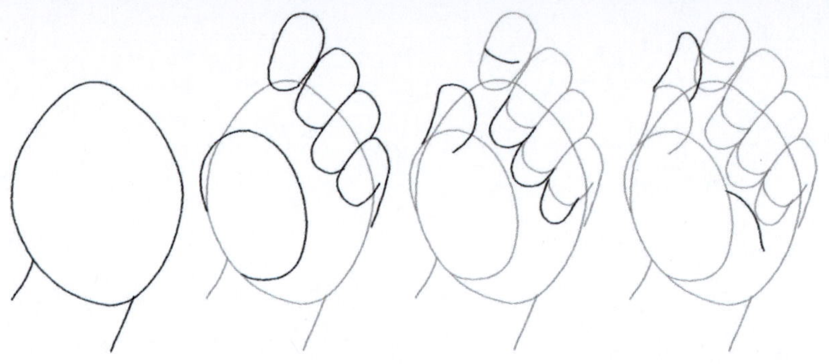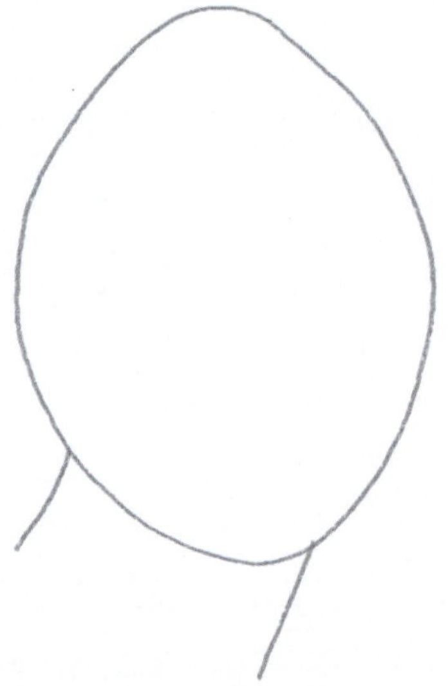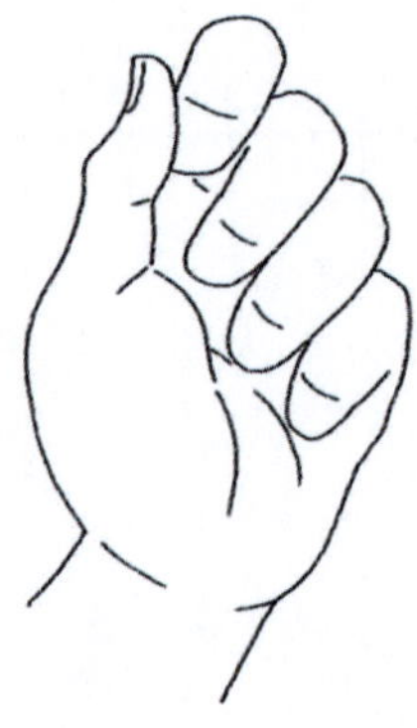

Fist

This pose is a soft, unclenched fist. The fingers are loose, but the thumb is held against the index finger, its base curved by the tension.

84 th day

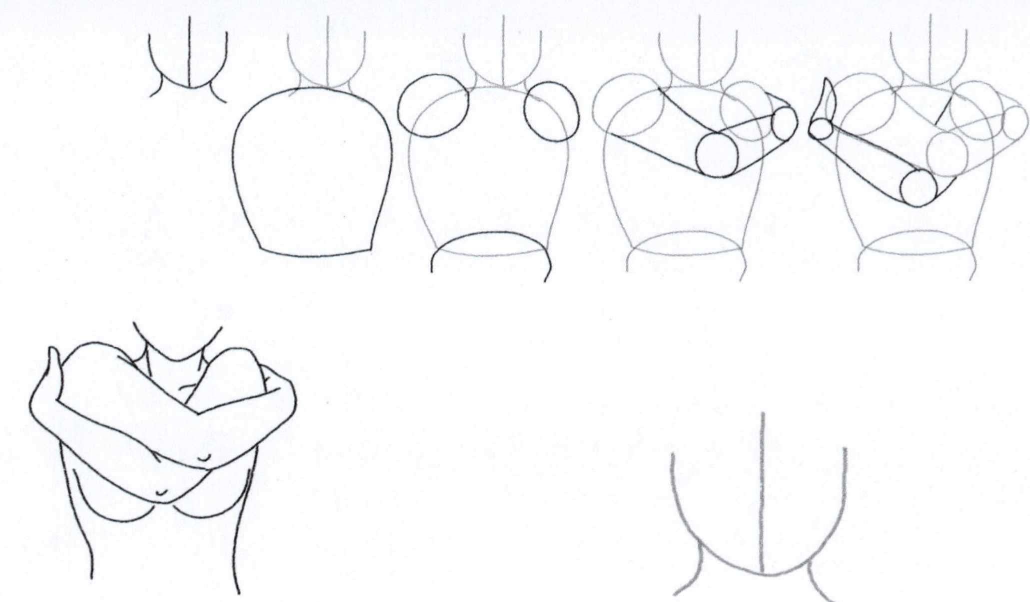

Woman's Torso

The arms are wrapped around
the shoulders, which point
upward, one slightly more than
the other. This accentuates the
narrowness of the torso.

85th day

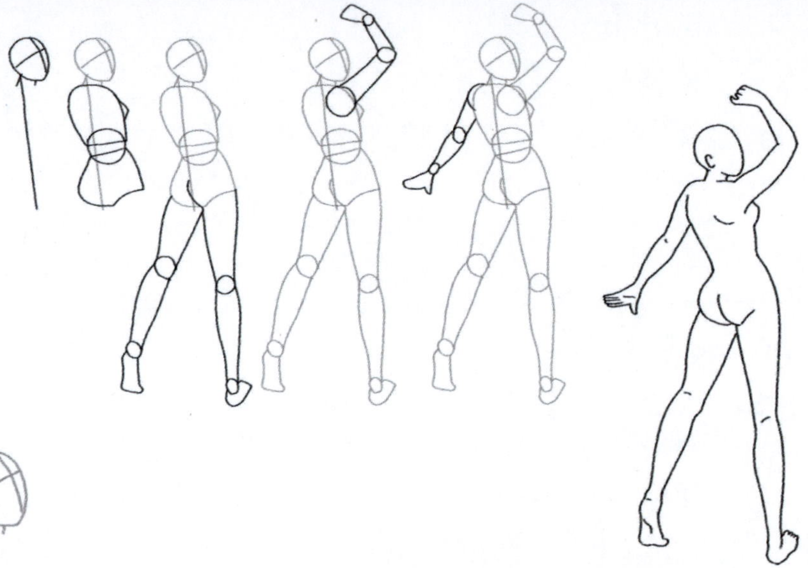

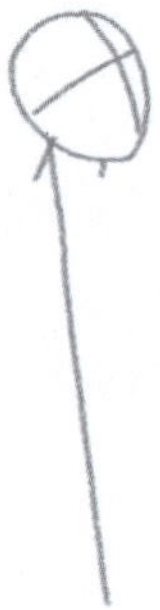

Woman from the Back

The overall effect of this pose, viewed in three-quarters from behind, is slightly swaying and in perspective.

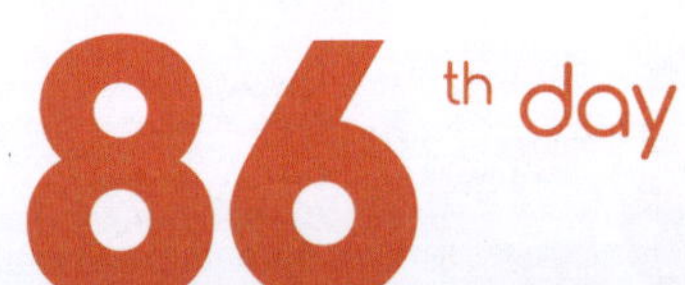

86th day

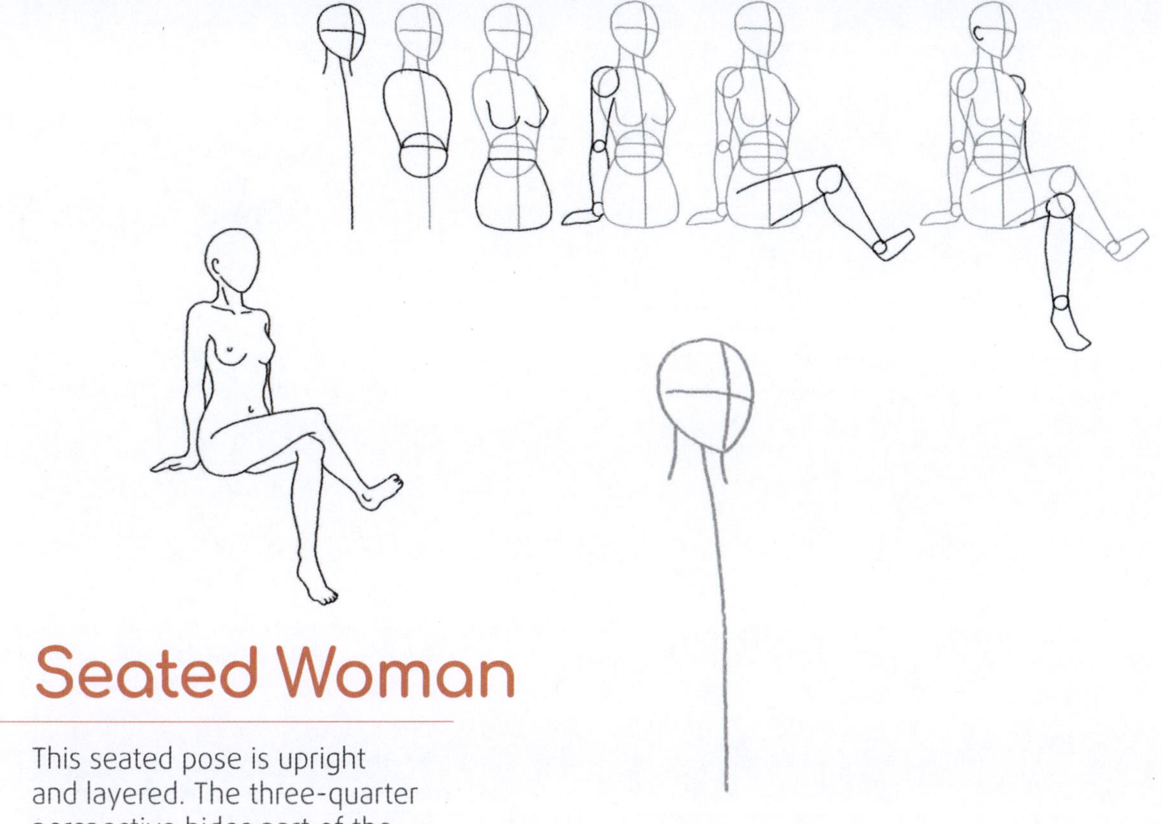

Seated Woman

This seated pose is upright
and layered. The three-quarter
perspective hides part of the
back arm and shapes the leg that
is crossed over the other.

87th day

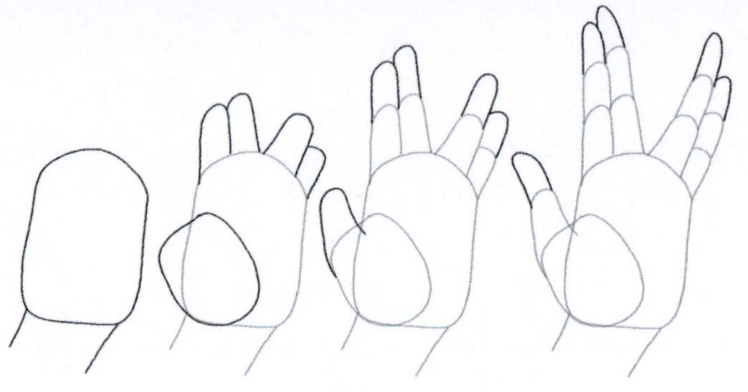

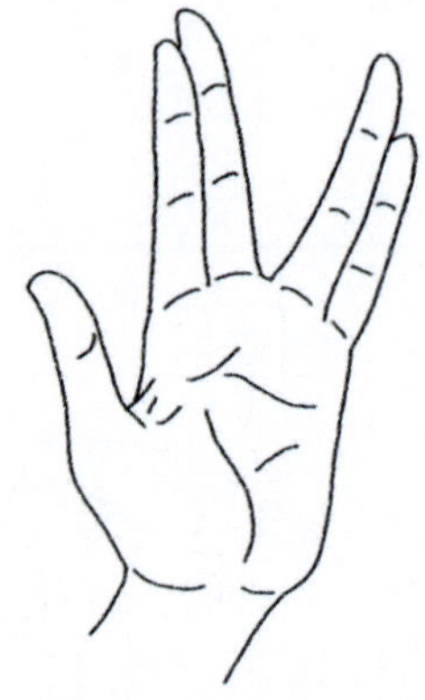

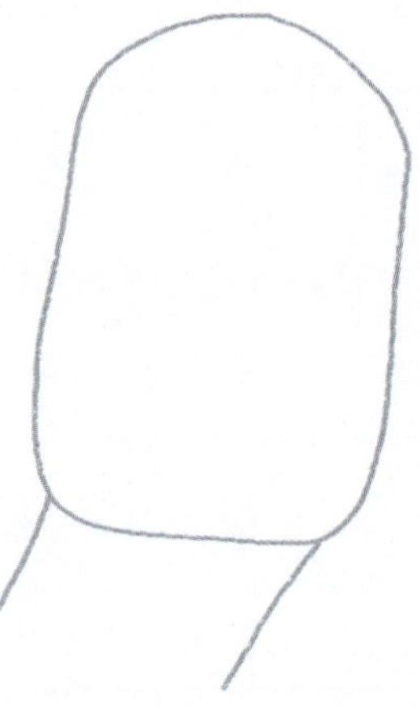

Hand

The elements of the hand in this pose are the same as one viewed from the front, but the fingers are pulled apart in the middle.

88th day

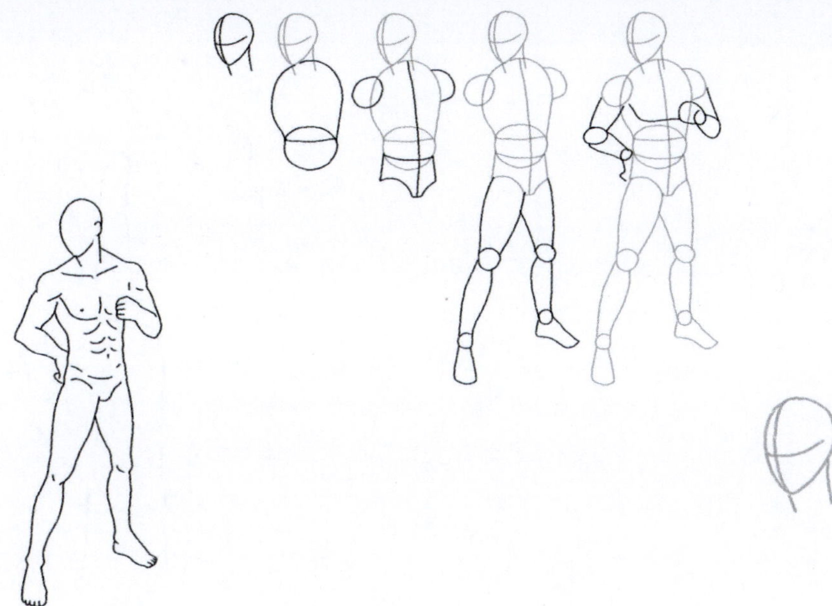

Standing Man

This figure's legs are firmly
planted on the ground and in
perspective. The upper torso is
turning in the opposite direction,
reorienting the shoulders.

89th day

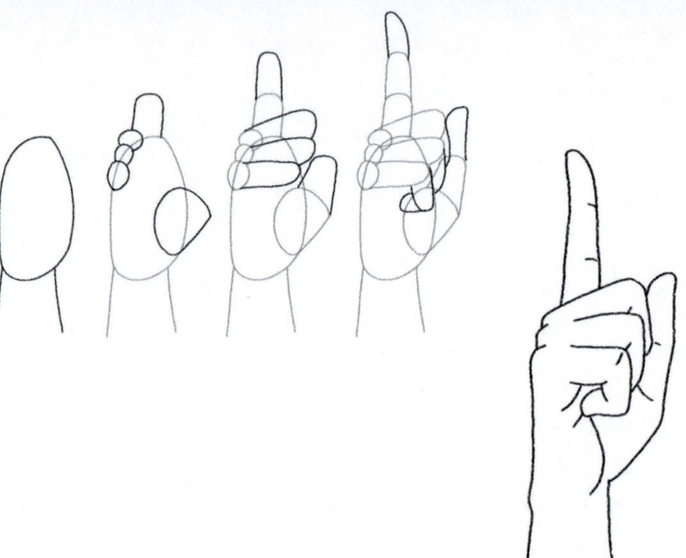

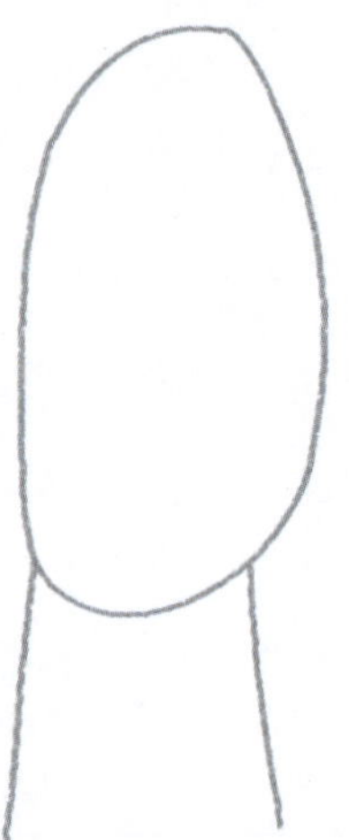

Hand

This hand is shown from the side. The folded fingers are clearly visible, but the rest of the hand is somewhat hidden.

90th day

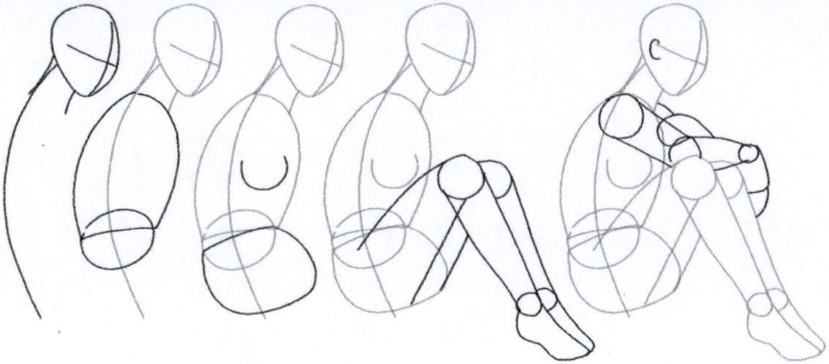

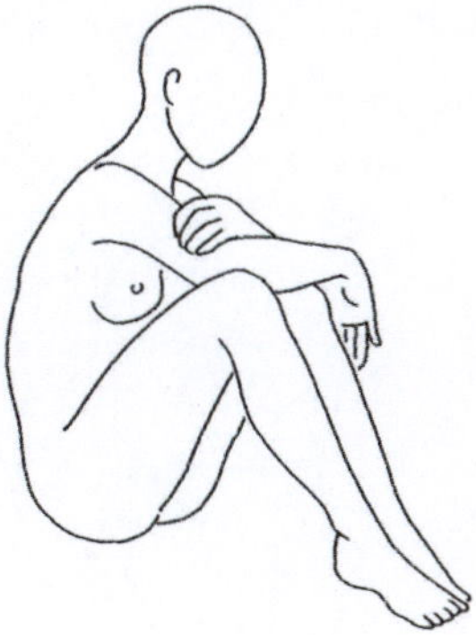

Seated Woman

This very compact, almost profile-like pose obscures much of one side of the figure's body.

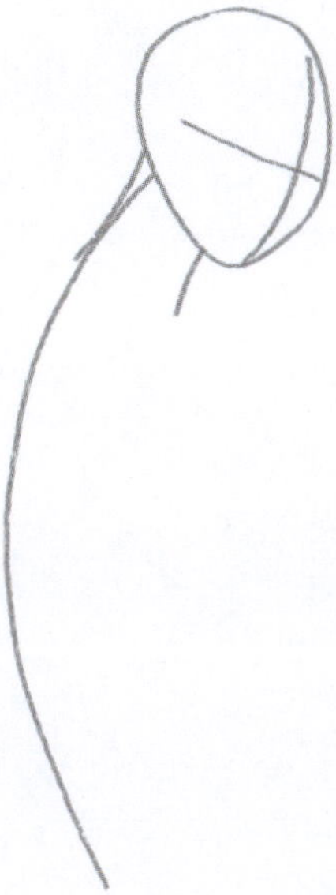

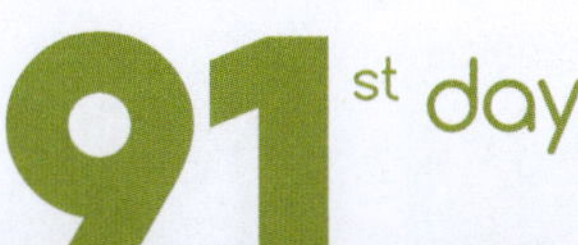

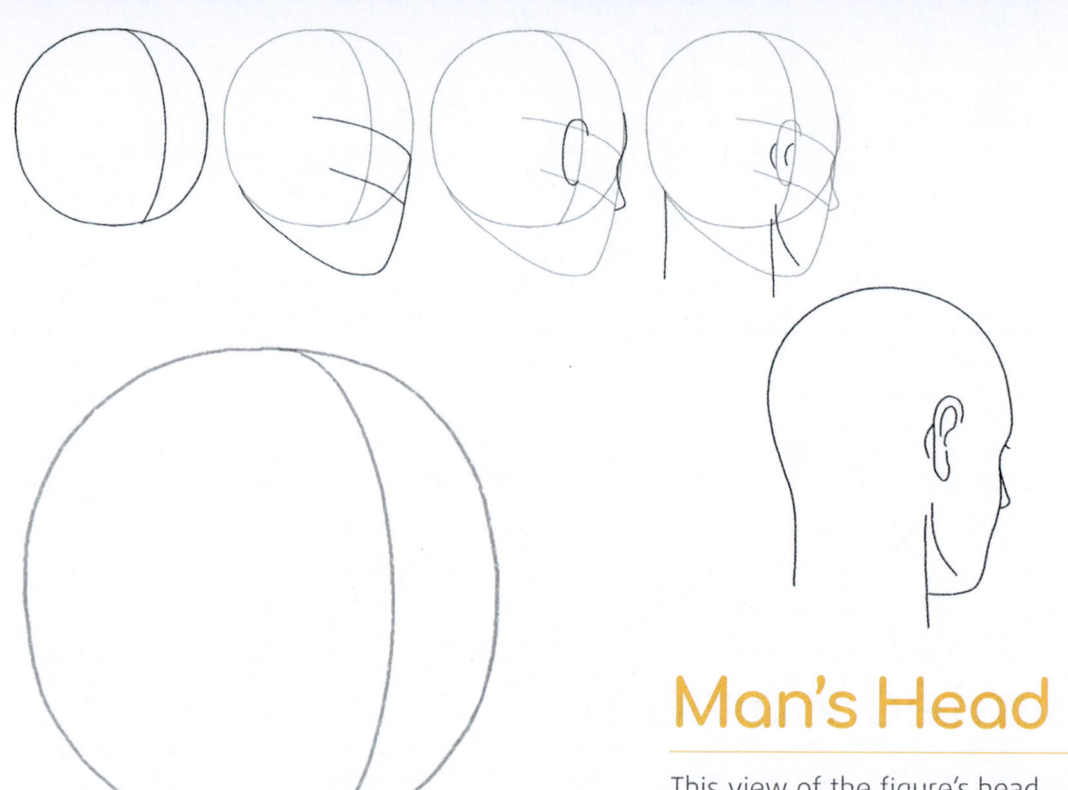

Man's Head

This view of the figure's head, almost from the back, hides much of the face. The inward curve above the cheek indicates the location of the eye.

92nd day

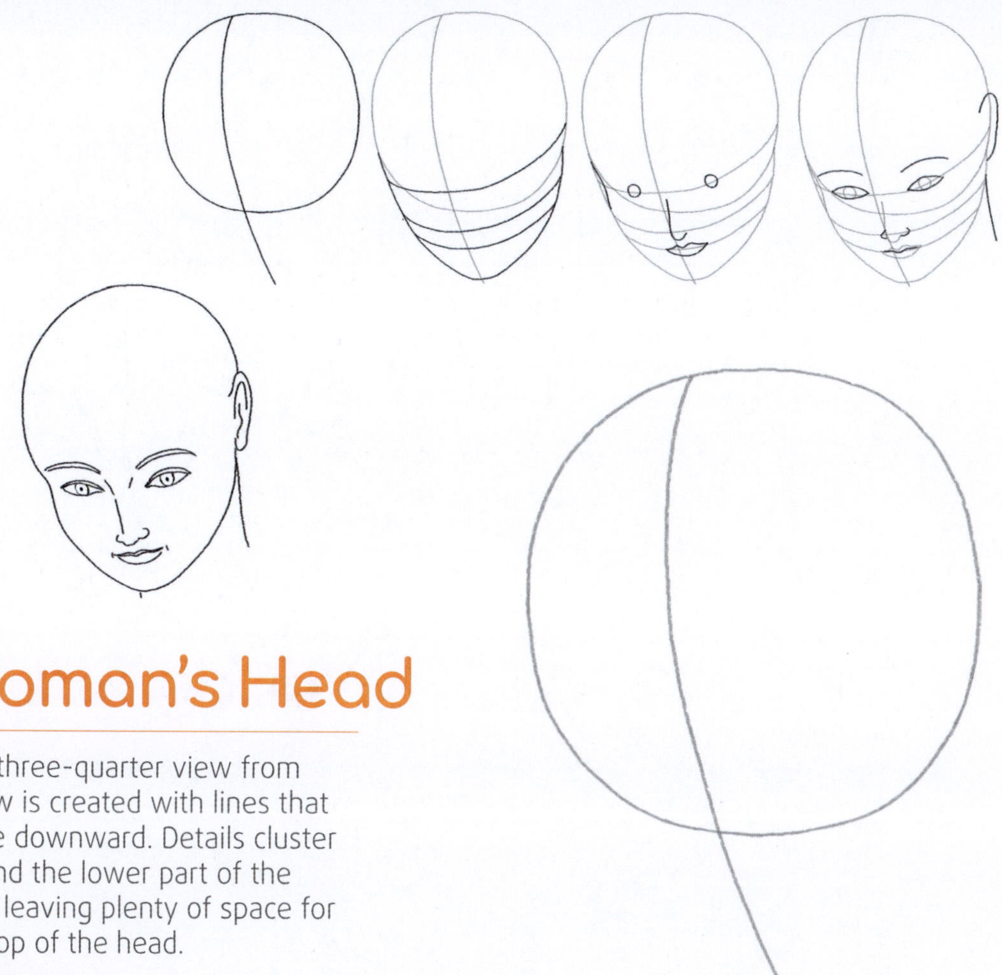

Woman's Head

This three-quarter view from below is created with lines that curve downward. Details cluster around the lower part of the face, leaving plenty of space for the top of the head.

93 rd day

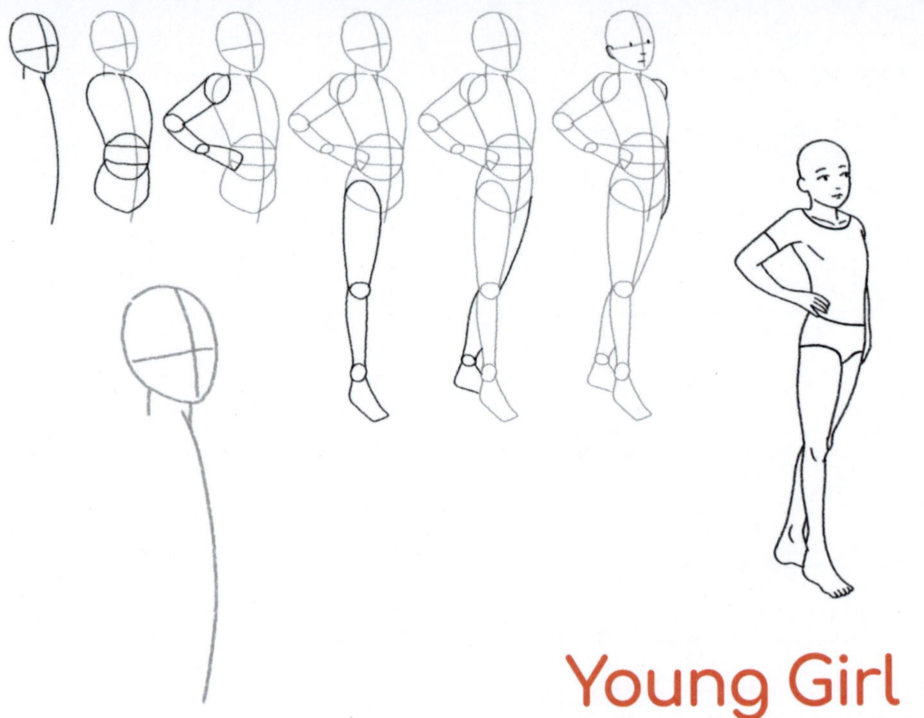

Young Girl

Before taking on a more womanly shape, a young girl's body is similar to that of a young boy.

94th day

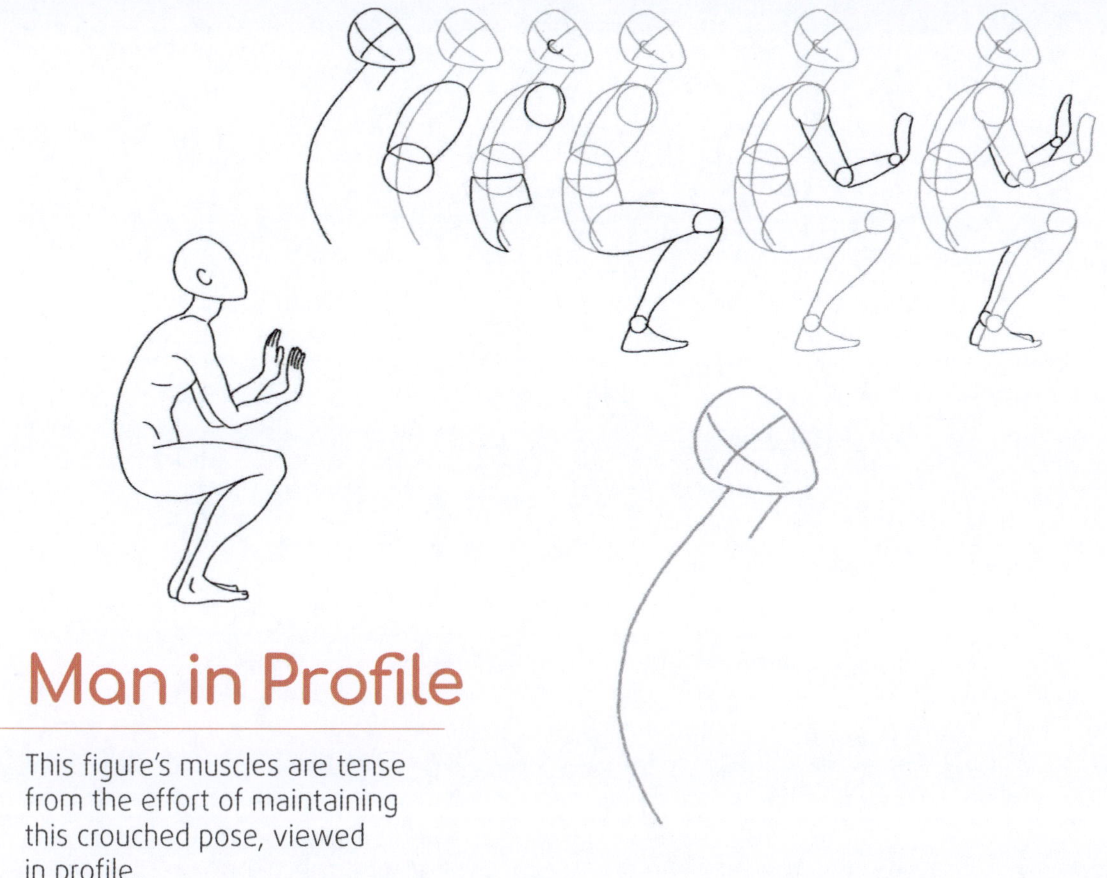

Man in Profile

This figure's muscles are tense
from the effort of maintaining
this crouched pose, viewed
in profile.

95th day

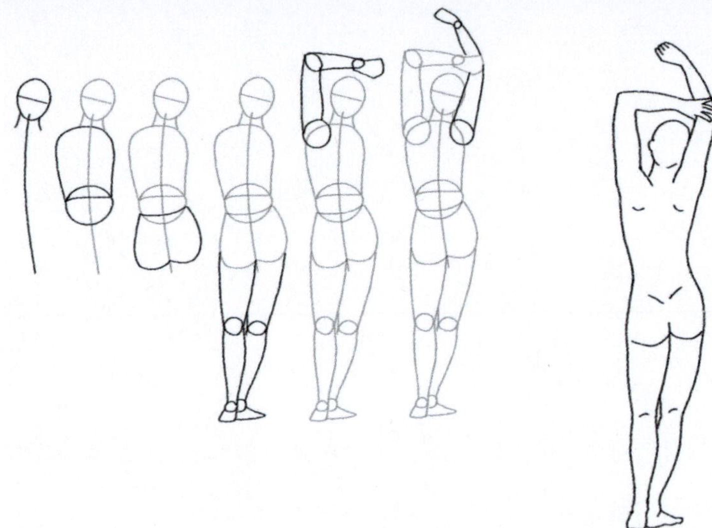

Woman from the Back

This view from behind is almost straight on. The figure has a very slight sway to the hips, barely twisting the spine.

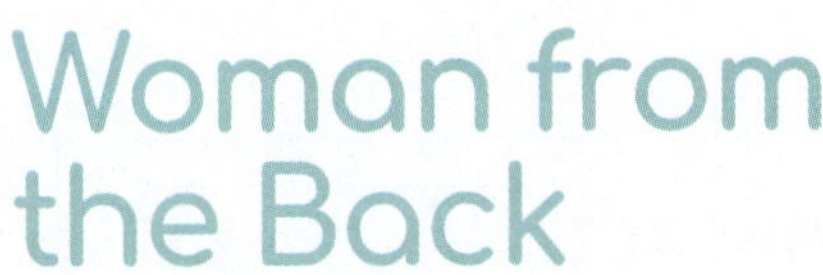

96 th day

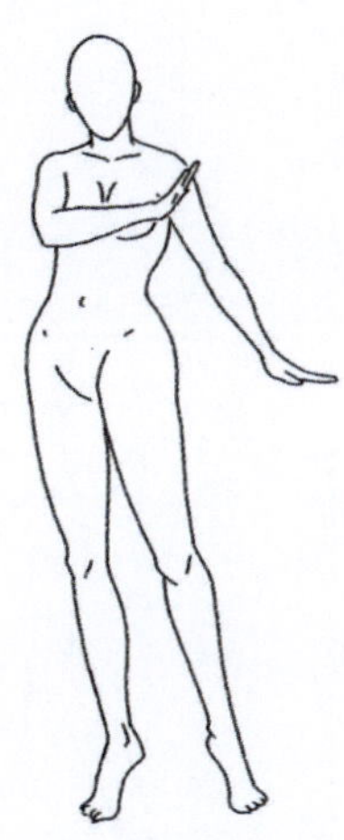

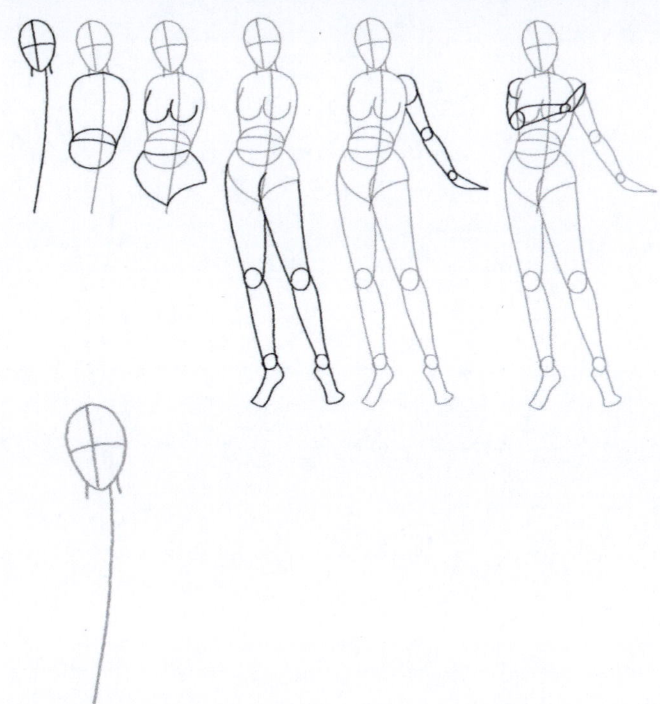

Standing Woman

This pose, viewed from a slightly three-quarter perspective, barely tilts the hipline backward. The pointed feet make the legs look long and lean.

97th day

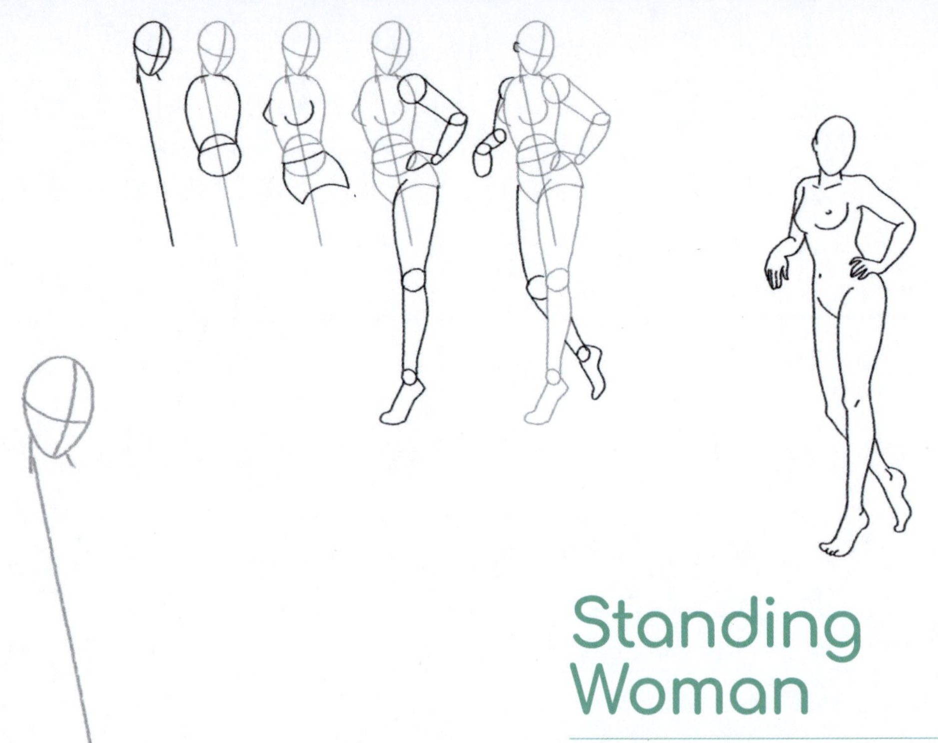

Standing Woman

Bending an arm to the back lifts the shoulders and stretches that side of the torso. The other side is swayed and curved.

98 th day

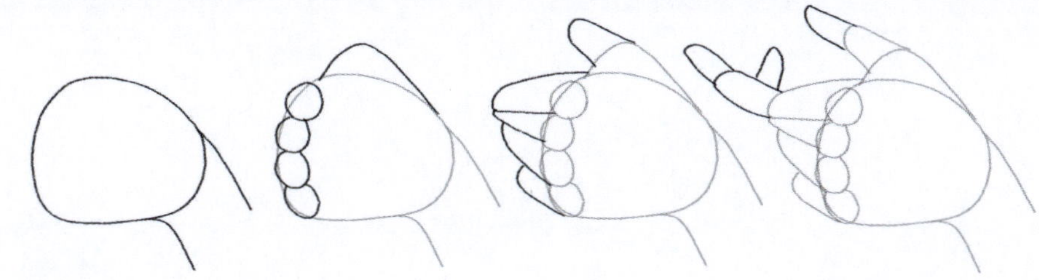

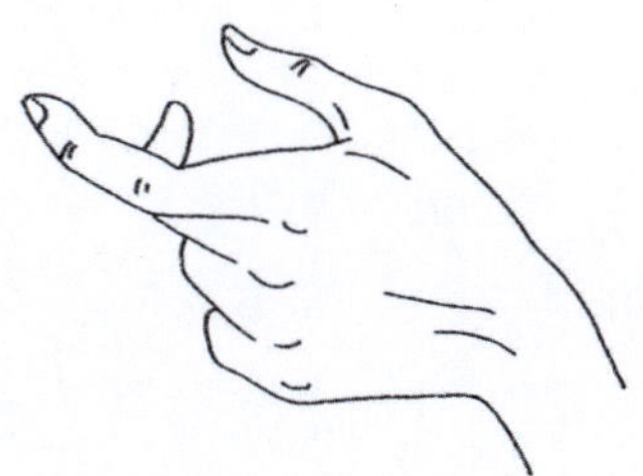

Outstretched Hand

This is a graceful pose. The wrist is curved, and the fingers stretch toward the index finger, which is slightly bent.

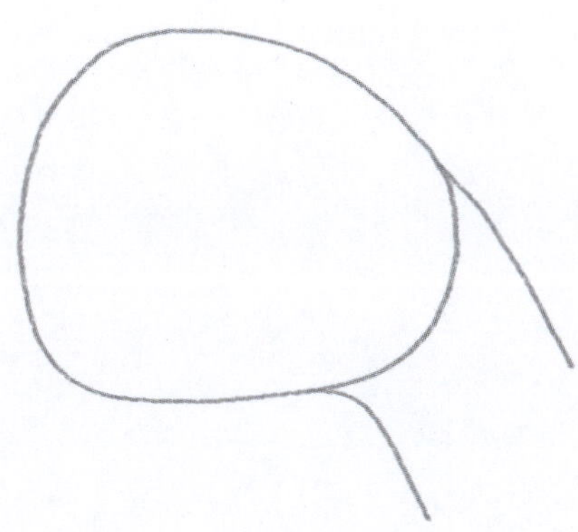

99th day

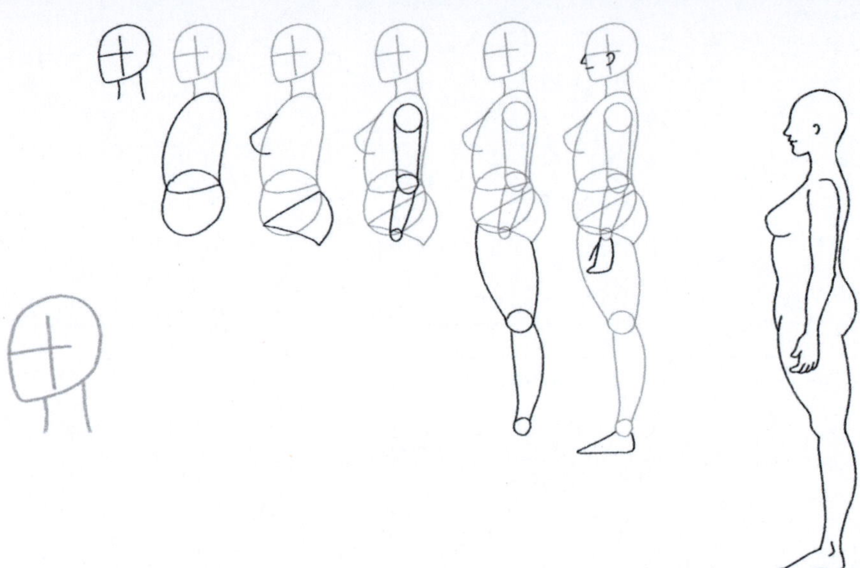

Woman
in Profile

This figure's generous curves are
still visible in profile. The feet
are slender, and the volumes
increase as you move up
the body.

100th day

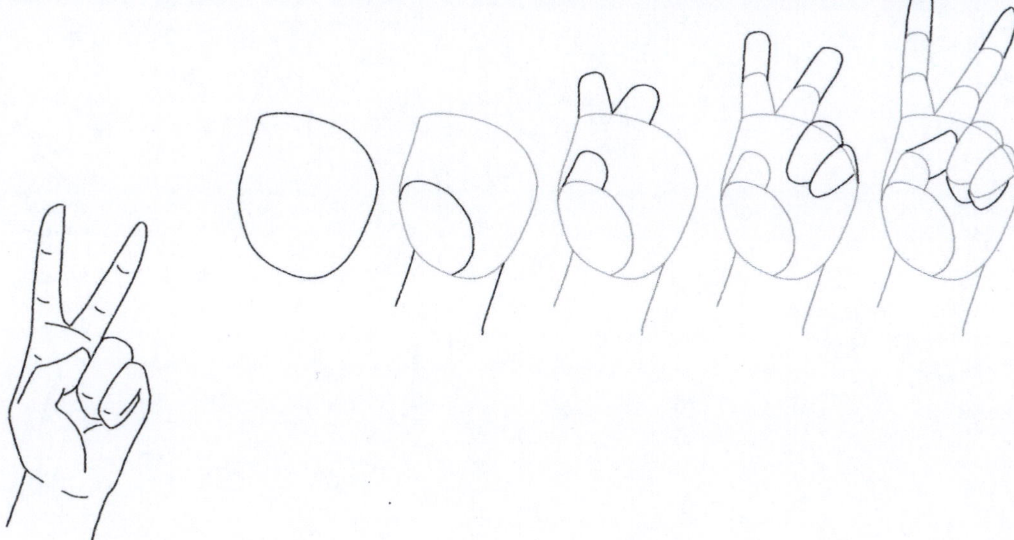

V Sign

To draw a hand forming the victory sign, fold the thumb and the last two fingers into the palm.

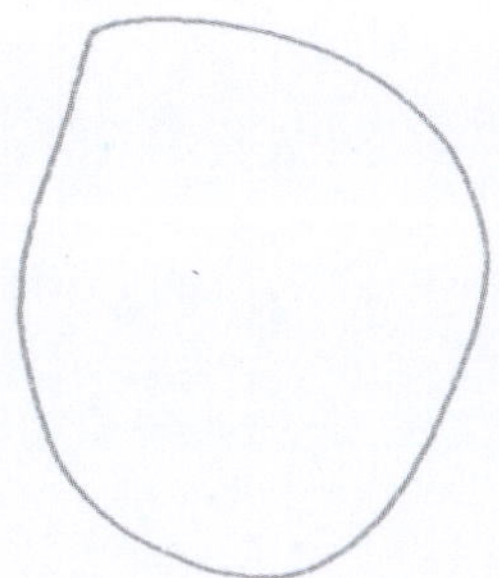

101st day

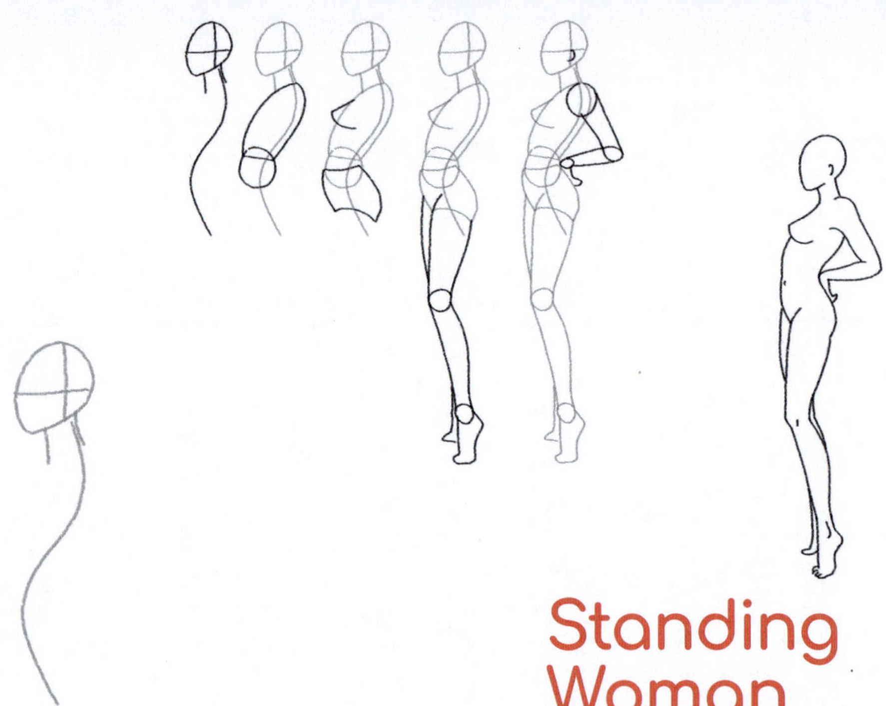

Standing
Woman

This very elegant pose is a barely
turned profile, revealing part of
the back of the body.

102nd day

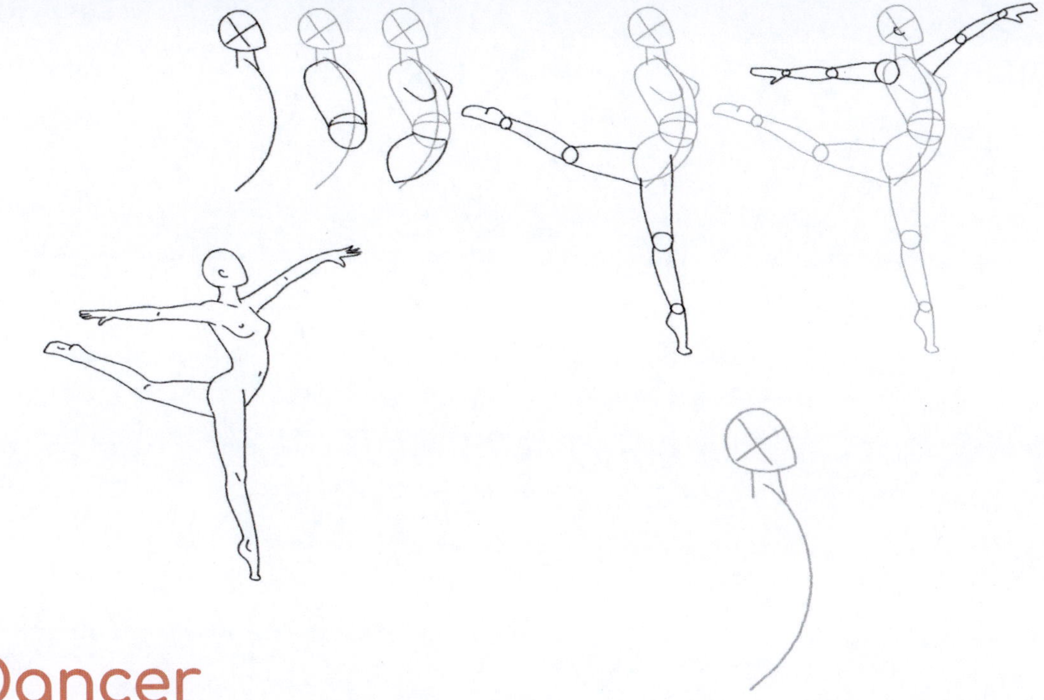

Dancer

This figure's pose twists the
whole body in an arc. The limbs
are stretched to their maximum,
from the tips of the toes to the
tips of the fingers.

103 rd day

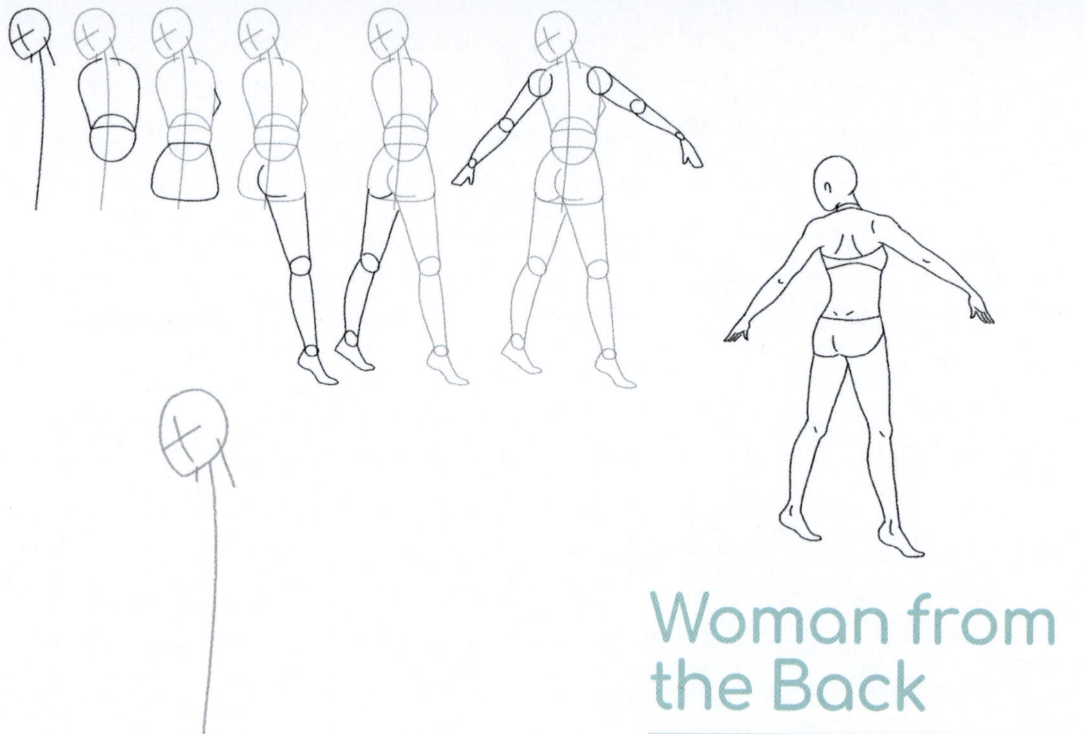

Woman from the Back

This rear-facing pose, with the figure's arms and legs spread apart, barely affects the proportions. The shoulder blades are clearly visible.

104 th day

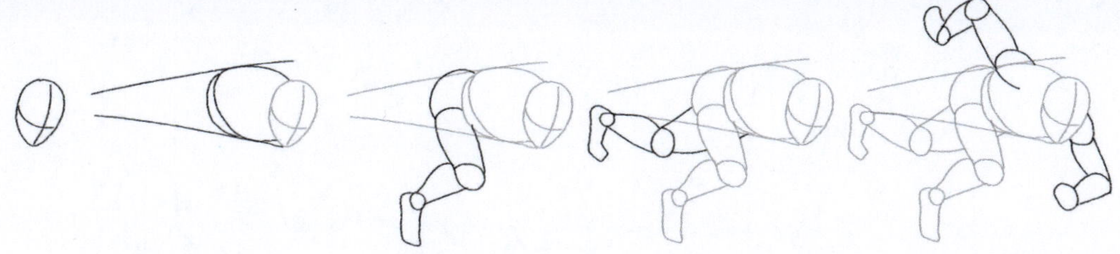

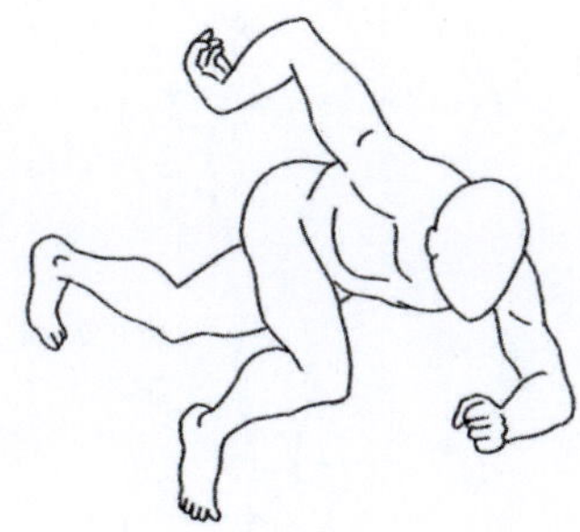

Running Man

The forward-leaning shape of
this pose accentuates the figure's
projecting movement.

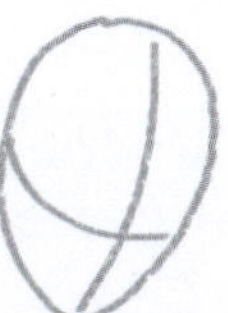

105th day

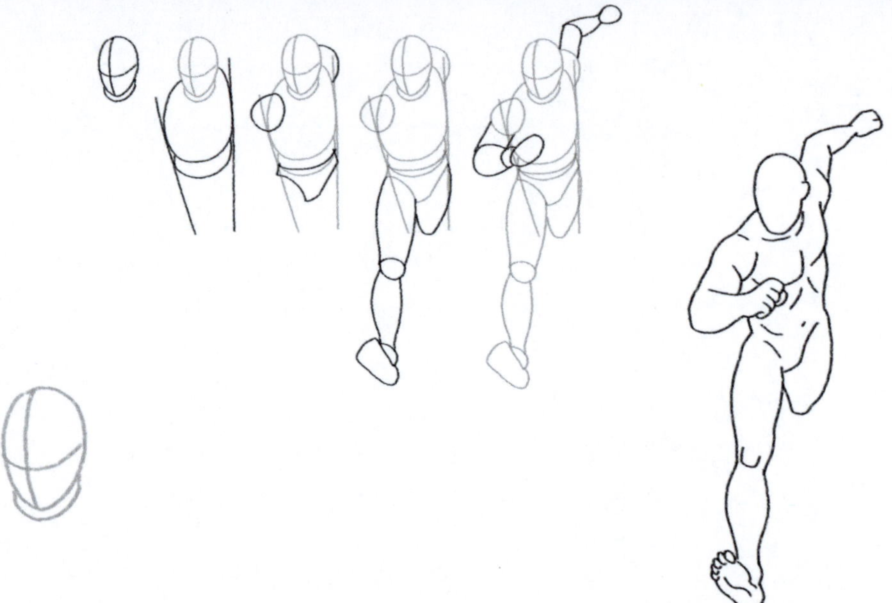

Running Man

The effect of perspective can help emphasize a particular pose or movement, such as running.

106 th day

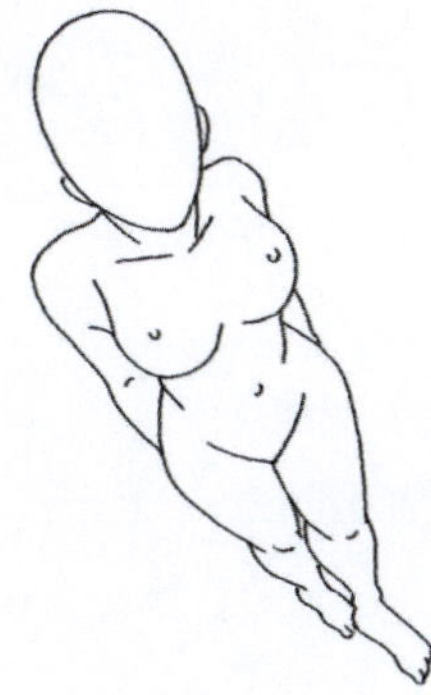

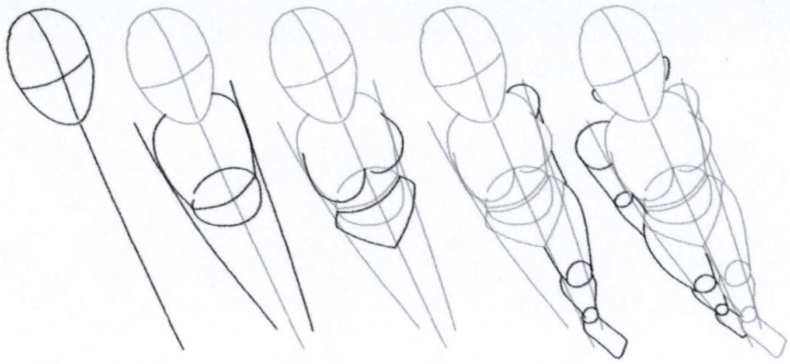

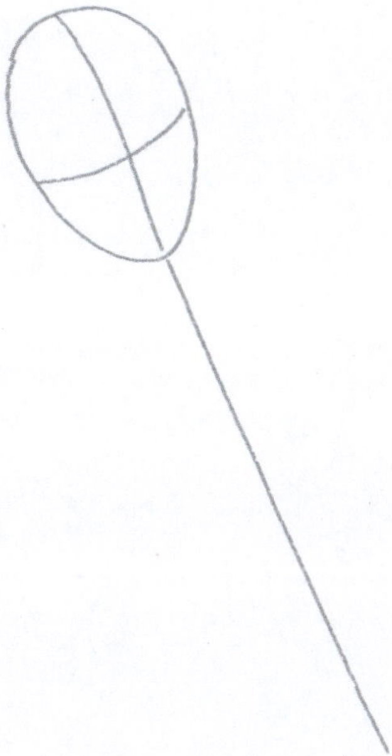

Woman
from Above

A dramatic perspective completely transforms the relationship between the body's proportions. The head looks enormous in relation to the feet. To help capture this effect, try sketching a line to the vanishing point.

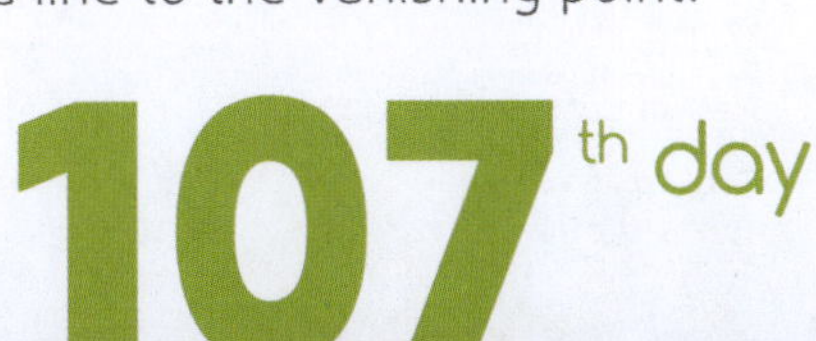

107th day

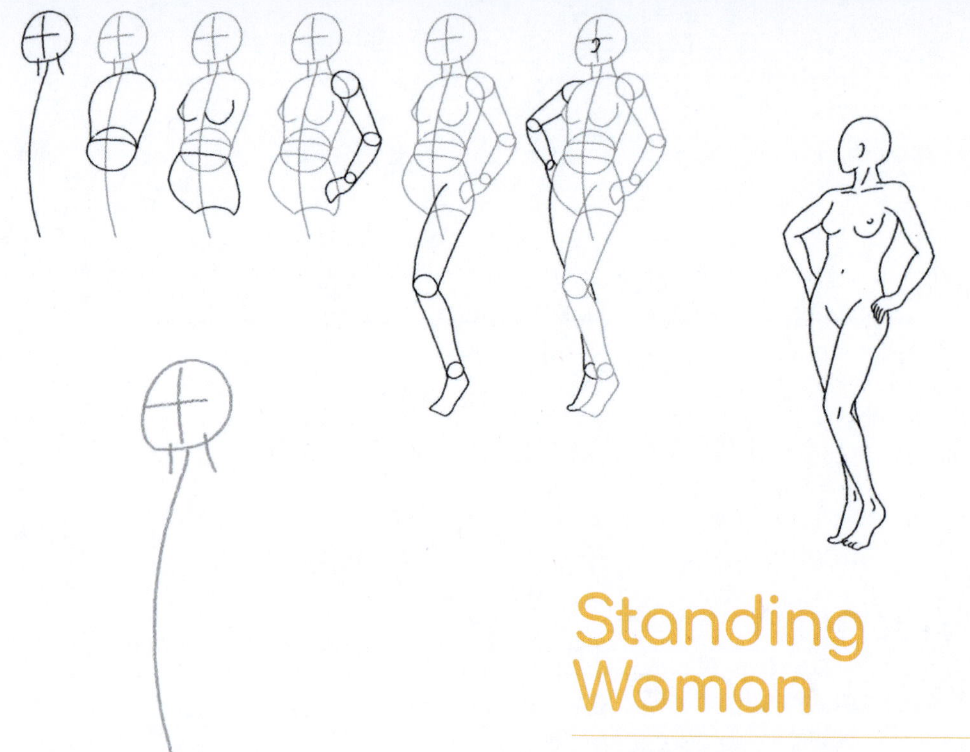

Standing Woman

A gentle curve arches
this figure's whole body
backward. The torso is slightly
in perspective.

108th day

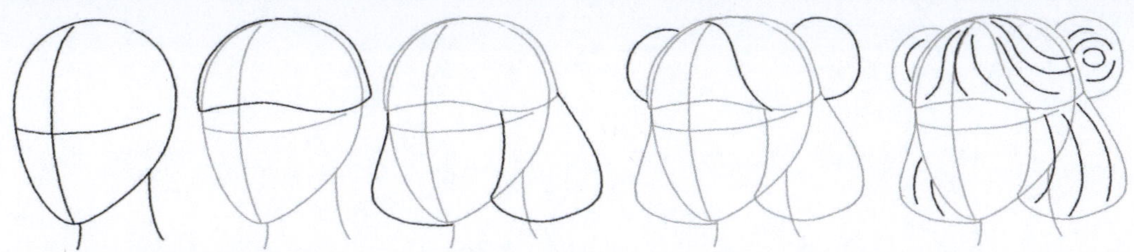

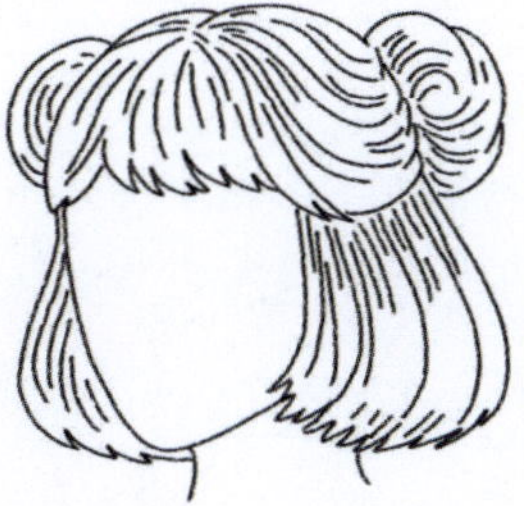

Bangs and Buns

Small curves emphasize the hair buns. The lines are compressed in the shaded areas.

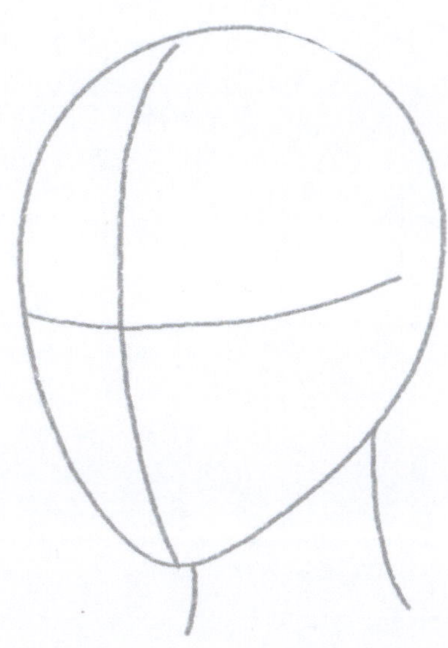

109 th day

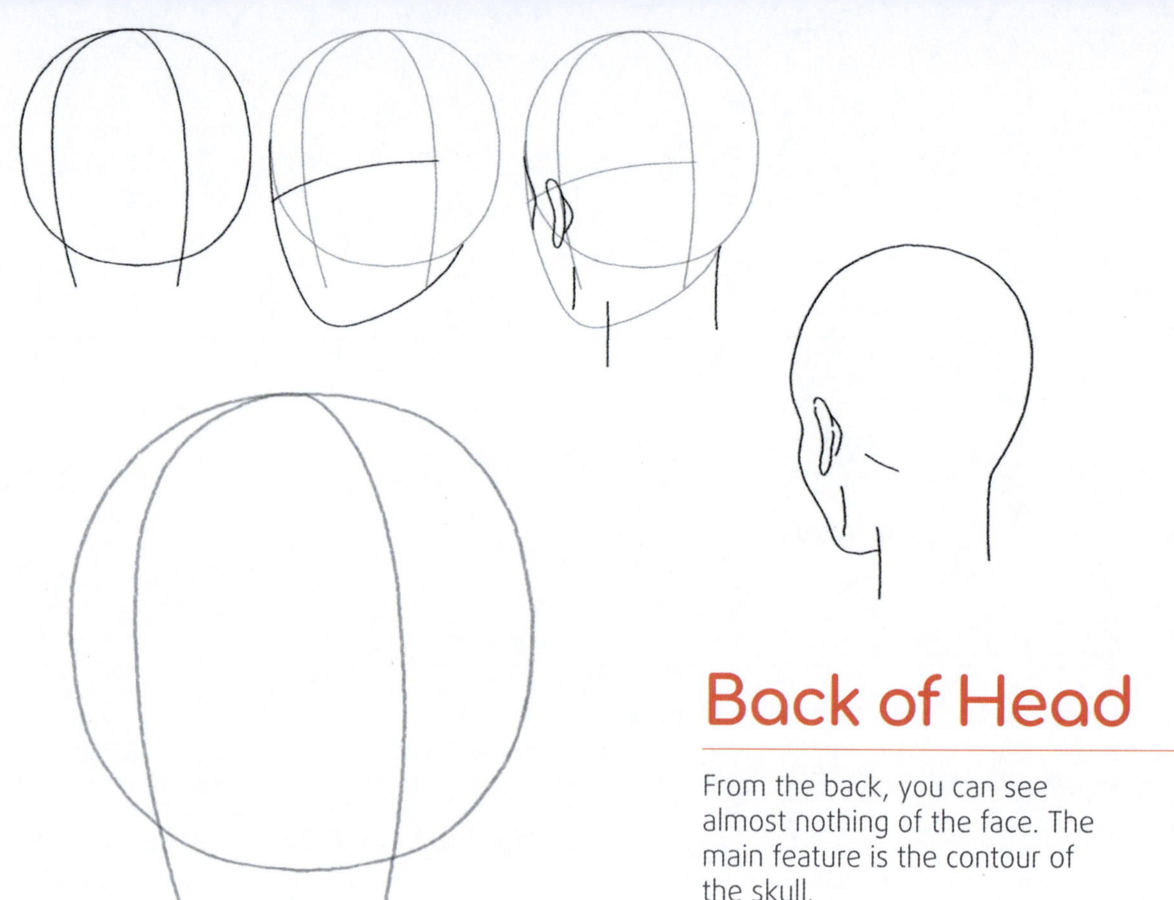

Back of Head

From the back, you can see
almost nothing of the face. The
main feature is the contour of
the skull.

110th day

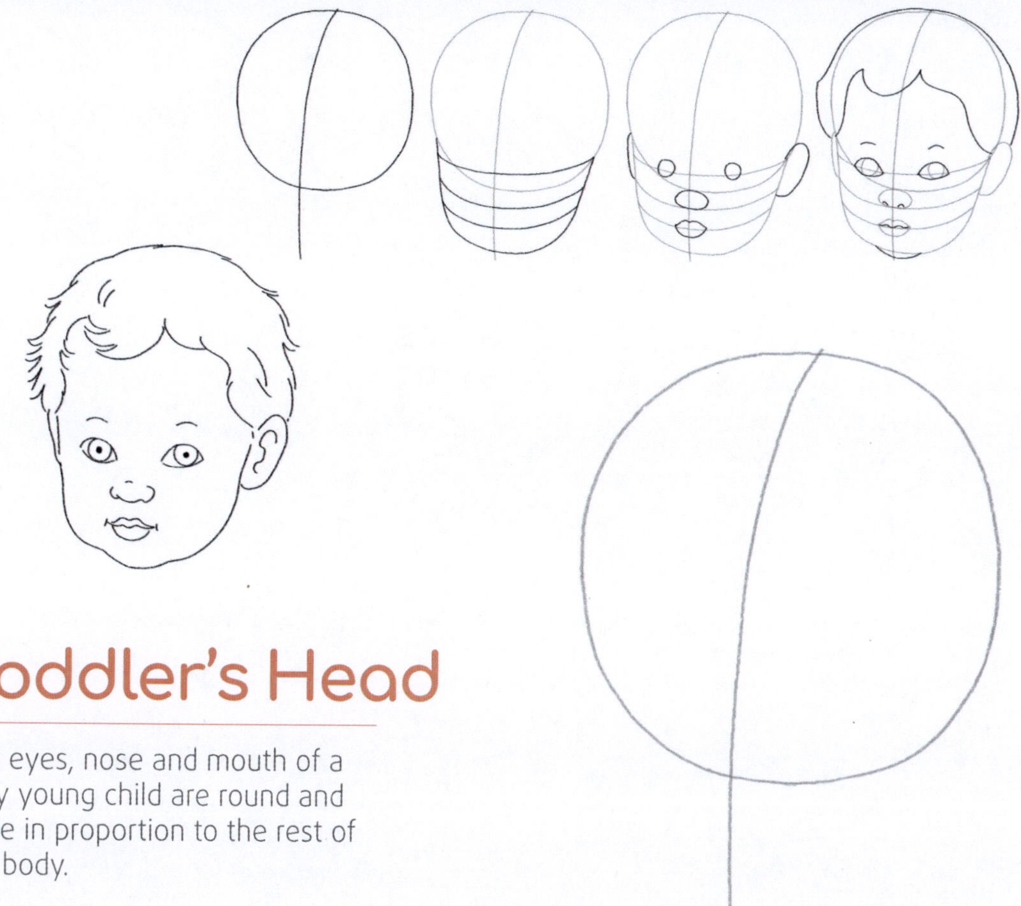

Toddler's Head

The eyes, nose and mouth of a very young child are round and large in proportion to the rest of the body.

111th day

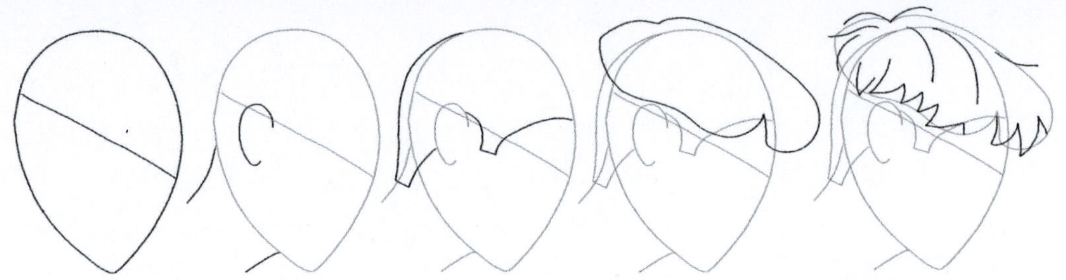

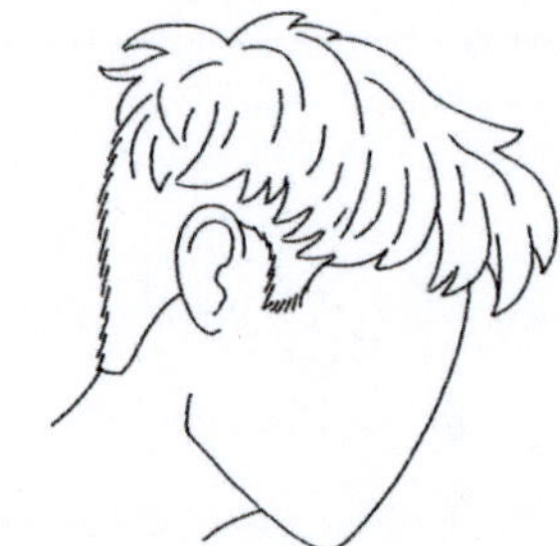

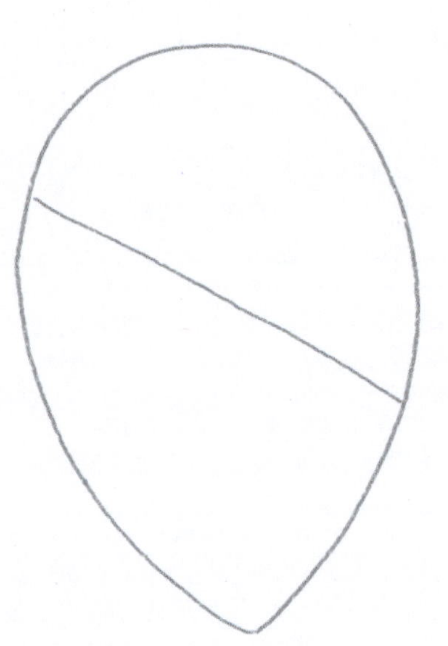

Shaved
Hairstyle

To mark the difference in length
between the bottom and top of
this hairstyle, use short straight
strokes and long flowing lines.

112th day

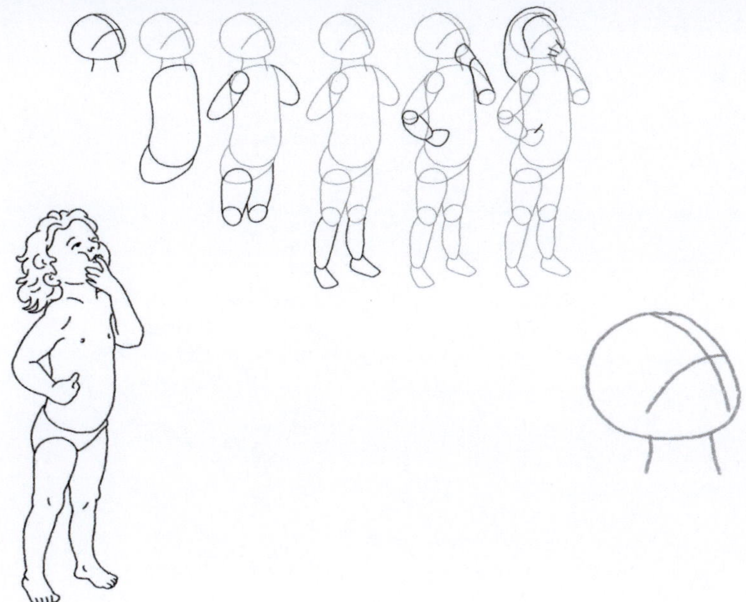

Toddler

This stretched-up pose reduces the length of the legs, which are already short in a toddler.

113 th day

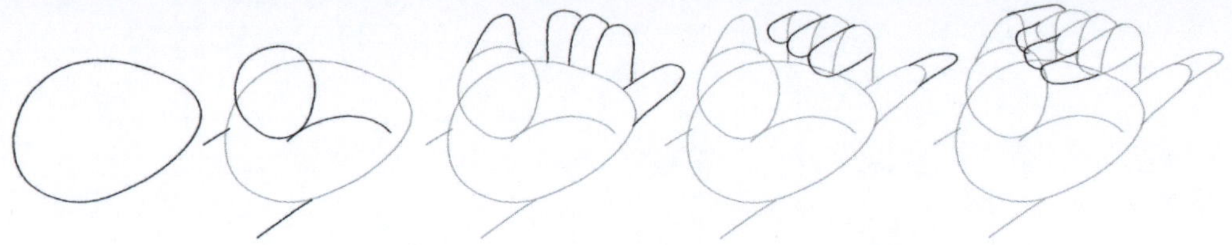

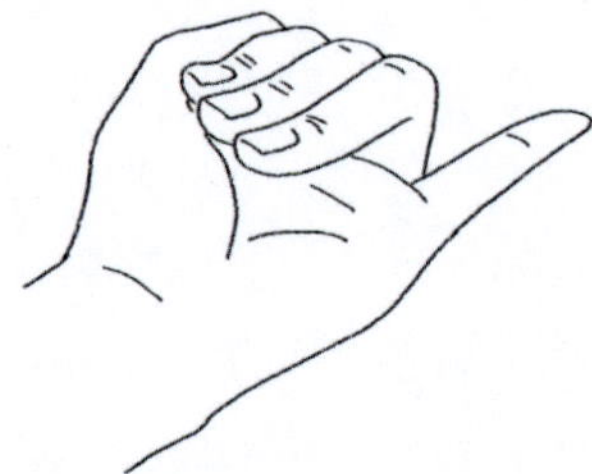

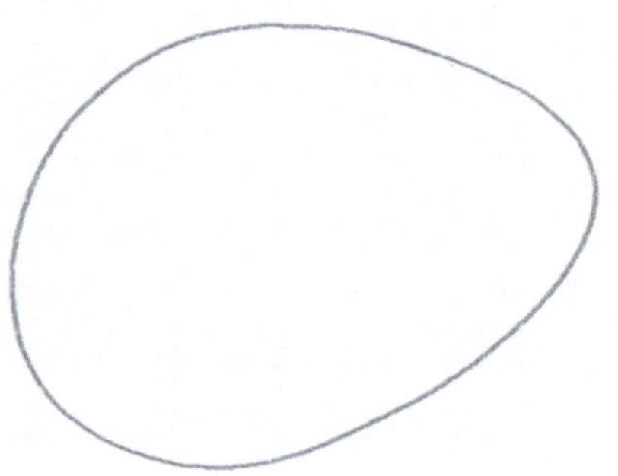

Hand

This hand is in perspective, with the palm and fingers extending in the same direction.

114 th day

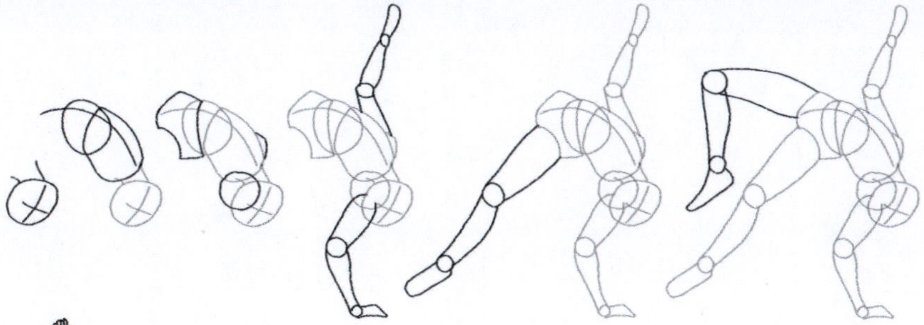

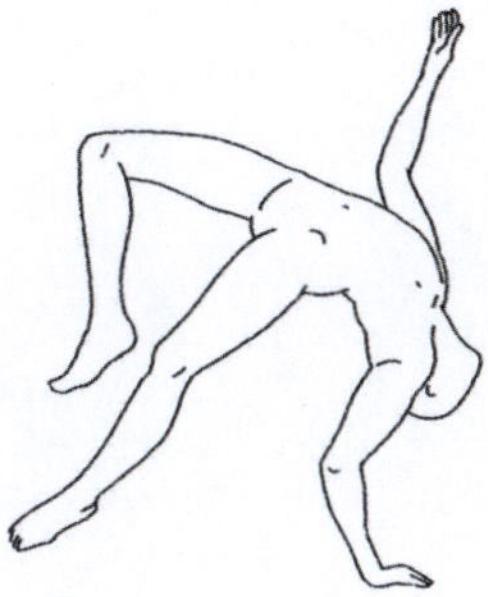

Gymnast

This contorted pose revolves around the arm that is resting on the ground. The entire body curves upward.

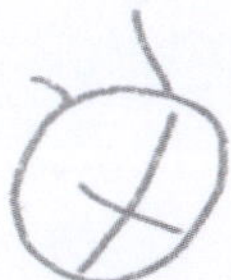

115 th day

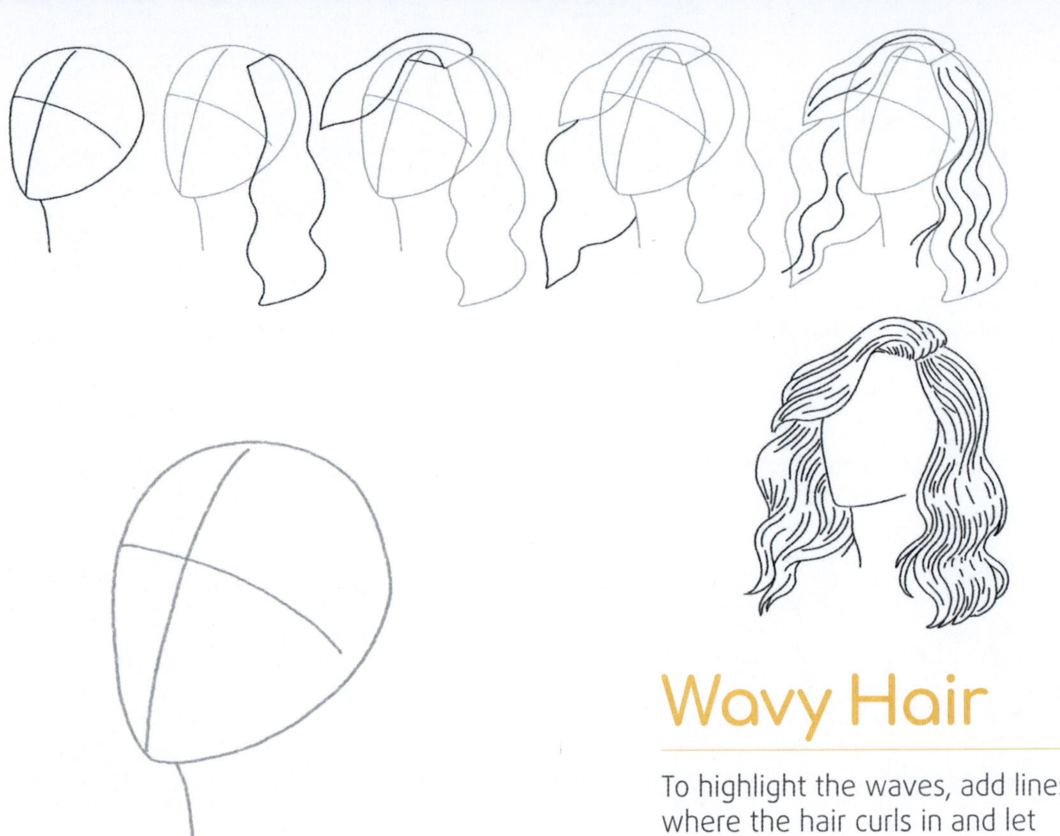

Wavy Hair

To highlight the waves, add lines where the hair curls in and let the light catch where the hair curls out.

116 th day

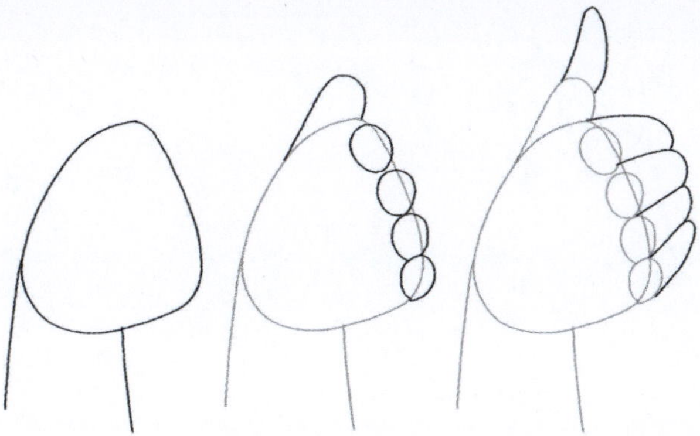

Thumbs-up

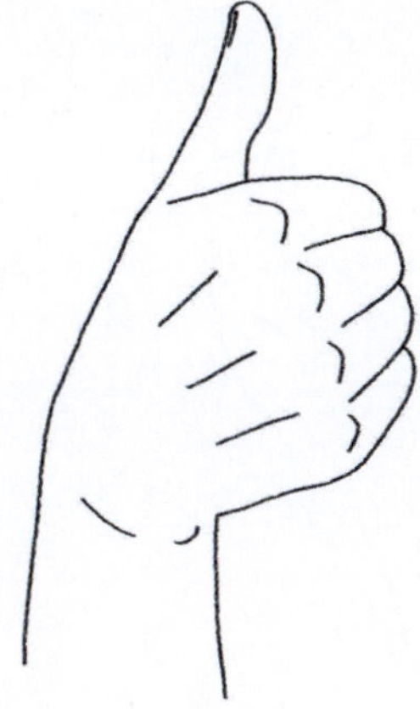

This hand is drawn from the
back. The proportions of
the raised thumb are clearly
visible. In contrast, the fingers
curled into the hand are
almost hidden.

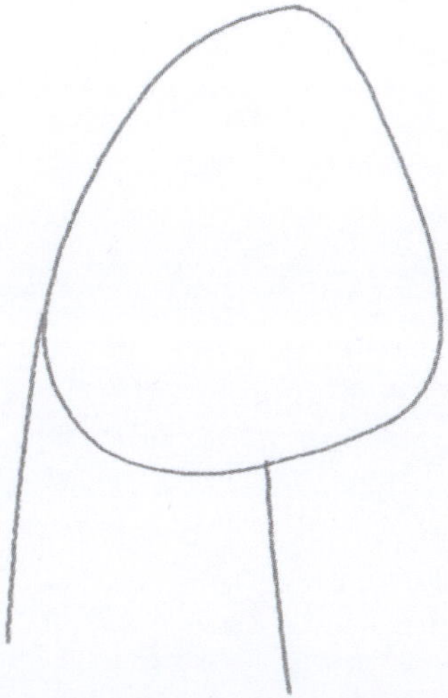

117 th day

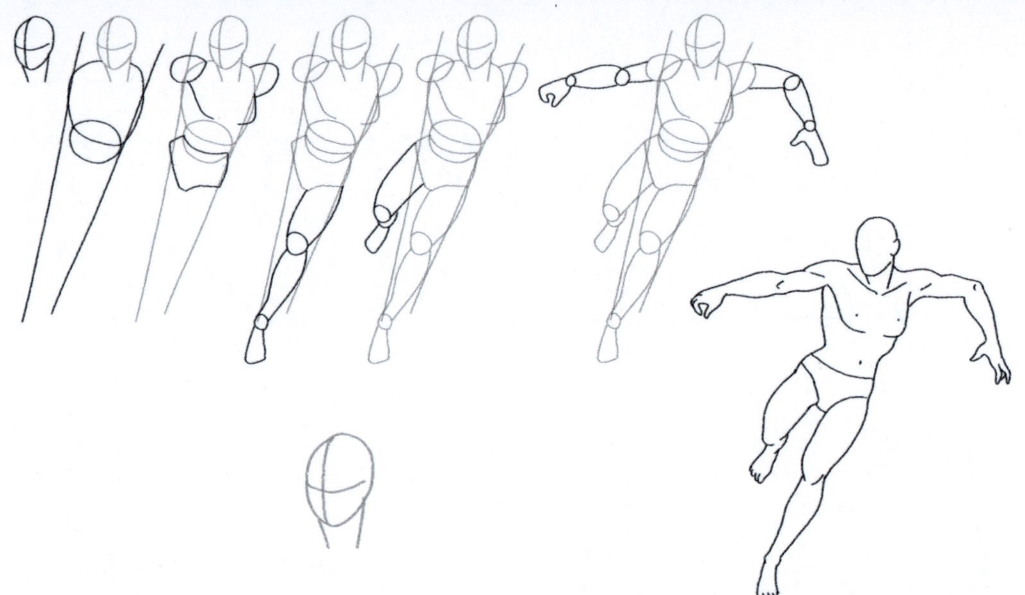

Soccer Player

The perspective has little effect on this figure, but the lower legs are still a bit smaller in proportion.

118 th day

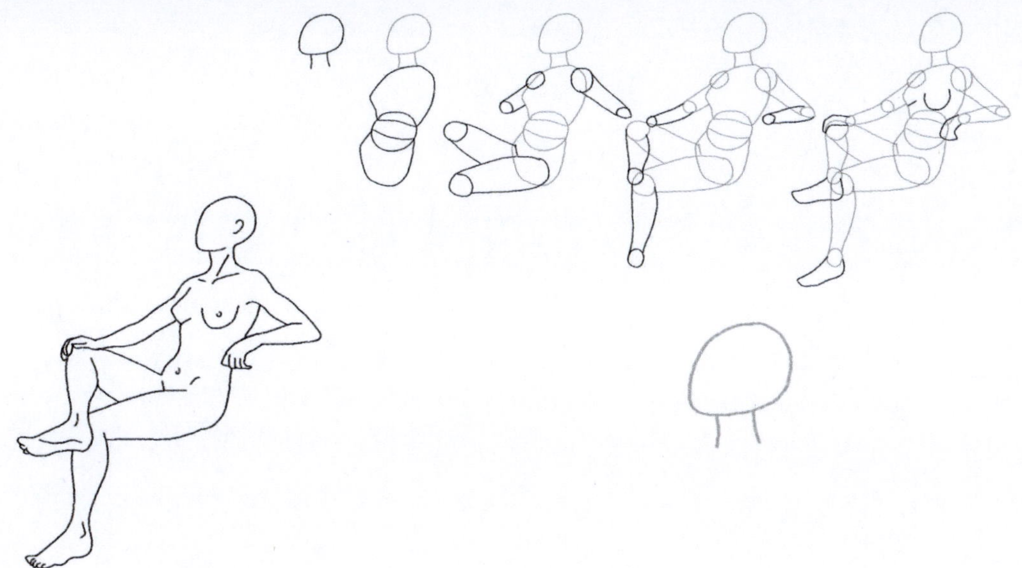

Seated Woman

In this seated pose viewed in three-quarters, the bent leg is shortened by the perspective. The arm resting on it also appears to be shorter.

119th day

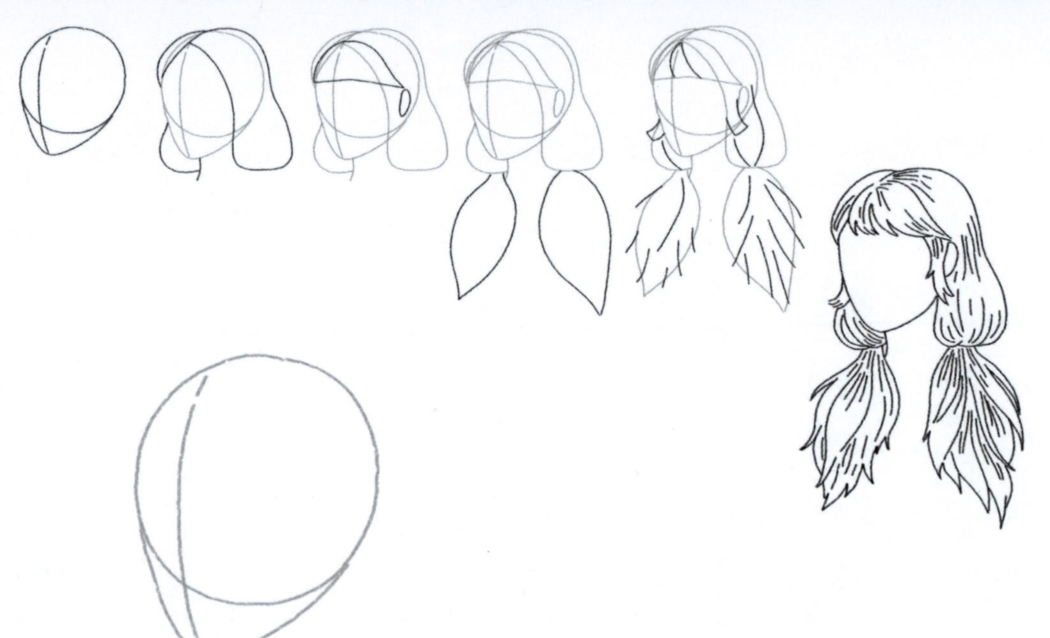

Pigtails

The lines that make up the hair
meet where the pigtails are tied,
accentuating the volume.

120th day

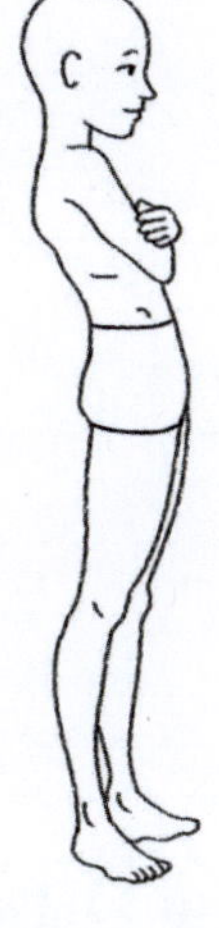

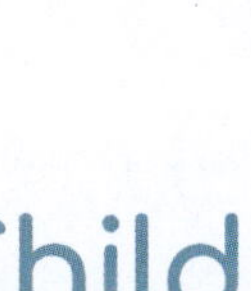

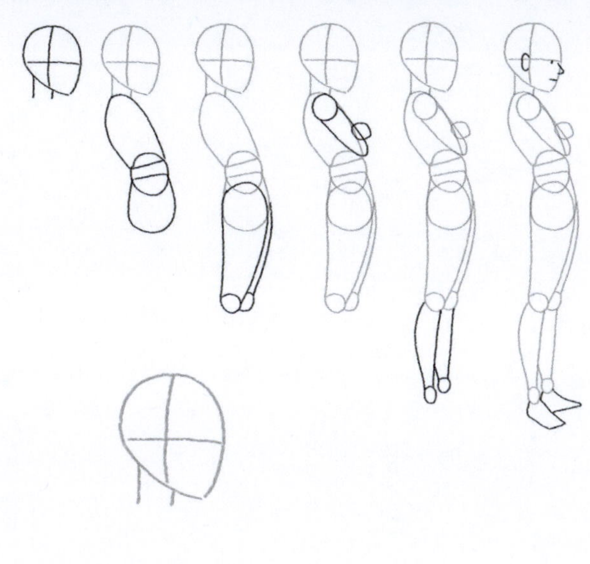

Child

In profile, a child's body displays
little volume. As a child grows,
the body lengthens, and the
adult masculine and feminine
forms become more pronounced.

121st day

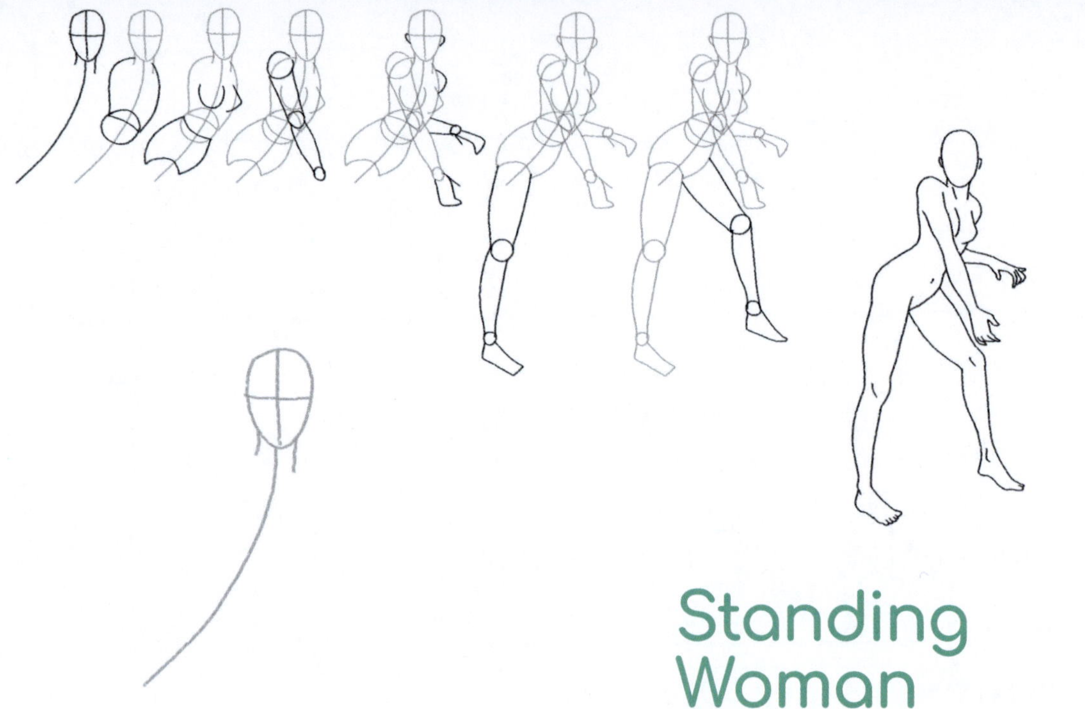

Standing Woman

This figure's swaying movement twists and curves the torso. One leg is straight, and the other is bent and in perspective.

122 nd day

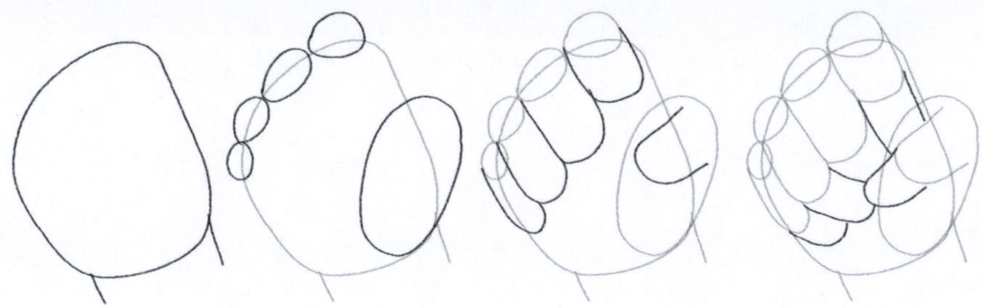

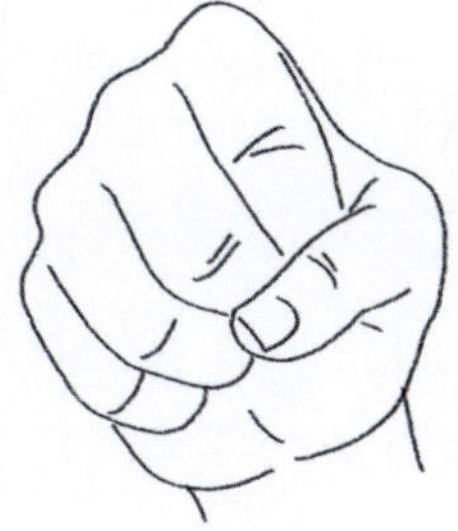

Fist

When making a fist, all of the
fingers come together and
squeeze into the palm.

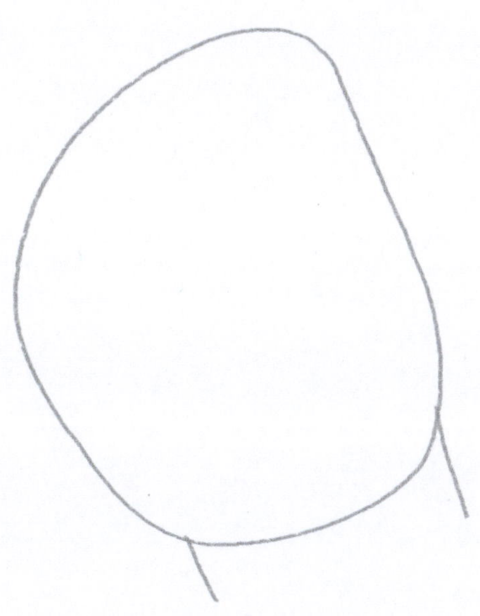

123rd day

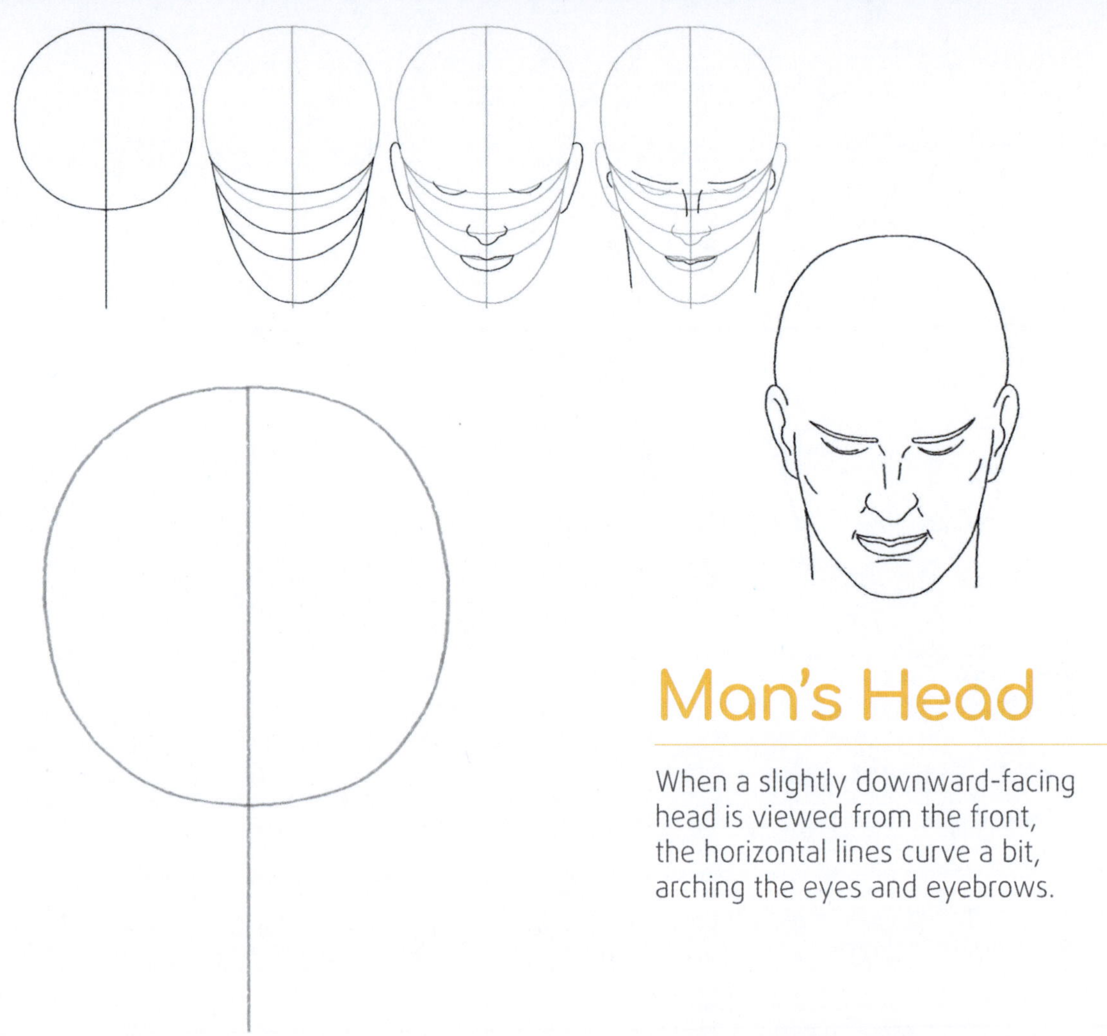

Man's Head

When a slightly downward-facing head is viewed from the front, the horizontal lines curve a bit, arching the eyes and eyebrows.

124th day

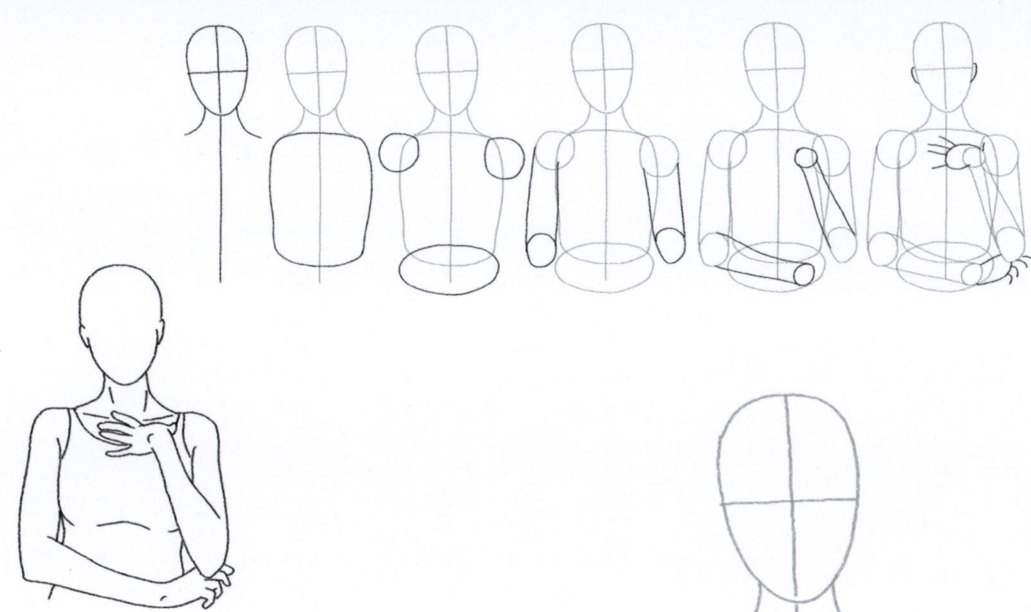

Woman's Torso

Up close, you can see the lines
of the collarbones and the neck,
the creases around the chest
and the details of the hands.

125th day

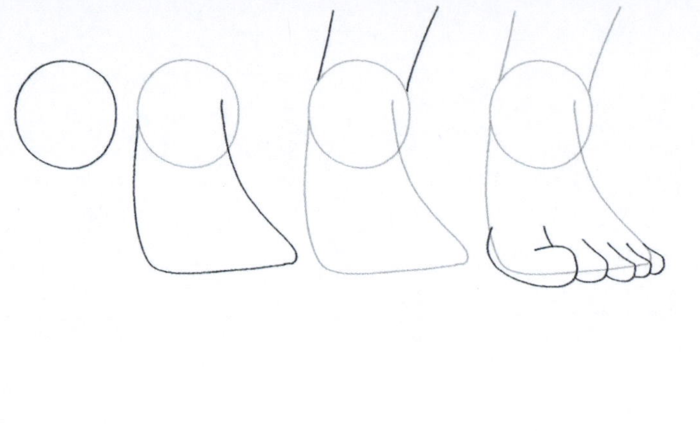

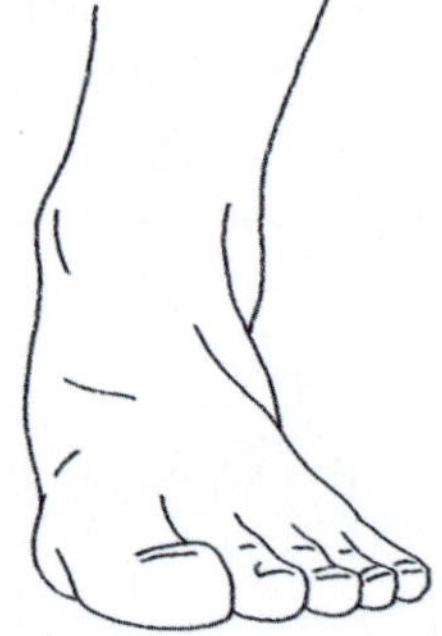

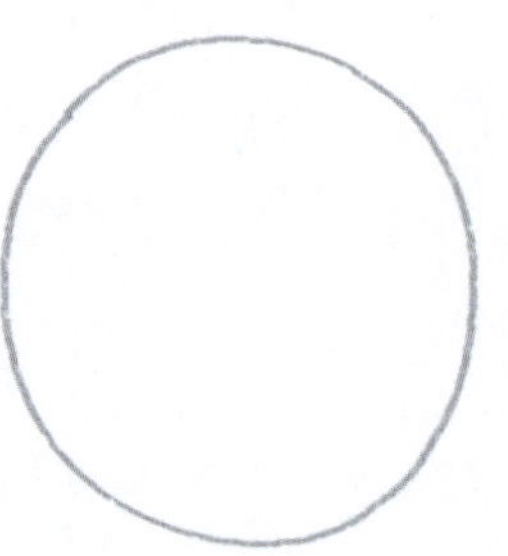

Foot

When a foot is viewed from the front and laid flat, the perspective conceals the heel. The length of the foot is also obscured.

126th **day**

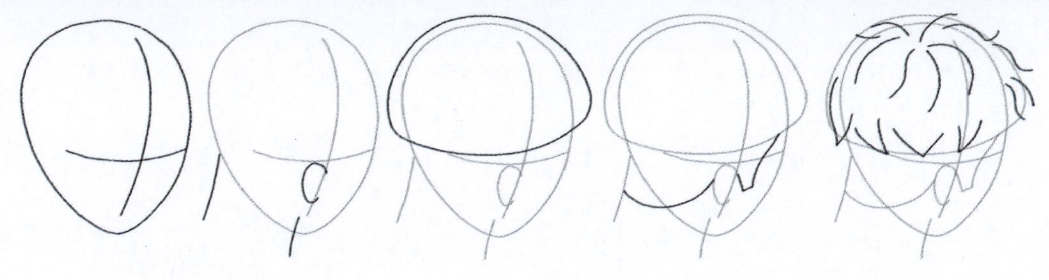

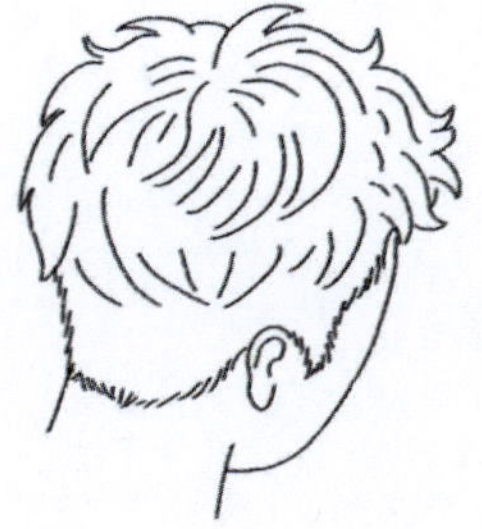

Short Hair

The bottom of this short haircut is highlighted with small strokes. The top is made up of soft, thick strands. You need only add a few lines.

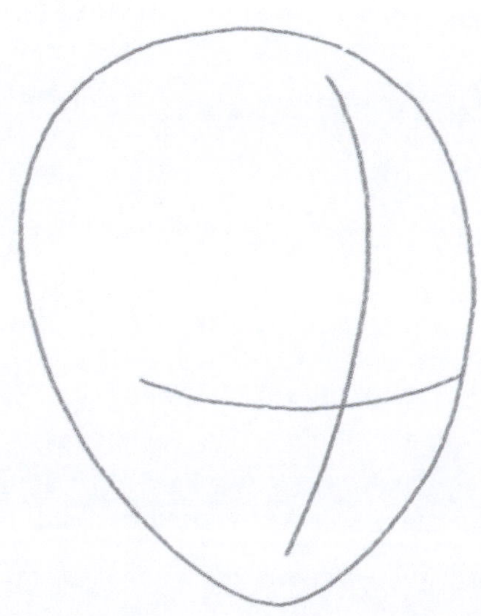

127th day

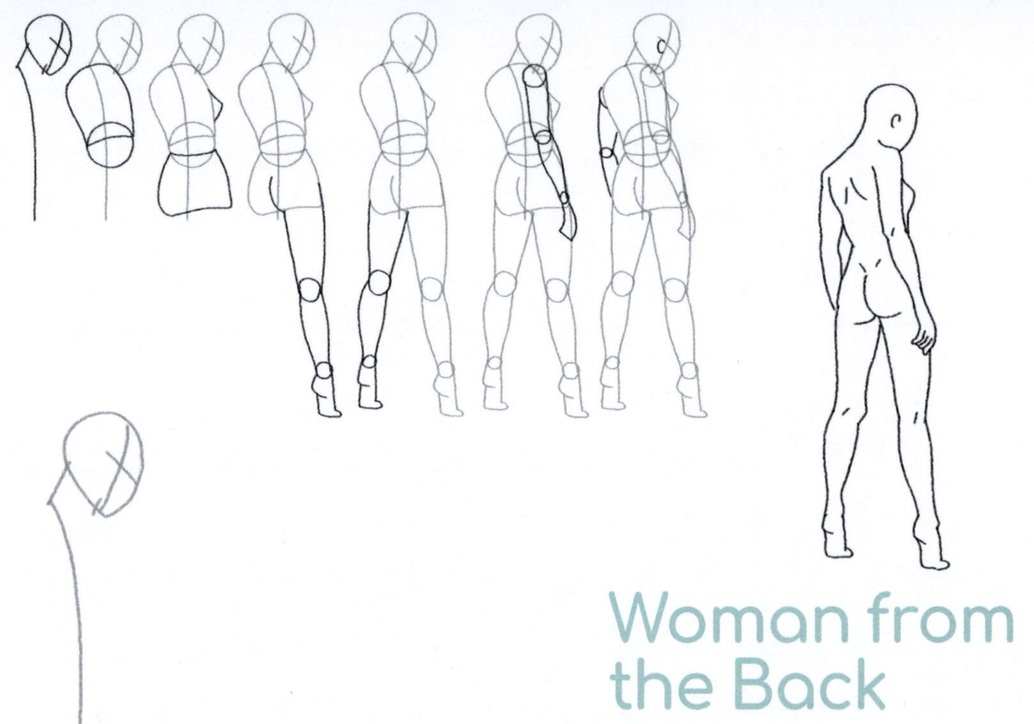

Woman from the Back

This pose is slightly swaying, and the three-quarter view tilts the shoulders and feet toward the vanishing point.

128th day

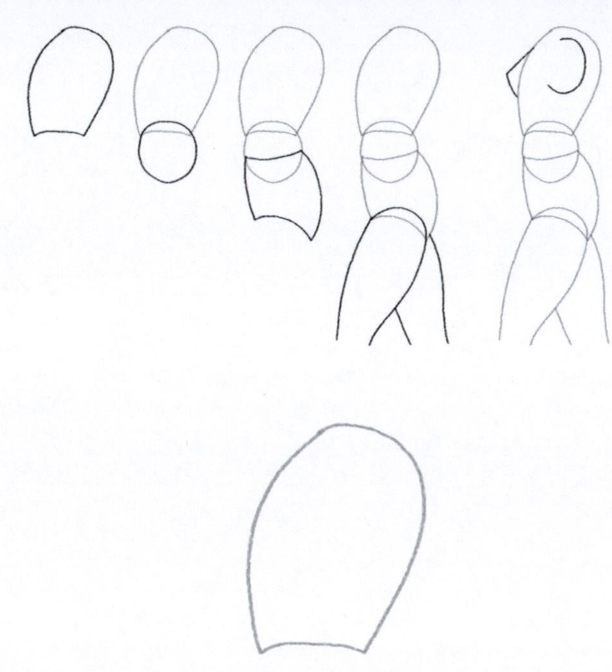

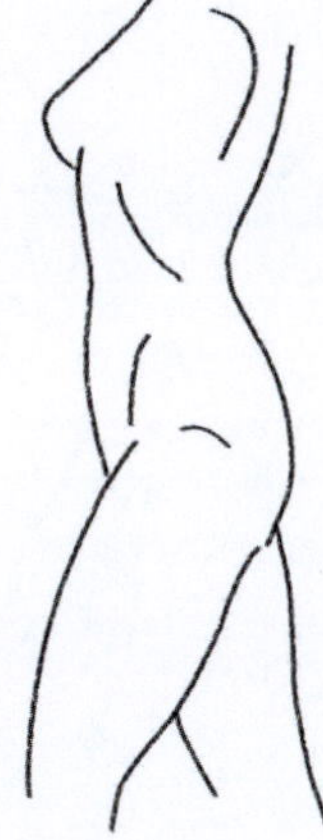

Woman
in Profile

A line can be used to emphasize
the ribs and hips when drawing
a figure in profile. The curves are
soft and subtle.

129 th day

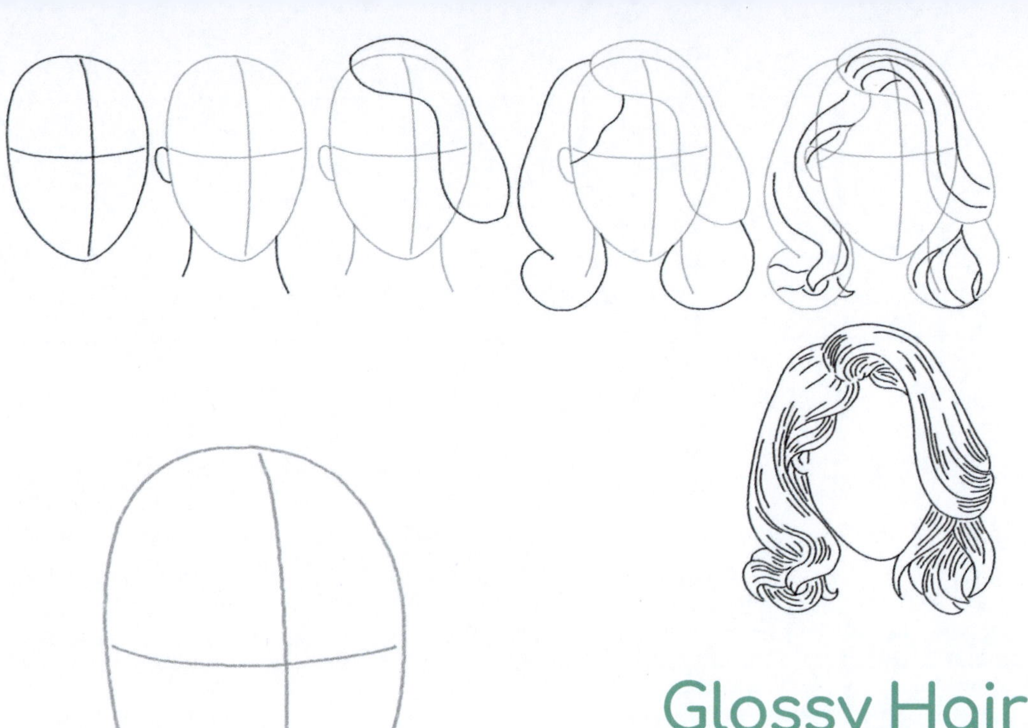

Glossy Hair

To create glossy hair, tighten the lines at the top and bottom of the strands, leaving plenty of empty space along the length to catch the light.

130th day

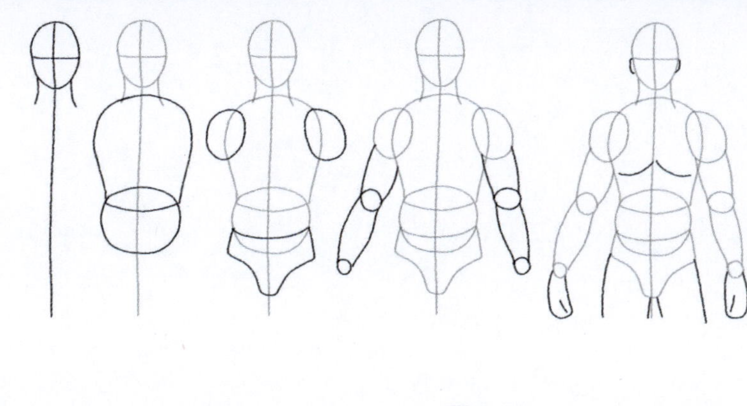

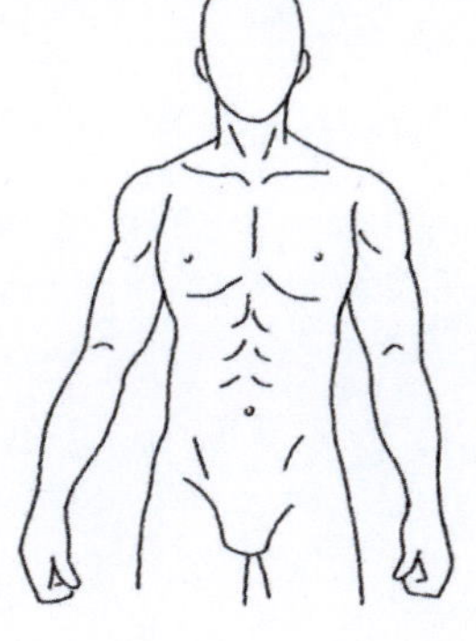

Man's Torso

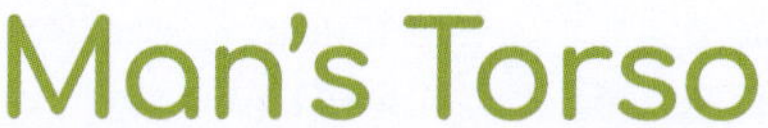

When focusing on the torso, you can emphasize the lines of its volumes and the lines of the collarbones and the neck.

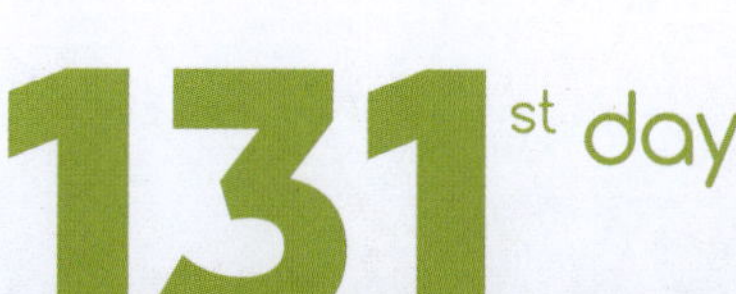

131st day

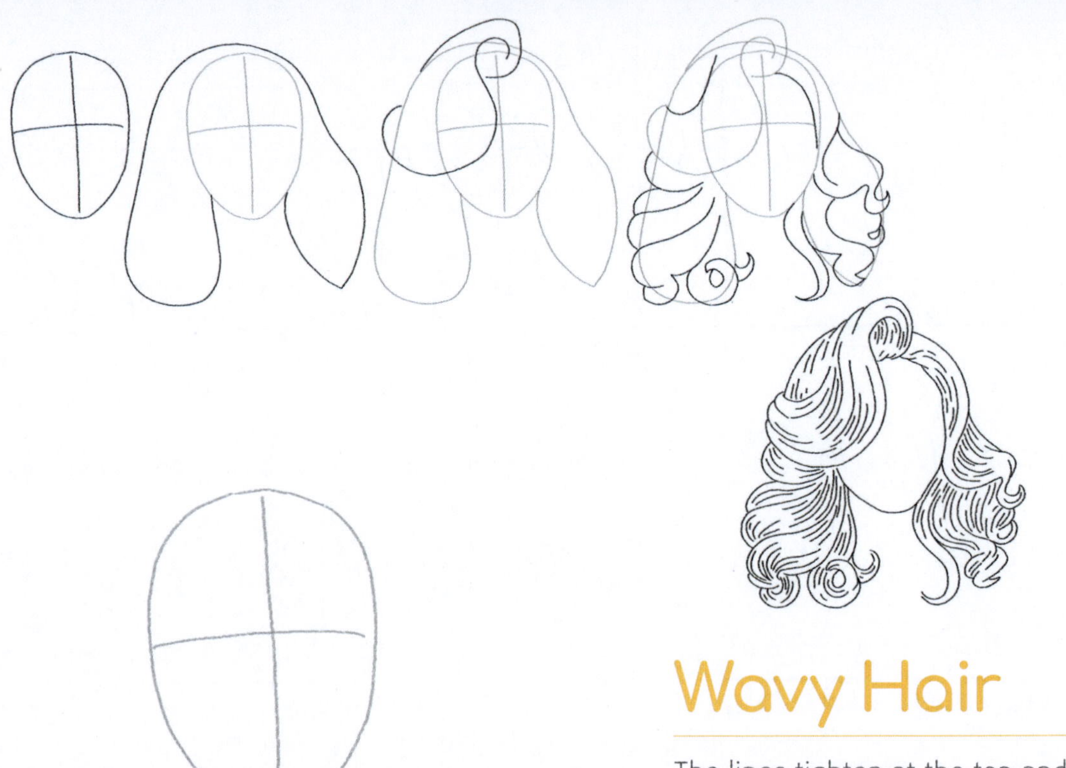

Wavy Hair

The lines tighten at the top and bottom of each strand of hair, allowing the volume to breathe. Each strand has its own direction, as does each curve.

132nd day

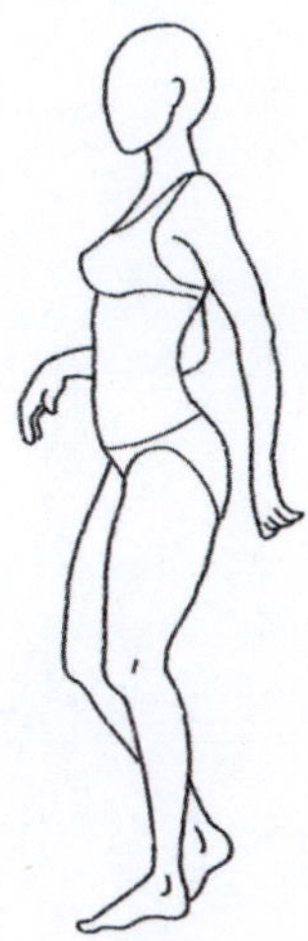

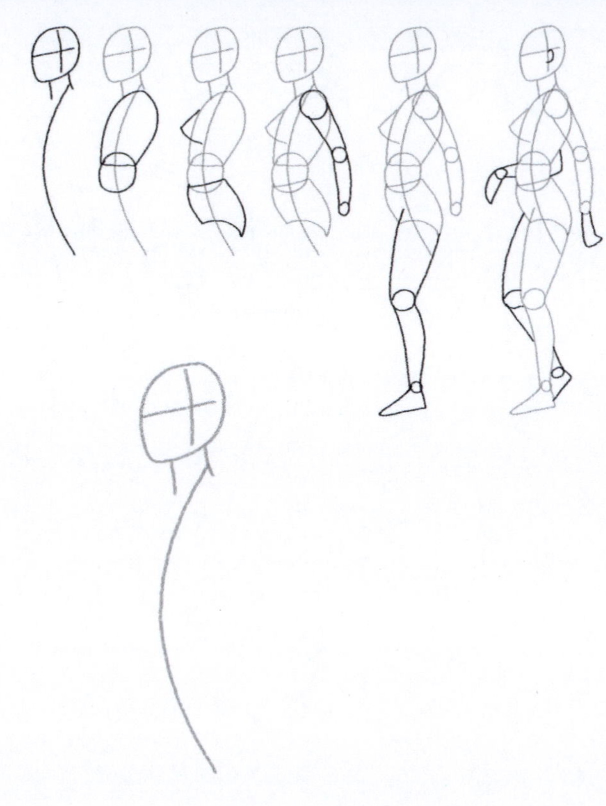

Woman
in Profile

This arched pose deepens
the back and emphasizes the
stomach. The profile partially
obscures one arm and one leg.

133 rd day

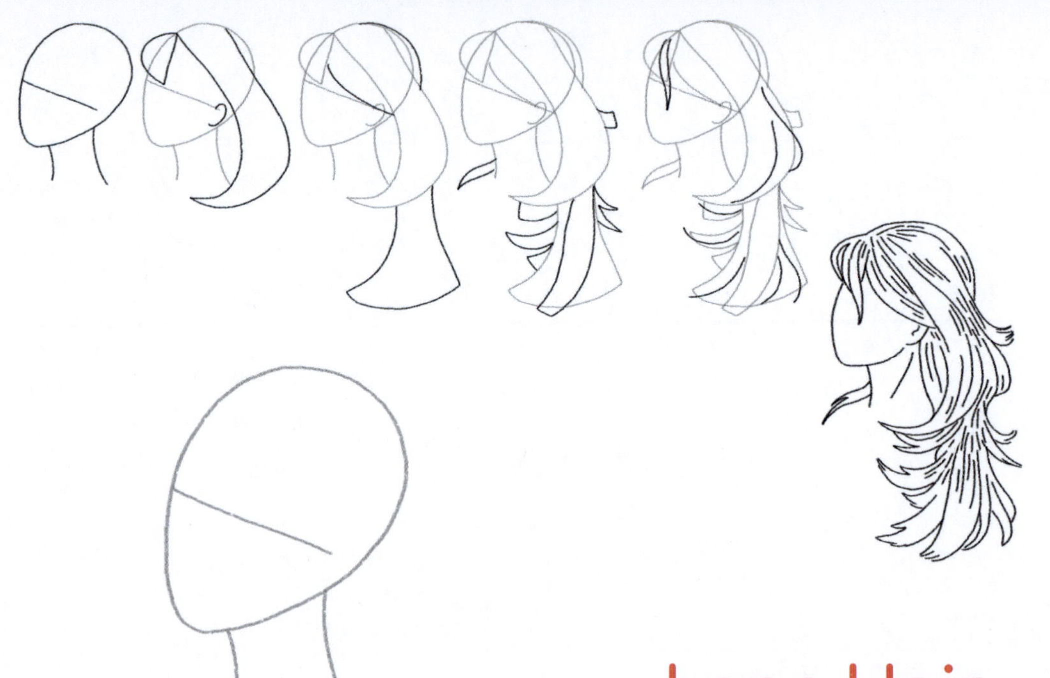

Long Hair

When drawing long strands of hair, draw longer lines within the sections of hair to create movement.

134th day

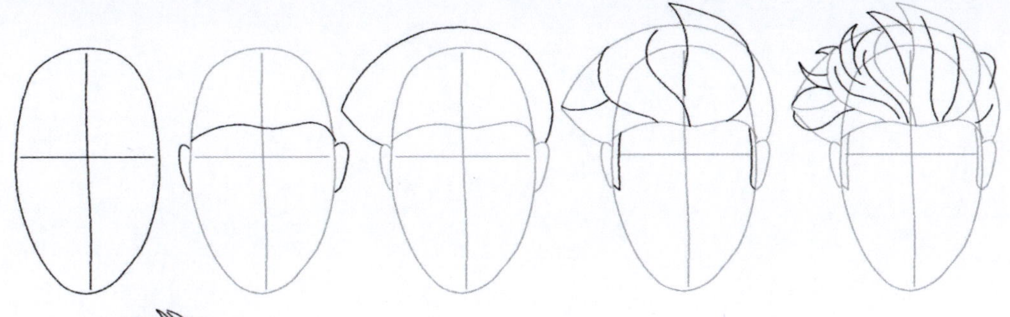

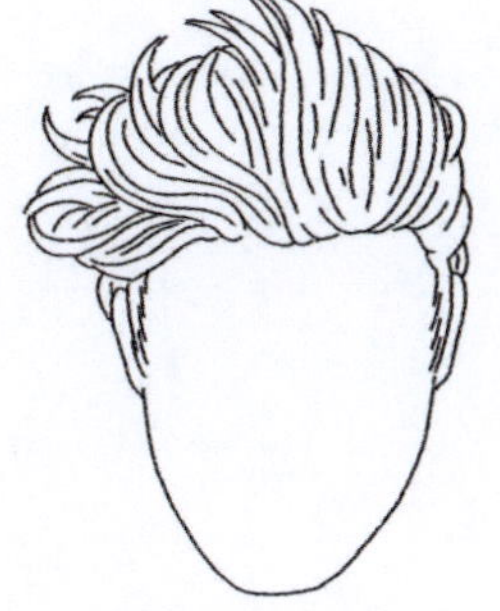

Short Hair

The movement of this hairstyle starts in the middle of the forehead and curves upward and to the sides in long strands.

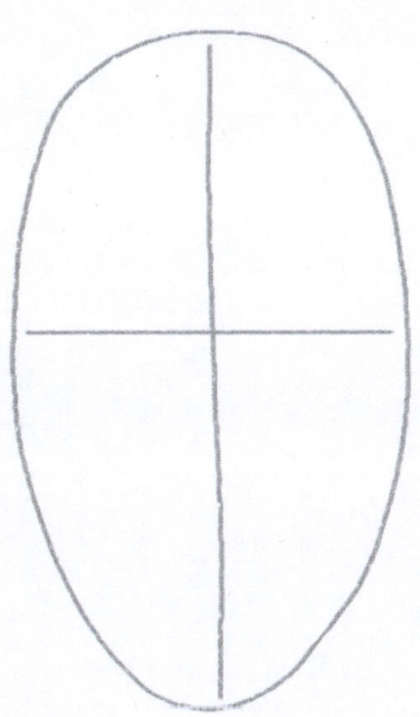

135th day

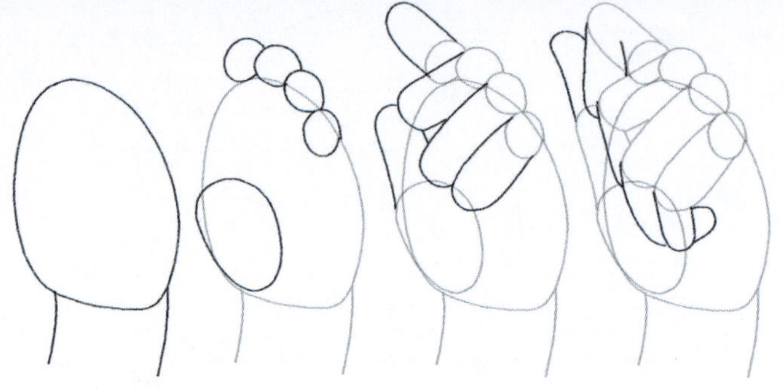

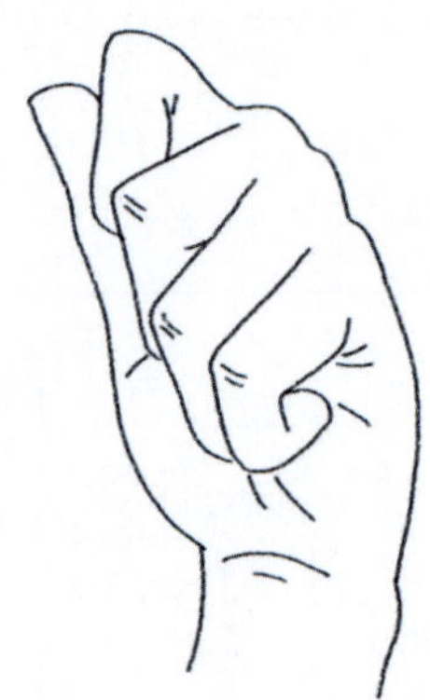

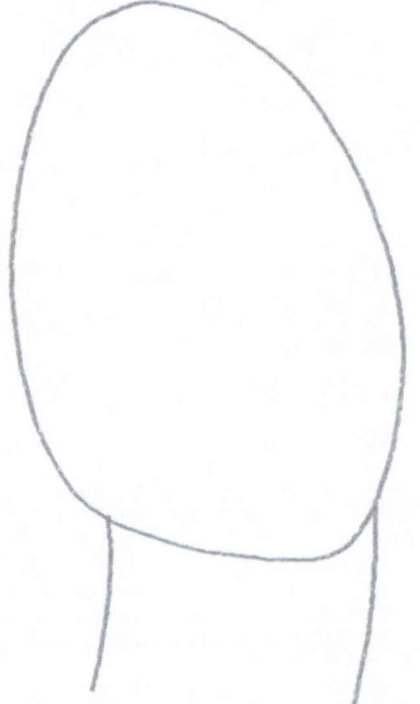

Fist

To draw a closed hand, curl the
fingers into the palm.

136th day

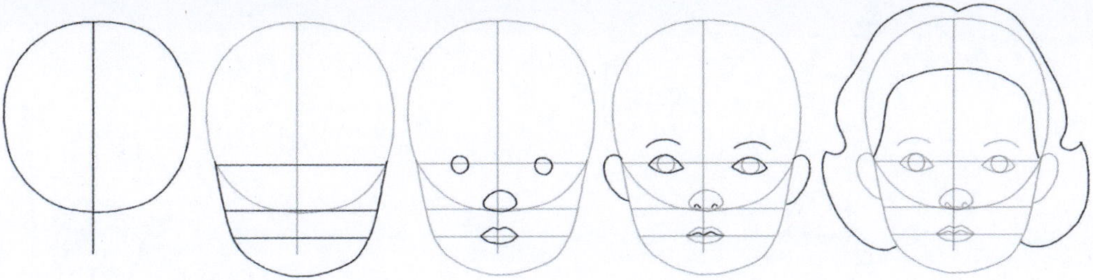

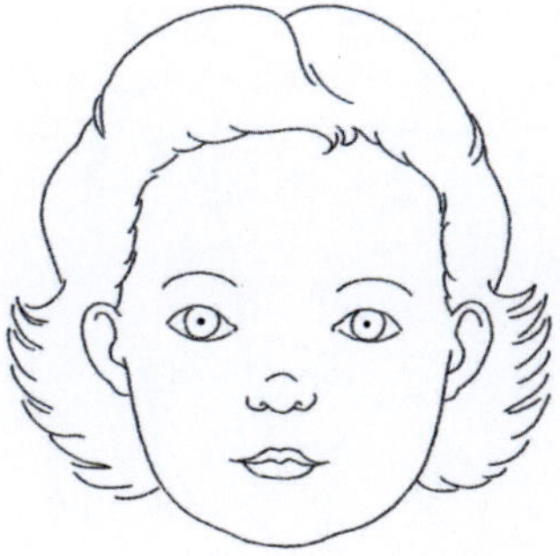

Toddler's Head

As toddlers, boys' and girls' faces look very similar. Adding details such as hair helps to differentiate them.

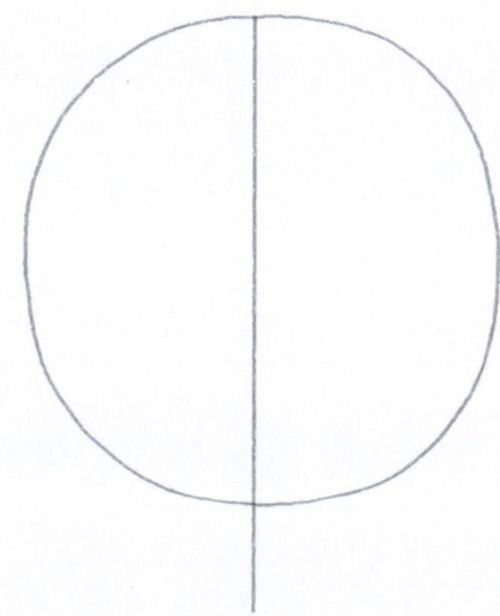

137th day

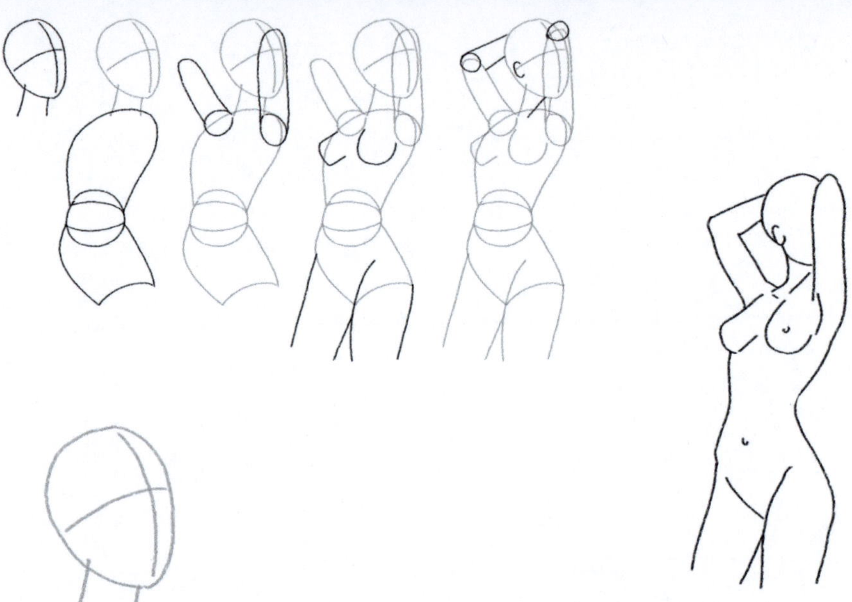

Woman's Torso

The arms of this figure are raised
and bent, partially obscuring
the forearms. The pose creates
a crease under the arm and
another crease near the neck.

138th day

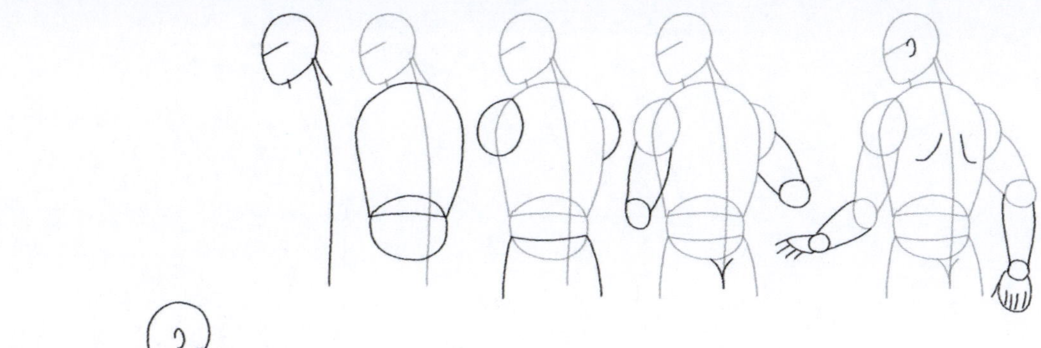

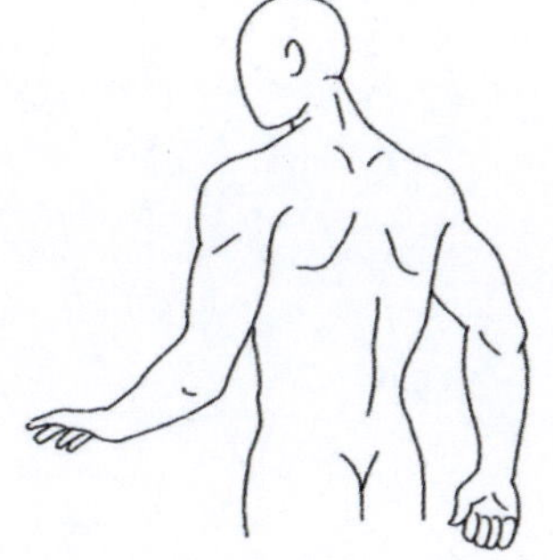

Man's Torso

Even when viewed at a three-quarter angle, a highly developed torso will look triangular.

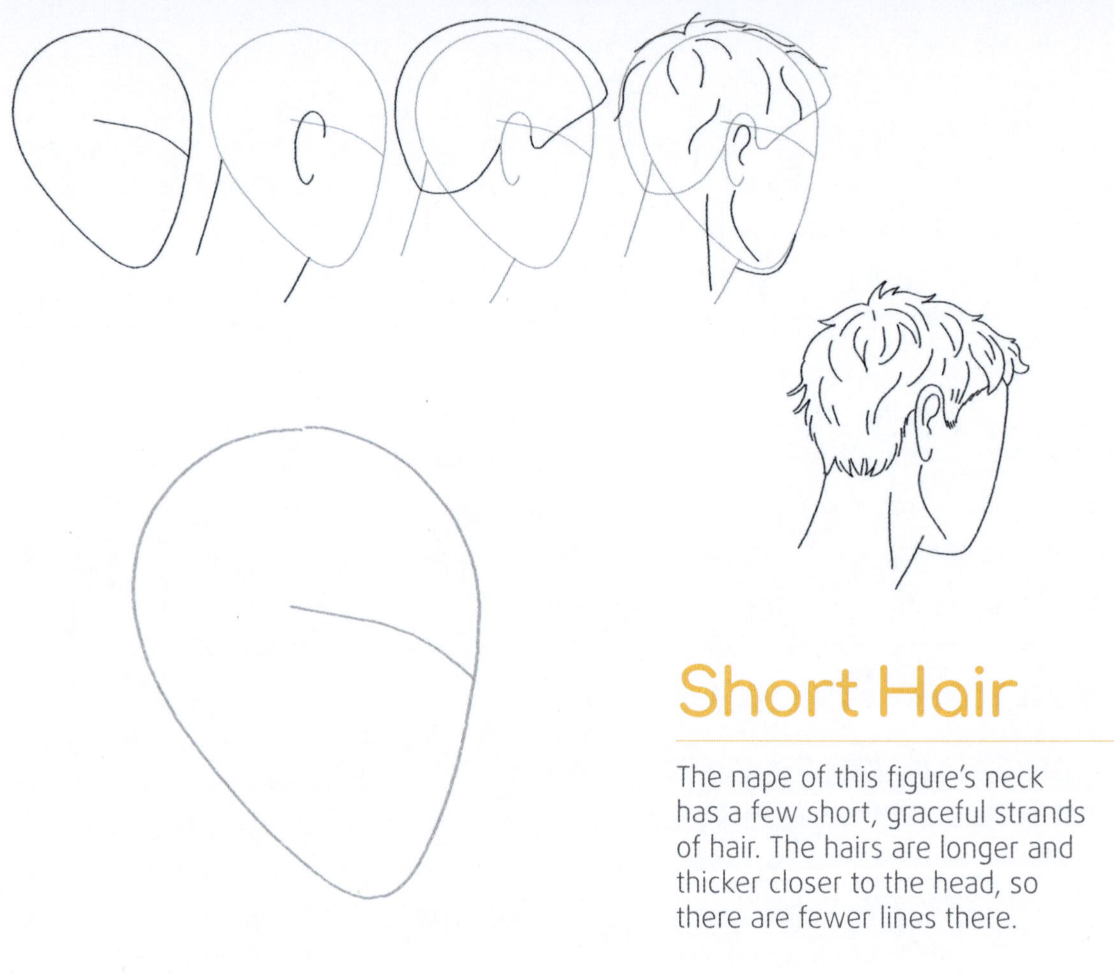

Short Hair

The nape of this figure's neck
has a few short, graceful strands
of hair. The hairs are longer and
thicker closer to the head, so
there are fewer lines there.

140th **day**

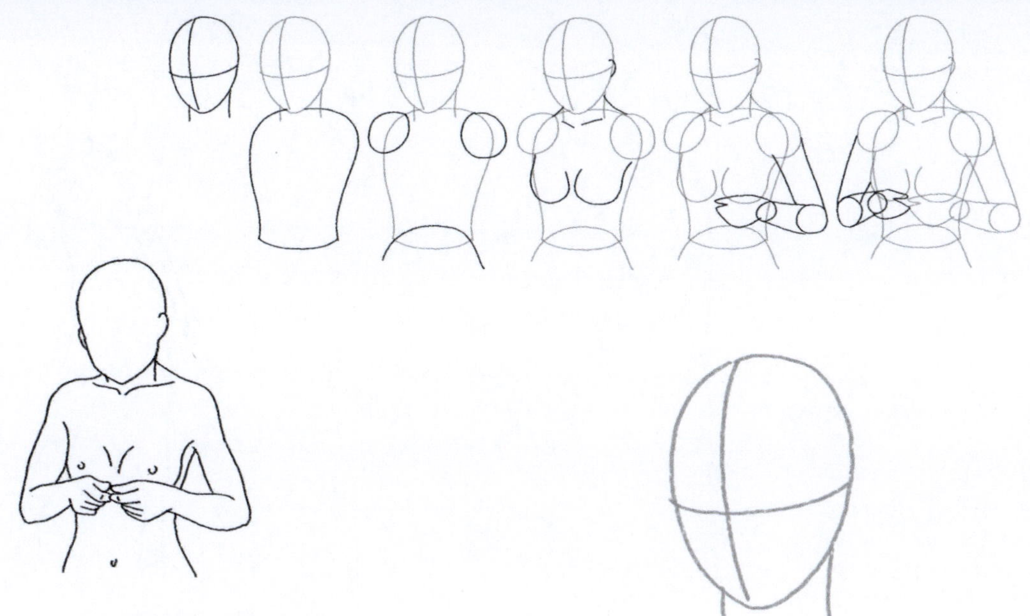

Woman's Torso

This pose tightens the chest
and creates a crease in the
middle of it.

141st day

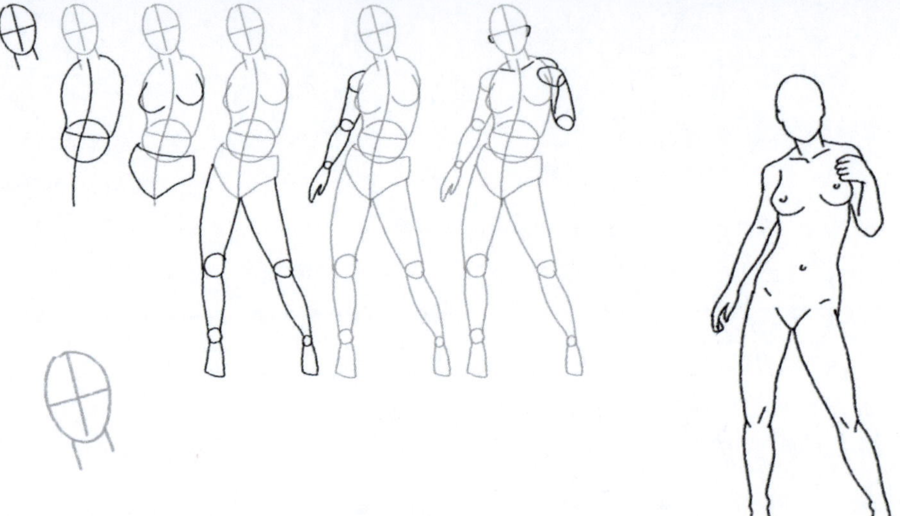

Standing Woman

A dynamic sway of the hips tilts the line of the shoulders and hips toward each other.

142**nd** day

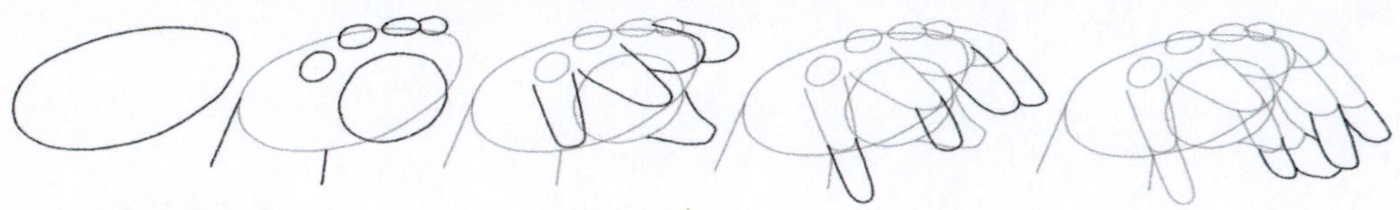

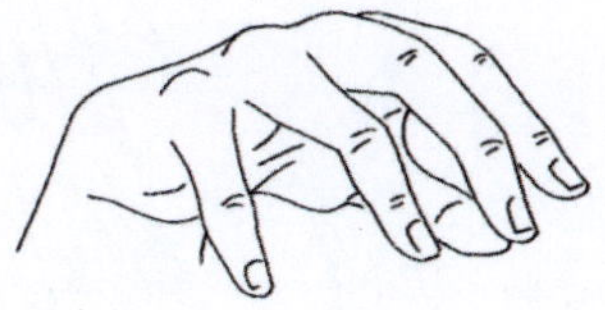

Hand

This hand is supple, and the fingers hang over the oval of the palm, partially concealing the thumb.

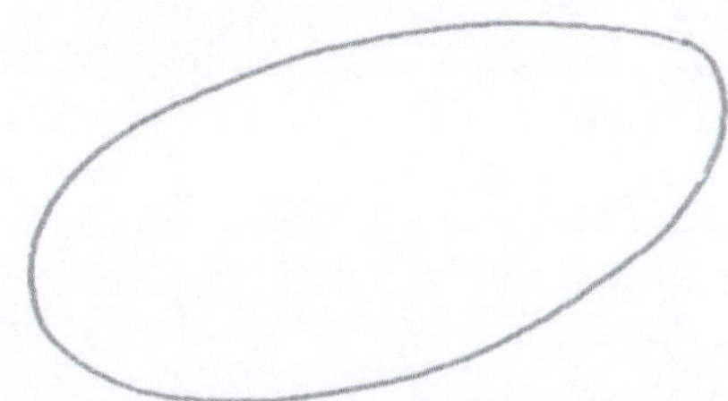

143 rd day

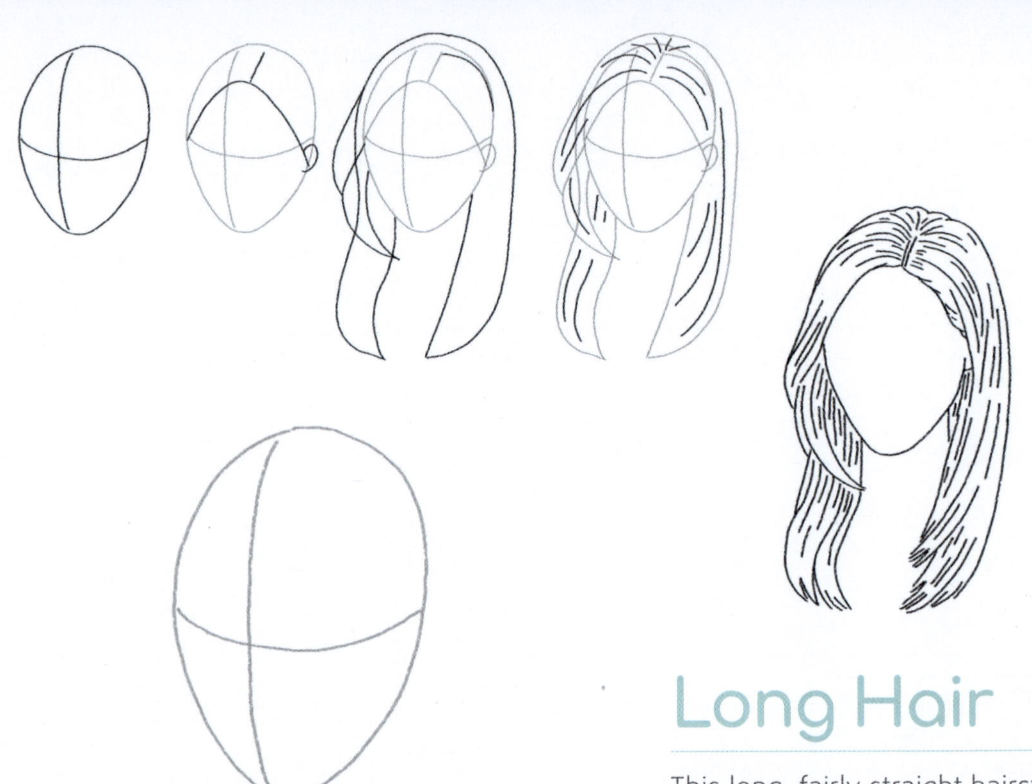

Long Hair

This long, fairly straight hairstyle wraps around the face, casting shadows around the neck. Add lines to create the shadows, and let the strands of hair breathe.

144 th day

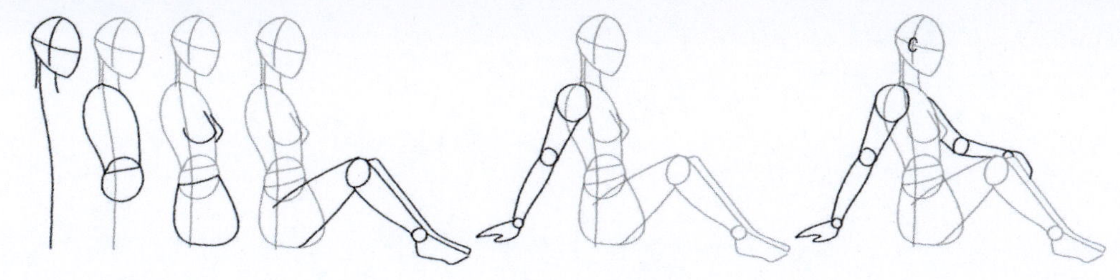

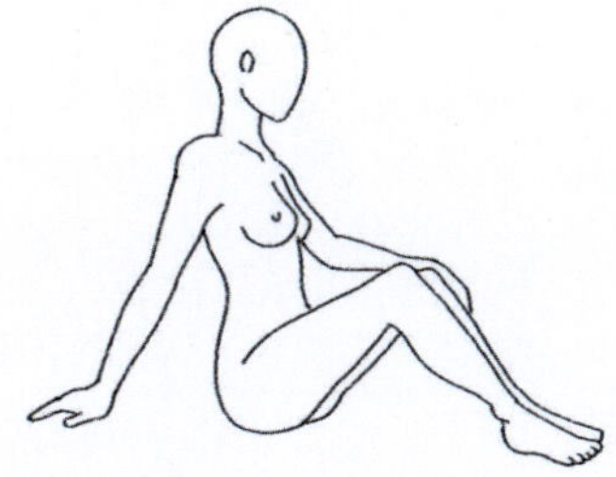

Reclining
Woman

This pose is in profile, almost
entirely obscuring one side of
the body.

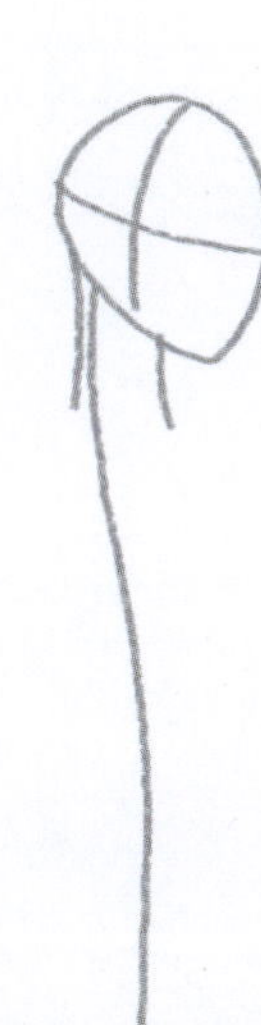

145th day

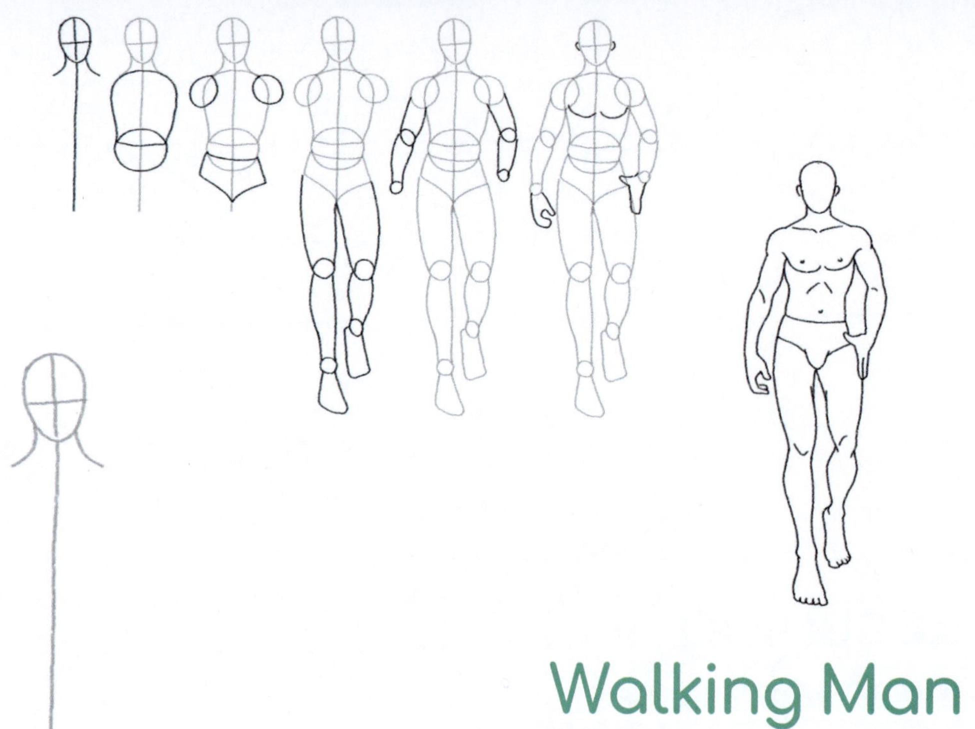

Walking Man

You can exaggerate the length of the legs to accentuate the movement.

146 th day

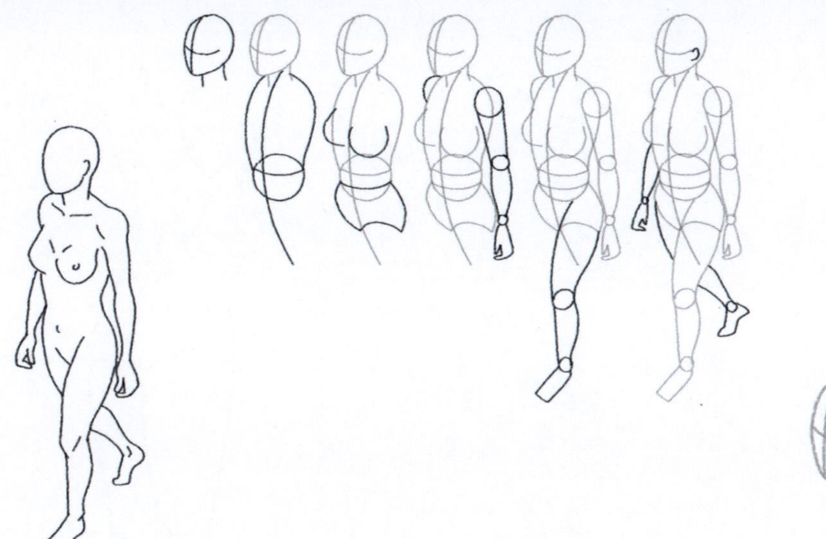

Standing Woman

This three-quarter bird's-eye view collapses the volumes on top of each other. The rear leg appears smaller in perspective.

147 th day

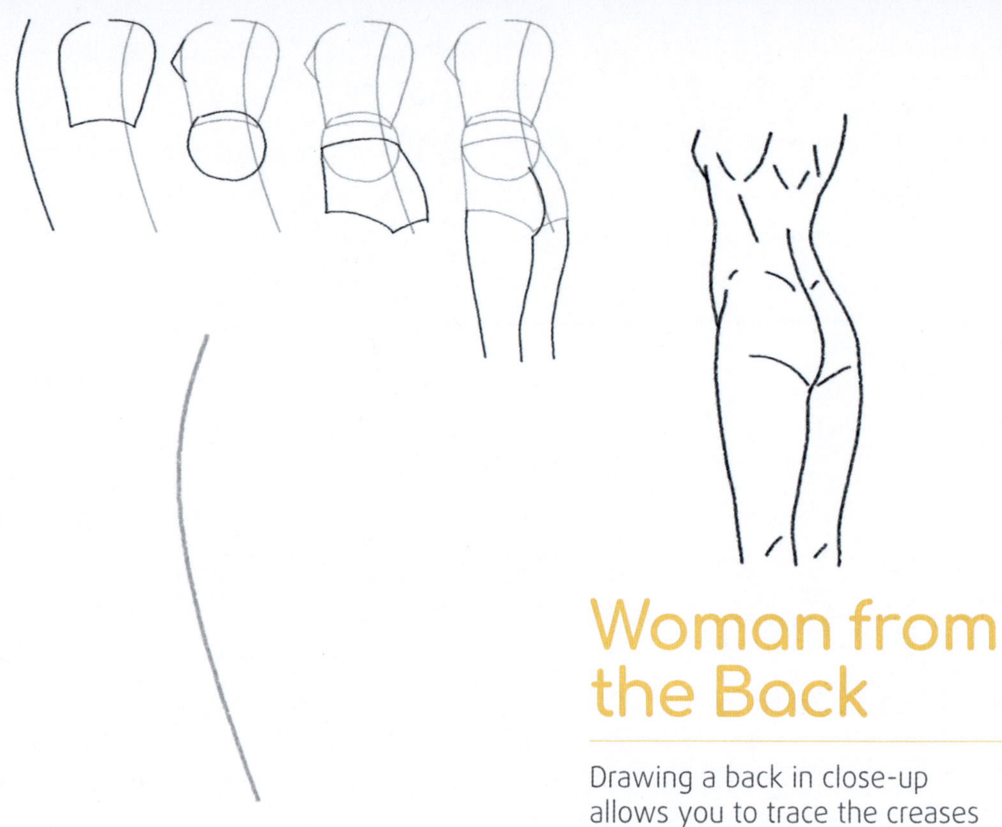

Woman from the Back

Drawing a back in close-up allows you to trace the creases and ridges of the ribs, spine, kidneys and knees.

148th day

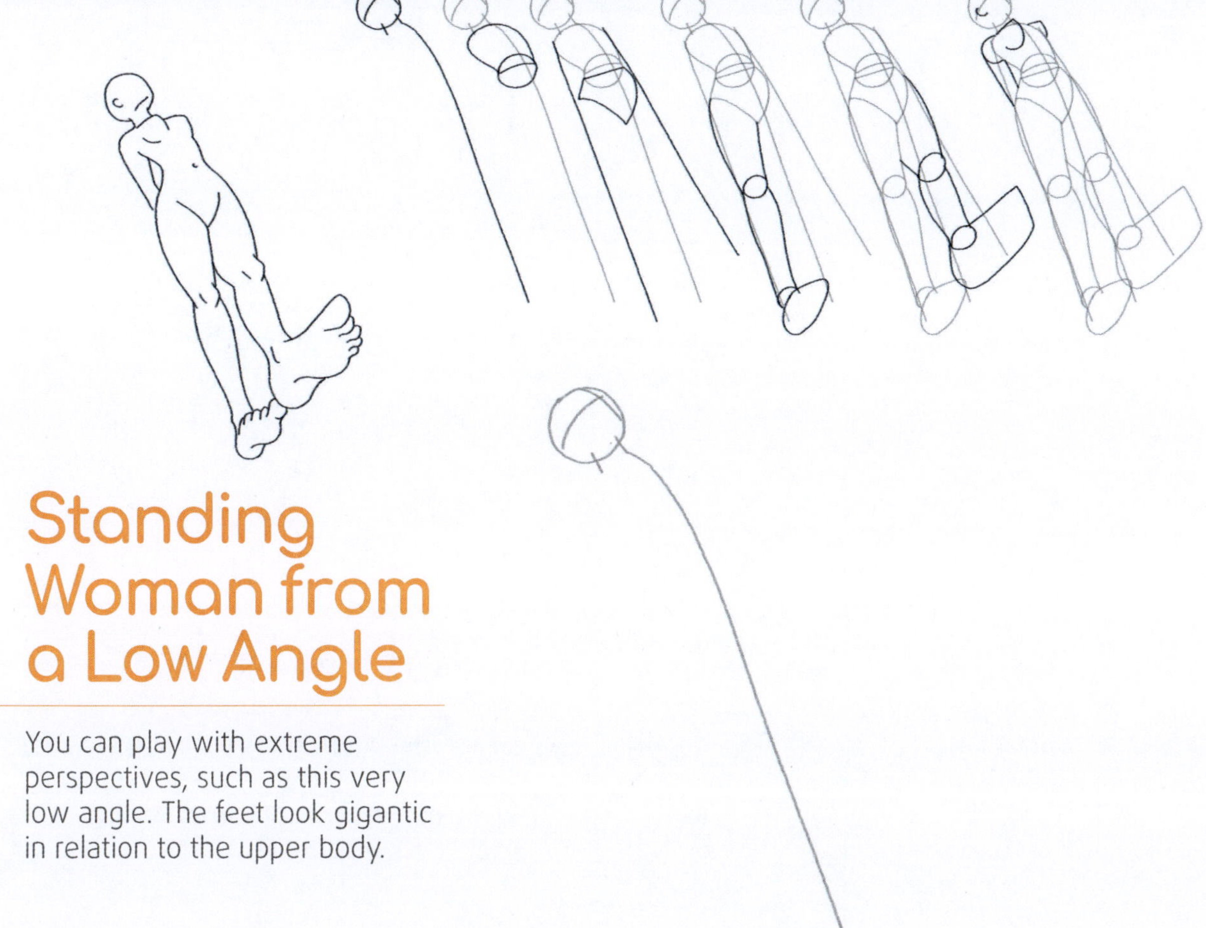

Standing
Woman from
a Low Angle

You can play with extreme
perspectives, such as this very
low angle. The feet look gigantic
in relation to the upper body.

149th day

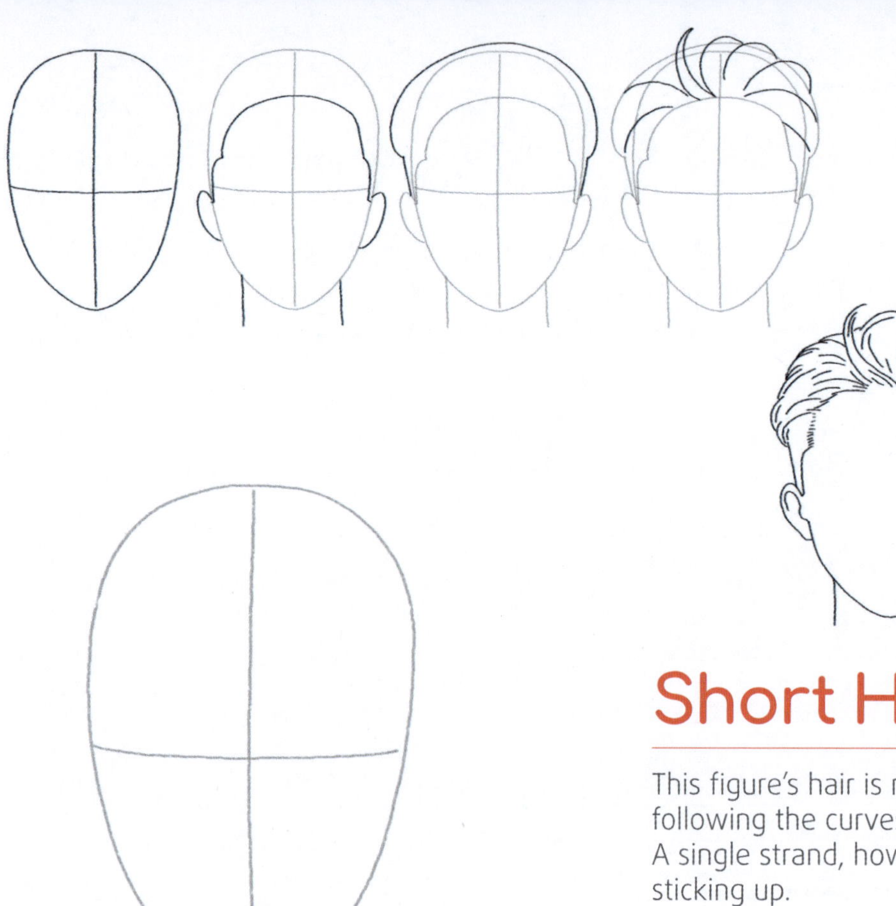

Short Hair

This figure's hair is neatly styled, following the curves of the head. A single strand, however, is sticking up.

150th day

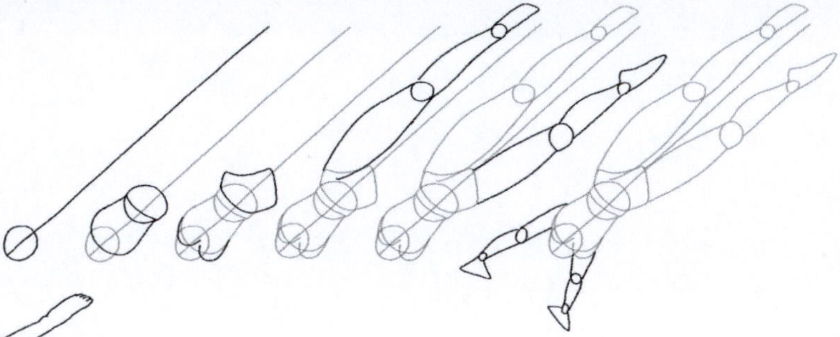

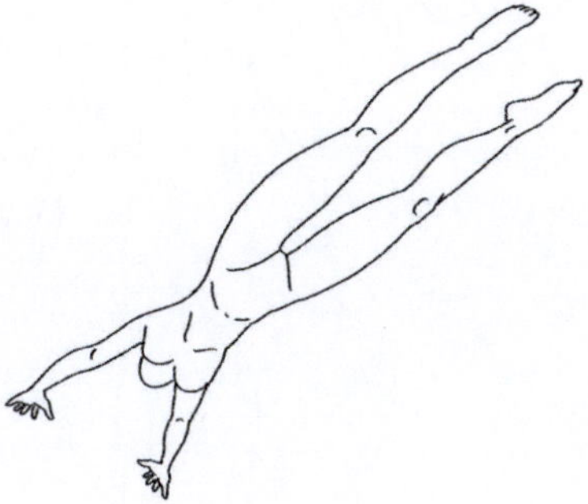

Diving Woman

The strong perspective of this pose, viewed from below, emphasizes the legs and greatly minimizes the upper body.

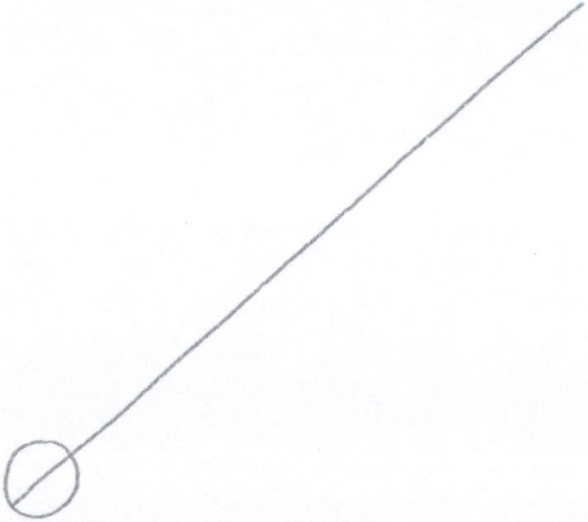

151st day

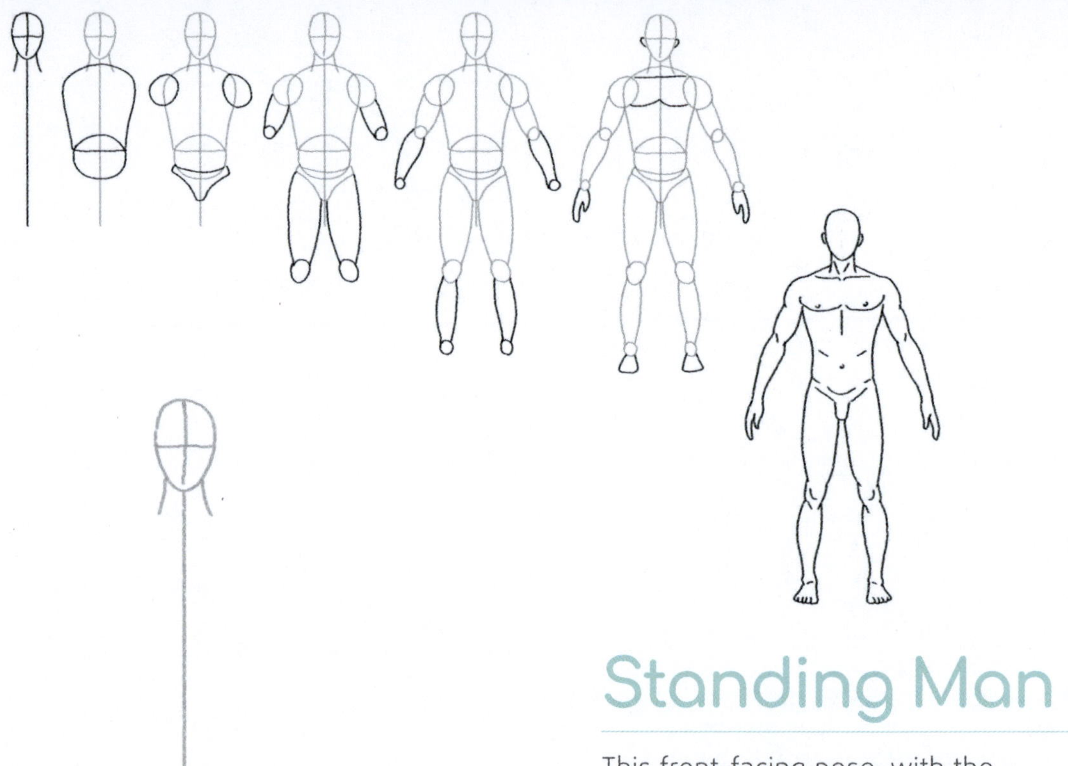

Standing Man

This front-facing pose, with the arms and legs slightly apart, clearly shows the triangular shape of the torso.

152nd day

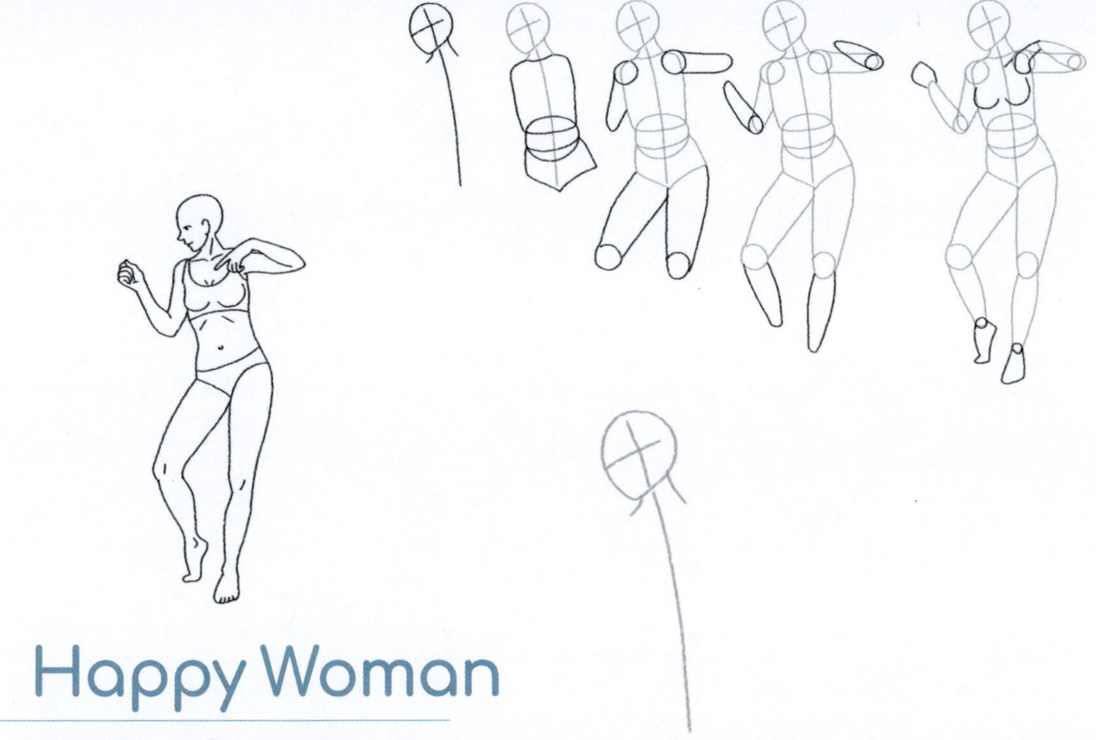

Happy Woman

This dancing pose tilts the shoulders and hips in the same direction. One leg is straight, while the other is flexed.

153 rd day

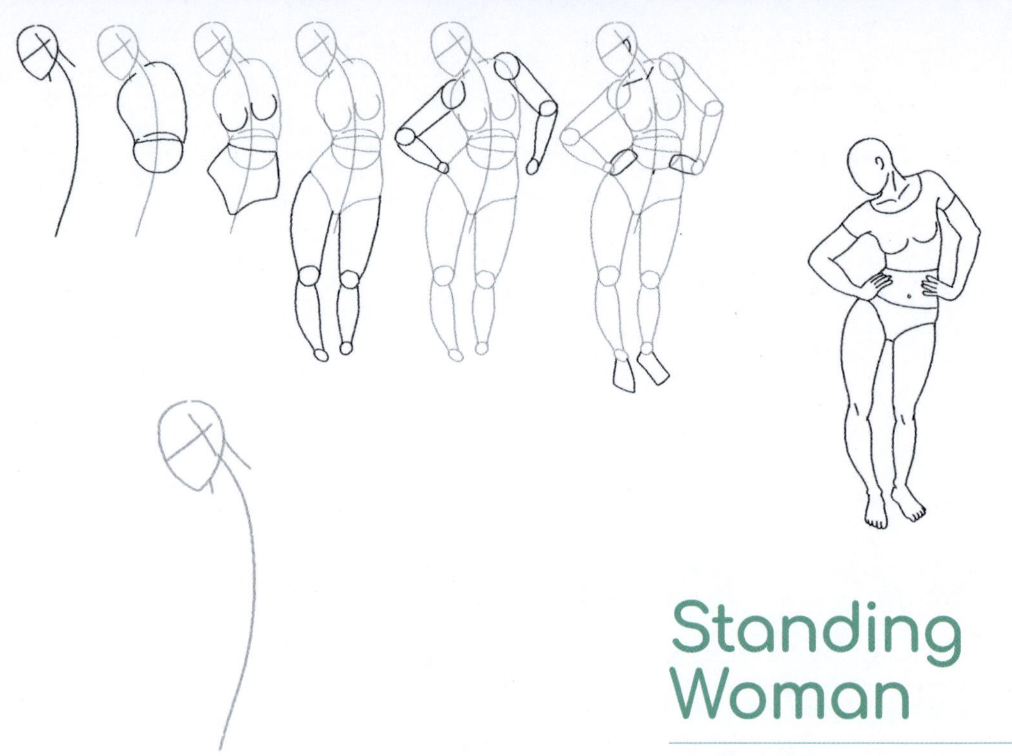

Standing
Woman

A dramatic sway tilts
the shoulder line
toward the raised hip.

154th day

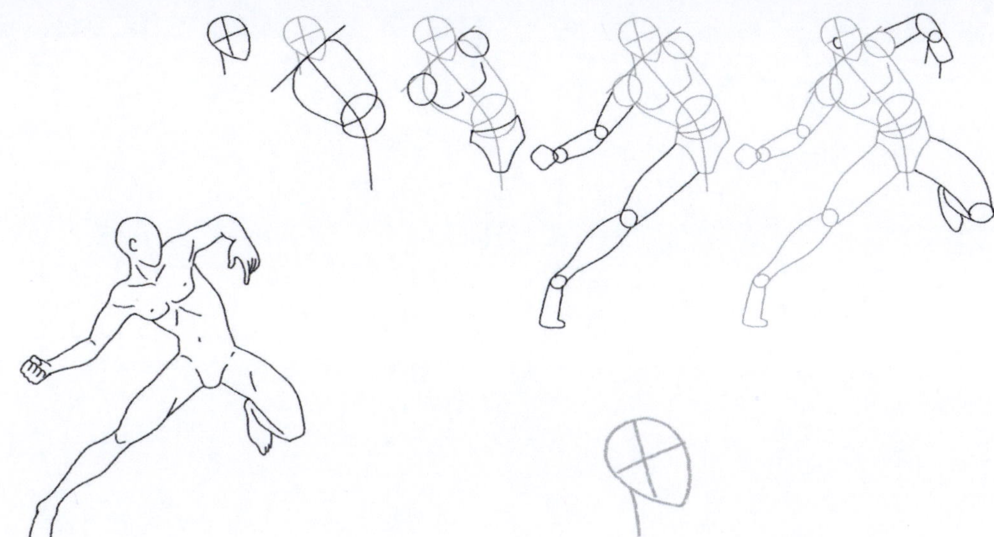

Man Throwing a Punch

The figure's weight is supported
by the grounded leg, projecting
the body forward, so he can shift
his weight as he punches.

155th day

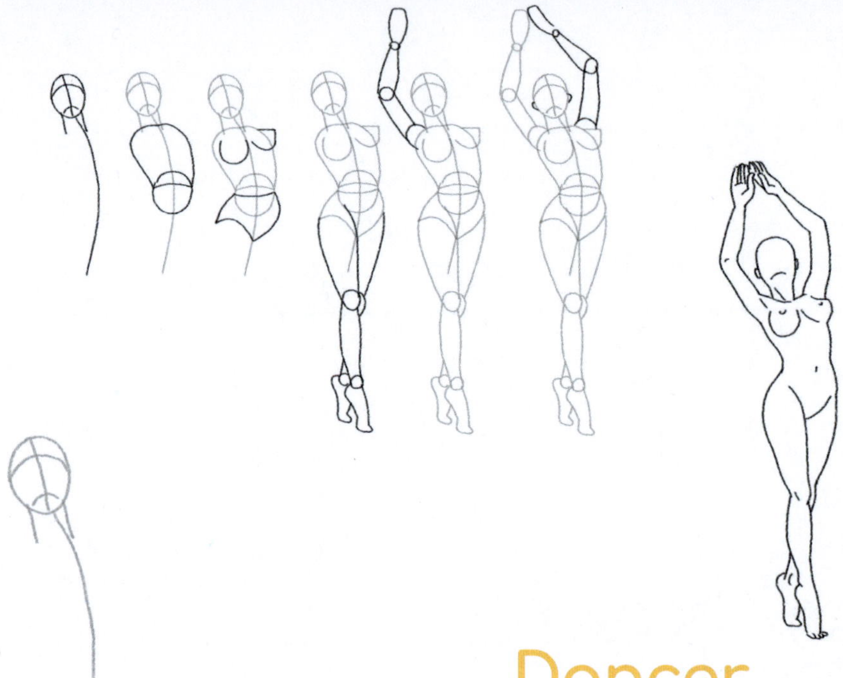

Dancer

This pose stretches the whole body toward the hands. The torso twists and arches upward.

156th day

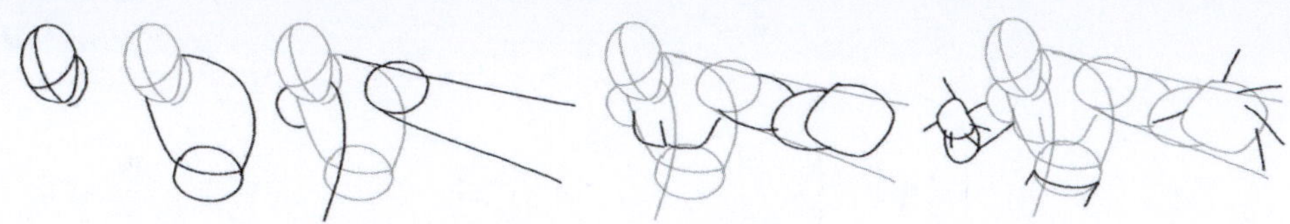

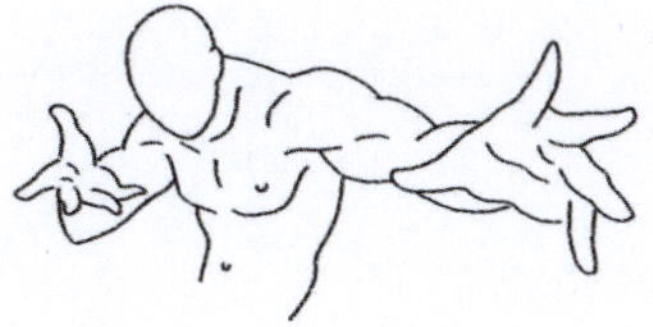

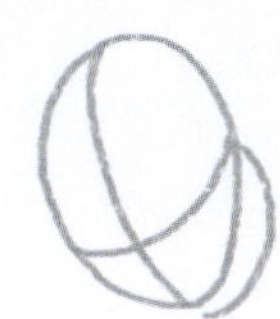

Man's Torso

The hand in the foreground is huge compared to the hand further back. It's the effect of perspective.

157th day

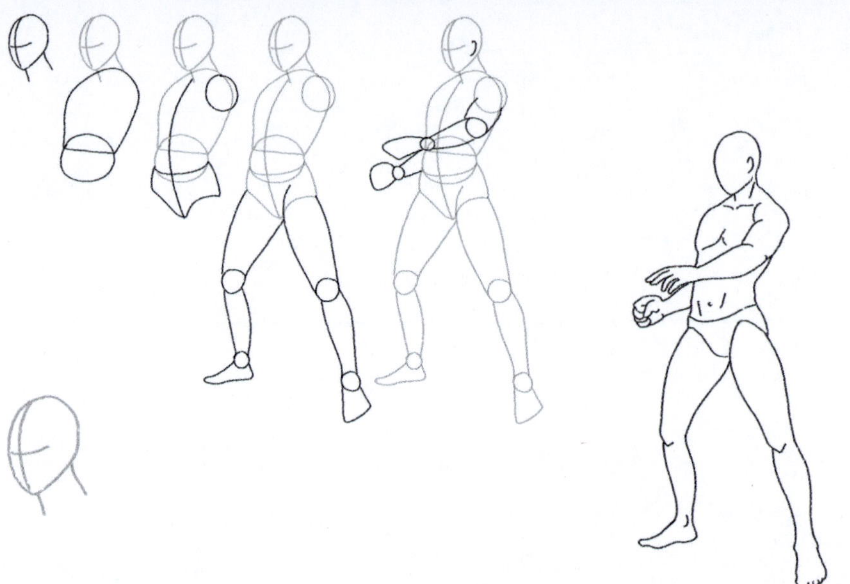

Standing Man

This figure's torso is arched backward. The foreground leg and arm are outstretched, and the rear leg and arm are slightly bent.

158th **day**

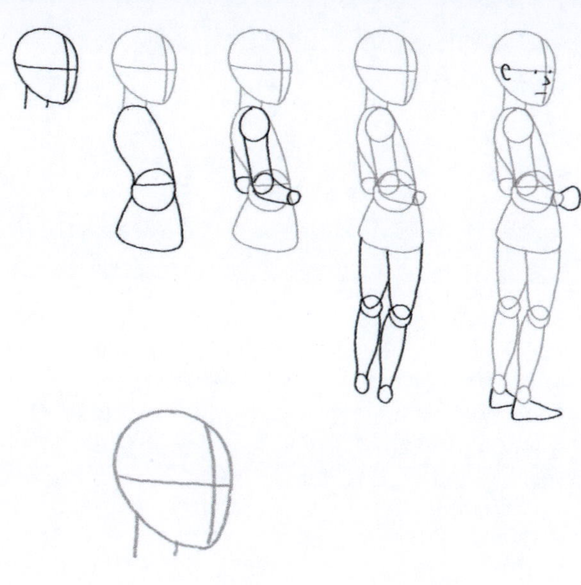

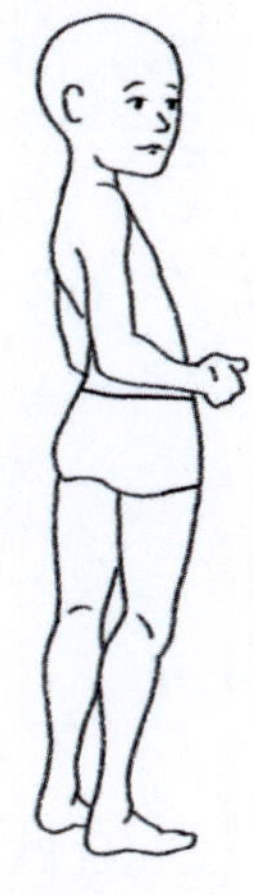

Child

Viewed from a three-quarter perspective, this pose obscures part of the torso, making it appear even thinner and the head appear larger.

159th day

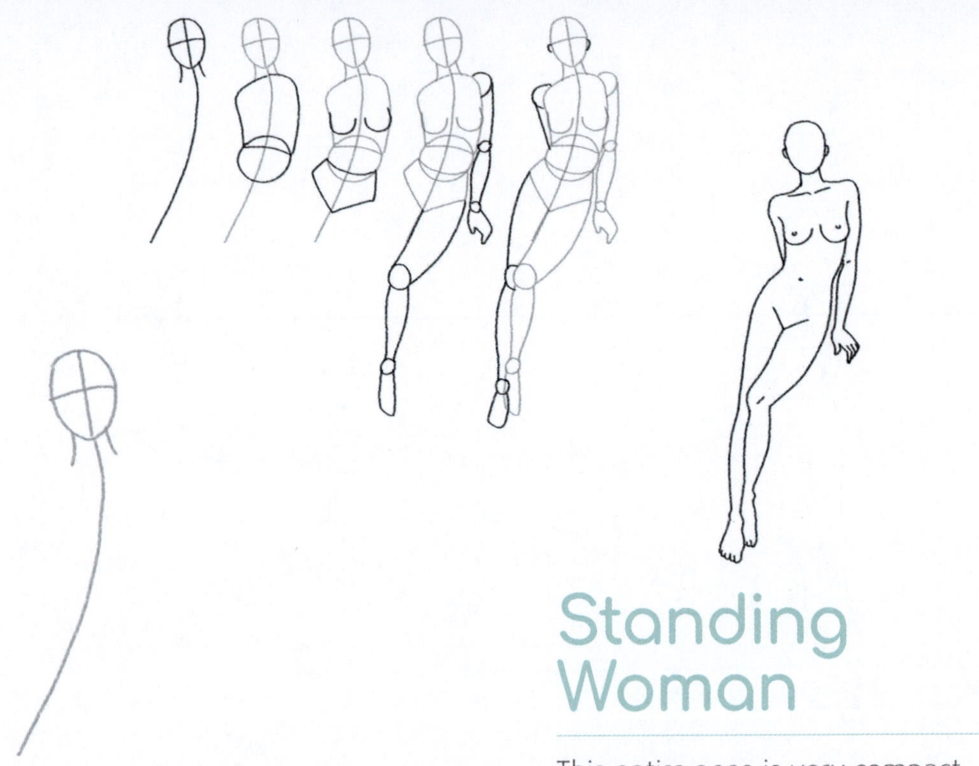

Standing
Woman

This entire pose is very compact
and entirely twisted along a
large curve.

160 — 160th day

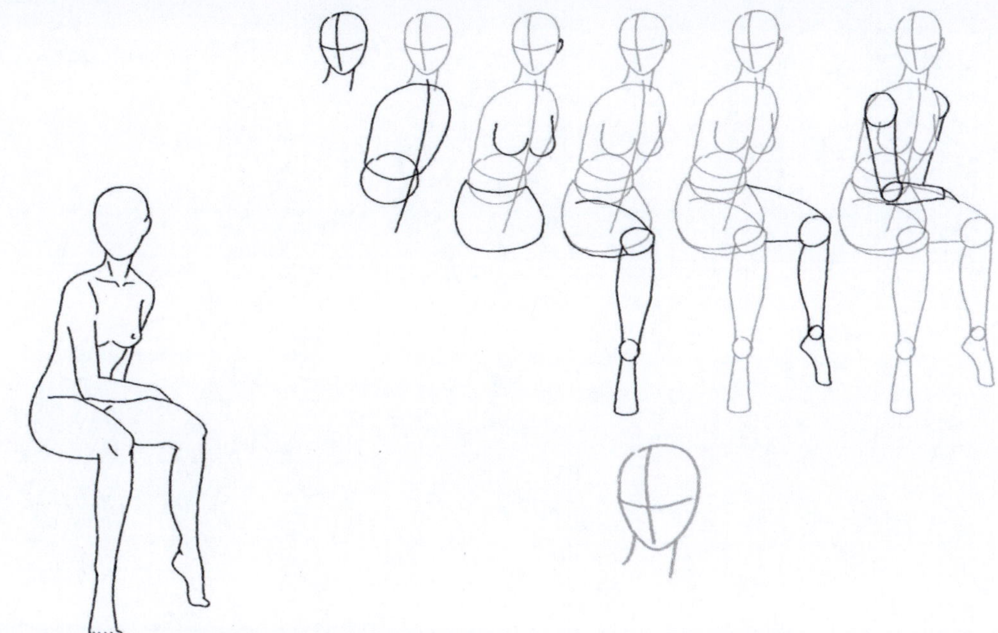

Seated Woman

Representing the surface on
which the figure is sitting can
help you create a pose. The legs
here are bent at right angles,
but the perspective reduces the
length of the thighs.

161st day

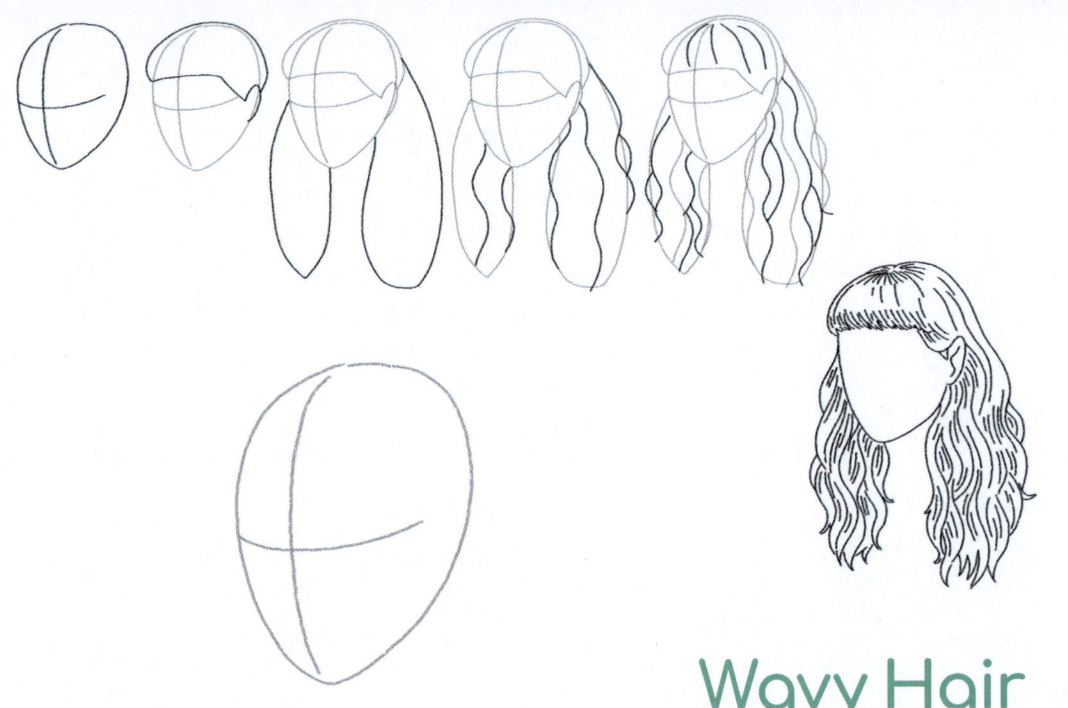

Wavy Hair

There are few lines near the top of the head, which helps catch the light. You can add more lines along the part, the bottom of the bangs and in the waves.

162nd day

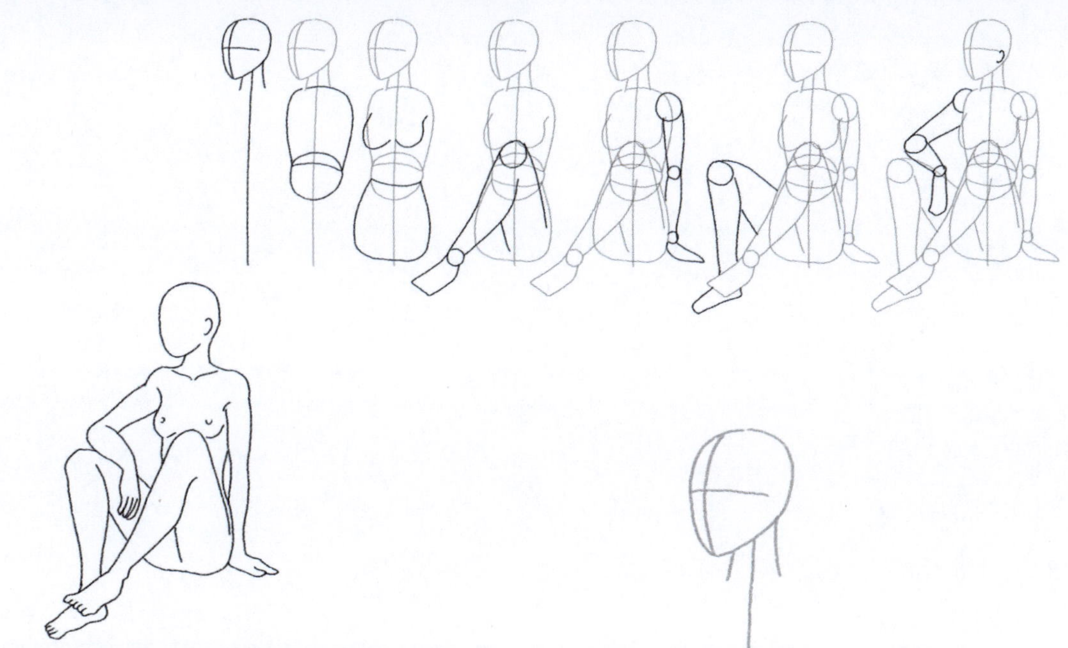

Seated Woman

In this pose, the stomach and the width of the hips are obscured.

163rd day

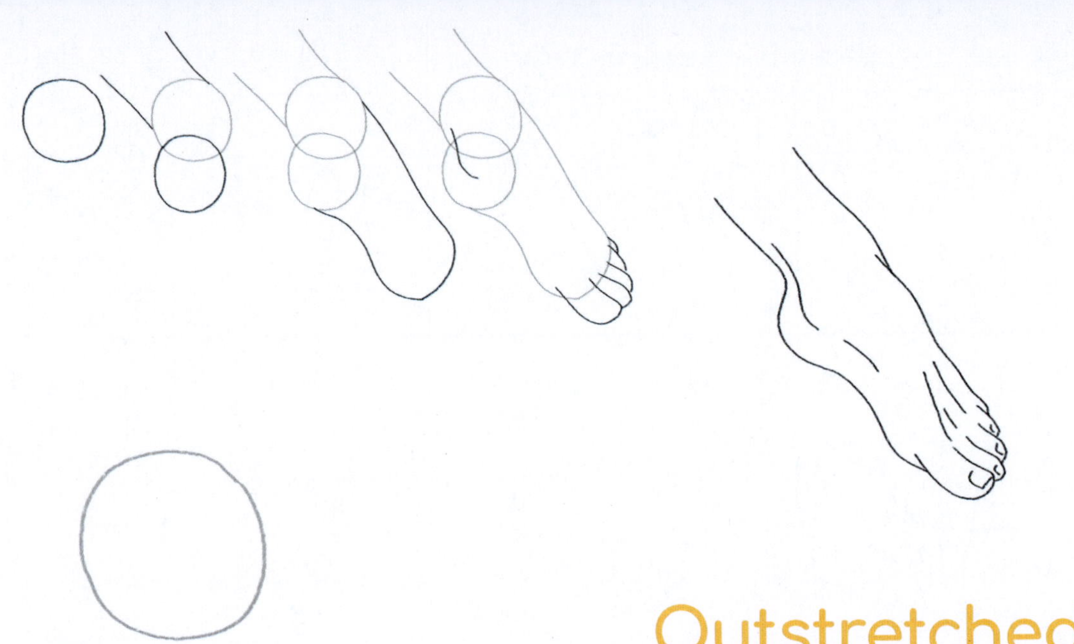

Outstretched Foot

When a foot is stretched, a bulge may be created along the top and an inward curve along the bottom. Creases appear near the toes.

164th day

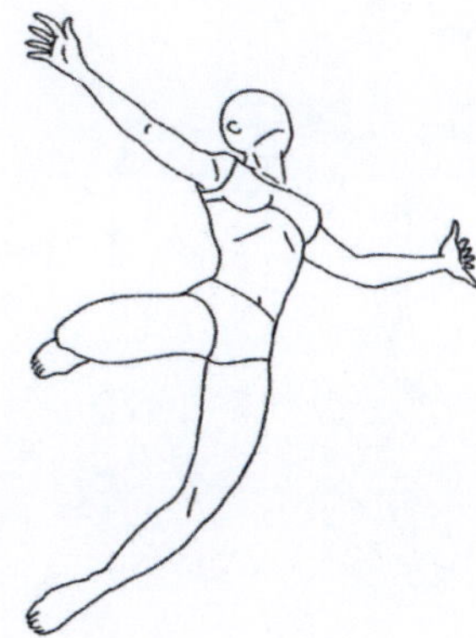

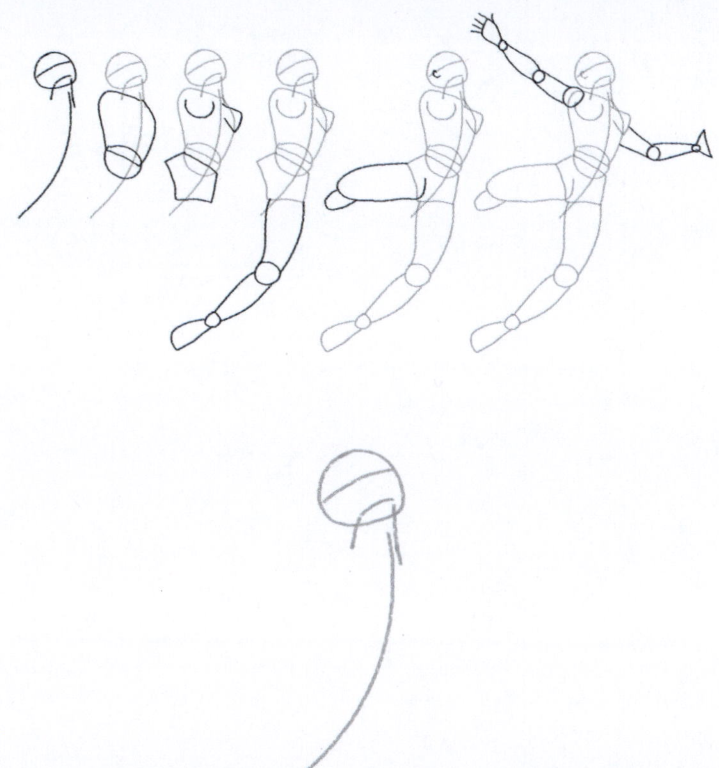

Jumping
Woman

The perspective of this pose
is quite complex. The jumping
posture is being viewed from
below, the bent legs are in
perspective and the torso is
stretched upward.

165th day

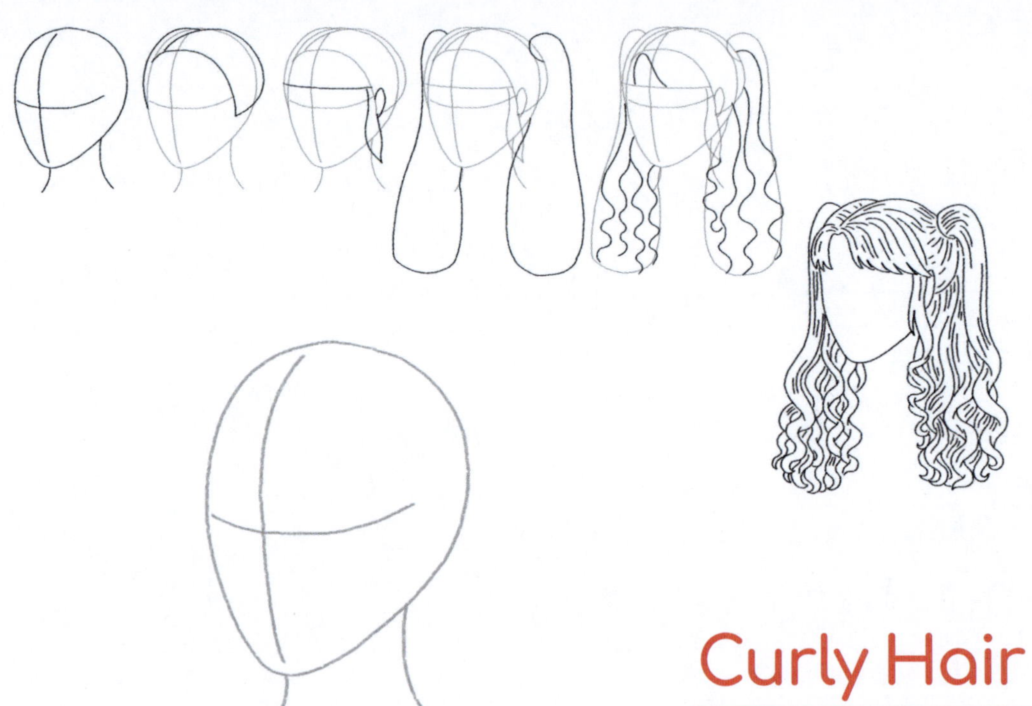

Curly Hair

To emphasize curls in hair,
separate as many strands
as possible into beautiful
tight spirals.

166th day

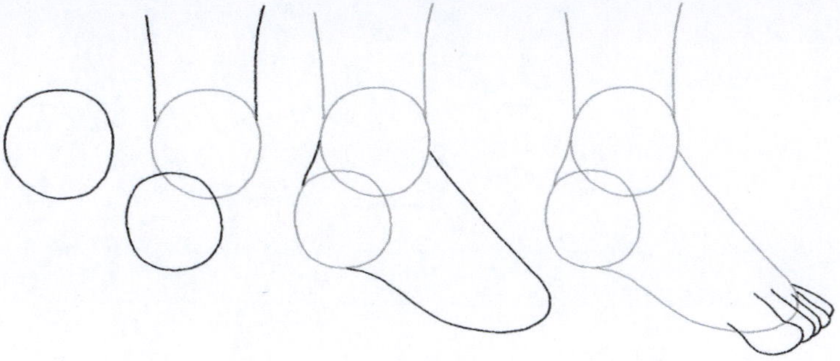

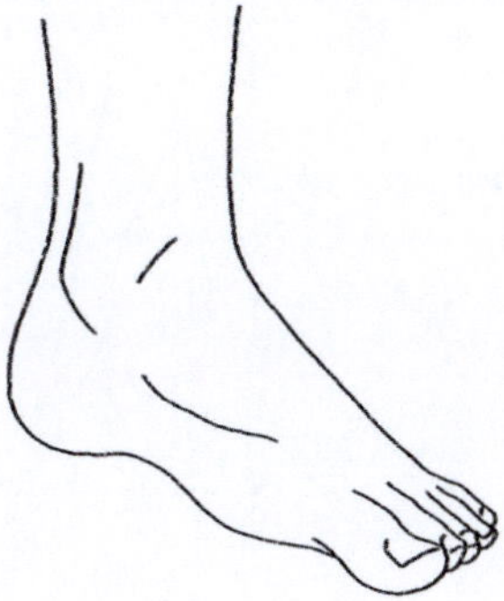

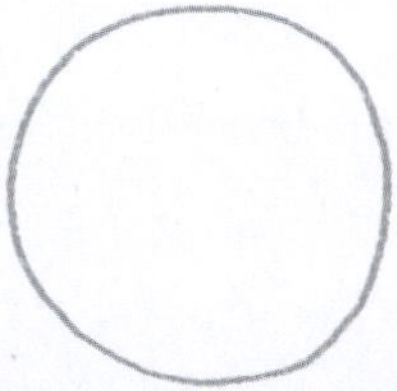

Foot

In this three-quarter view from above, you can see the length of the foot as well as the alignment of the toes.

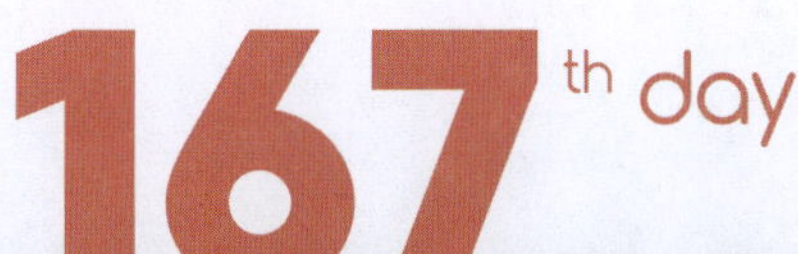

167th day

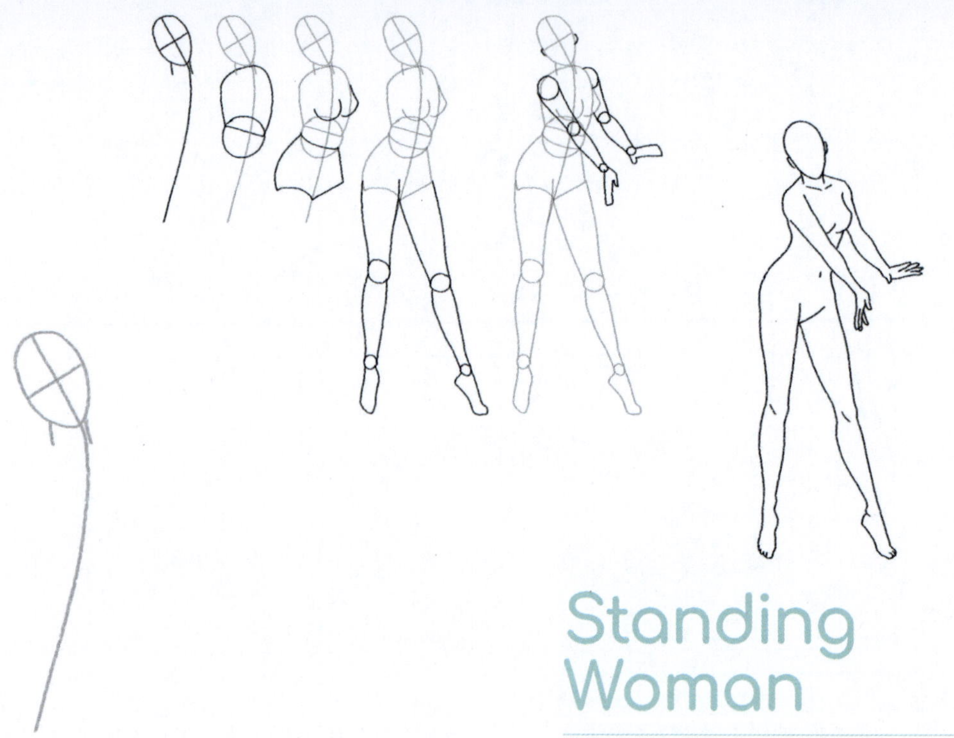

Standing Woman

Standing on tiptoes extends the legs and exaggerates their length.

168 th day

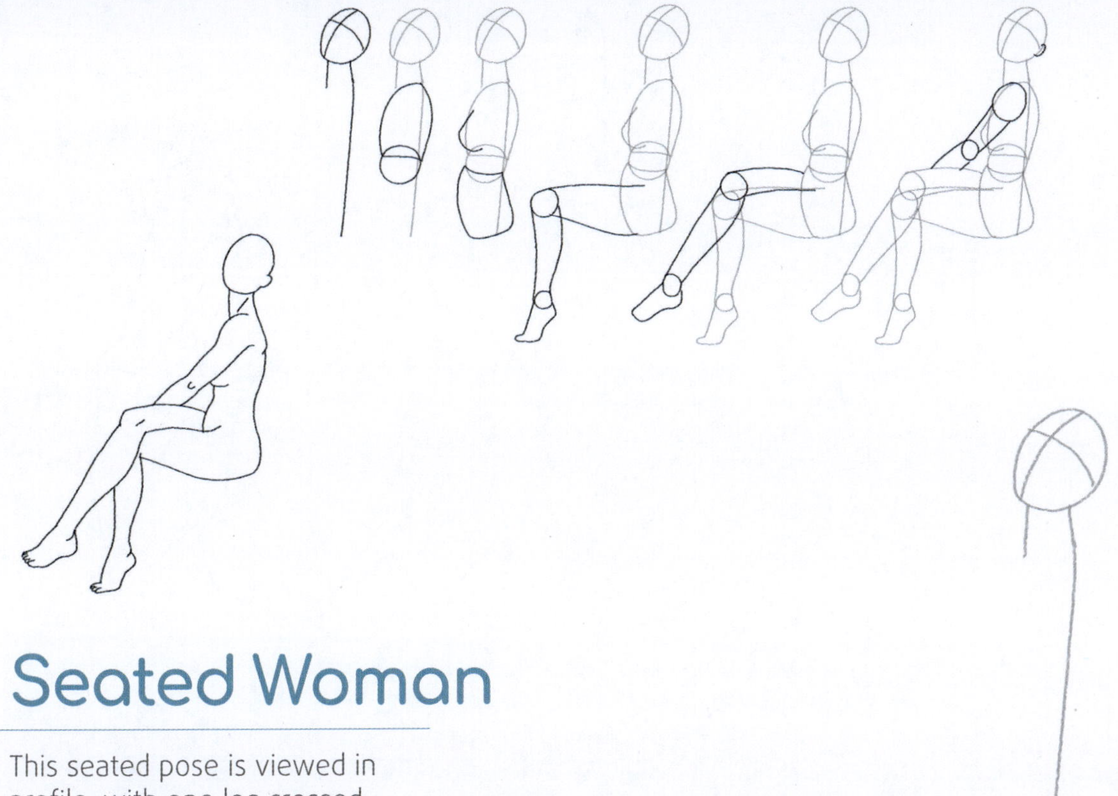

Seated Woman

This seated pose is viewed in
profile, with one leg crossed
over the other. The thigh of
the crossed leg is viewed in
perspective and partly hidden.

169th **day**

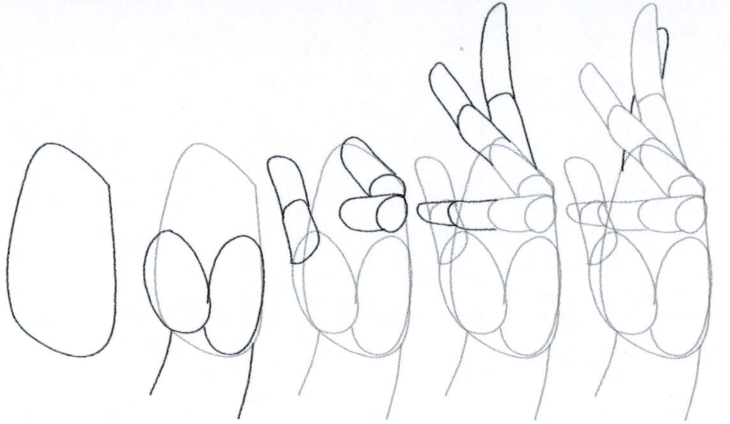
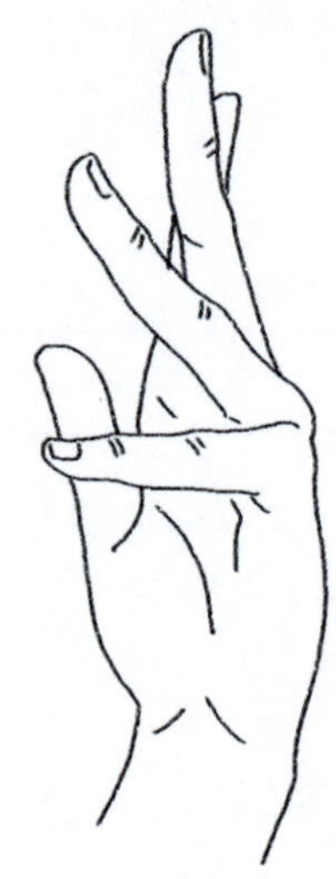
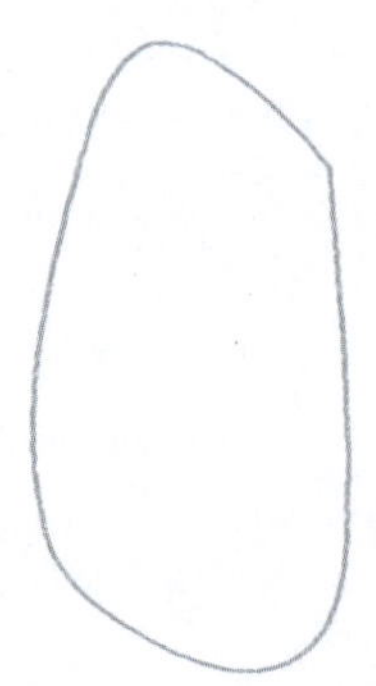

Hand

The whole hand is twisted and
spiraling upward in this pose.

170th **day**

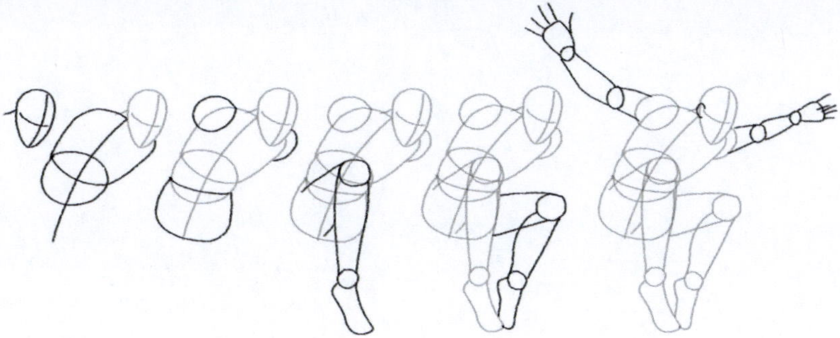

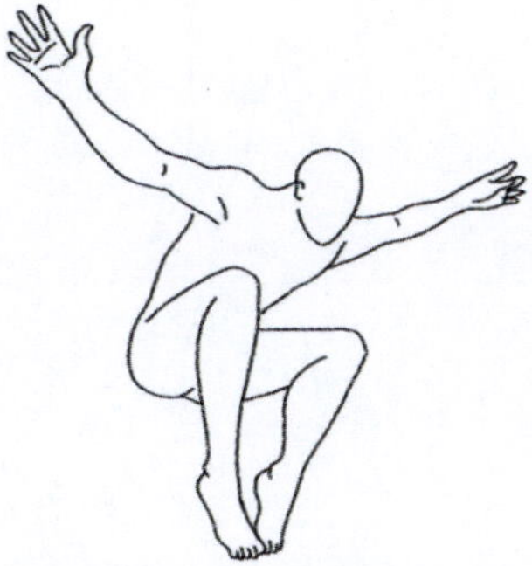

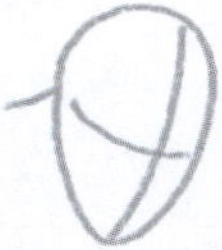

Jumping Man

The feet in this pose point downward. The outstretched arms are in perspective, giving the impression that one arm is larger than the other.

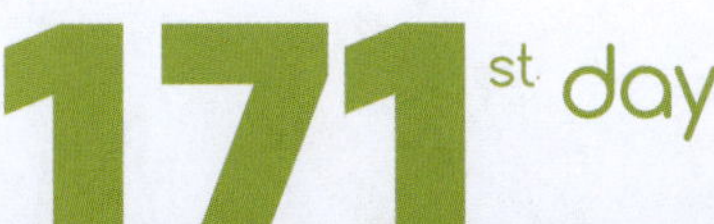

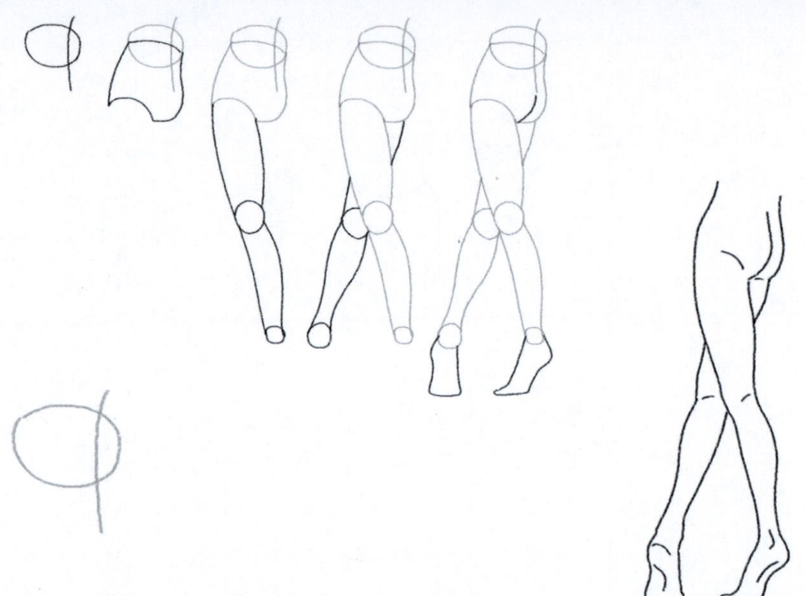

Woman's Legs

The figure is twisting her legs in this pose. The foot turning backward pulls the whole body along with it.

172nd day

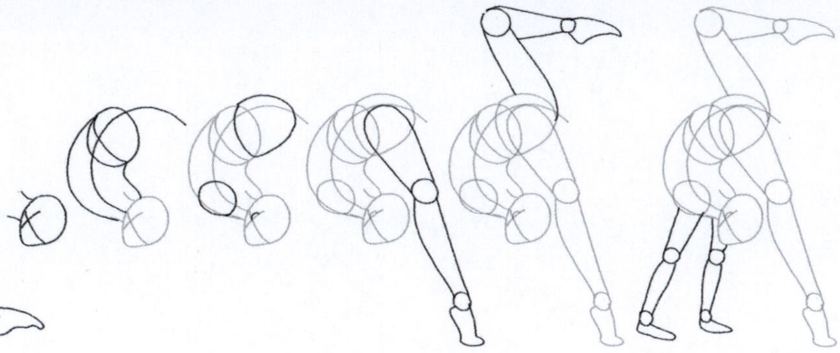

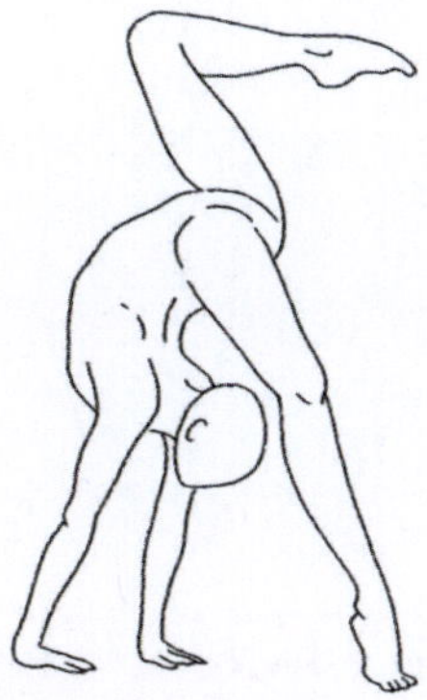

Gymnast

This contorted pose curves the
back as the limbs stretch to
touch the ground.

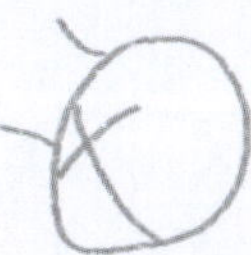

173rd day

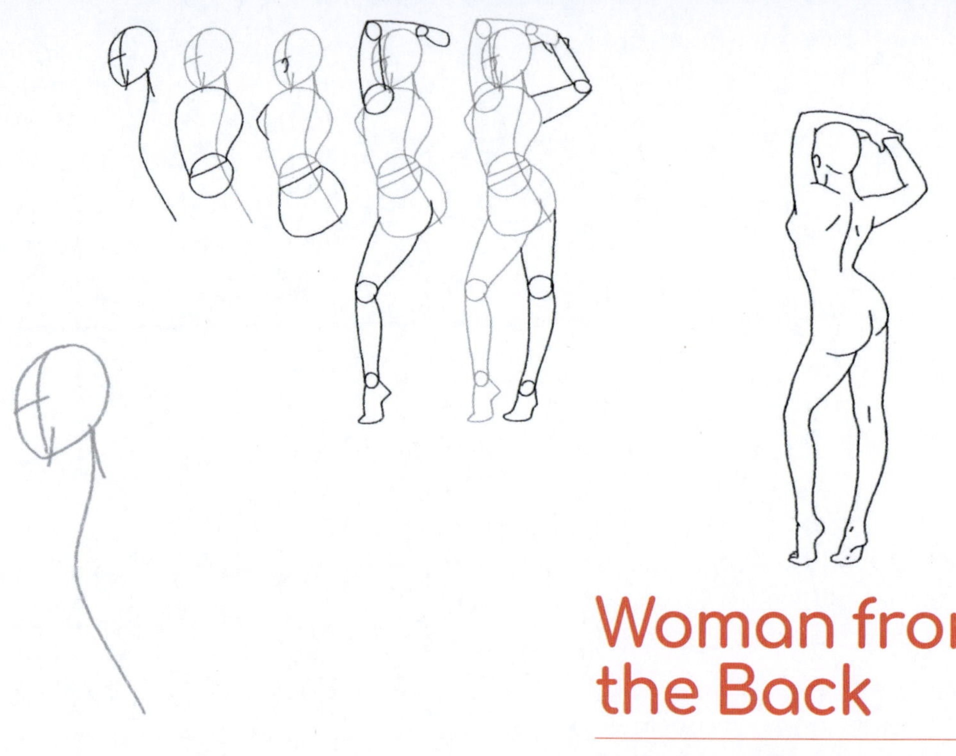

Woman from the Back

A deep sway tilts the hipline, stretching one leg and bending the other.

174th day

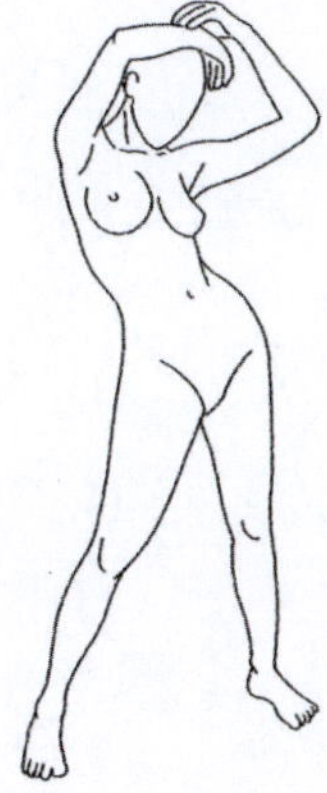

Standing Woman

This figure's pronounced hip sway twists the torso into an S shape. You can sketch a line along the ground to help you draw the legs in perspective.

175th day

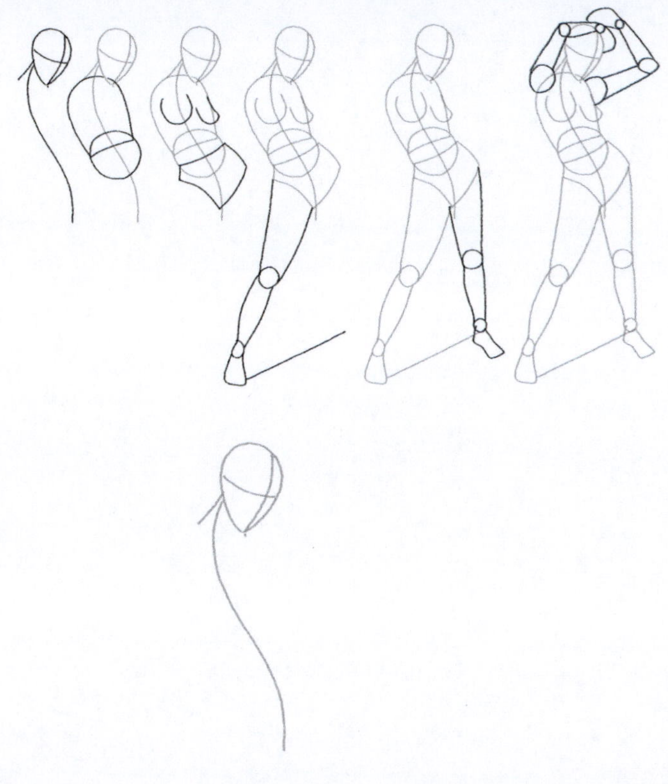

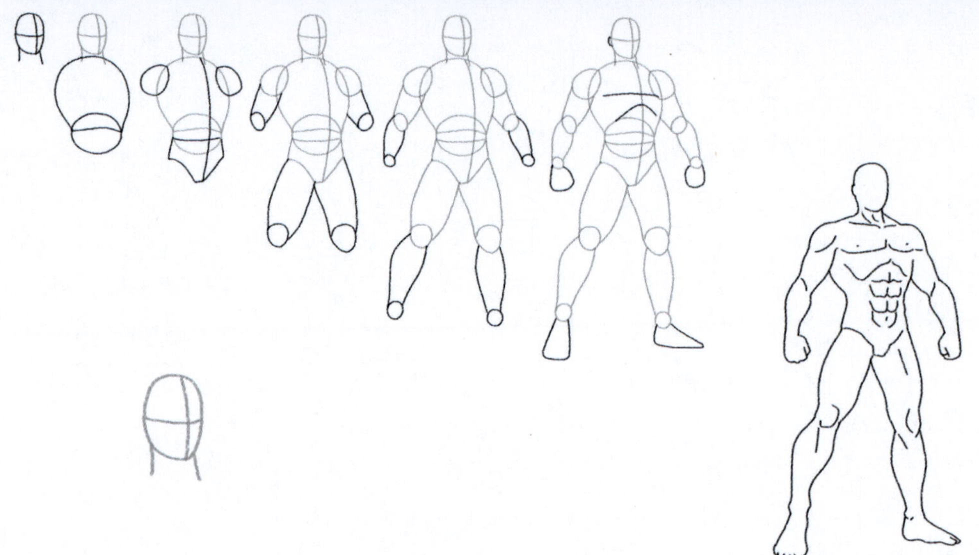

Muscular Man

This figure's muscles are highly developed and contoured.

176th day

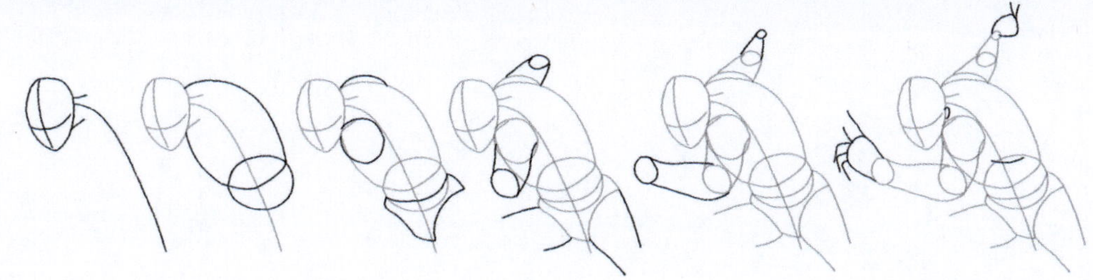

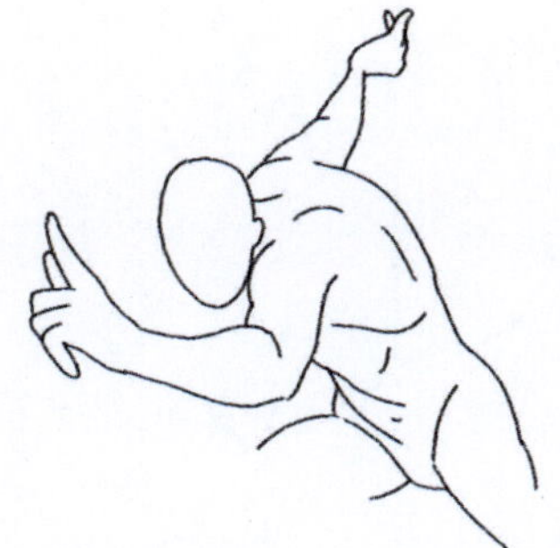

Running Man

This dynamic pose projects one arm forward and curves the torso. The rear hand seems very small in perspective.

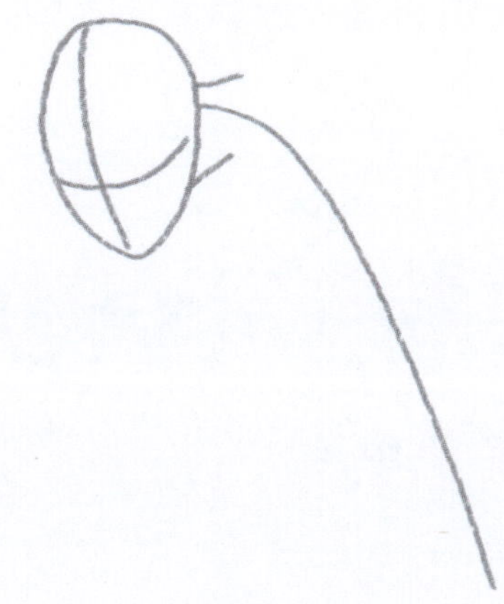

177th day

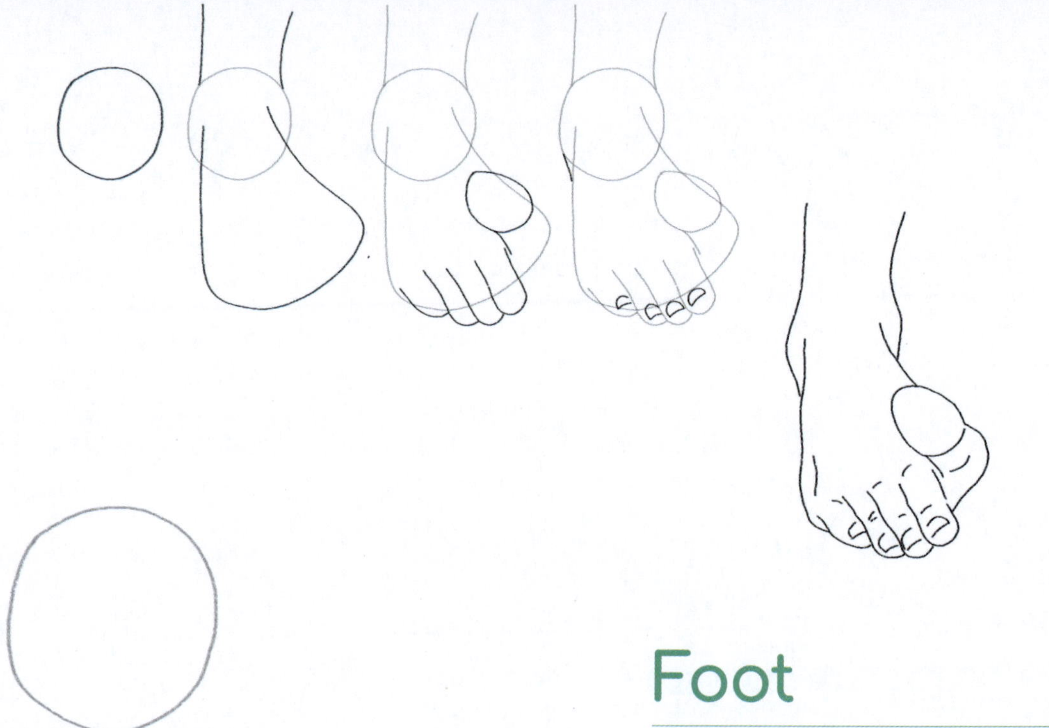

Foot

Viewed in perspective, the front of the foot and the toes appear larger.

178th day

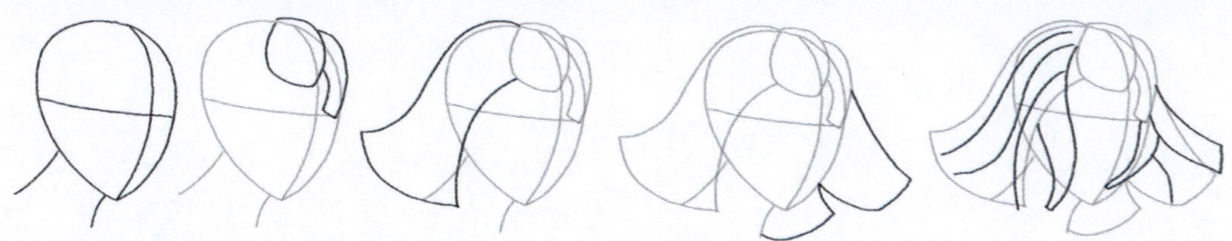

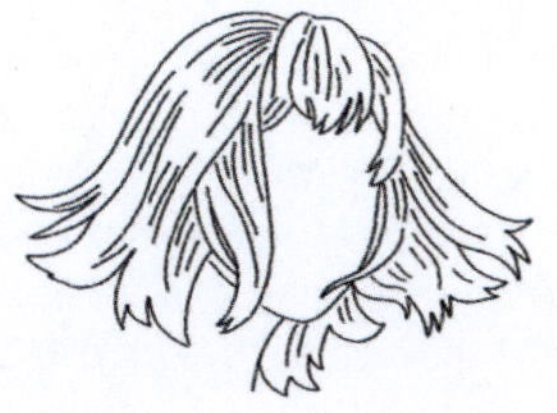

Wind-Blown Hair

With somewhat straight hair, strands in motion create very few curves.

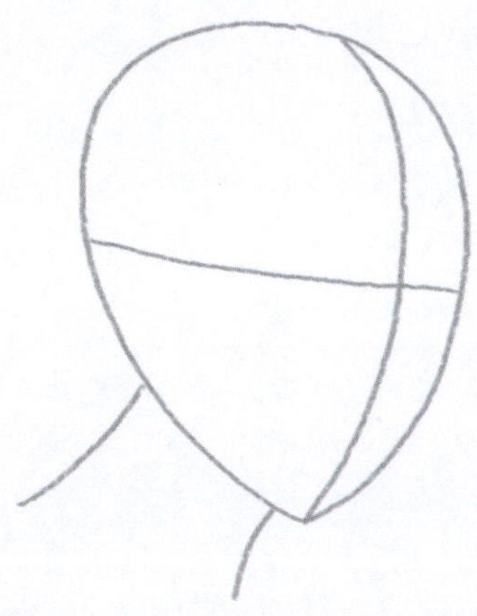

179th **day**

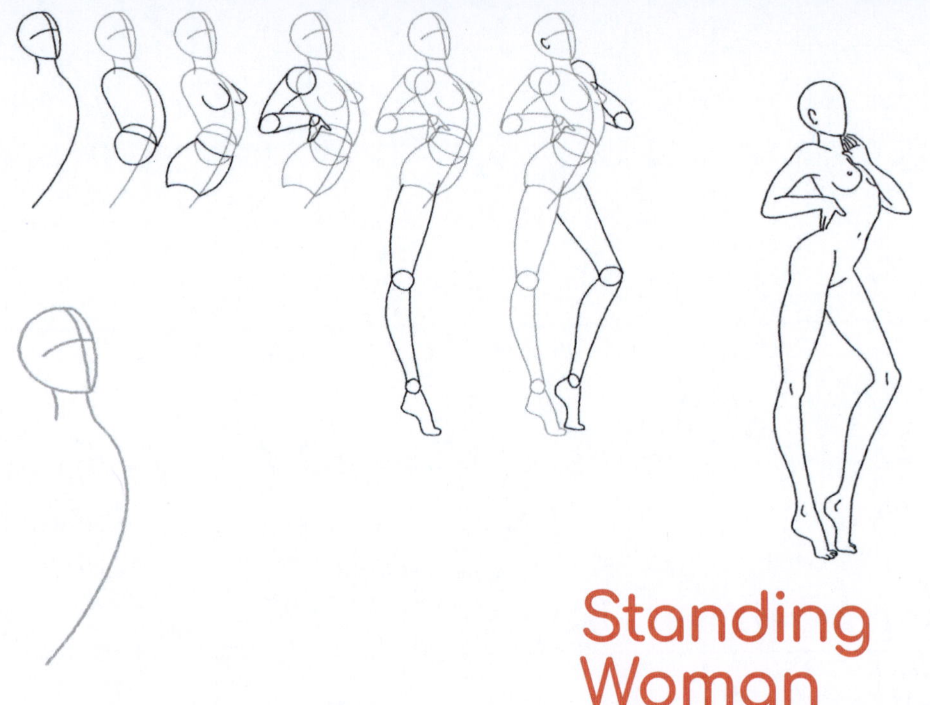

Standing
Woman

This figure's deeply curved back and very long legs are typical of fashion illustrations.

180 th day

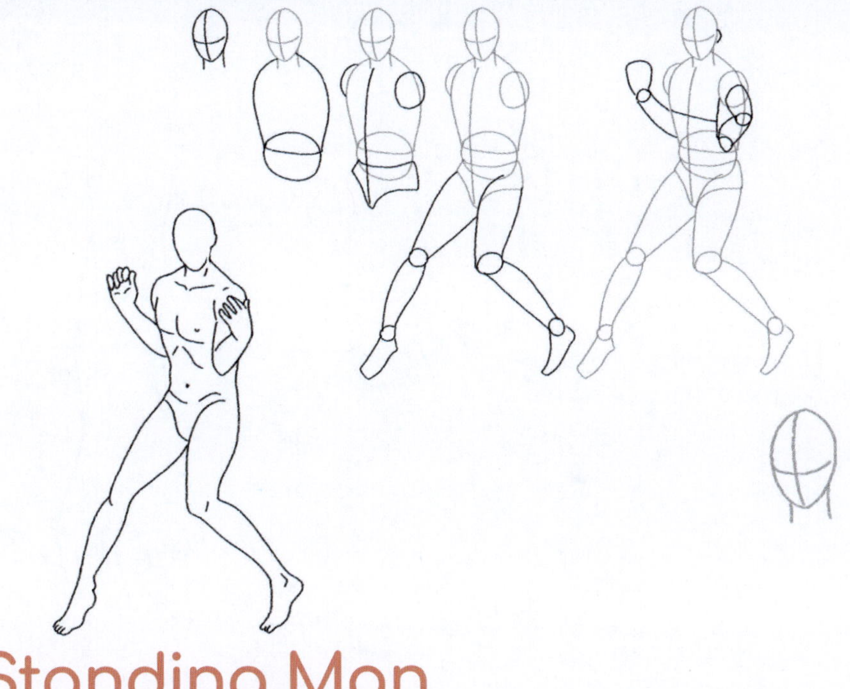

Standing Man

In this pose the entire body is twisted, as if it's rotating.

181 st day

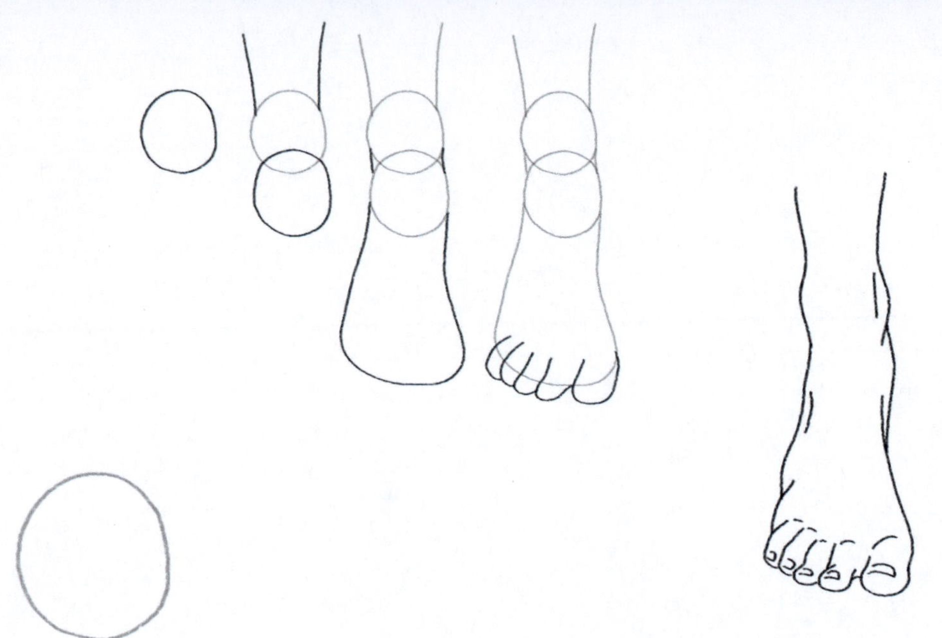

Foot

A foot's length is not obvious
when it is viewed head-on. As
the foot is pressed down, the
toes become slightly flexed.

182nd day

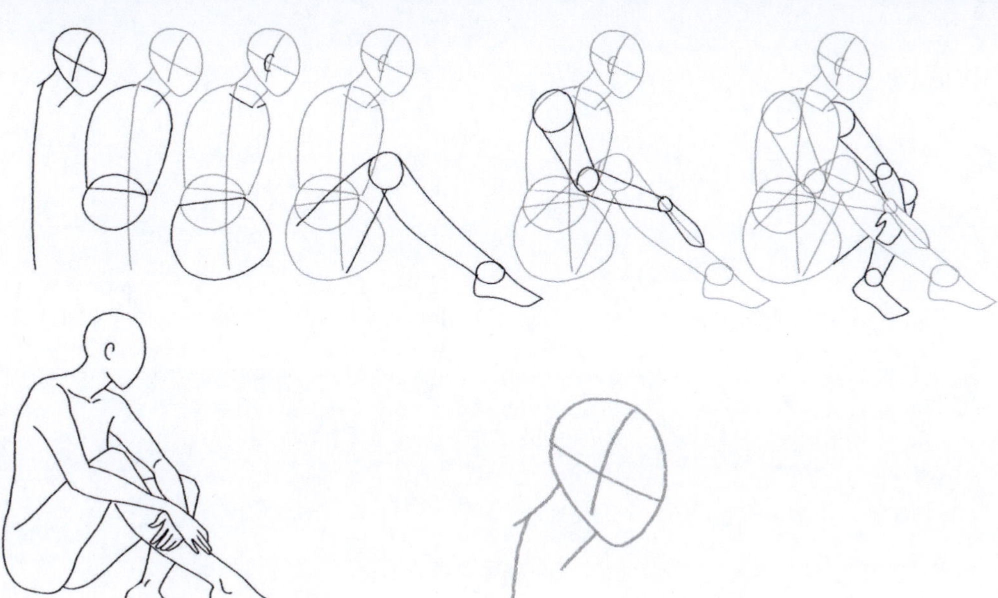

Seated Woman

The three-quarter view of this seated pose obscures part of the torso and creates a sense of perspective.

183rd **day**

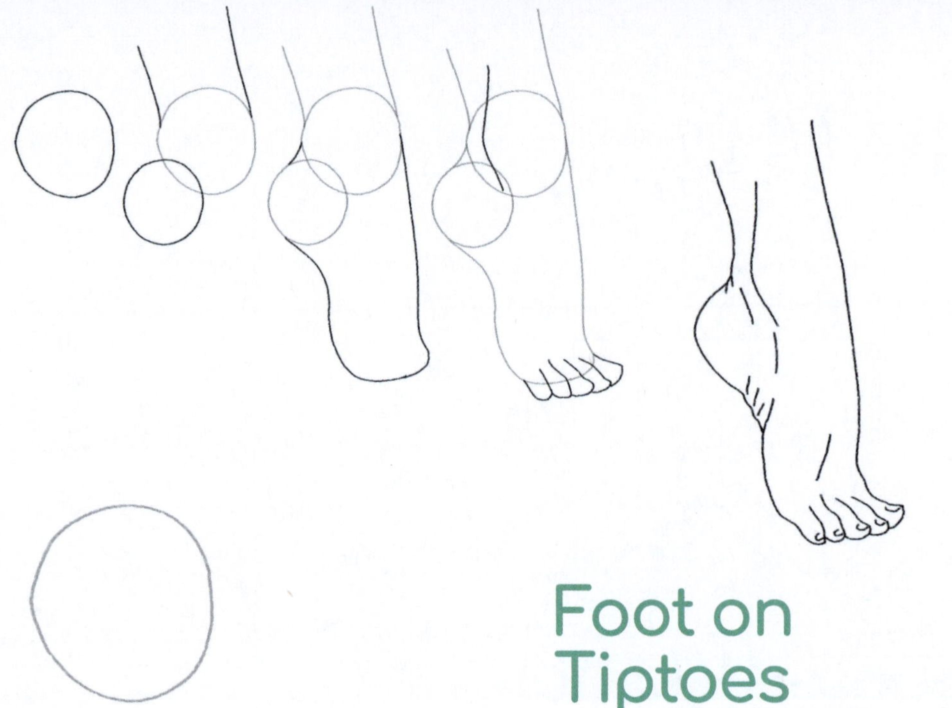

Foot on Tiptoes

This very flexed pose creates creases in the curve of the sole of the foot.

184th day

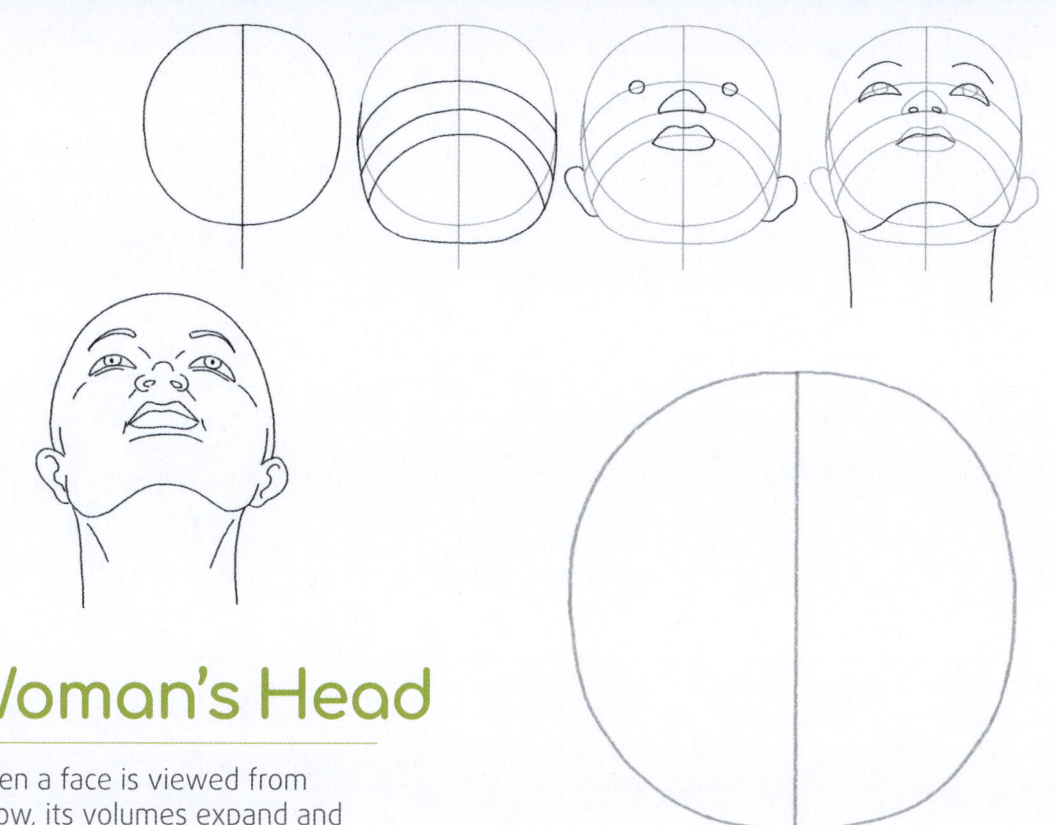

Woman's Head

When a face is viewed from
below, its volumes expand and
the elements align in upward-
facing curves.

185 th day

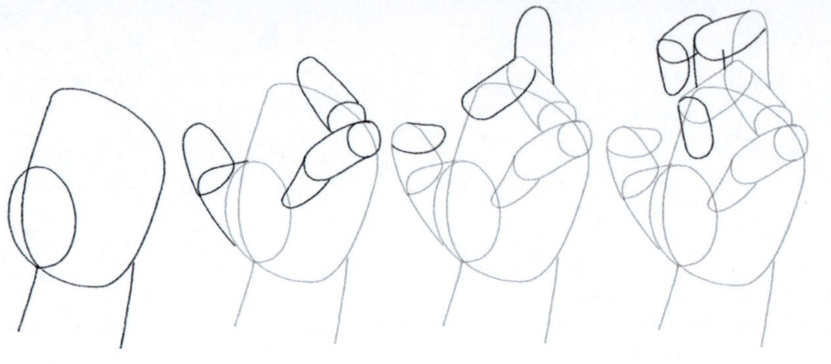

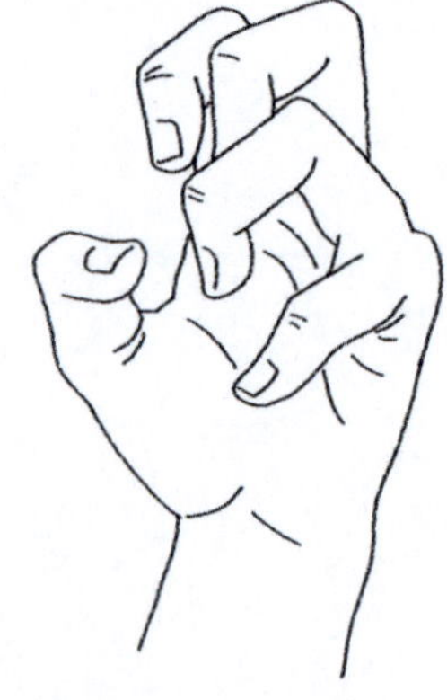

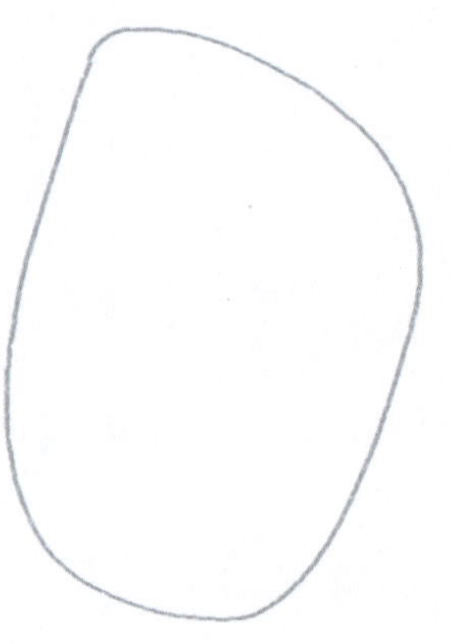

Clenched Hand

The creases in the palm and the angles formed by the fingers give this hand a tense, clenched appearance.

186th day

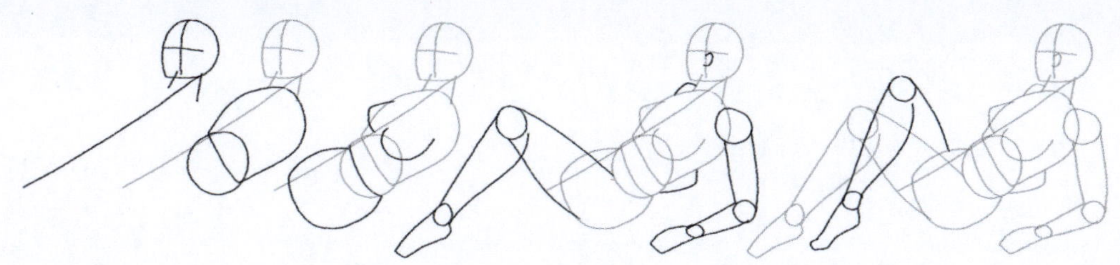

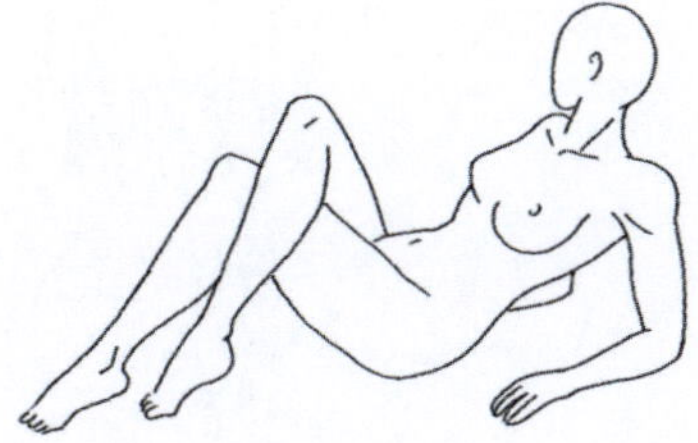

Reclining
Woman

This slightly overhead view puts
the torso in perspective and
obscures part of it.

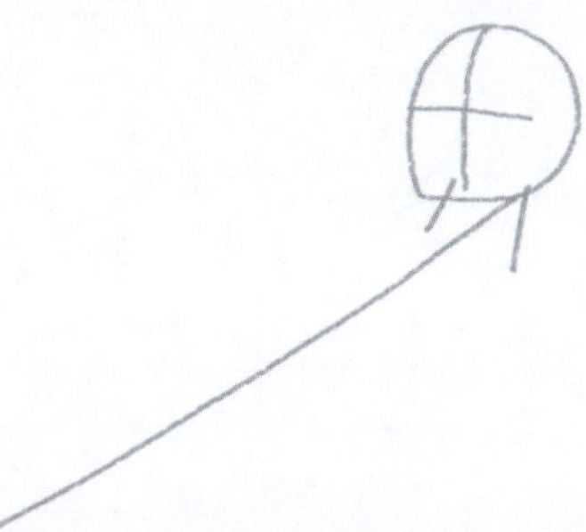

187th day

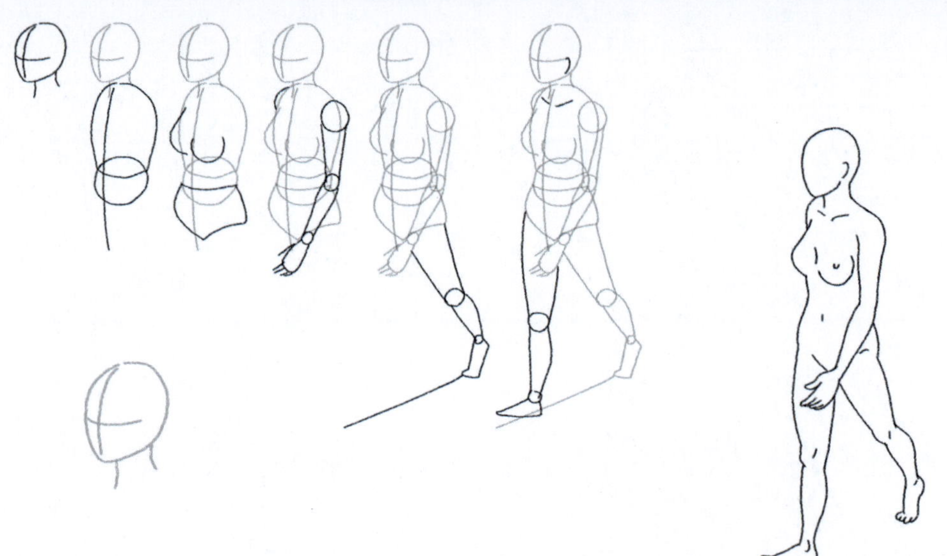

Walking Woman

From this perspective, one leg stretches behind the figure. Sketching a line on the ground can help you get the proportions right.

188th day

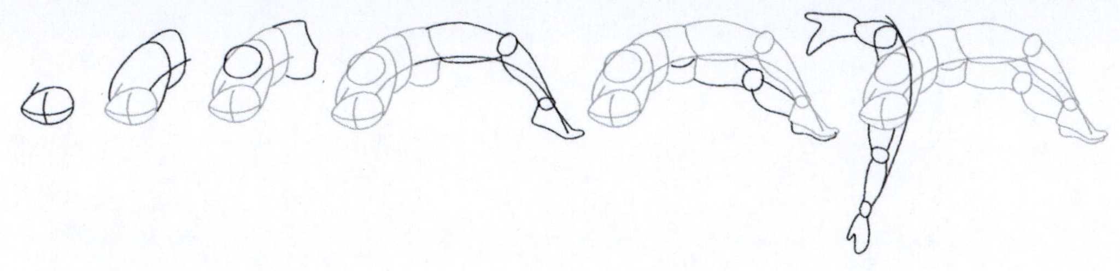

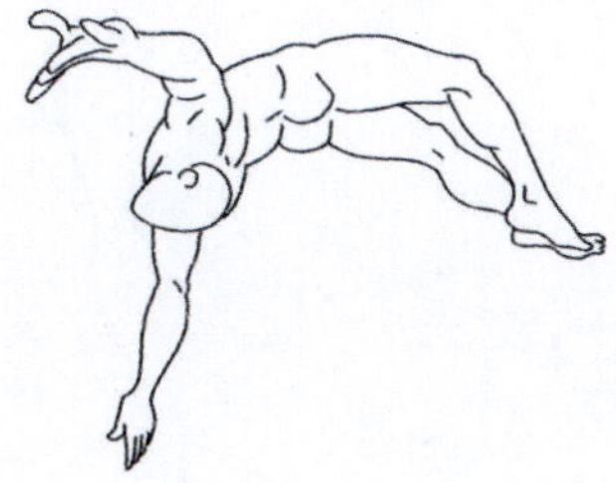

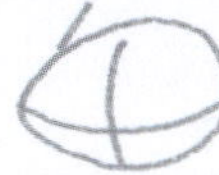

Backflip

This perspective shows a
curved figure whose body
is turned upside down. The
arms are closest to us, so they
seem larger.

189 th day

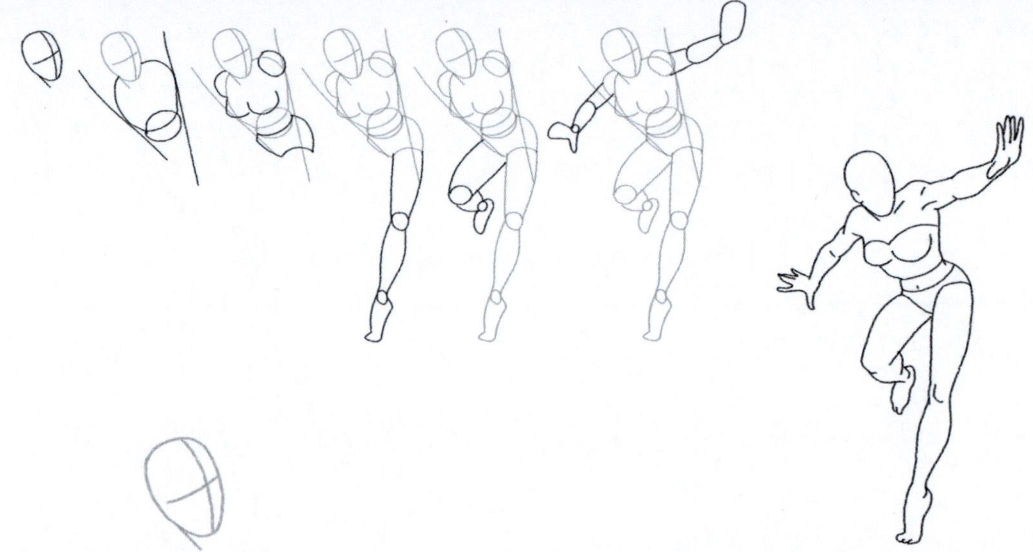

Running
Woman

The figure's upper body is facing us, and the legs are stretched downward and behind her. This dynamic pose conveys speed and movement.

190th day

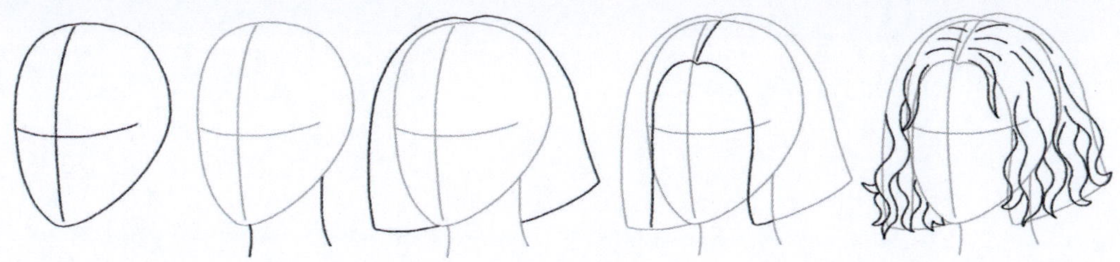

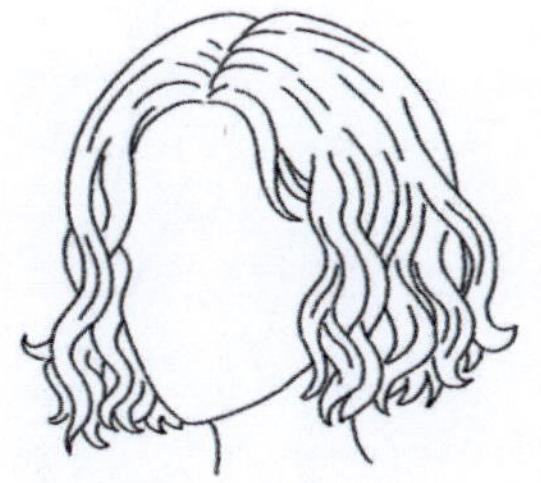

Wet Hair

To create the look of wet hair, carefully separate the strands.

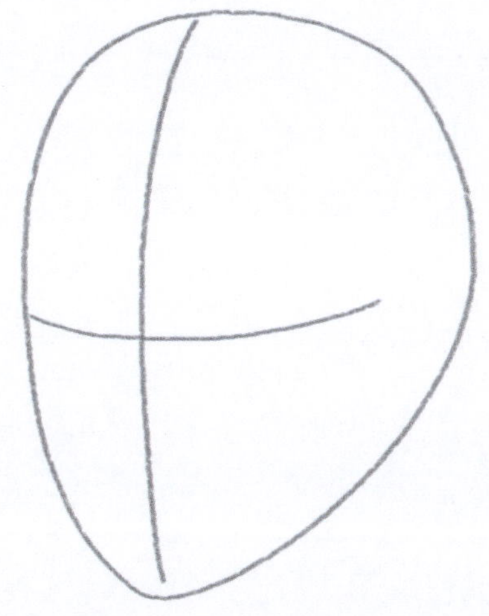

191st day

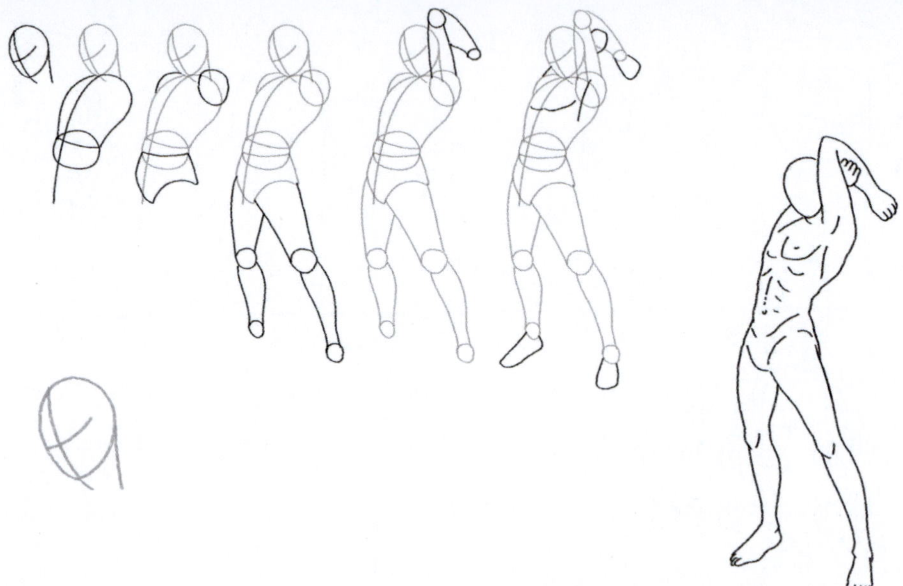

Standing Man

The raised arms stretch this figure's whole torso and accentuate the lines of his abdominal muscles. The well-grounded legs are in perspective.

192nd day

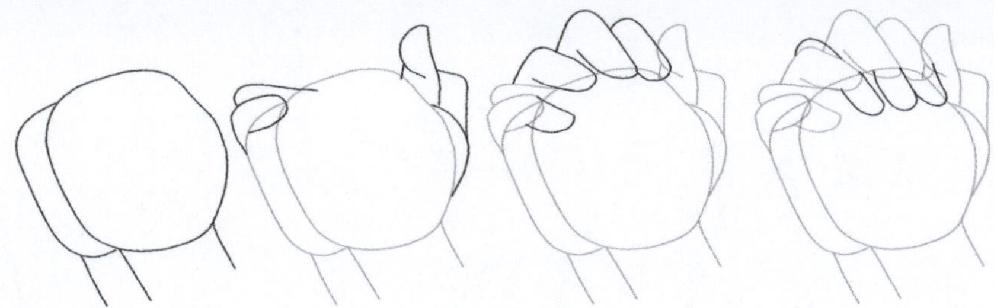

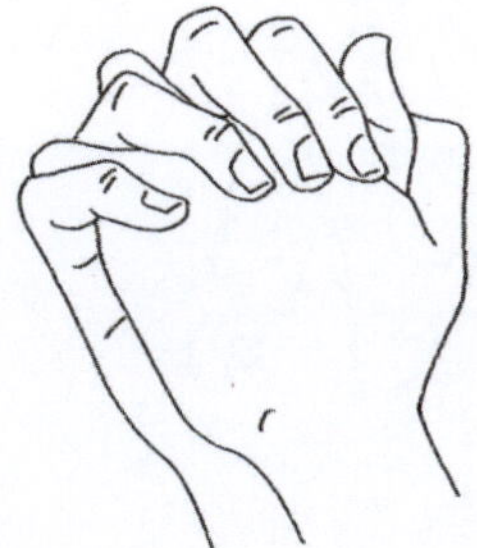

Clasped
Hands

To draw two clasped hands,
place them one against the other.
The fingers of one hand cross
over the fingers of the other.

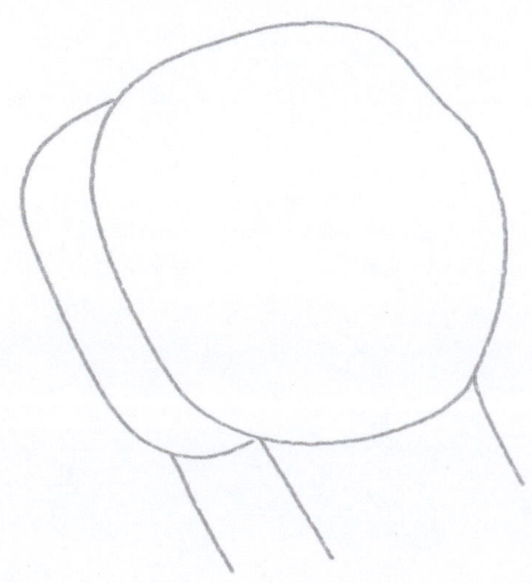

193 rd day

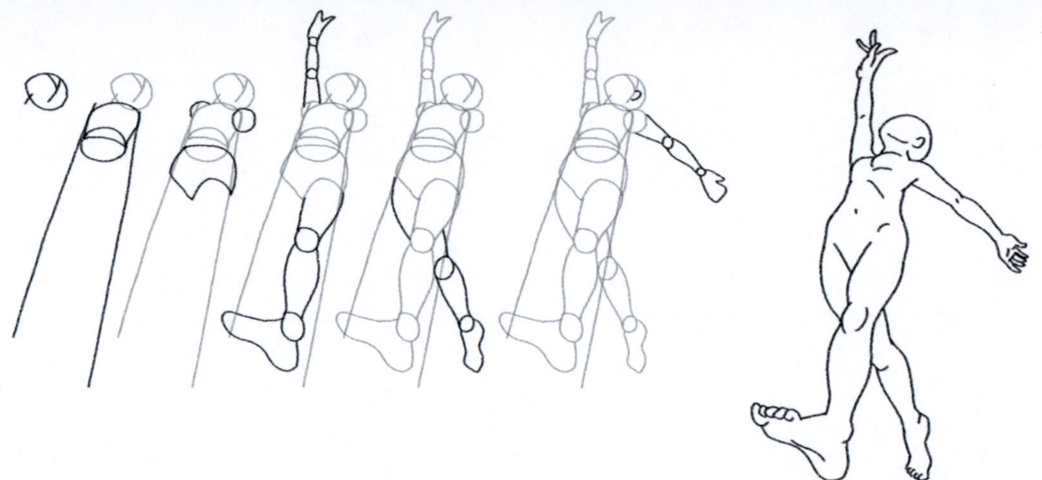
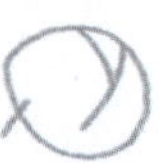

Standing Woman from Low Angle

This low-angle view exaggerates the proportions of the foot in the foreground. The hands look tiny in comparison.

194th day

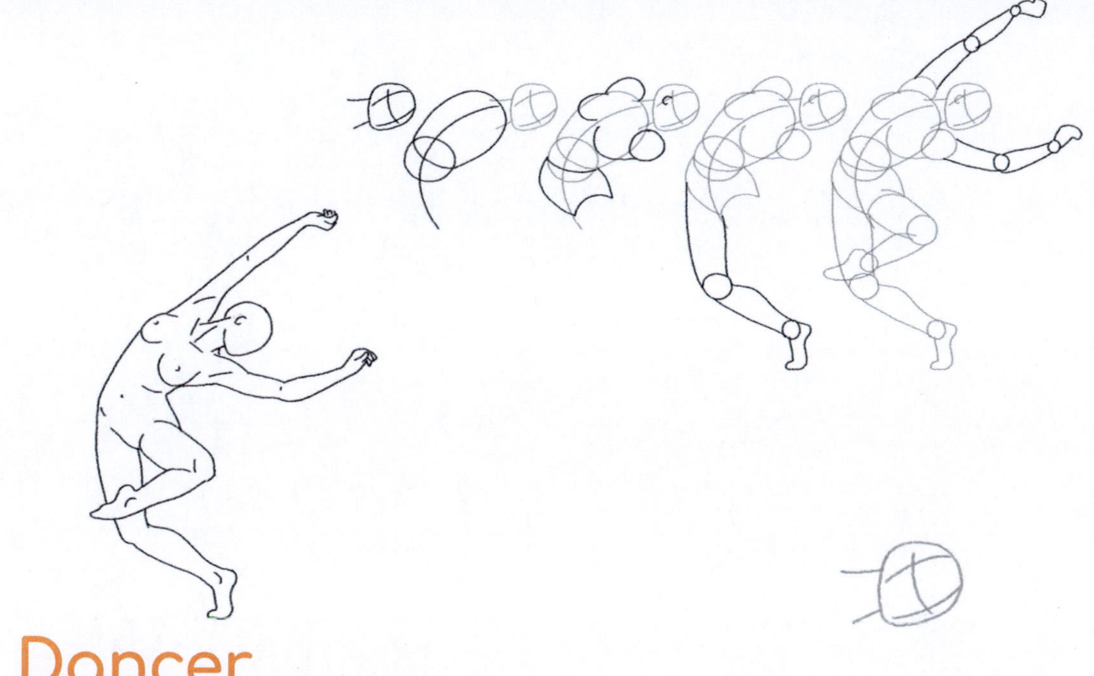

Dancer

This figure is twisting her whole
body in a large C-shaped arc.

195th day

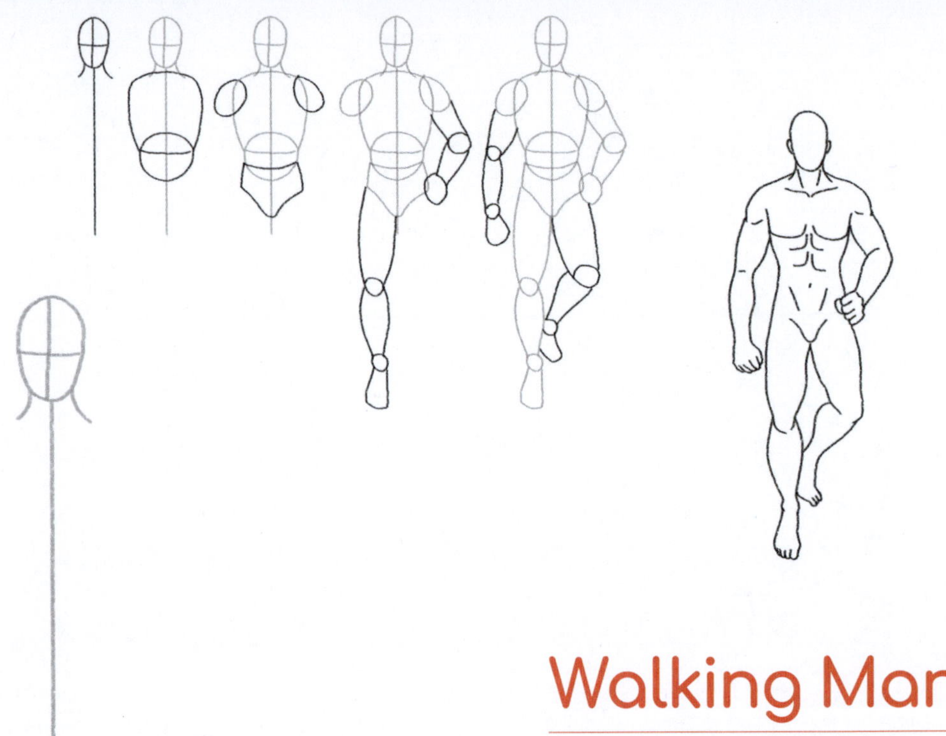

Walking Man

When viewed from the front, a walking figure moves one leg and the opposite arm together in the same direction.

196th day

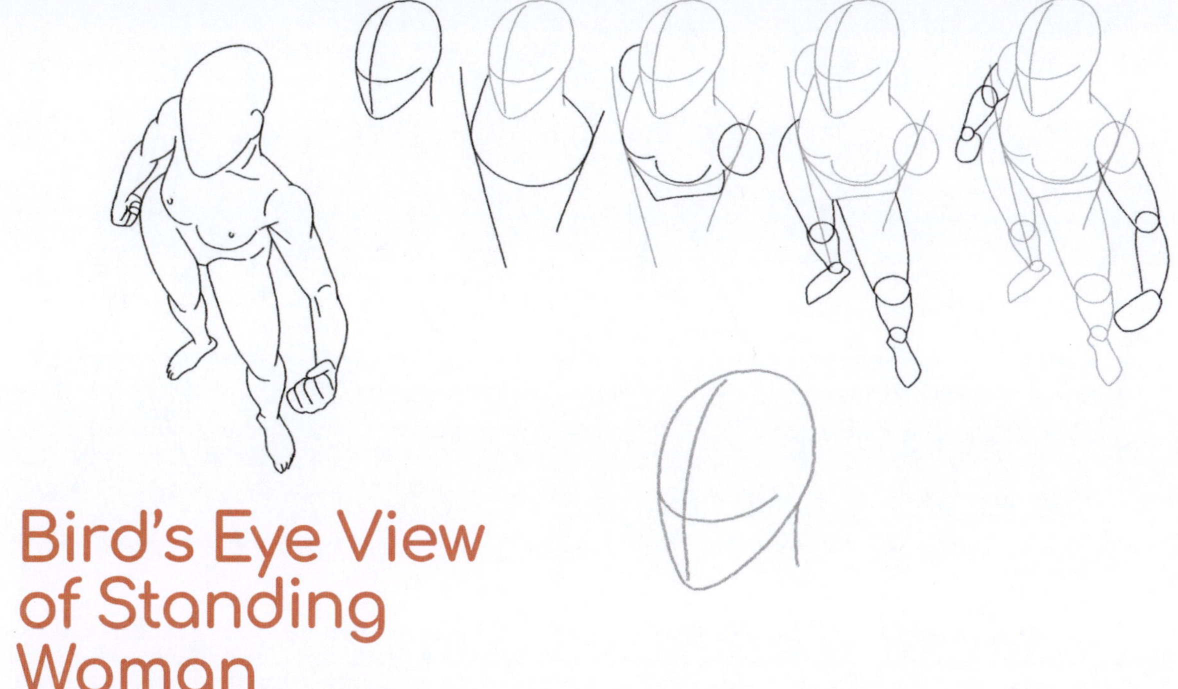

Bird's Eye View of Standing Woman

Viewed from above, the parts of the body that are closest to us obstruct our view of those below, which become progressively smaller.

197th day

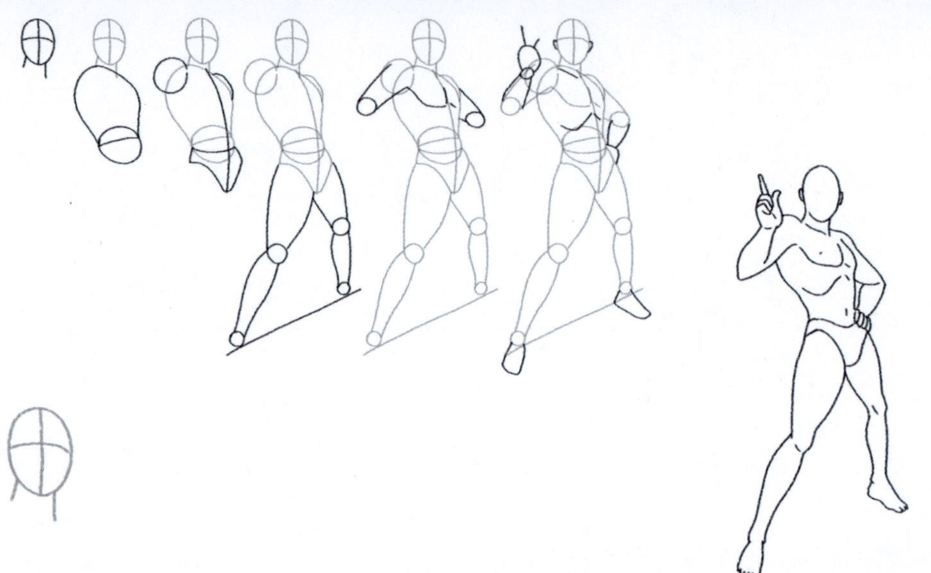

Happy Man

This three-quarter pose is very arched and in perspective. The horizontal lines run quite sharply. Sketching a line on the ground toward the vanishing point can help you get the perspective and proportions right.

198th day

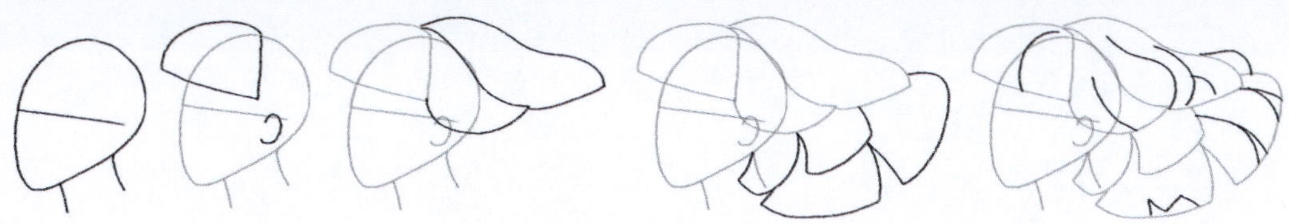

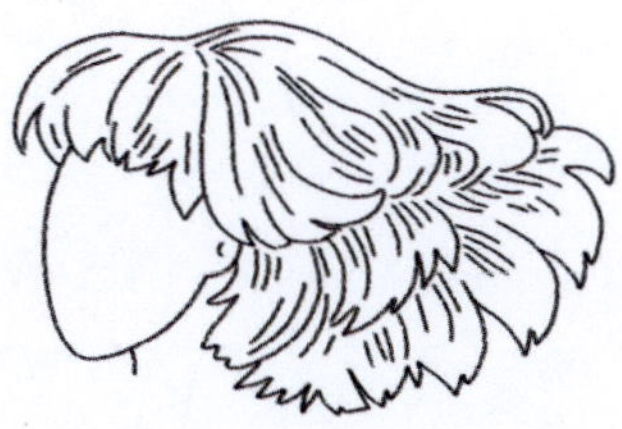

Wind-Blown Hair

If the figure is jumping or skipping, the hair bounces and curls.

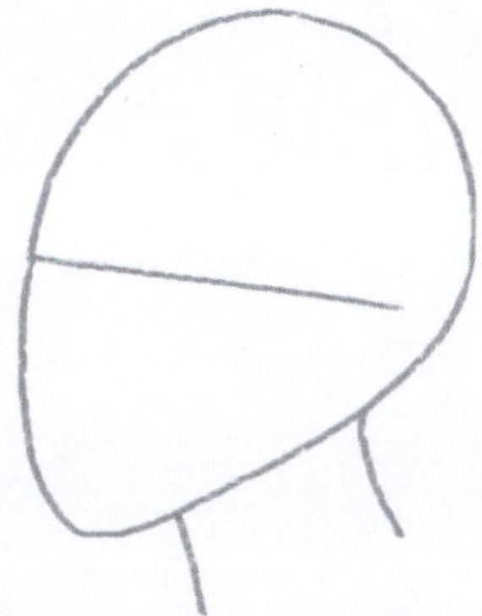

199 th day

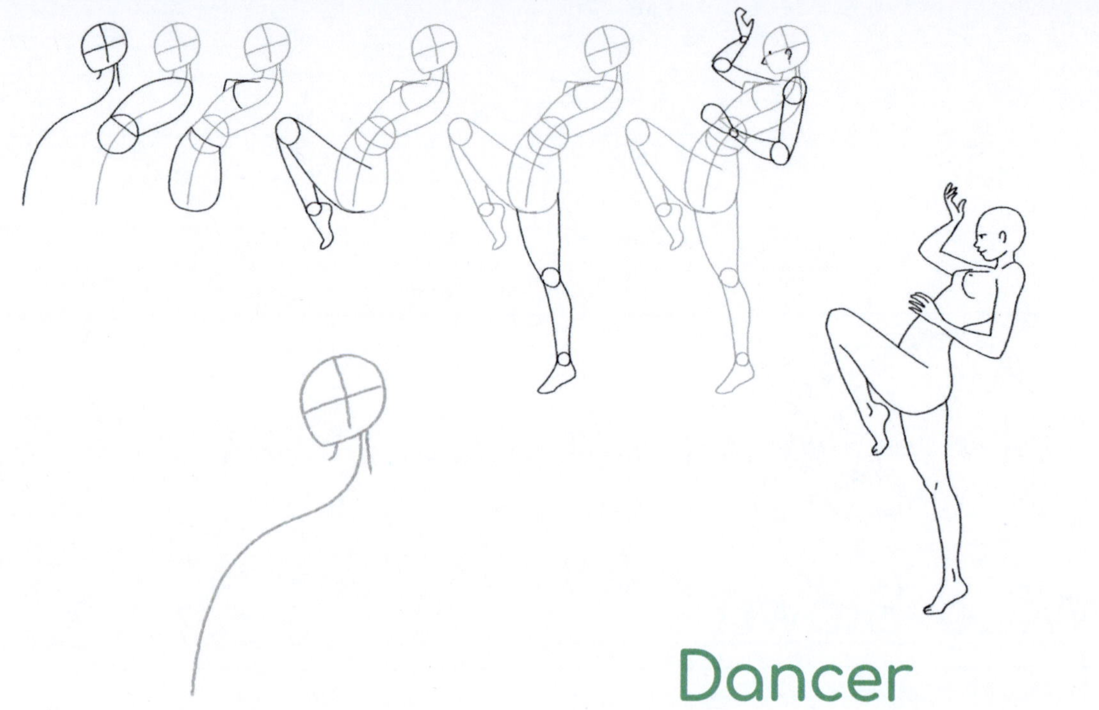

Dancer

This pose articulates the whole body into an inverted S shape.

200th day

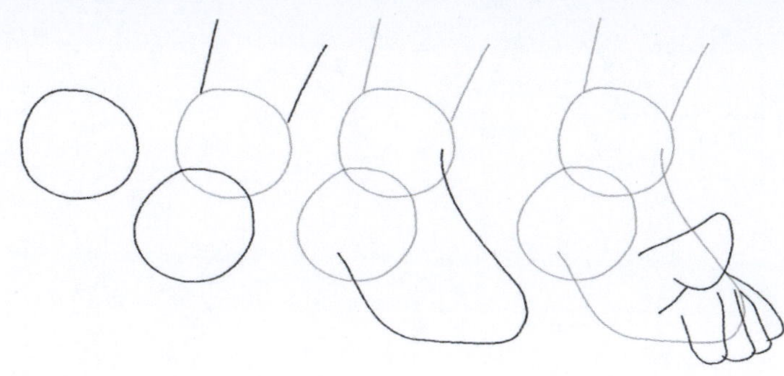

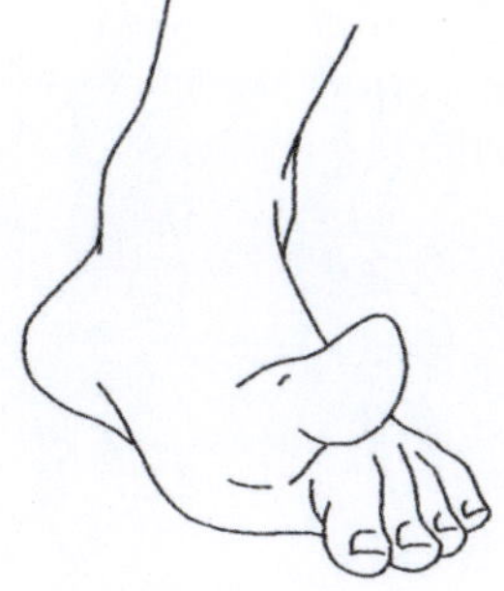

Foot

In a three-quarter view, you can't see the whole length of the foot. The big toe is quite fleshy compared to the rest of the toes, which are thinner and more delicate.

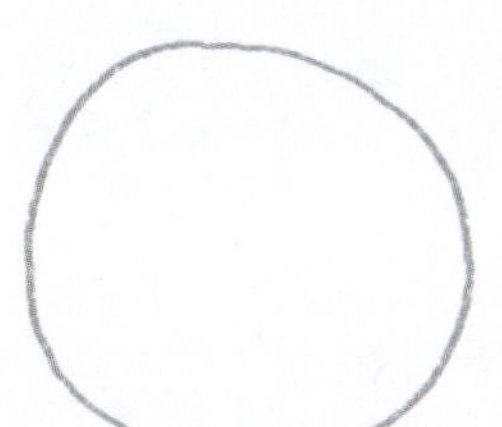

201

201st day

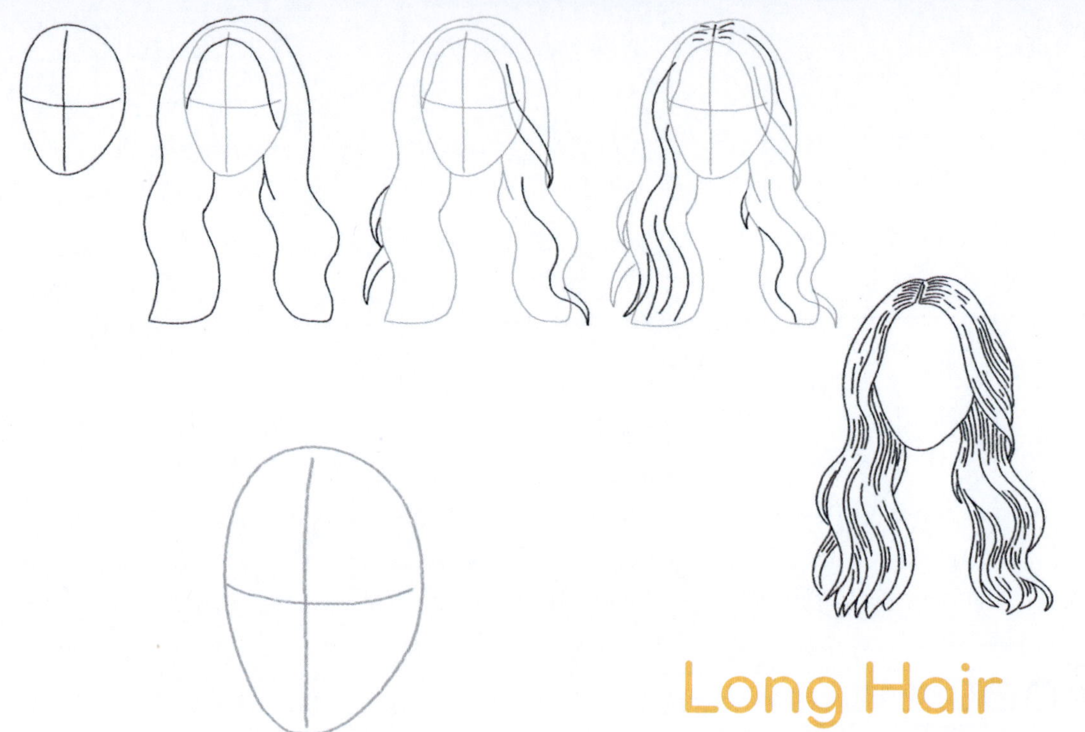

Long Hair

You can add lines near the neck to add shading and depth and, by contrast, give volume to the rest of the waves.

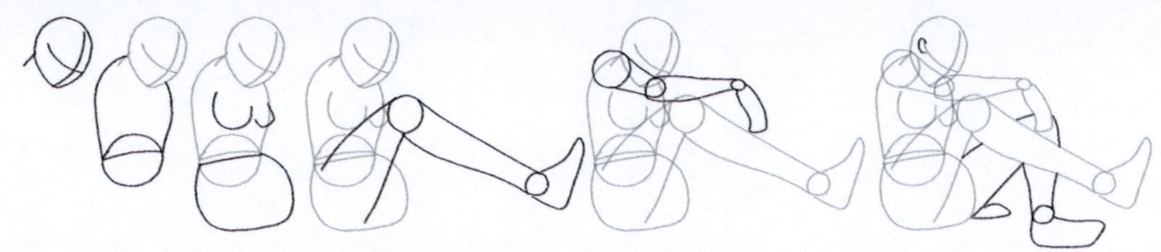

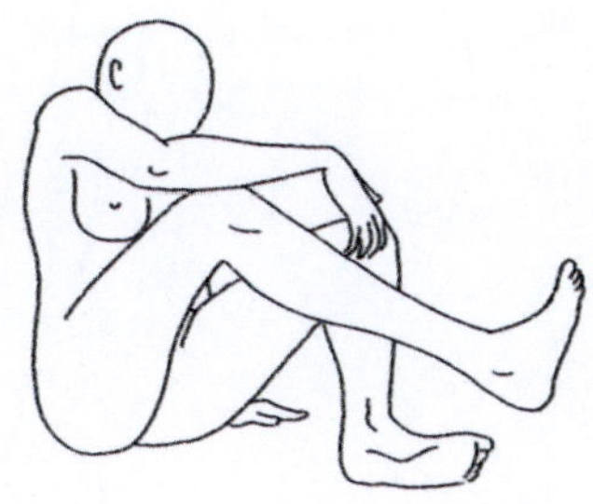

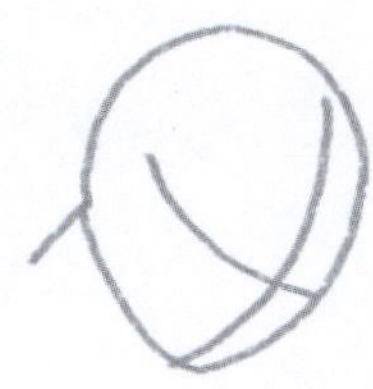

Seated Woman

In this pose, only one side of the
torso is visible, and the body tilts
backward.

203rd day

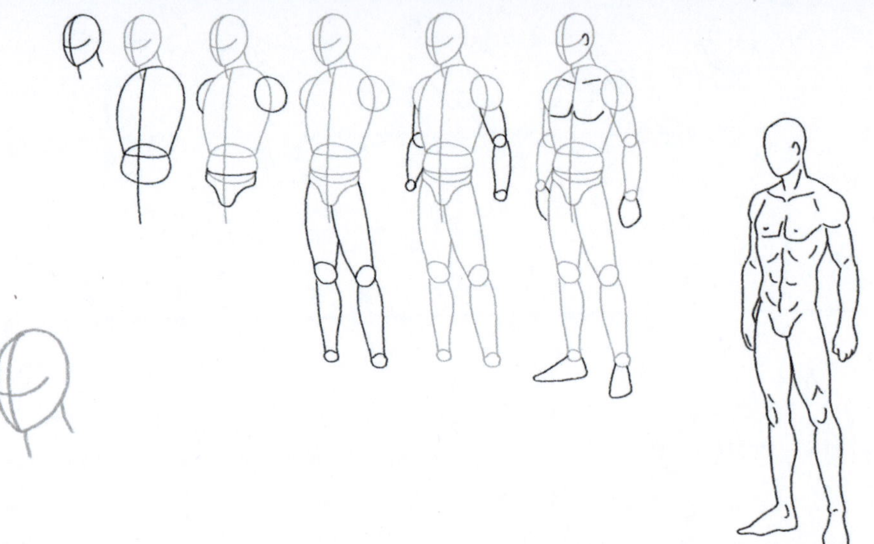

Standing Man

All of the volumes appear thinner when viewed in three-quarters, since the perspective reduces them.

204th day

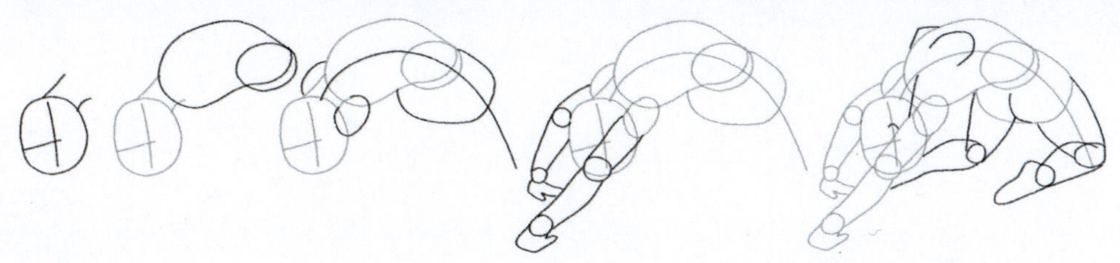

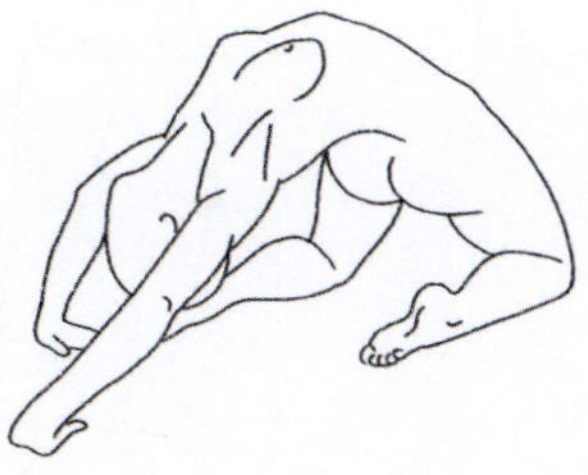

Gymnast

You can create a backward contortion by articulating each of the figure's volumes along a curve.

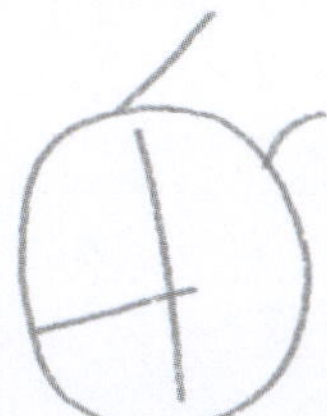

205th day

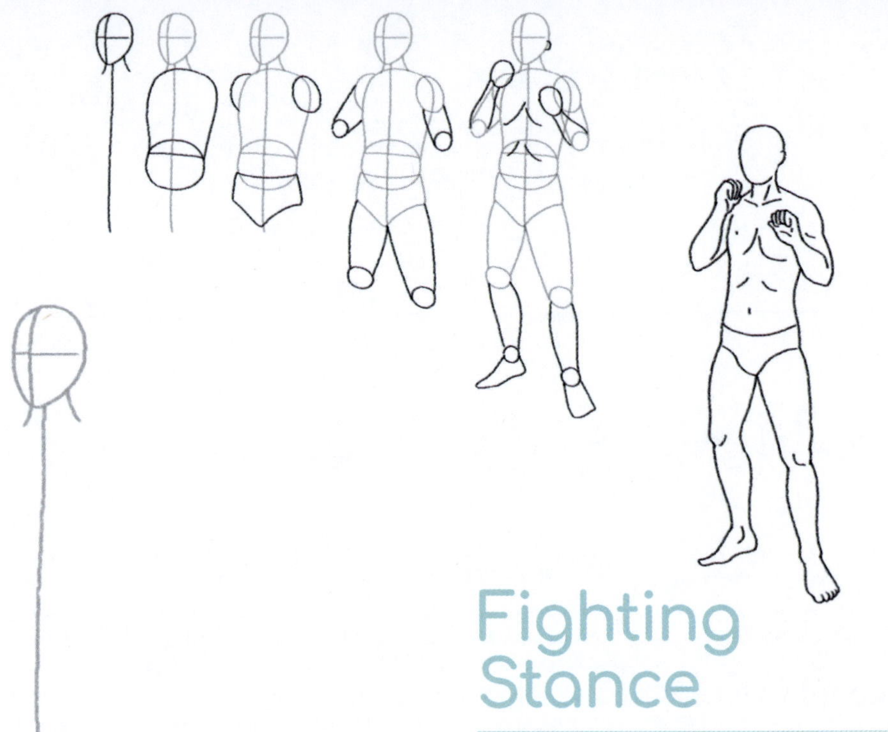

Fighting Stance

This figure's folded forearms obscure his upper arms. One leg is behind him, in perspective.

206 th day

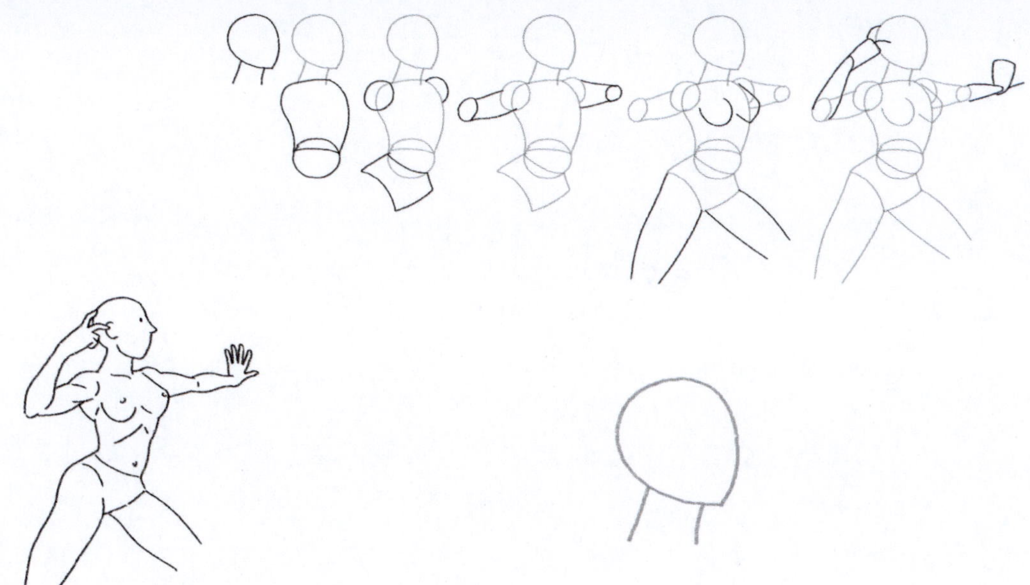

Woman's Torso

This figure's muscular torso creates volumes around the chest and shoulders. The rear arm is in perspective and therefore looks smaller.

207th day

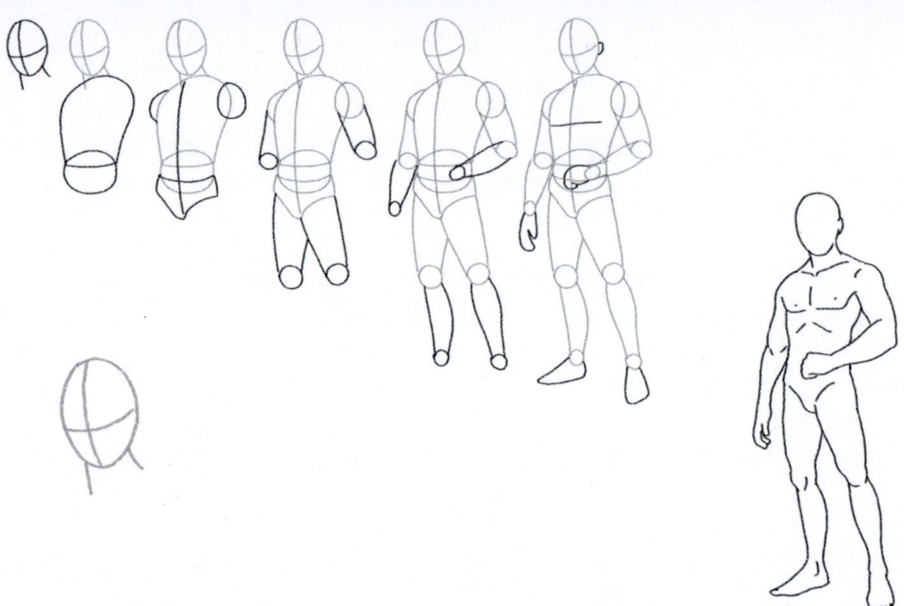

Standing Man

This three-quarter pose is very much in perspective. The lines of the shoulders, hips and between the feet extend toward the vanishing point.

208th day

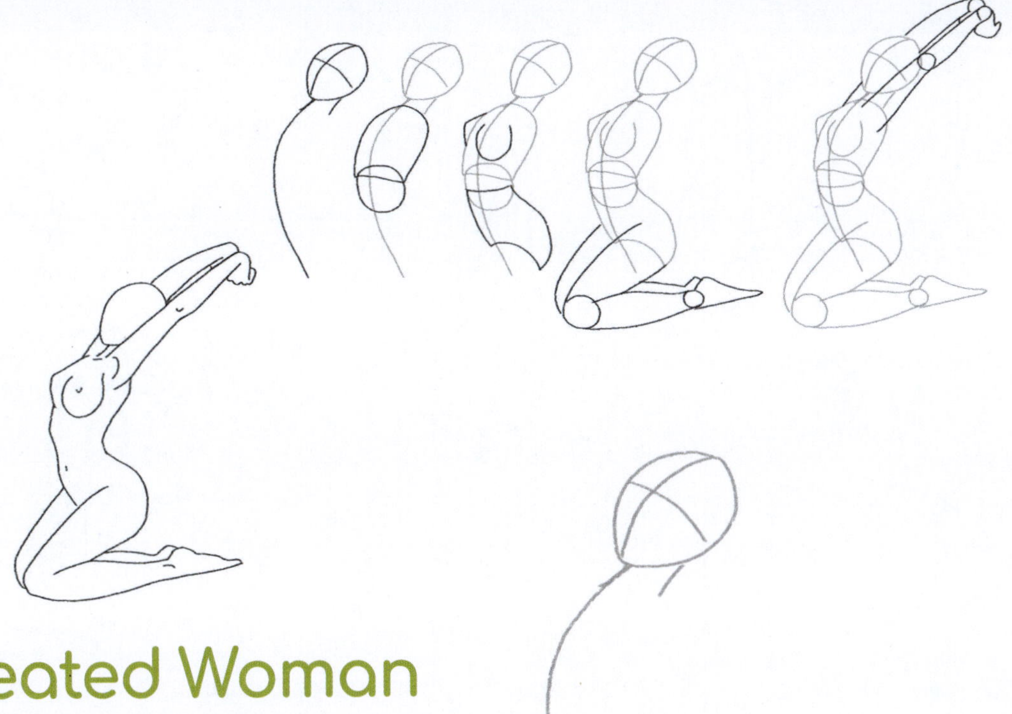

Seated Woman

This figure's upper body is fully arched and stretched along a curve. Each volume of the torso is elongated.

209th **day**

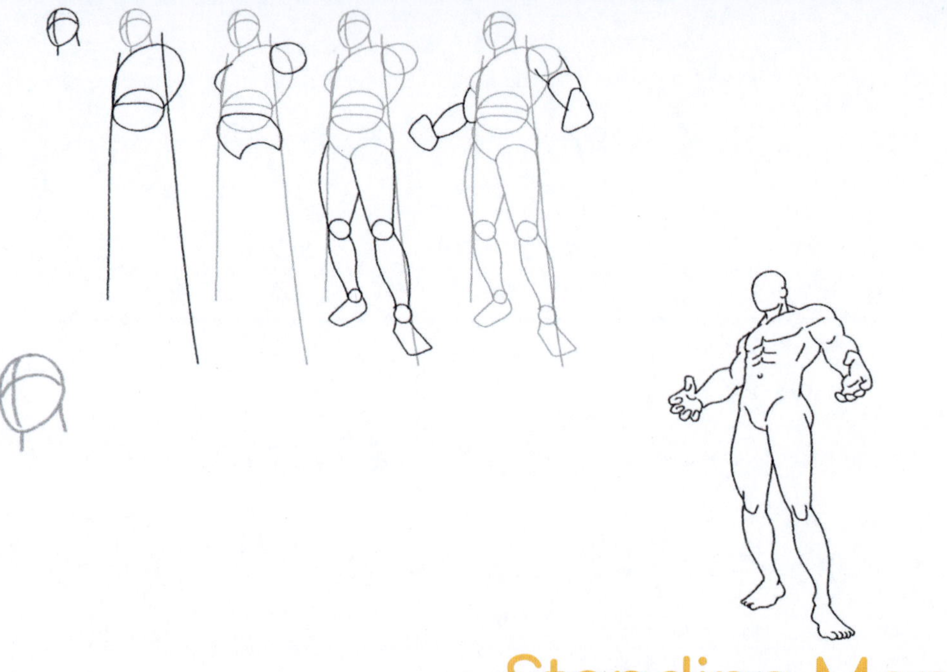

Standing Man

The perspective created by this low-angle view makes the hands look huge.

210th **day**

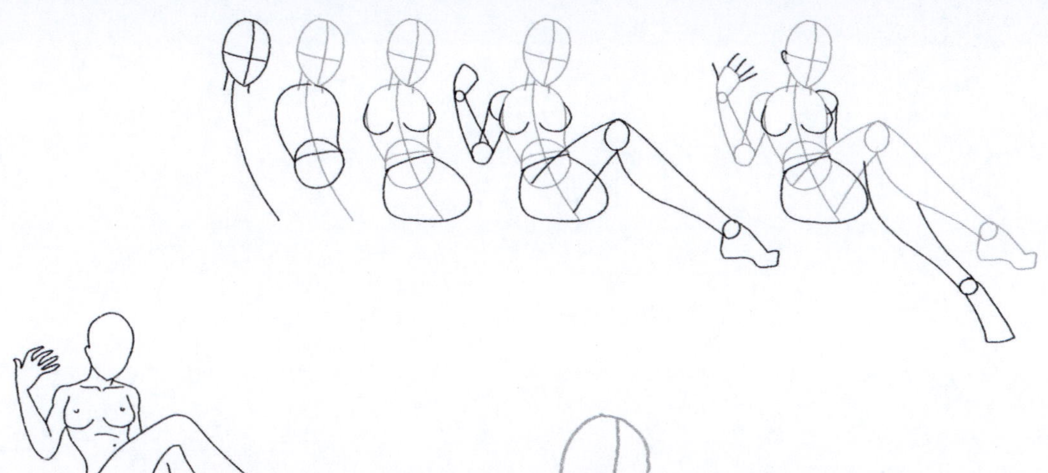

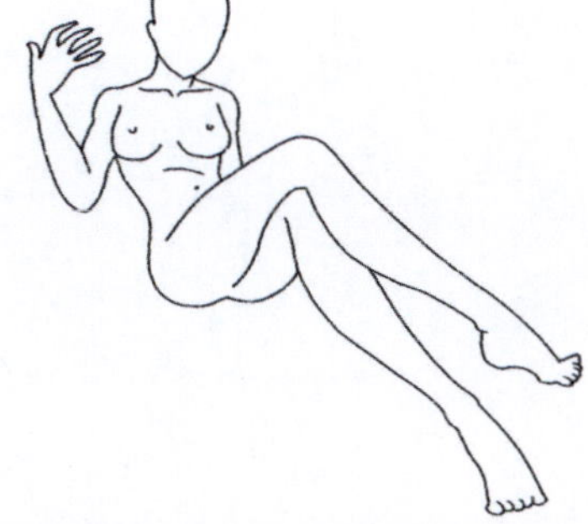

Seated Woman

This figure's long legs are in the foreground, so they're stretched by the perspective. The upper part of the torso seems very small in comparison.

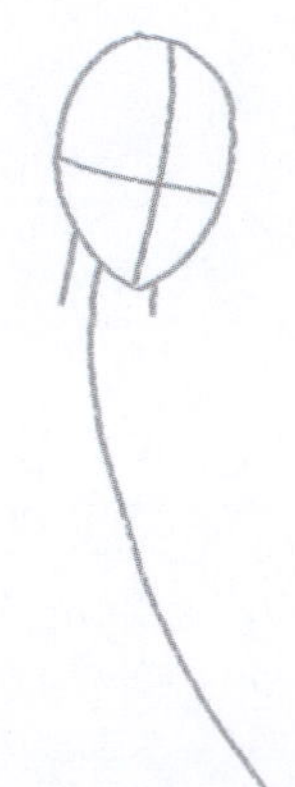

211th day

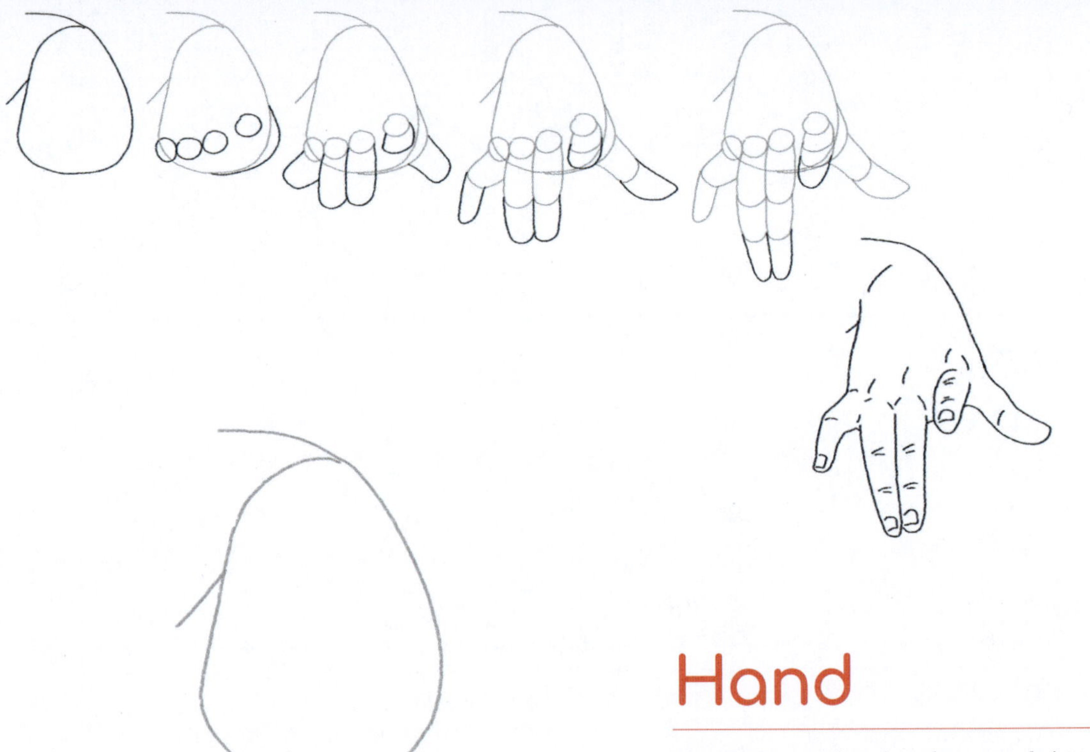

Hand

The palm and index finger of this hand are shown in perspective. The palm is tapered, and the index finger is smaller.

212th day

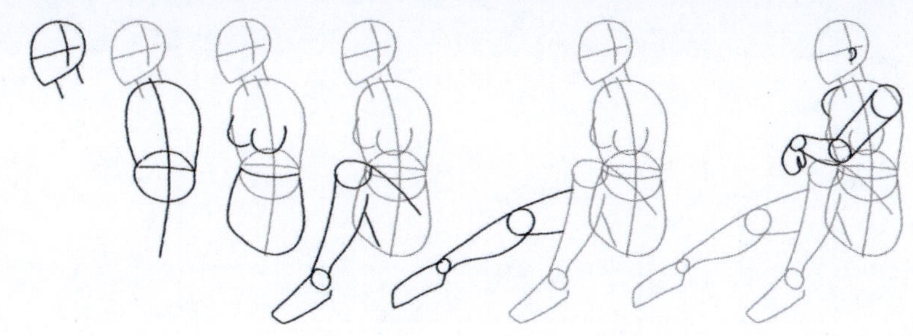

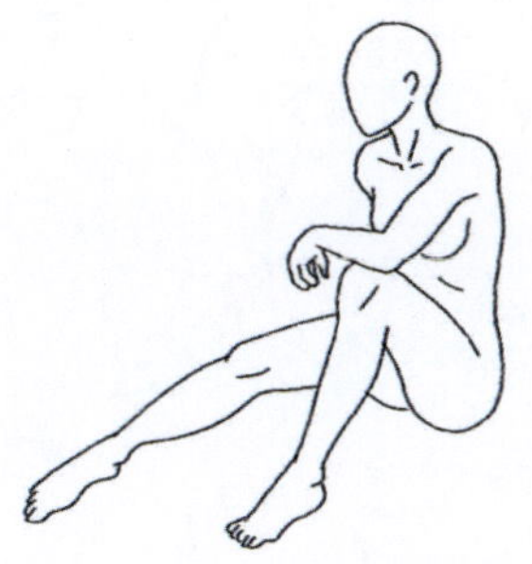

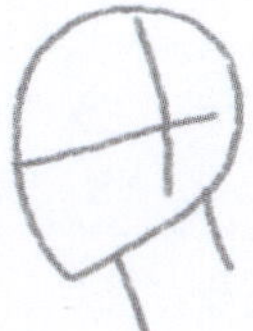

Seated Woman

This seated pose puts the front thigh in perspective and twists the torso backward, obscuring one arm.

213th day

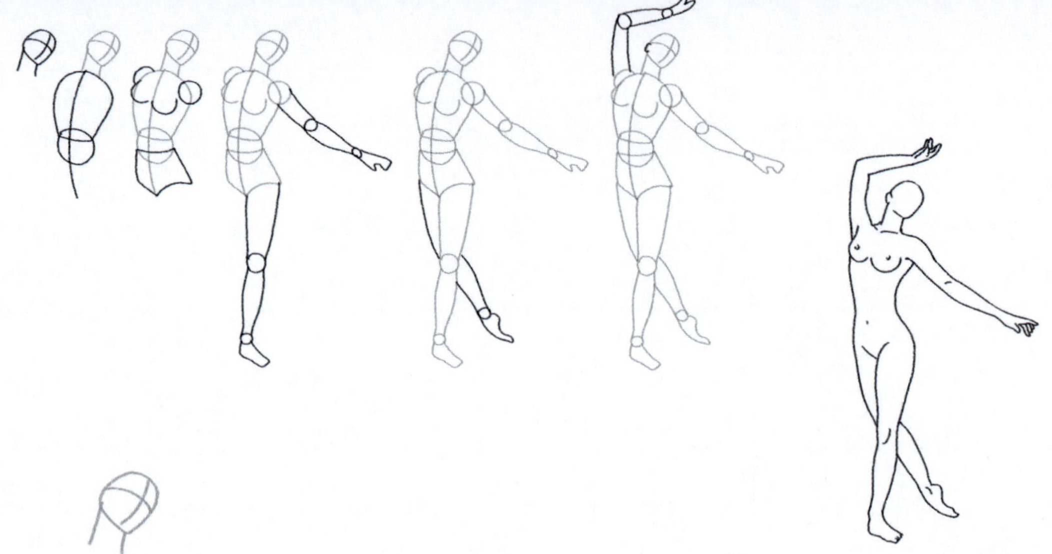

Dancer

This figure is stretching backward, rotating her body around the foot on the floor.

214 th day

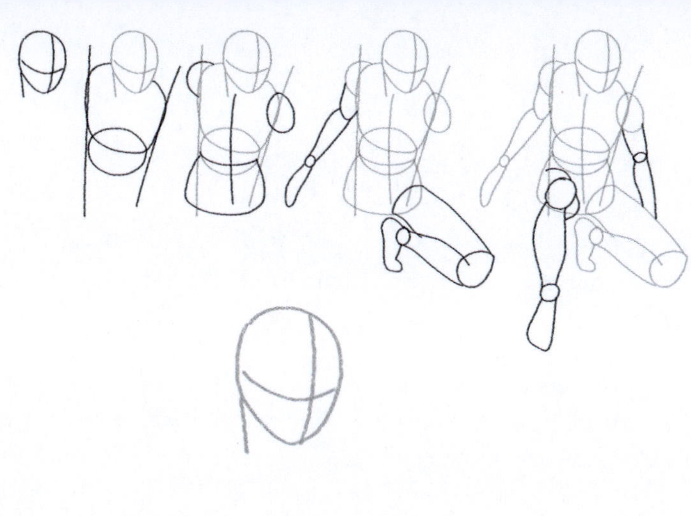

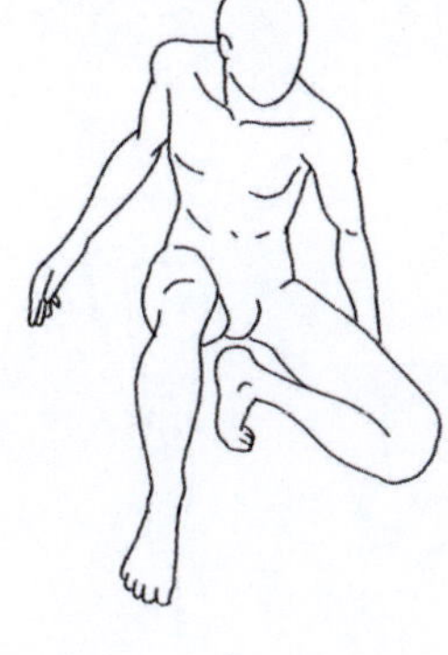

Crouching Man

This figure's upper torso and bent leg are projecting forward. The arms and foot on the ground extend behind him, making them appear smaller.

215 **th day**

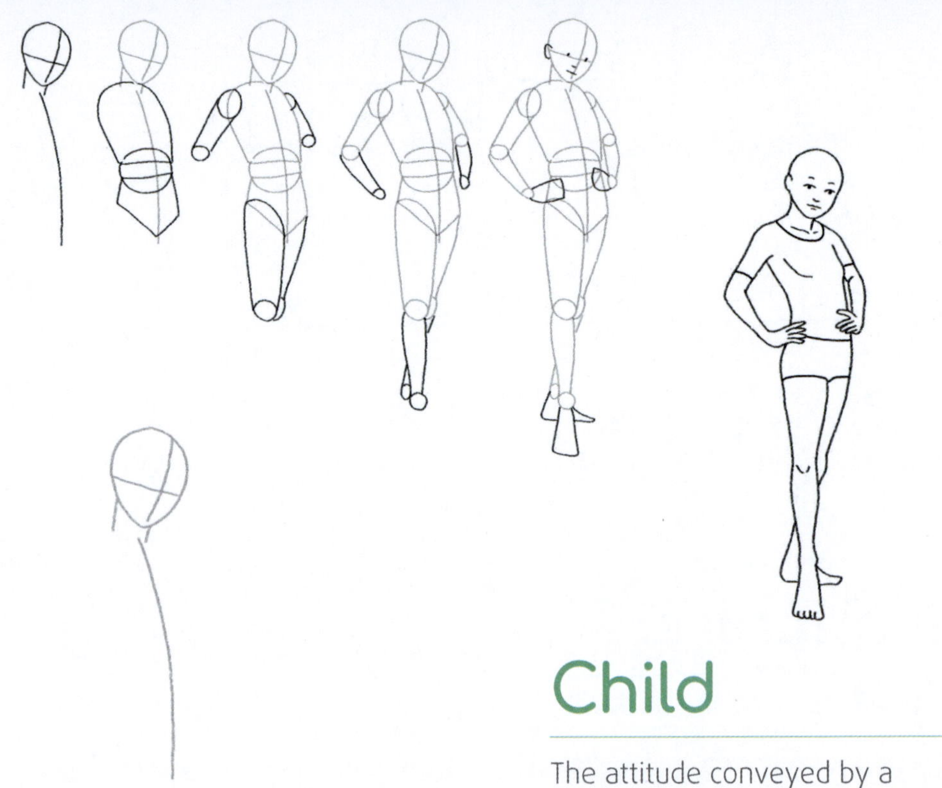

Child

The attitude conveyed by a pose can give a figure a more feminine form.

216th day

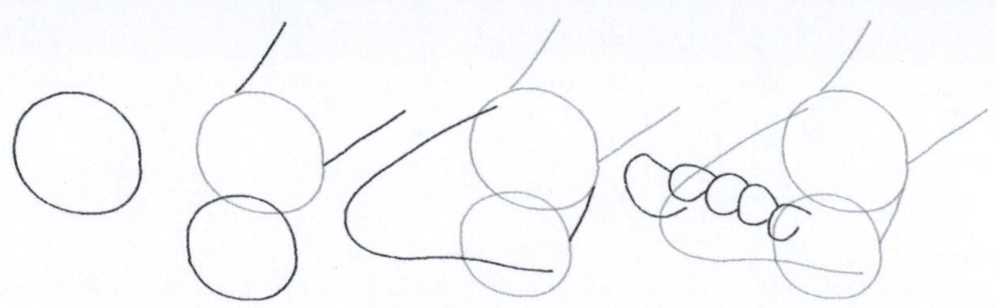

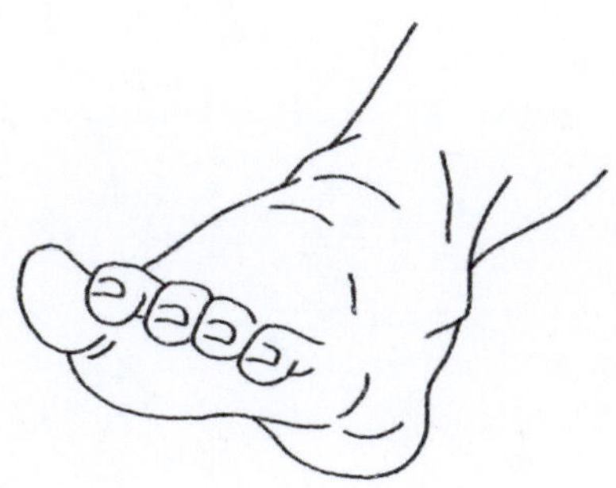

Foot

This front view of the toes obscures the length of the foot. The various bumps and indentations are easily recognized.

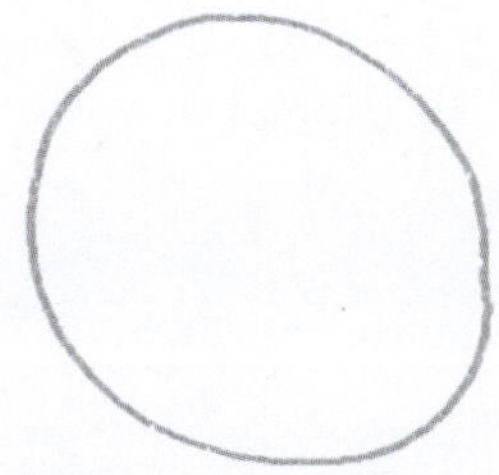

217th day

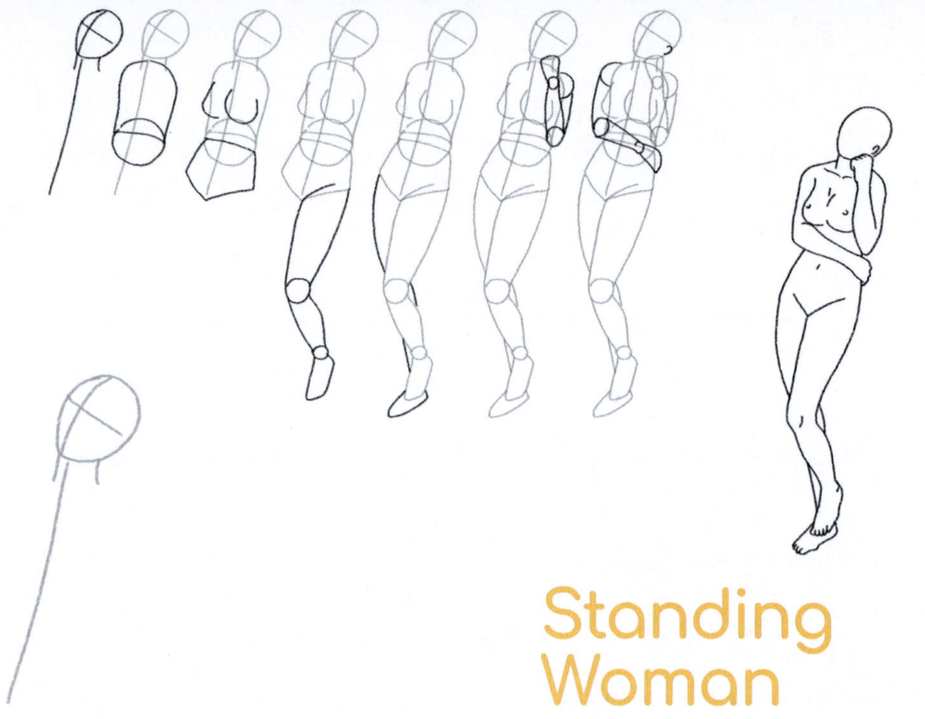

Standing Woman

This figure is tilting her torso slightly to one side, which offsets the sway of the hips and the three-quarter perspective of the pose.

218 th day

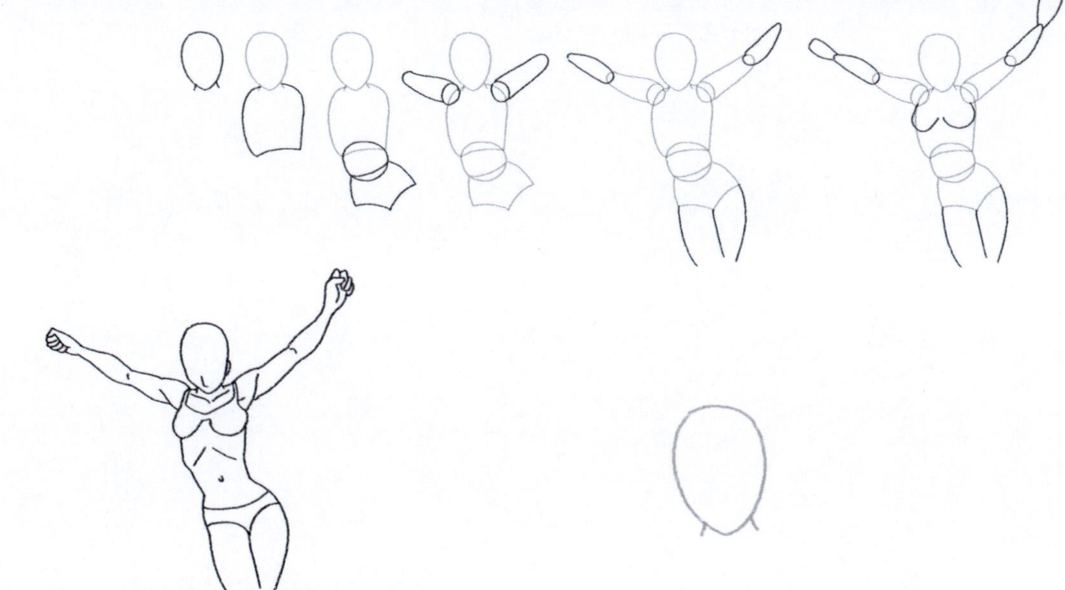

Woman's Torso

If your drawing isn't too small, you can add lines to highlight creases and muscles. Raised arms stretch the torso and emphasize the ribs.

219th day

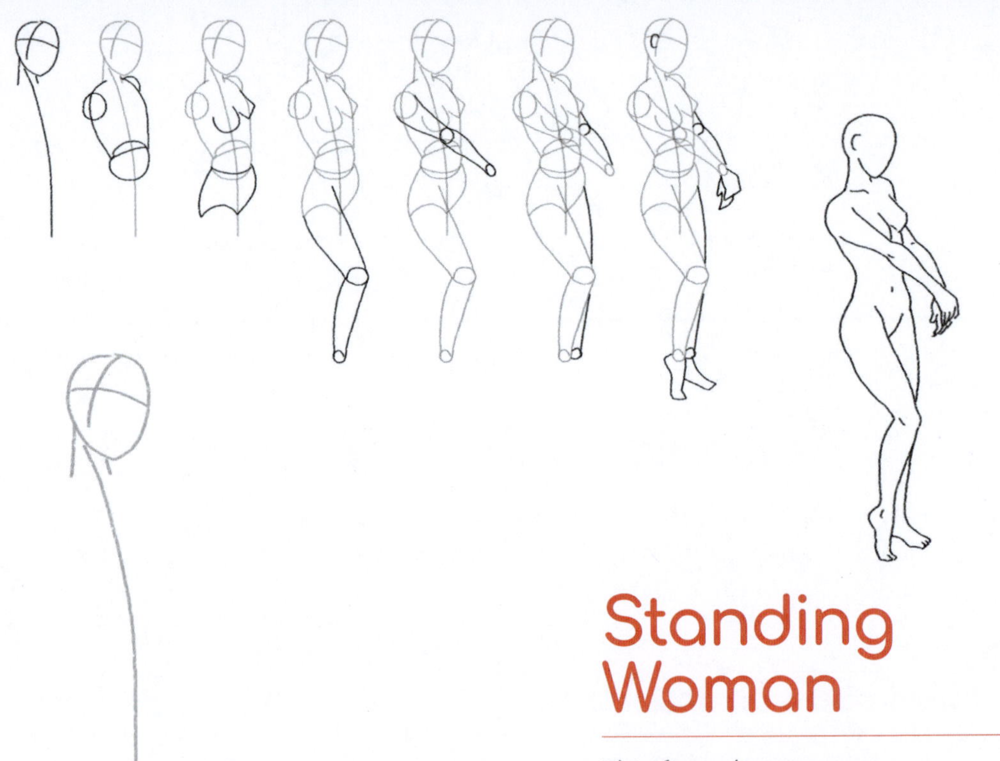

Standing Woman

This figure's arms are outstretched and one leg is bent, giving the body a slight sway around the hips. The whole body is curved forward slightly.

220th day

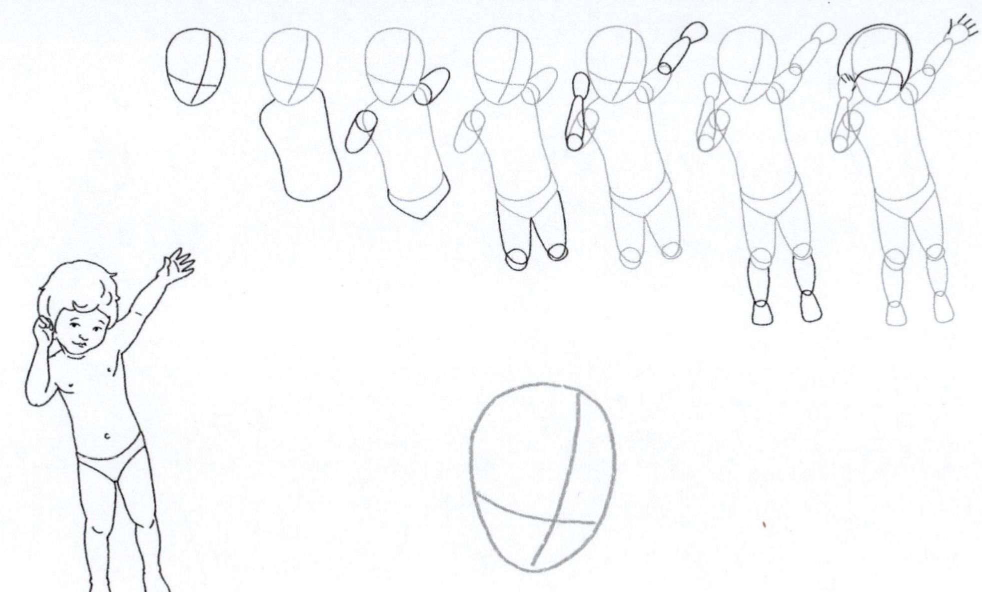

Toddler

This figure's left arm is in perspective, so it is partially obscured. The head is large in relation to the rest of the body, typical of a toddler's proportions.

221st day

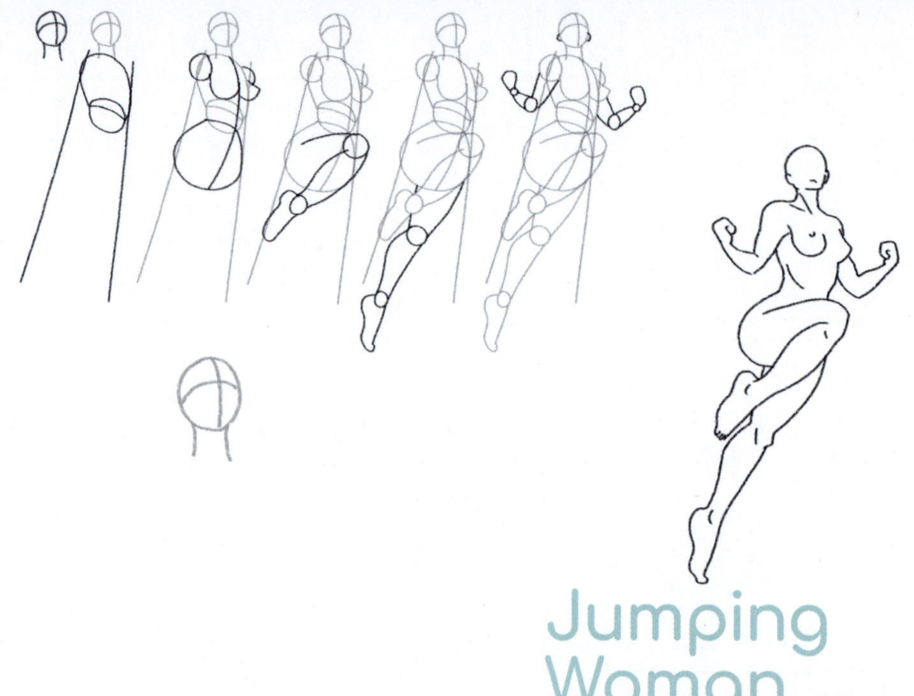

Jumping
Woman

This entire pose flows upward, and the lower body is larger in proportion to the upper body. To help you draw a pose such as this, you can sketch a line to the vanishing point.

222nd day

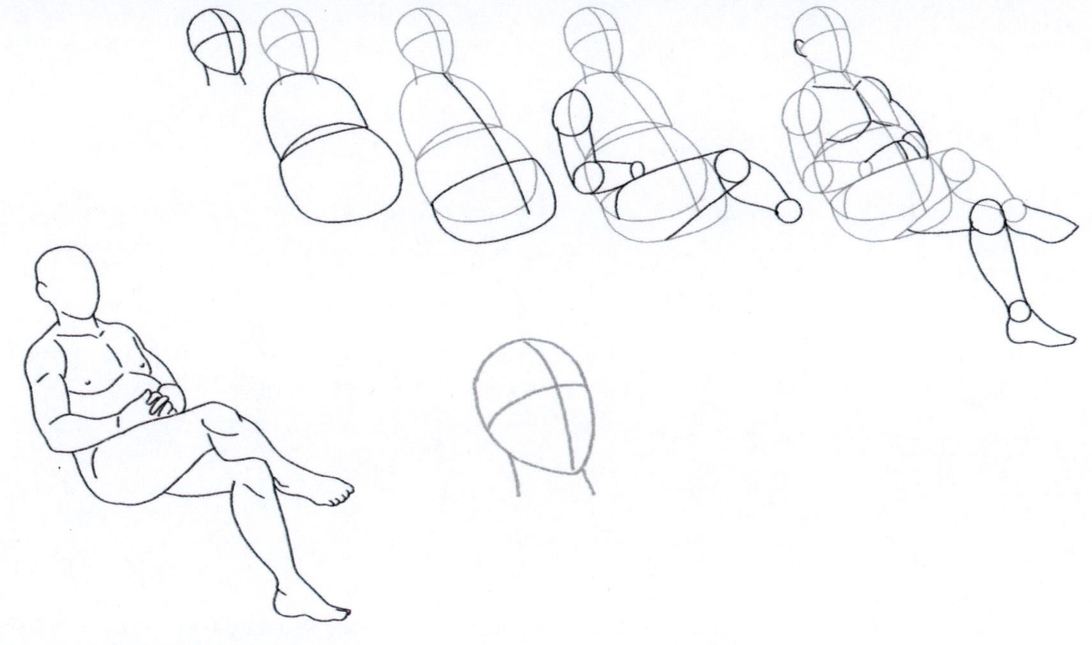

Seated Man

The figure in this seated pose
has a round shape. The crossed
leg is in perspective, and one
arm is slightly hidden by the
chest and stomach.

223 rd day

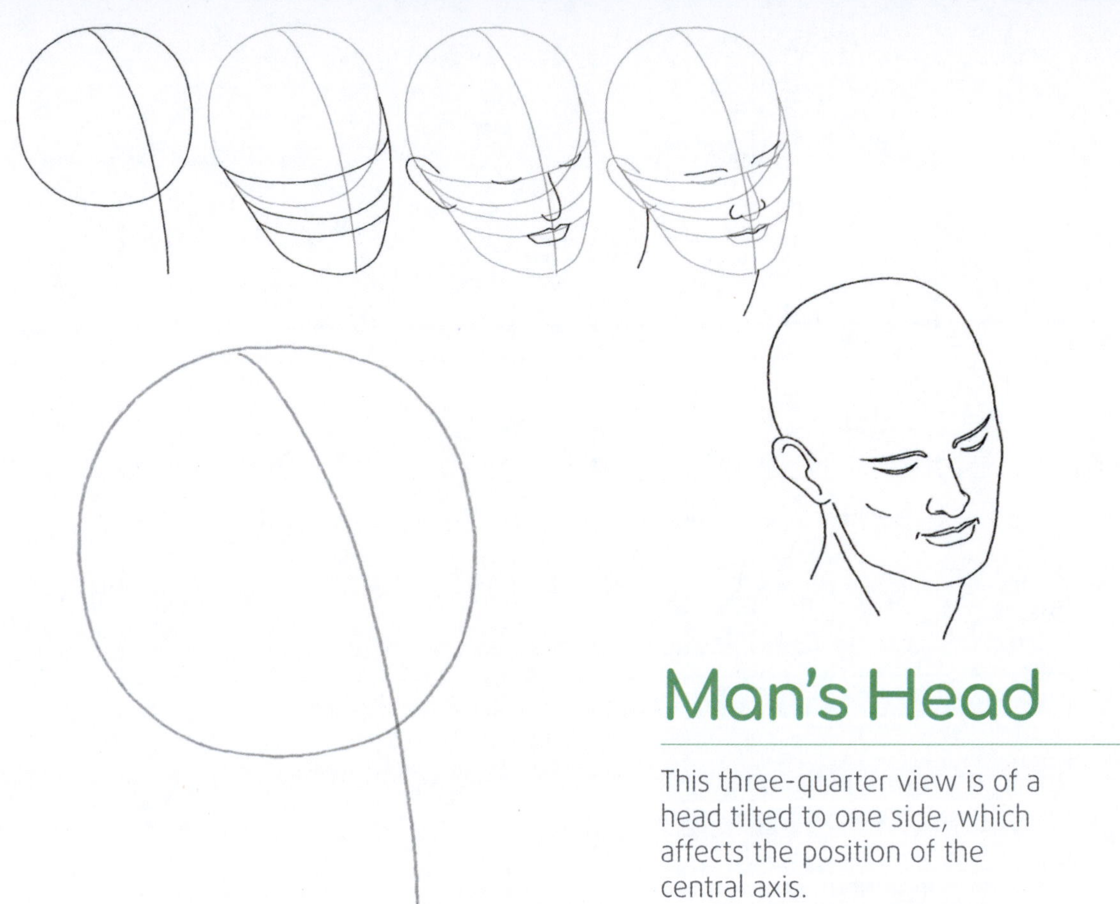

Man's Head

This three-quarter view is of a head tilted to one side, which affects the position of the central axis.

224 th day

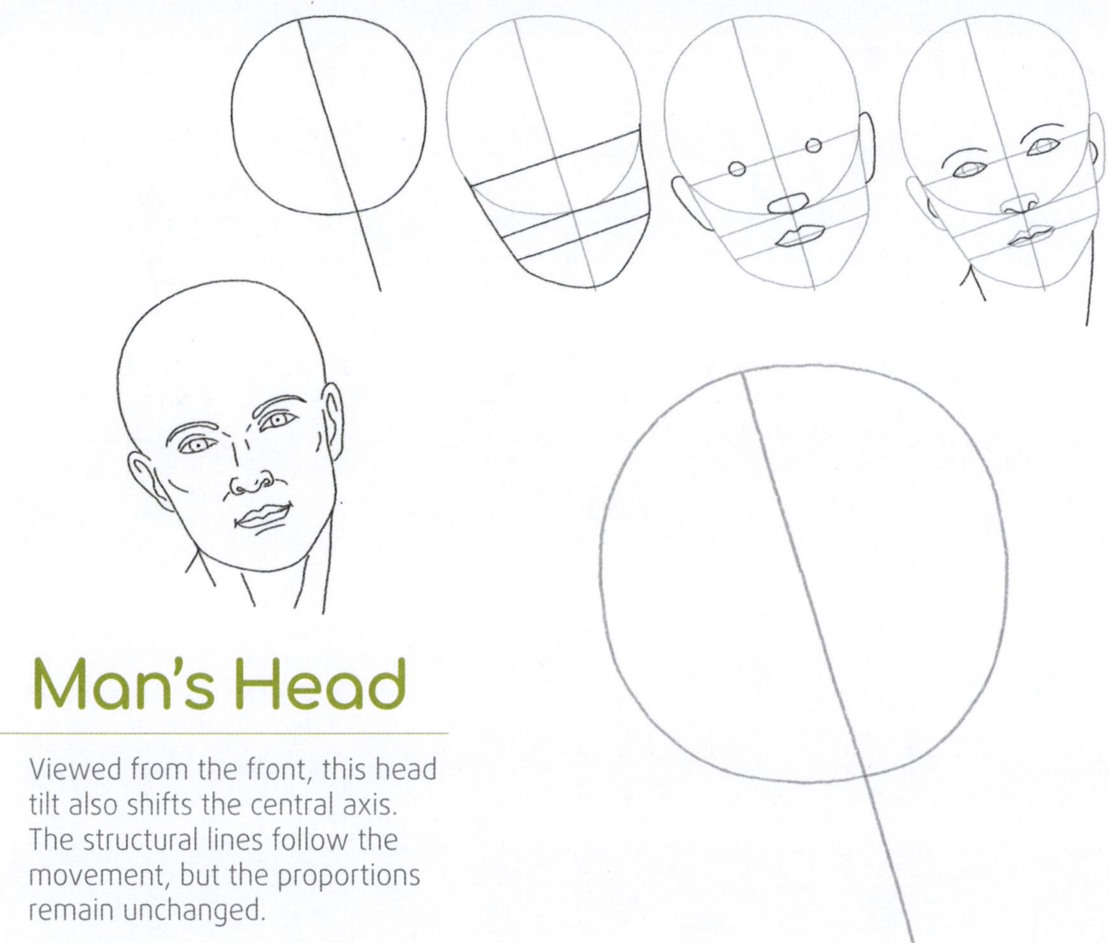

Man's Head

Viewed from the front, this head tilt also shifts the central axis. The structural lines follow the movement, but the proportions remain unchanged.

225th day

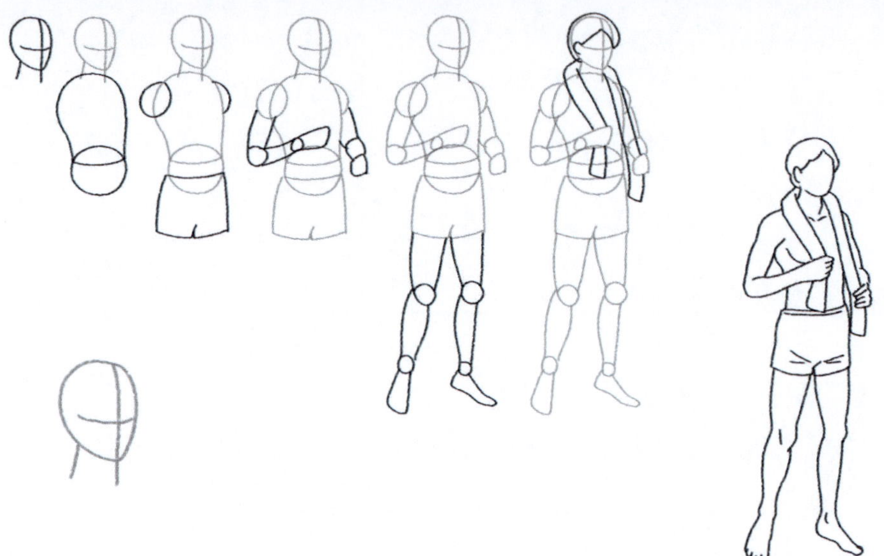

Standing Man

You can add a few accessories
to suggest a scene and enhance
a pose.

226th day

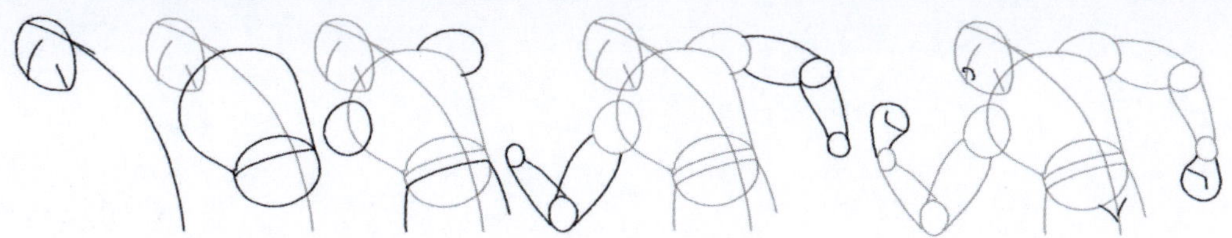

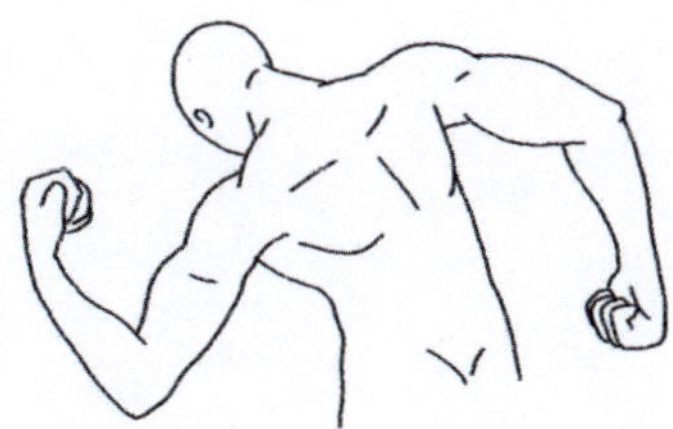

Man's Torso

This pose emphasizes the
muscles of the back and arms.

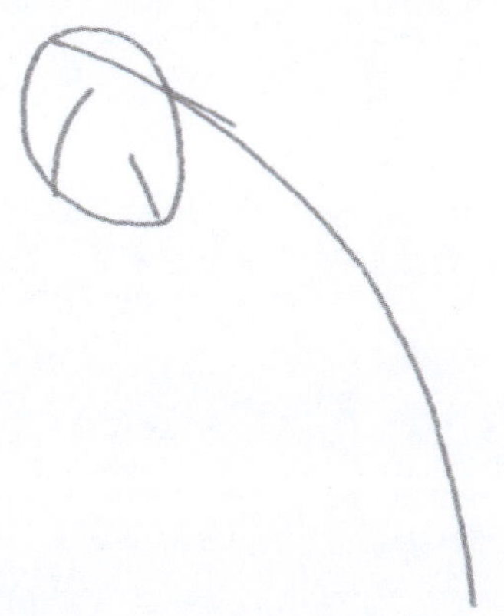

227th day

227th day

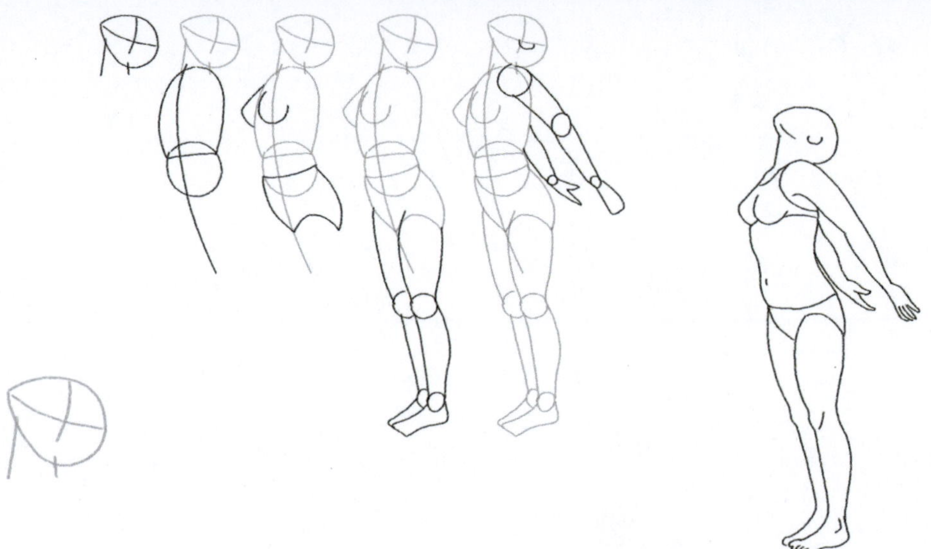

Woman in Profile

Positioning the feet flat on the ground makes the legs appear shorter. The slight three-quarter angle puts the whole body in perspective and reduces the size of one arm and one leg.

228th day

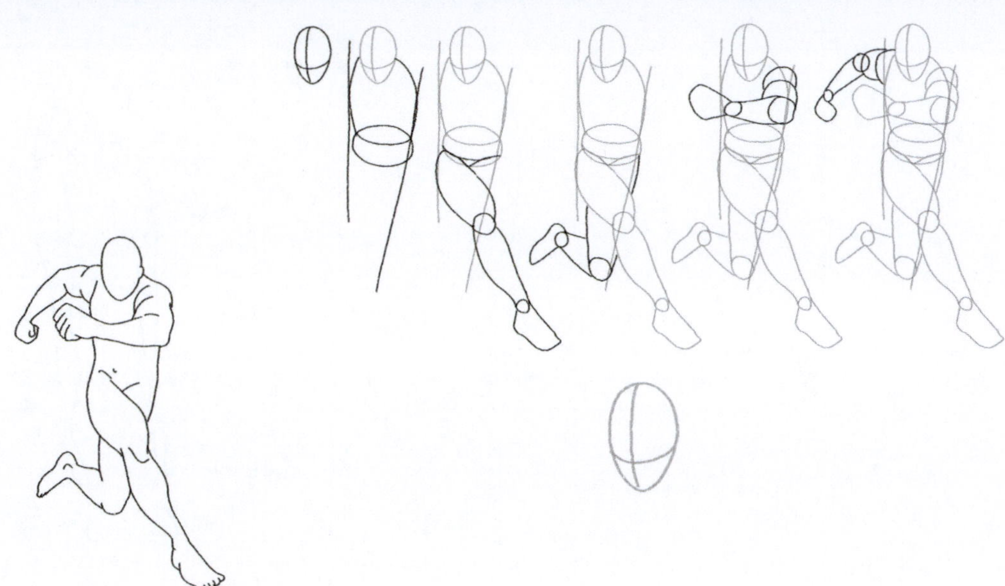

Running Man

The arm and leg in the foreground
project toward us and look larger.

229th day

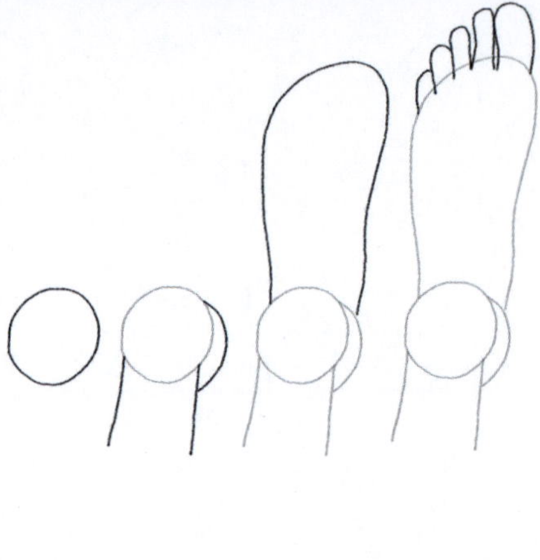
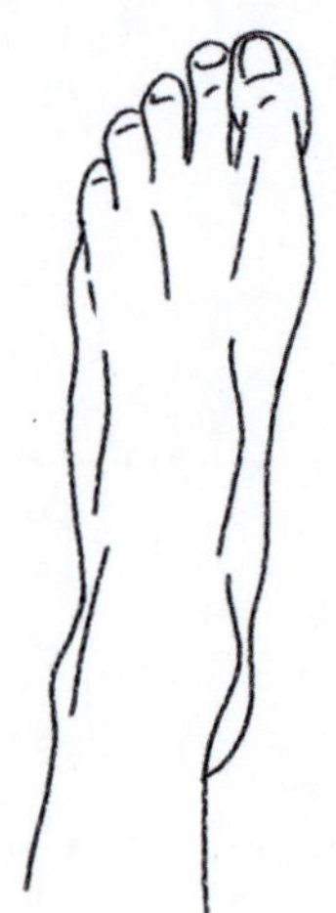

Foot

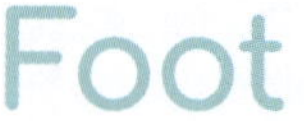

You can't see much of the heel when looking at a foot from above, but you can make out the ridges on the top of it.

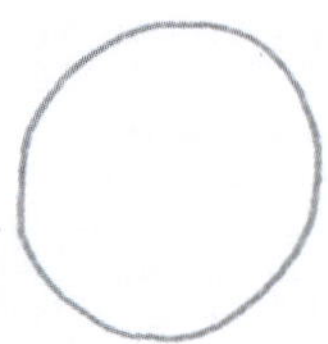

230th day

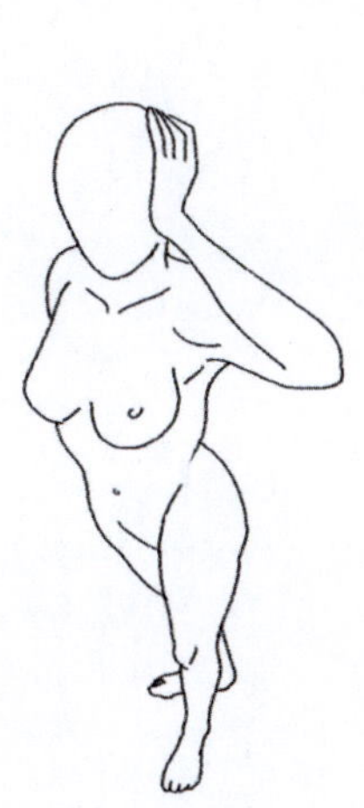

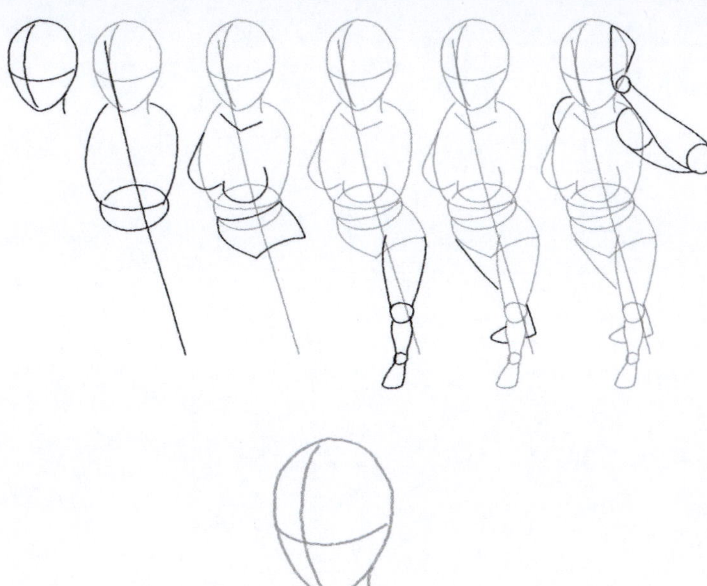

Standing Woman

This highly exaggerated three-quarter view stacks volumes one on top of the other. The dramatic perspective reduces the size of the legs and feet.

231st day

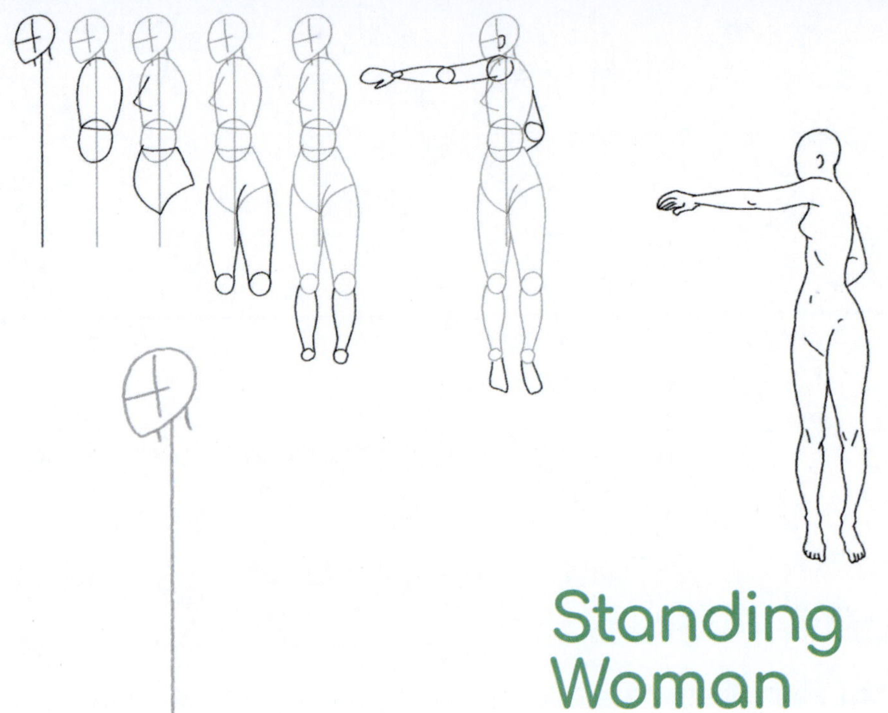

Standing Woman

This figure's upper body is in profile, so we cannot see its width, while the lower body is turned and gradually faces the front.

232nd day

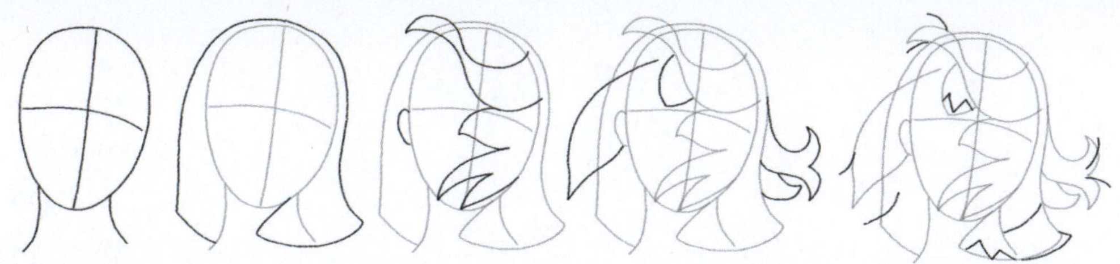

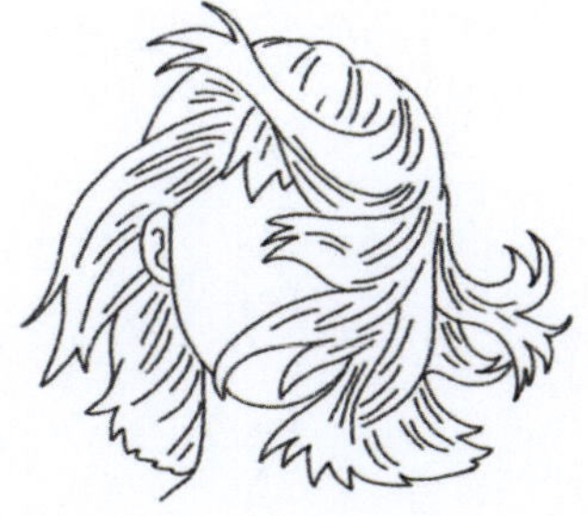

Wind-Blown Hair

You can create joyful movement by aiming strands of hair in several different directions using small curves.

233rd day

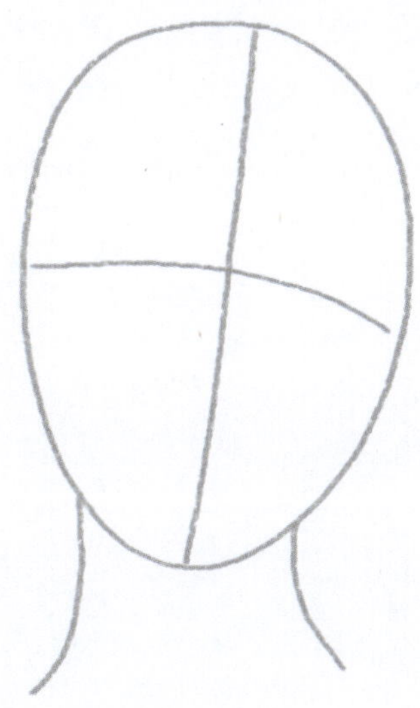

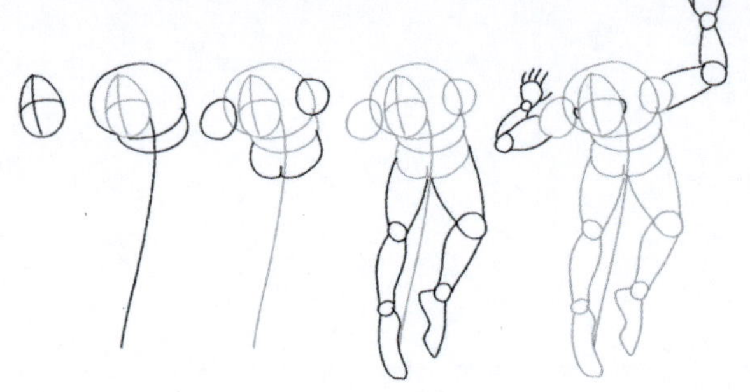

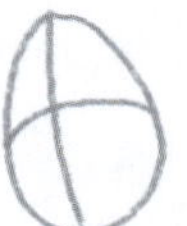

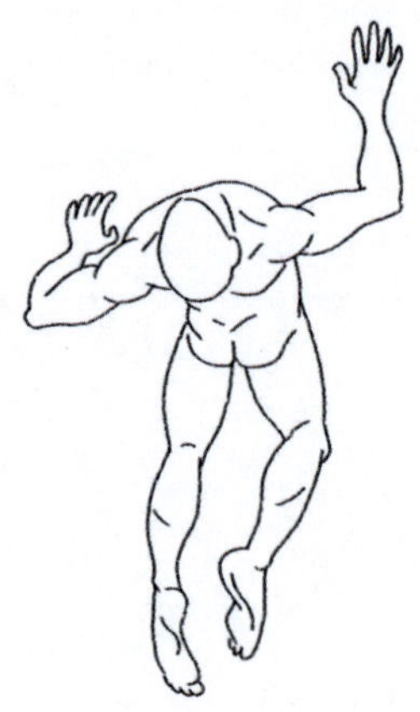

Backflip

This figure's upper body is twisted and bending back, toward us. The shoulders, head and arms are therefore larger.

234th day

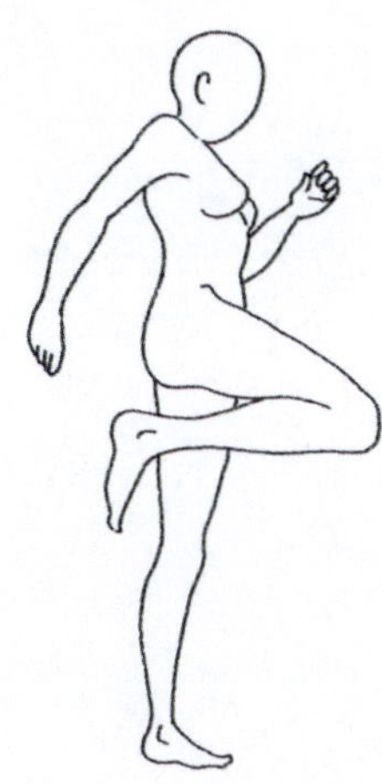

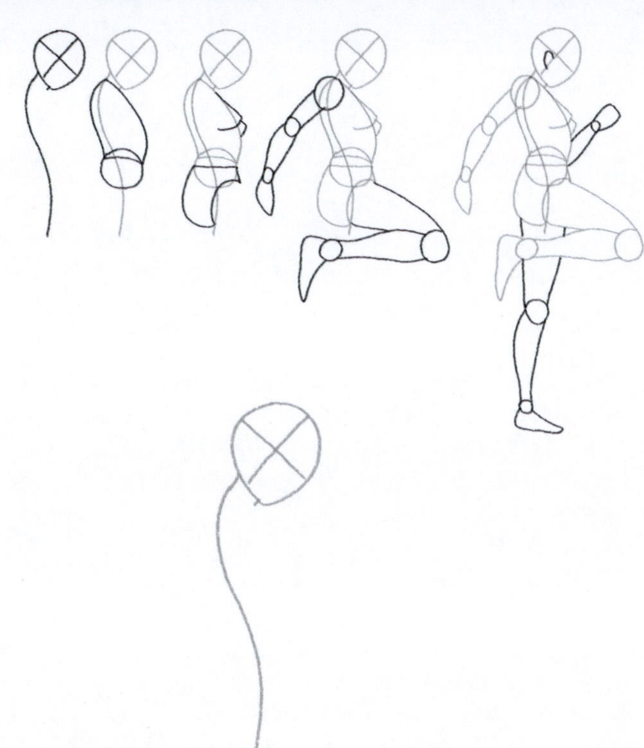

Running Woman

The bent leg, viewed in profile, makes the back leg visible. The figure is holding her arms away from her body and lightly twisting her torso.

235th day

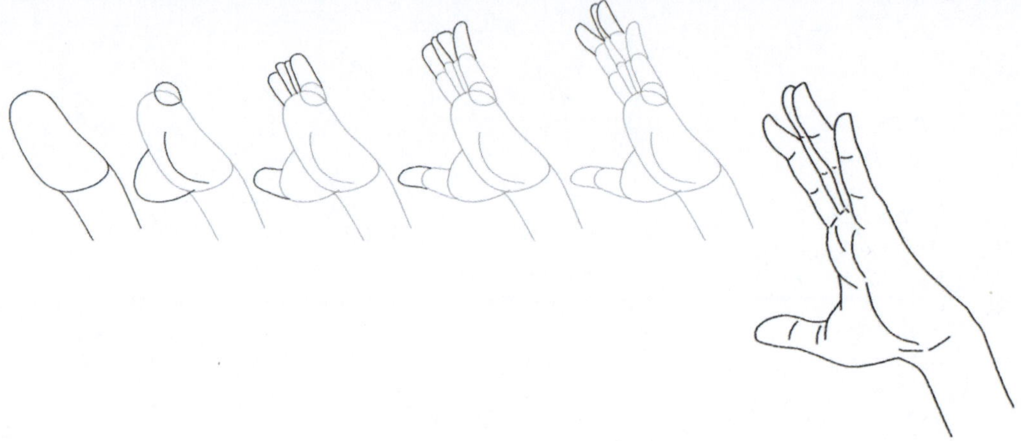

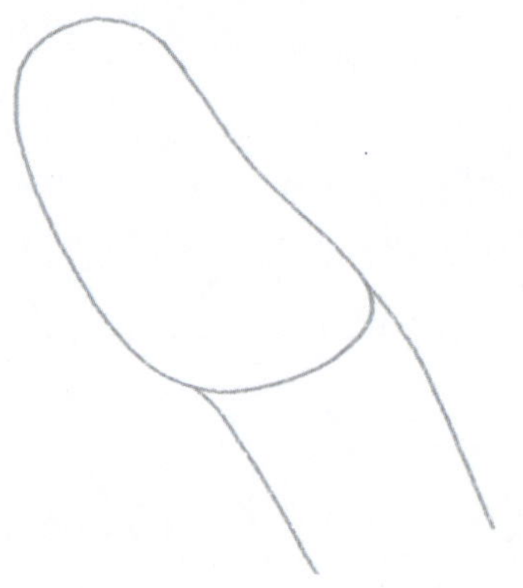

Hand

In this three-quarter view of a hand, the fingers are partially obscured. The creases in the palm indicate that the thumb is slightly bent.

236th day

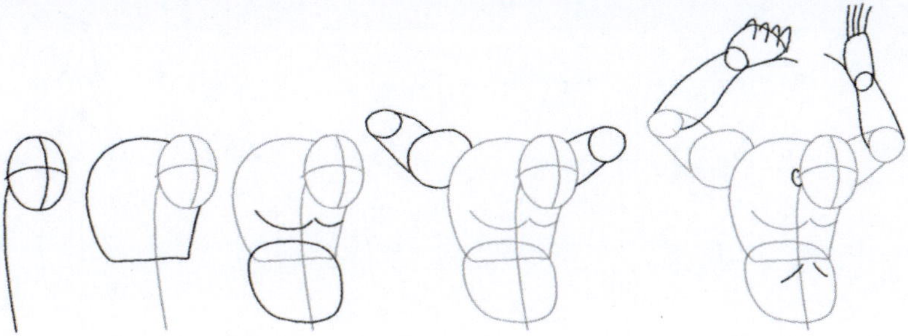

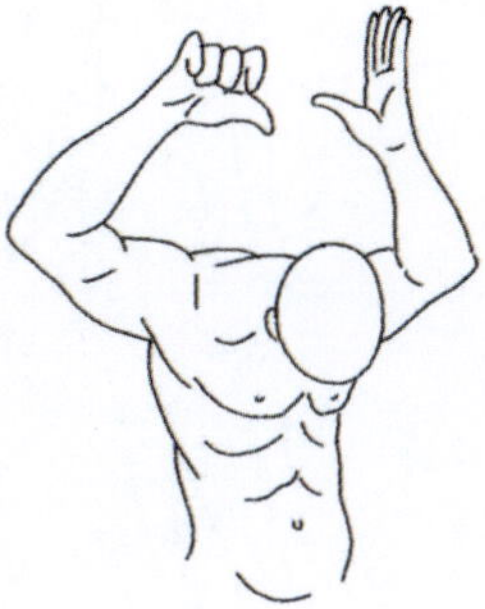

Man's Torso

In a close-up view, you can see the different muscles of the stomach, arms and shoulders.

237th day

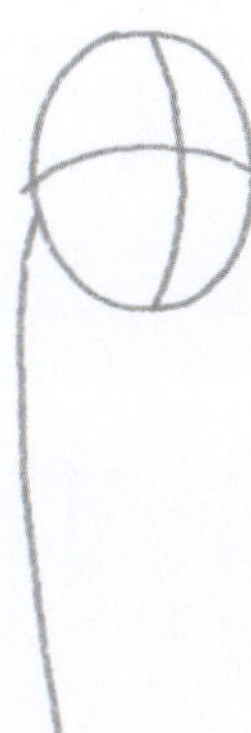

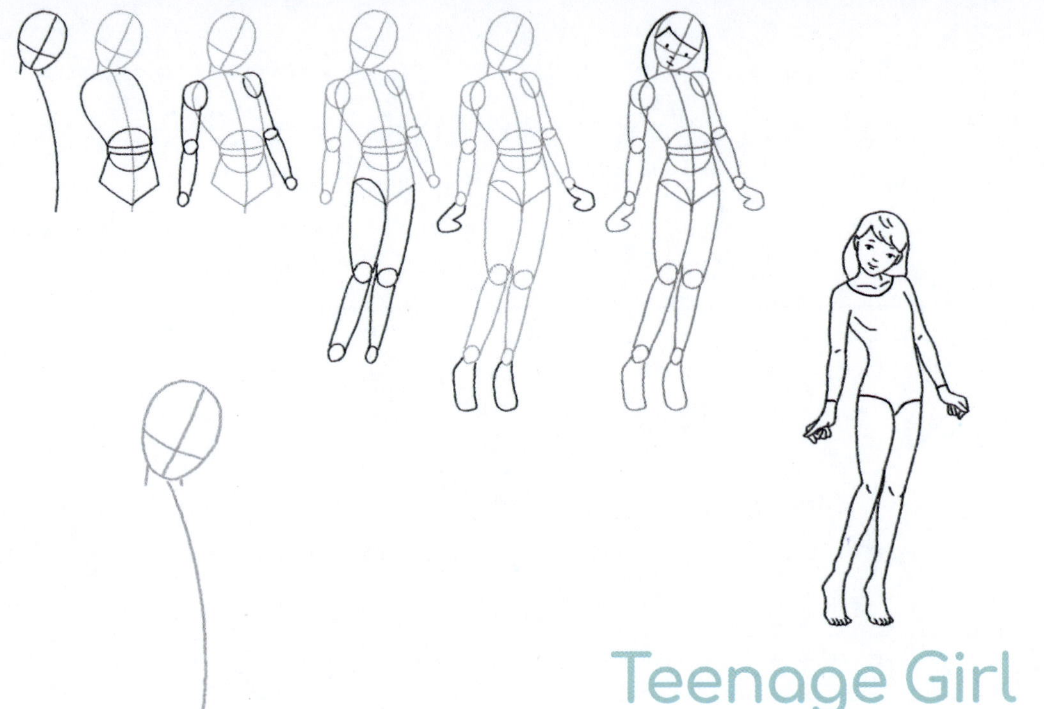

Teenage Girl

This is a graceful pose, with a slight sway to the hips, the hands gently closed and the shoulders and head softly arched.

238 th day

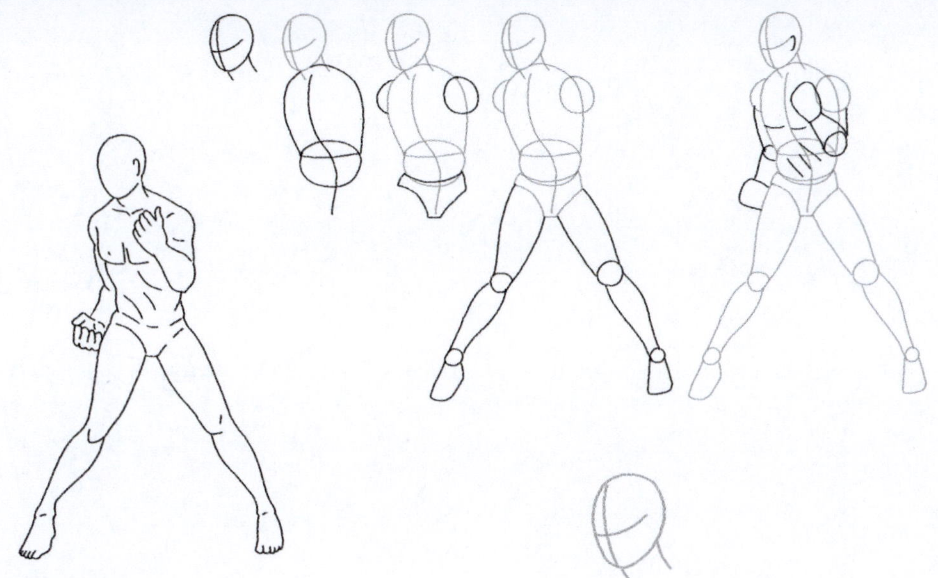

Fighting Stance

In this pose, the legs are facing the front and the torso is twisted, creating creases along the stomach. One arm is curving to the back.

239th day

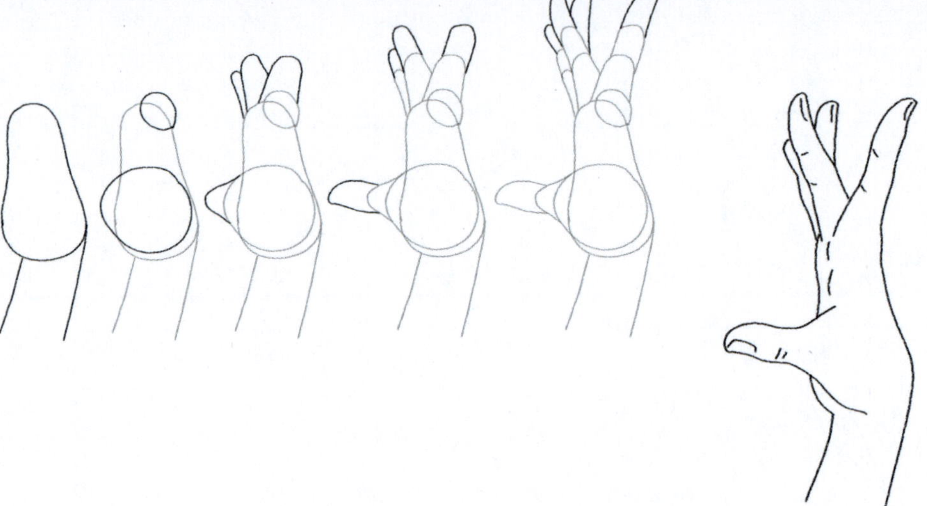

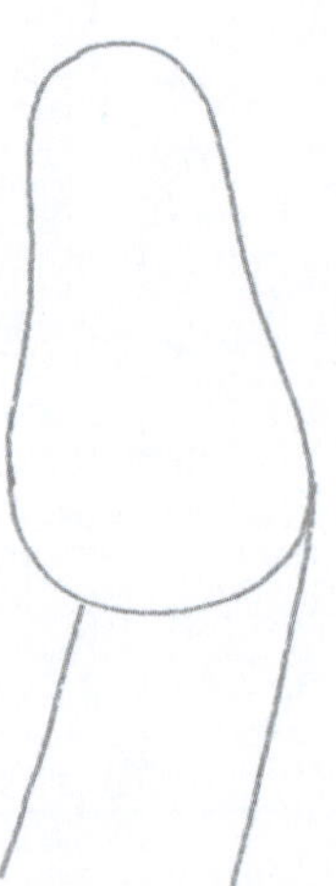

Hand

In this elegant pose the little finger is raised, the top of the hand is curved inward and the wrist is flexed. The entire hand is stretched upward.

240th day

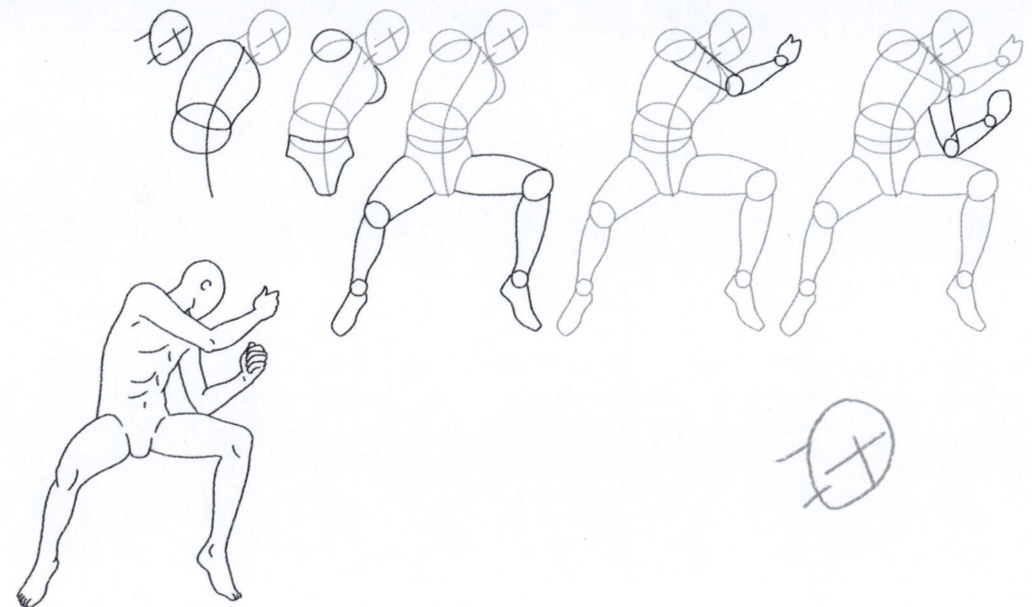

Rower

This pose shows the movement
of a figure paddling a boat.
The upper body pivots to one
side, while the legs remain
firmly planted.

241st day

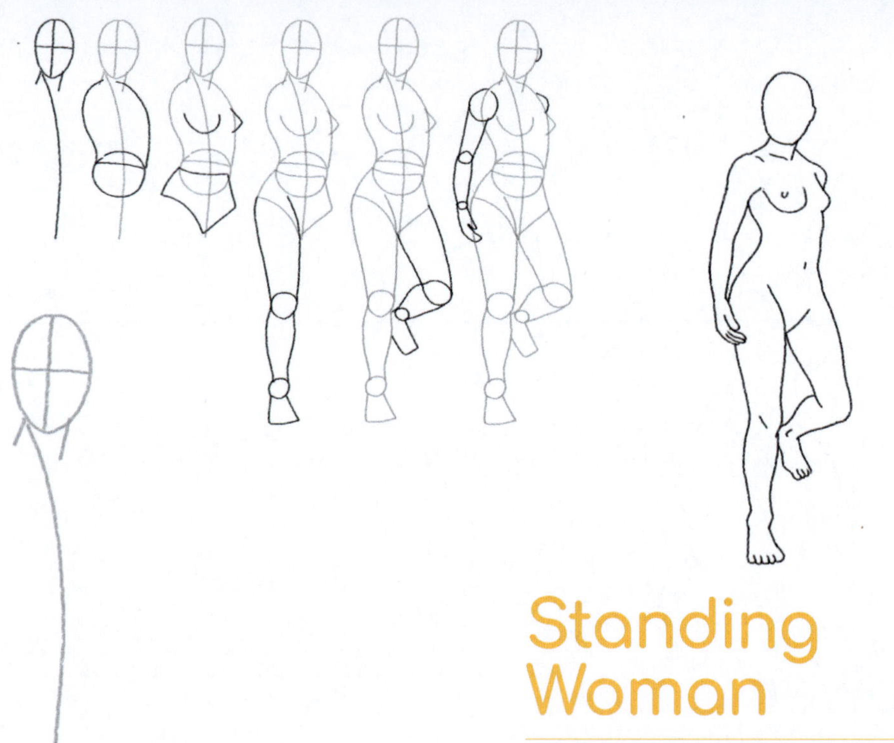

Standing Woman

In this pose, the figure's body is slightly twisted, and part of the torso and one arm are obscured.

242nd day

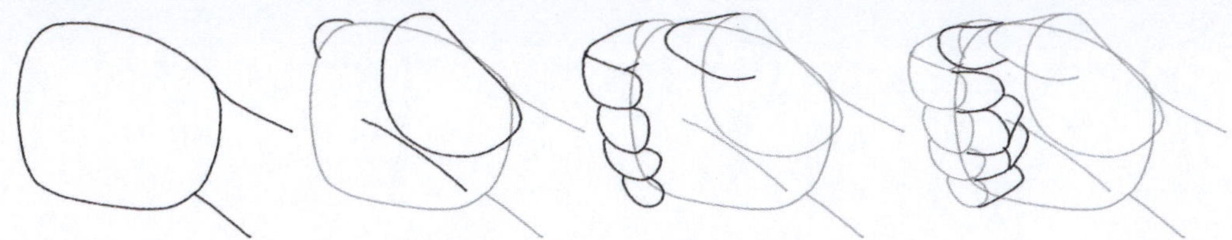

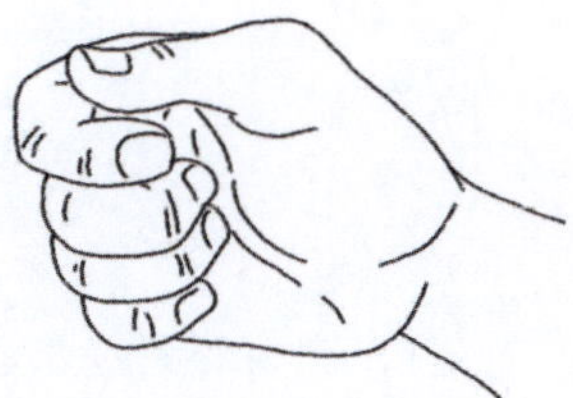

Fist

As the fingers curl into the palm,
they create creases in the skin.

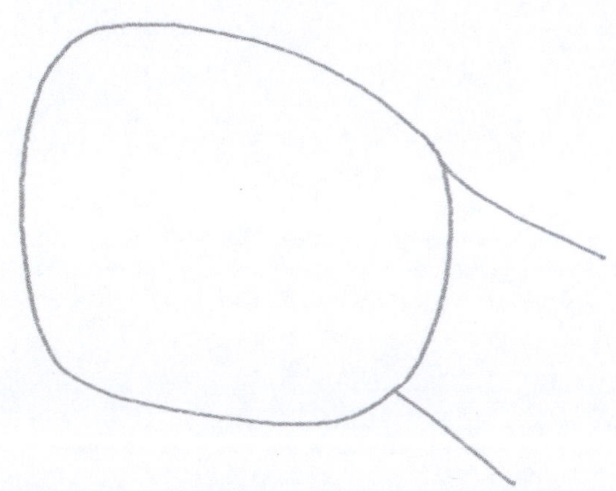

243rd day

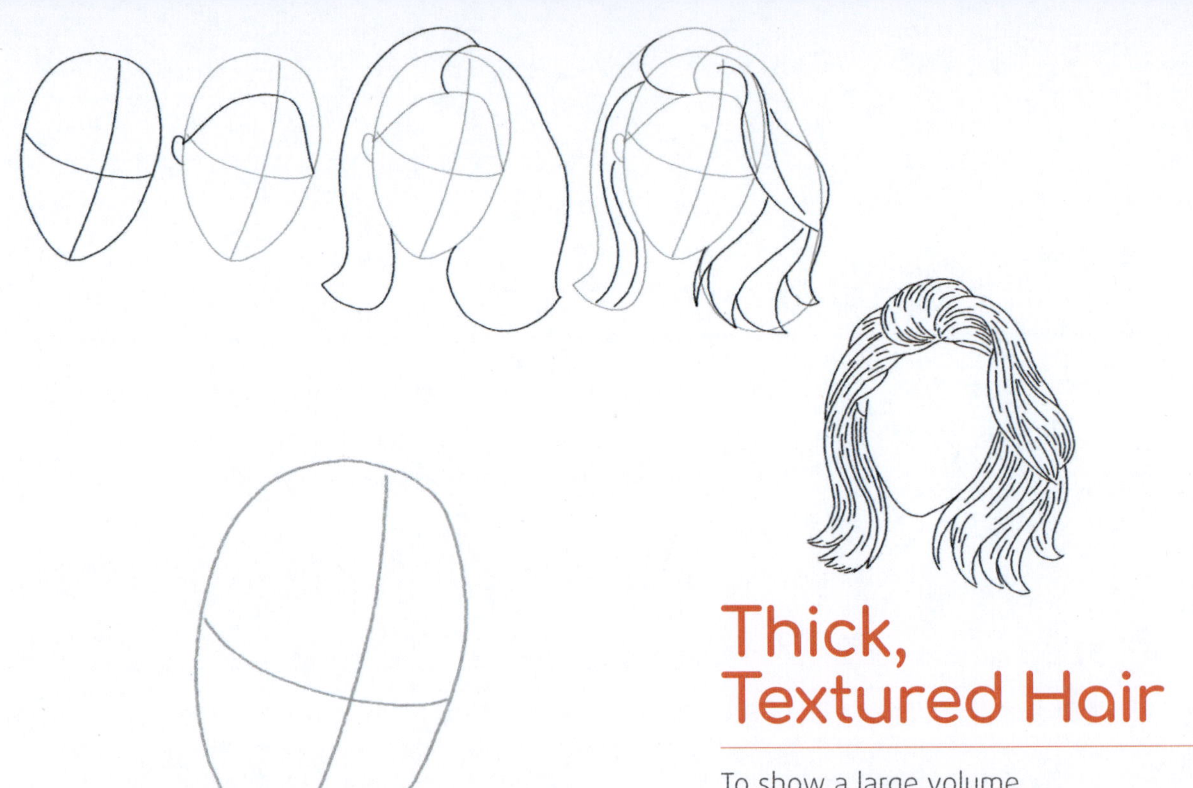

Thick, Textured Hair

To show a large volume
of hair, draw lines in many
different directions.

244th **day**

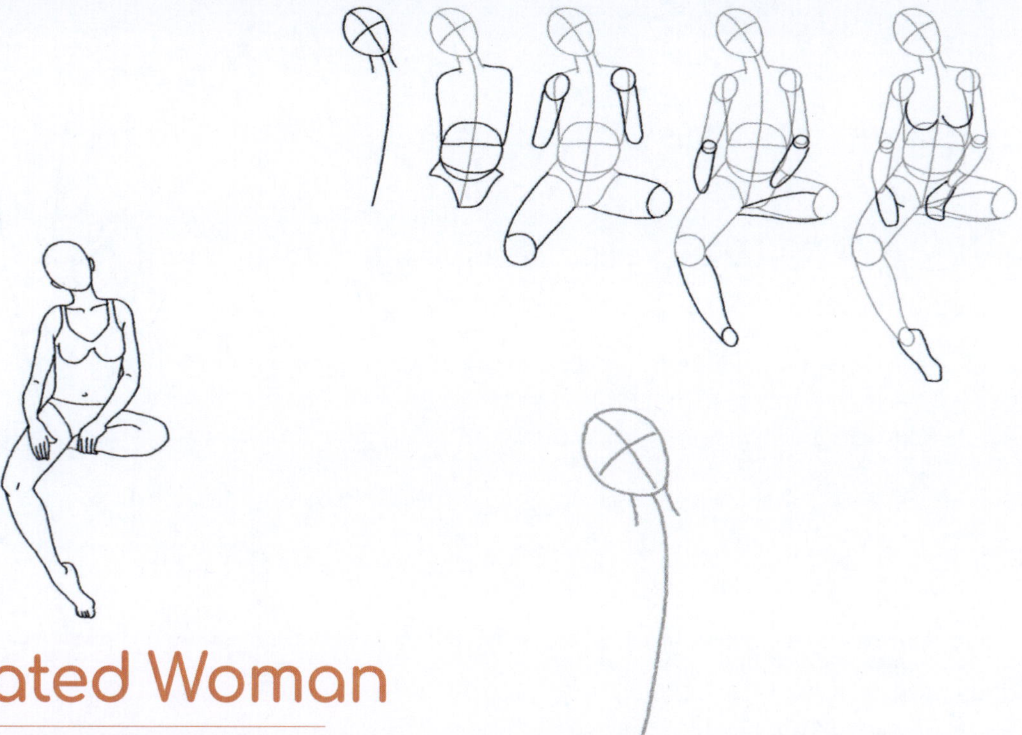

Seated Woman

This figure's torso is slightly curved to the side. The bent leg looks smaller because of the perspective.

245th day

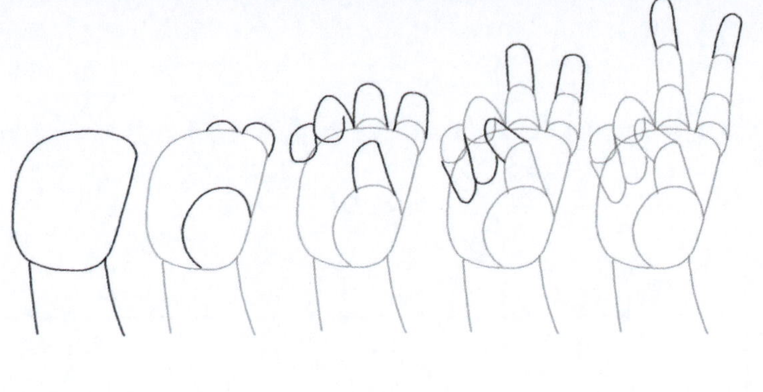

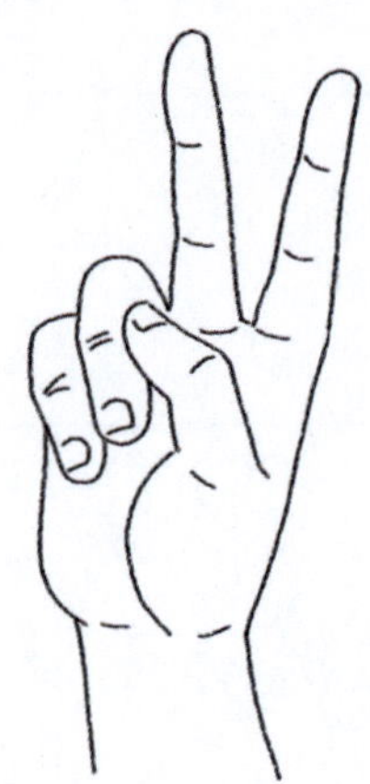

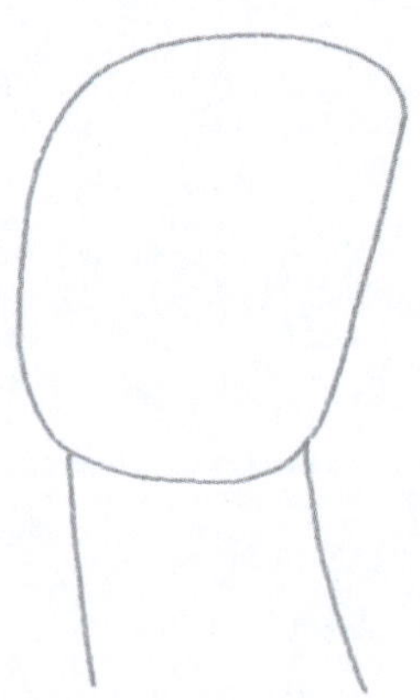

V Sign

When making the victory sign, the hand is quite supple. The thumb doesn't wrap completely around the hand, and the two raised fingers aren't quite straight.

246th day

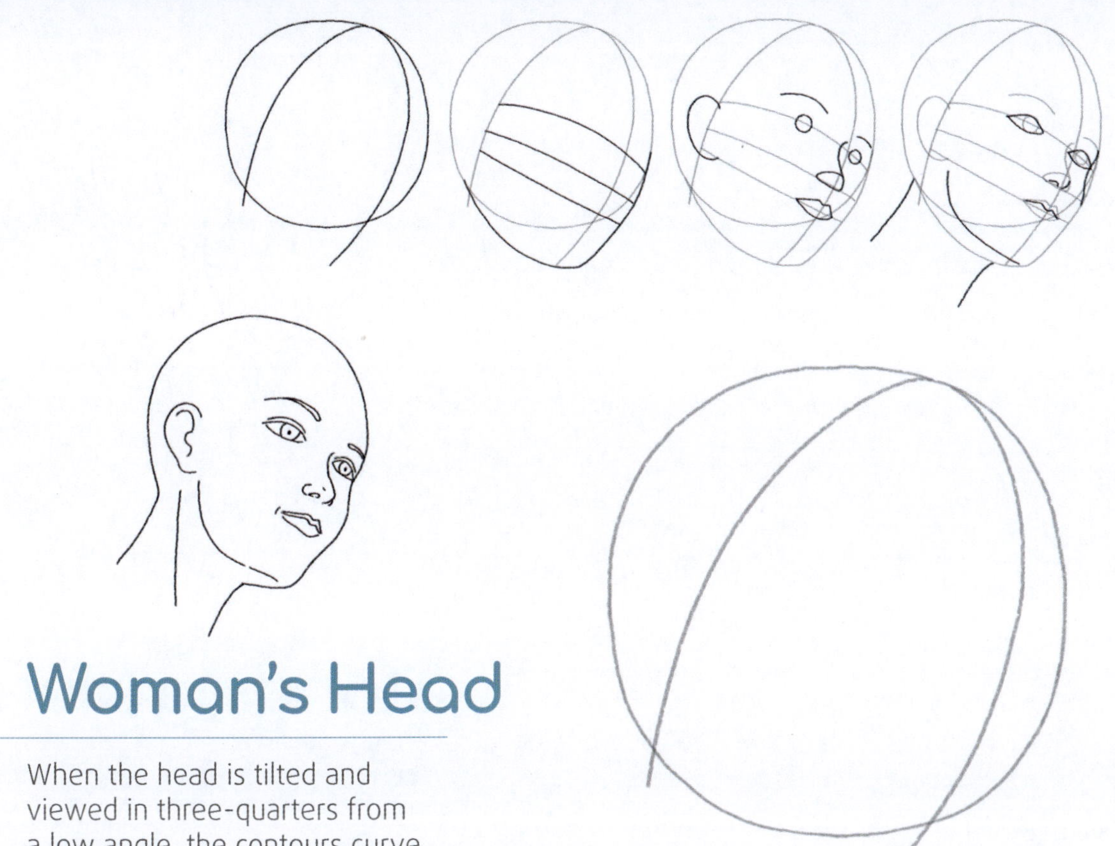

Woman's Head

When the head is tilted and viewed in three-quarters from a low angle, the contours curve downward.

247th day

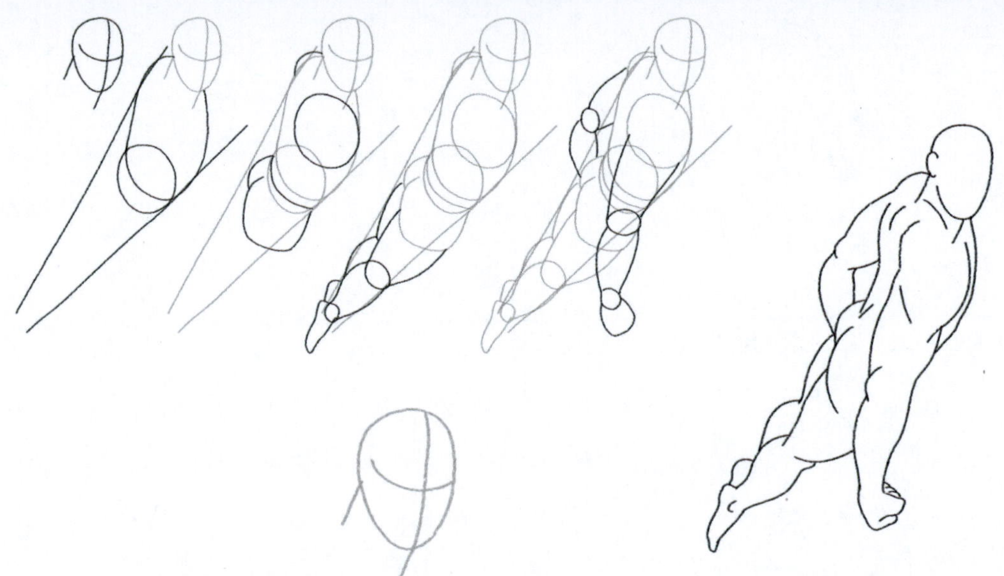

Standing Man

When the arms and legs are held against a very compact body, the perspective is very striking. The arm closest to us looks thicker than the legs.

248 th day

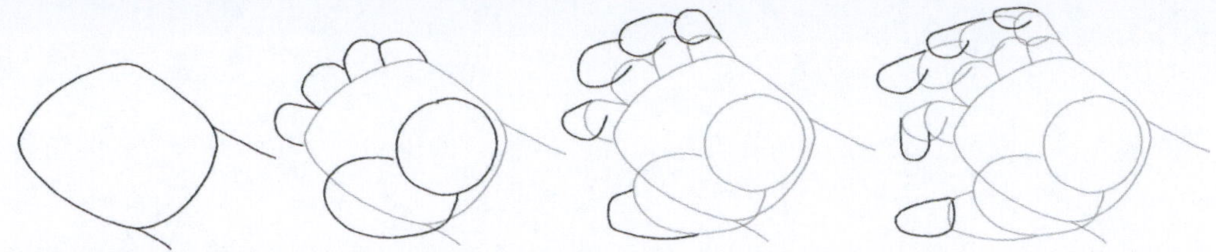

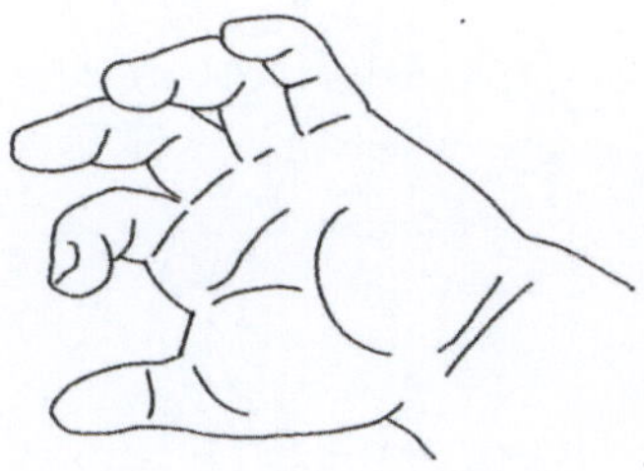

Child's Hand

The inside of a young child's palm is very round, as is the underside of each finger.

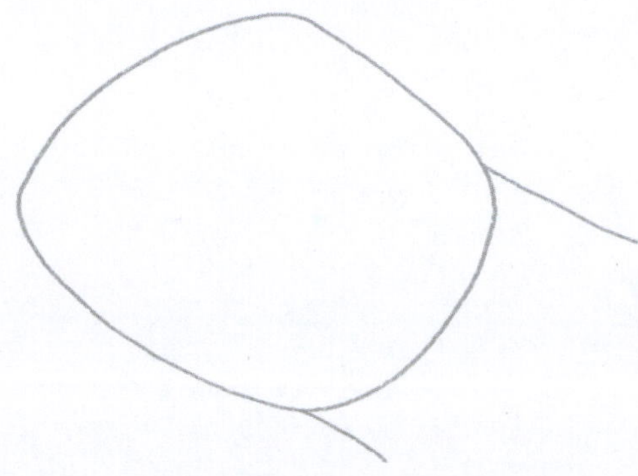

249th day

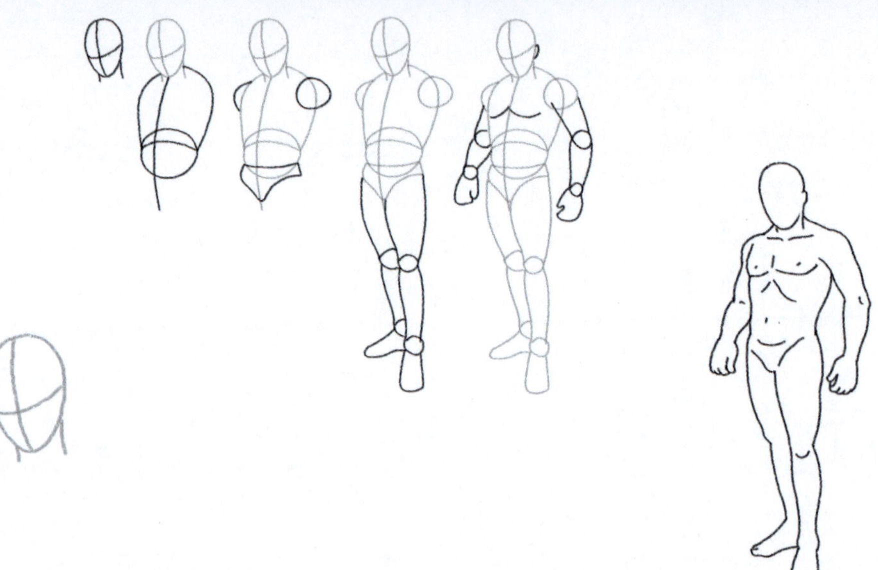

Standing Man

This morphology presents a strong torso, and the entire body is fairly compact. The rear leg is smaller in perspective.

250 th day

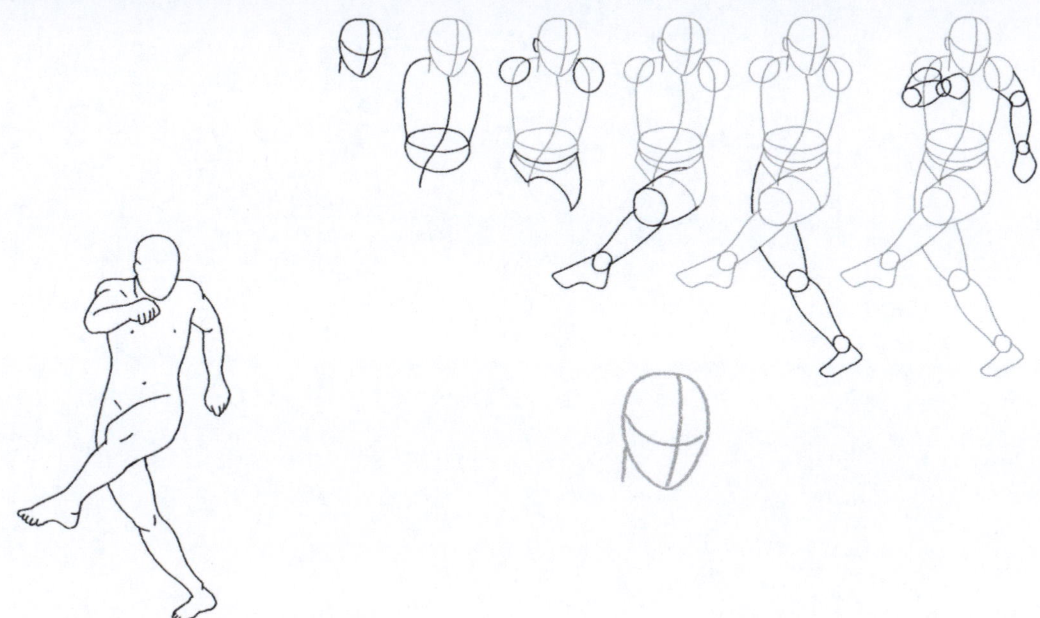

Soccer Player

The foot on the ground acts as a
pivot on which the whole body
can turn to kick the ball. The
figure's upper torso and legs are
oriented in different directions.

251st day

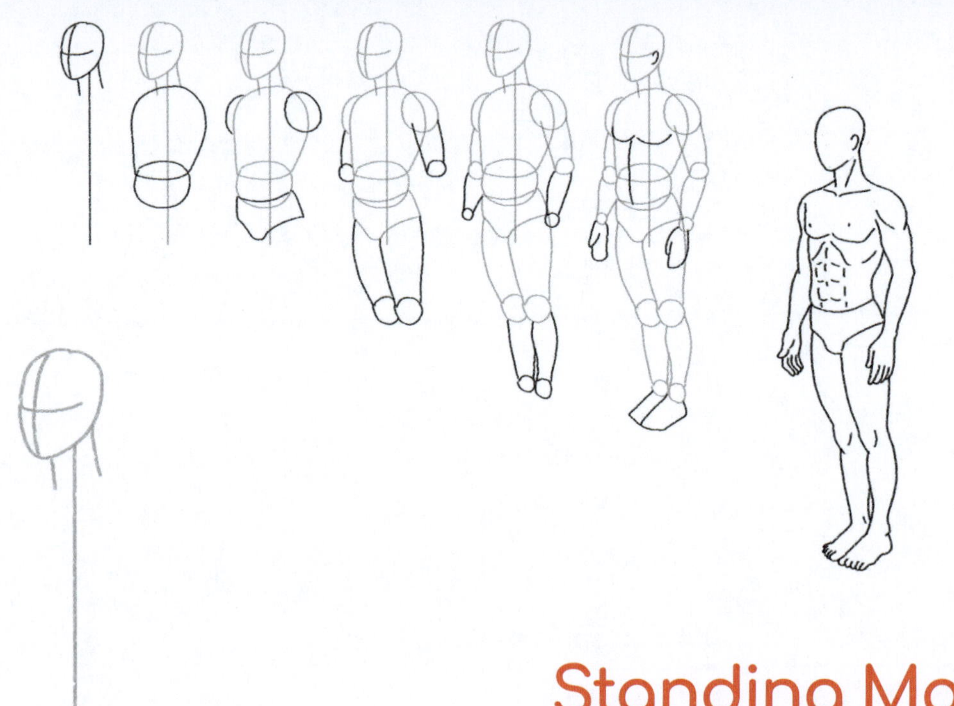

Standing Man

In a three-quarter view, the perspective reduces one side of the body in relation to the other. You can emphasize the abdominal muscles by drawing a few lines.

252 nd day

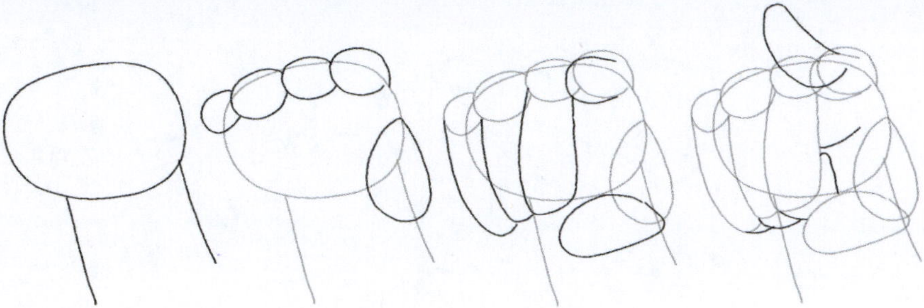

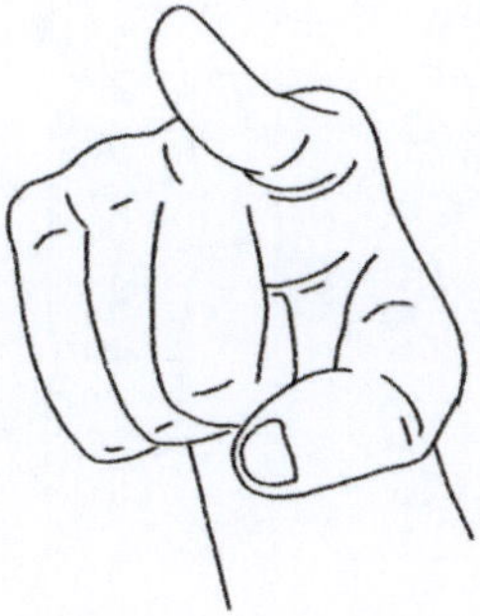

Pointing Finger

In this pose, the index finger is pointed at us and in perspective, so we can't see all of it.

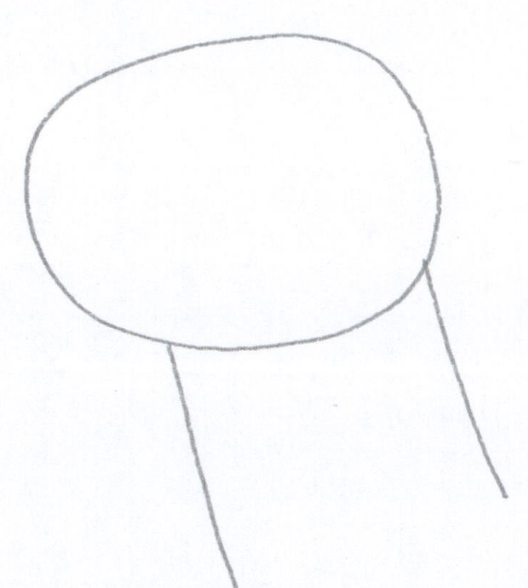

253 rd day

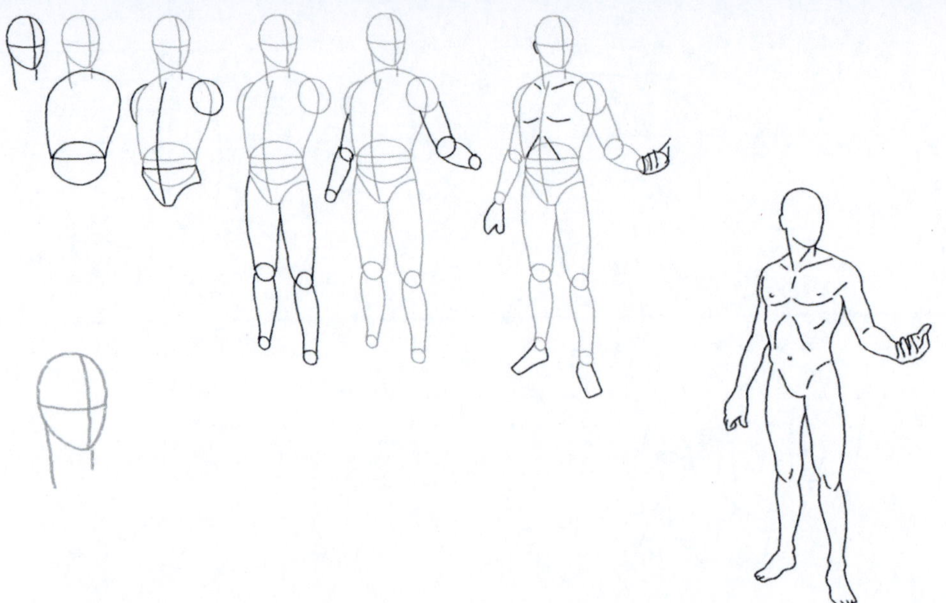

Standing Man

Puffing the chest sucks in
the belly and makes the ribs
stand out.

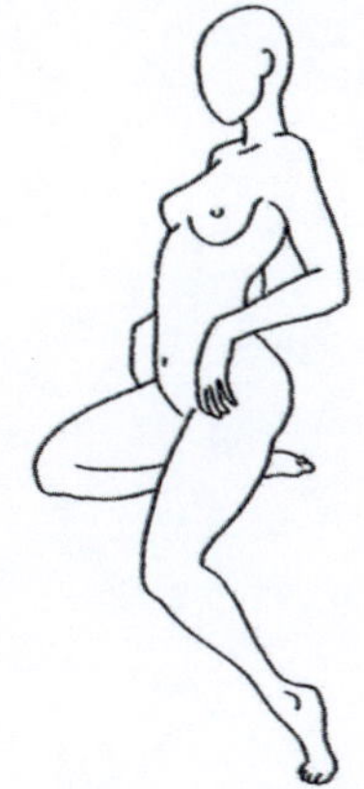

Seated Woman

This figure's back follows a
sweeping inward curve. The
arms and bent leg appear to be
resting on something.

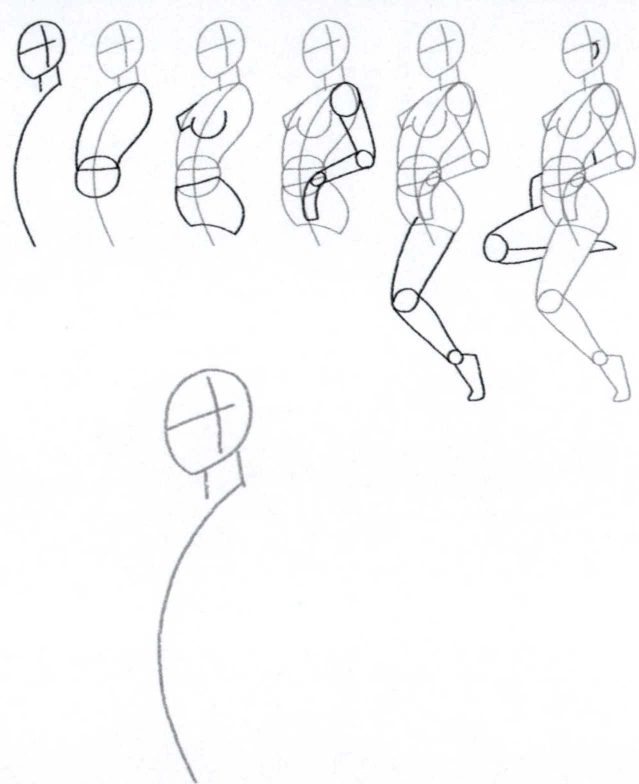

255th day

255th day

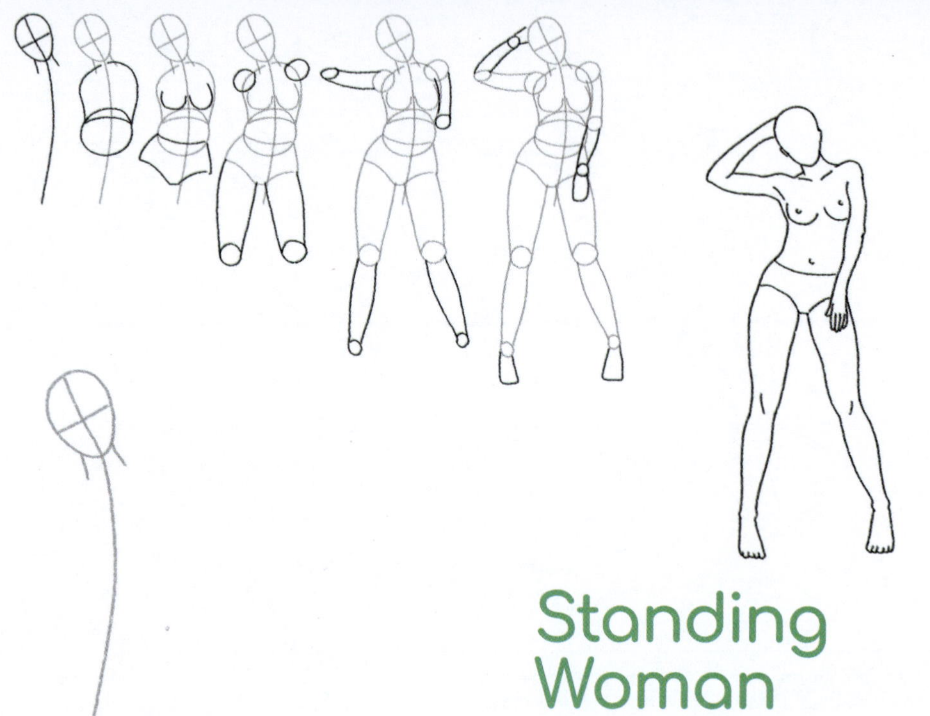

Standing Woman

You can exaggerate certain parts of the body, such as lengthening the legs, to create a more stylized drawing, typical of fashion illustrations.

256 th day

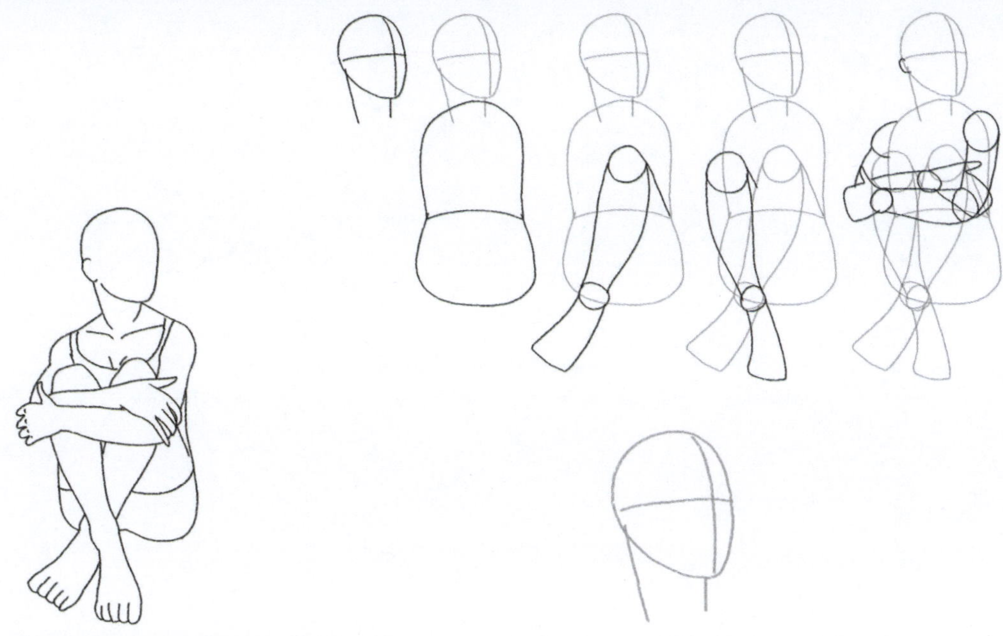

Seated Woman

The torso is mostly hidden in this compact pose.

257

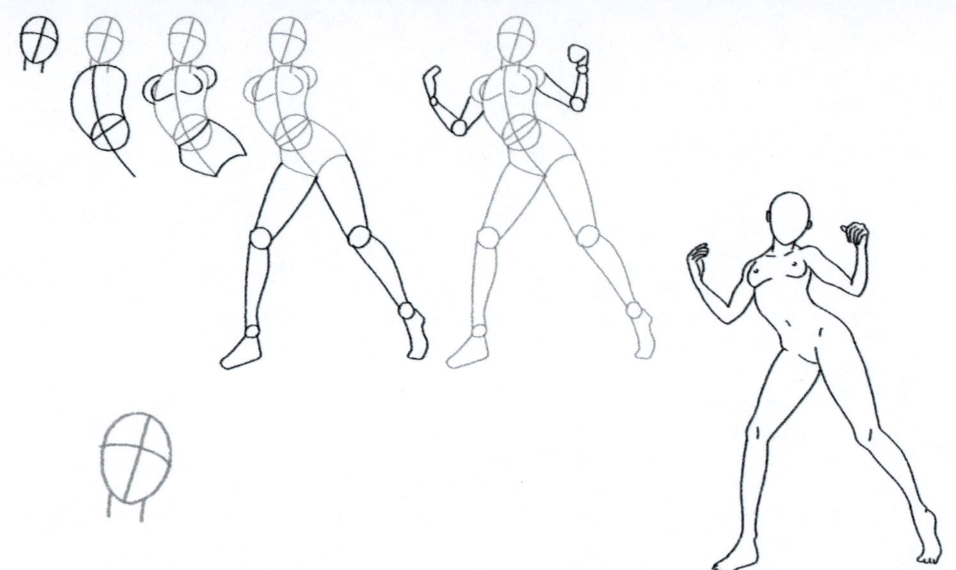

Dancer

This figure is resting her weight on one leg before shifting it to the other. The upper body is leaning back.

258th day

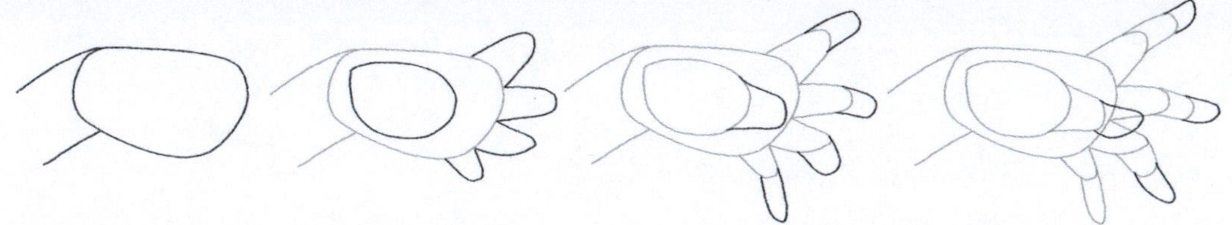

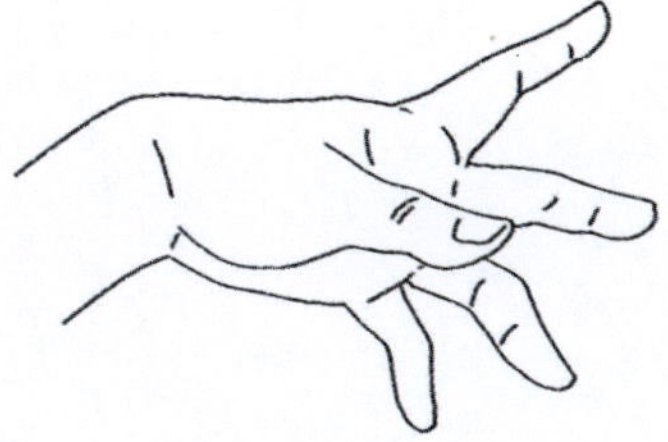

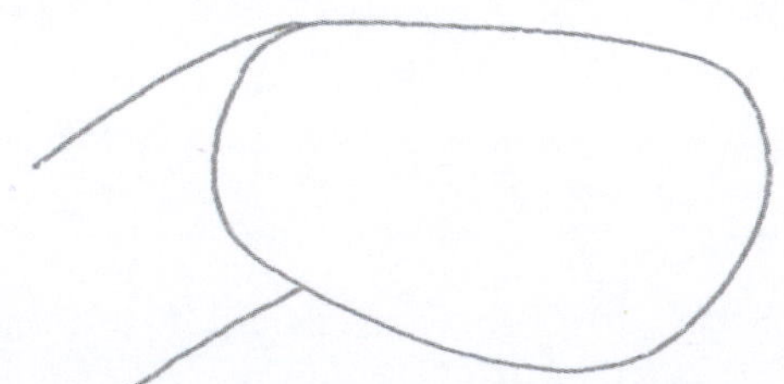

Hand

This hand is tense, with each finger pointing and reaching out in a different direction.

259th day

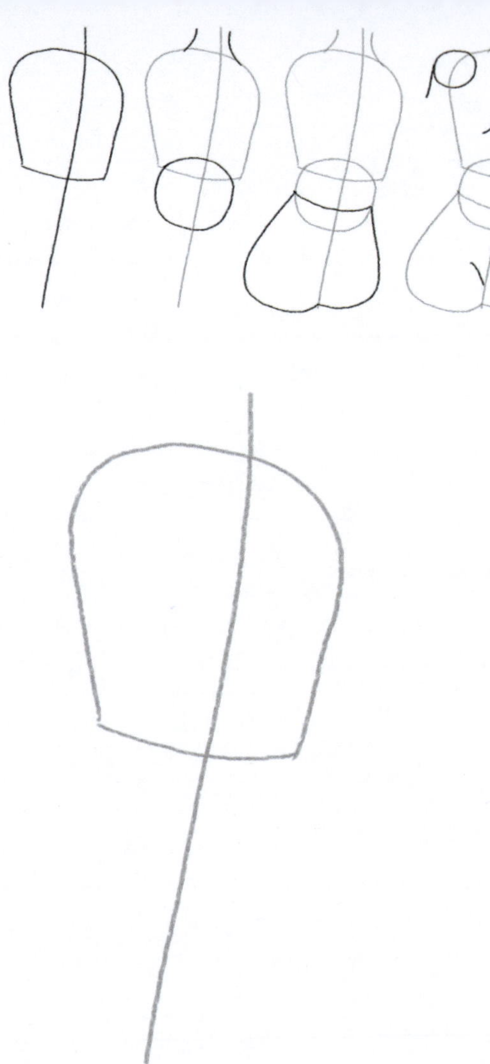

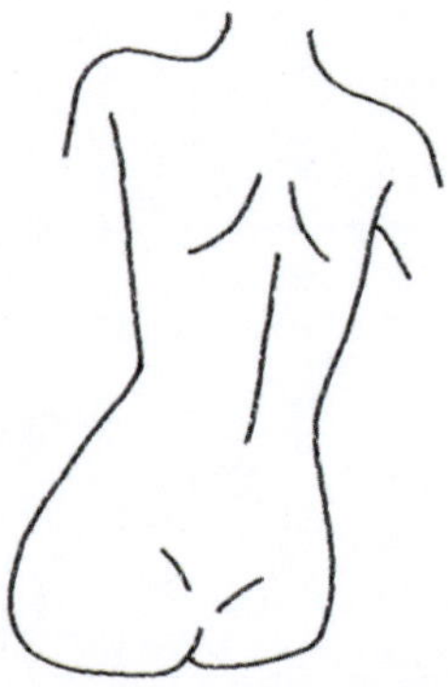

Woman from the Back

When viewed from the back, a seated pose creates creases over the buttocks.

260th day

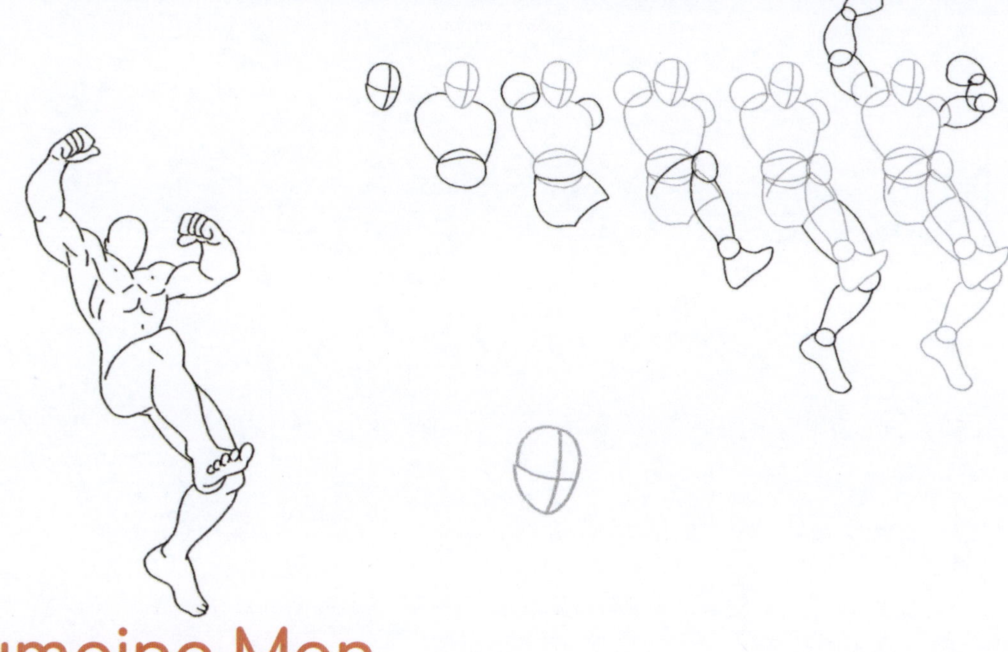

Jumping Man

The feet in the foreground are large in relation to the upper body. The bulging muscles emphasize the effort associated with this movement.

261st day

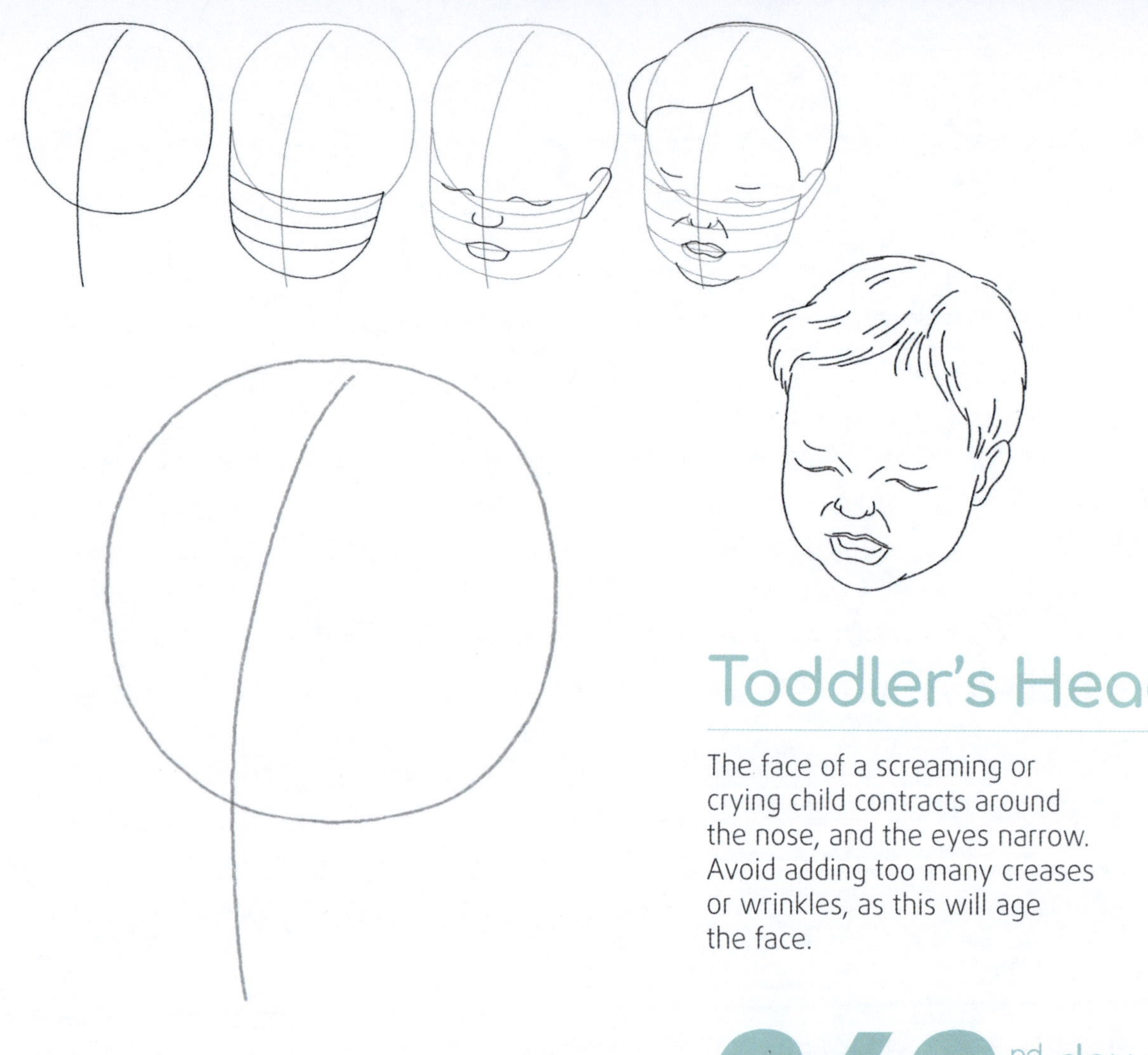

Toddler's Head

The face of a screaming or crying child contracts around the nose, and the eyes narrow. Avoid adding too many creases or wrinkles, as this will age the face.

262nd day

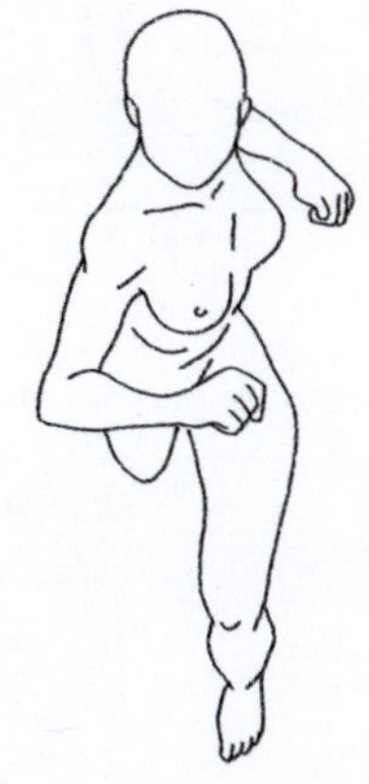

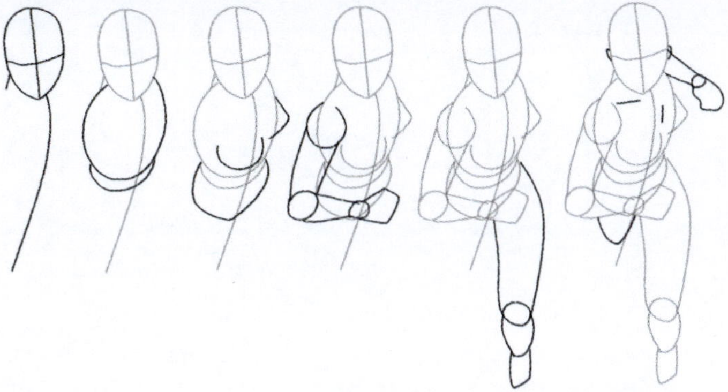

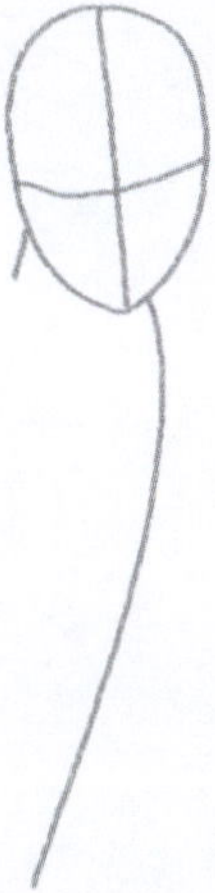

Running
Woman

This running pose, viewed from
above, puts the lower body in
perspective. One leg disappears,
and the other is greatly reduced.

263rd day

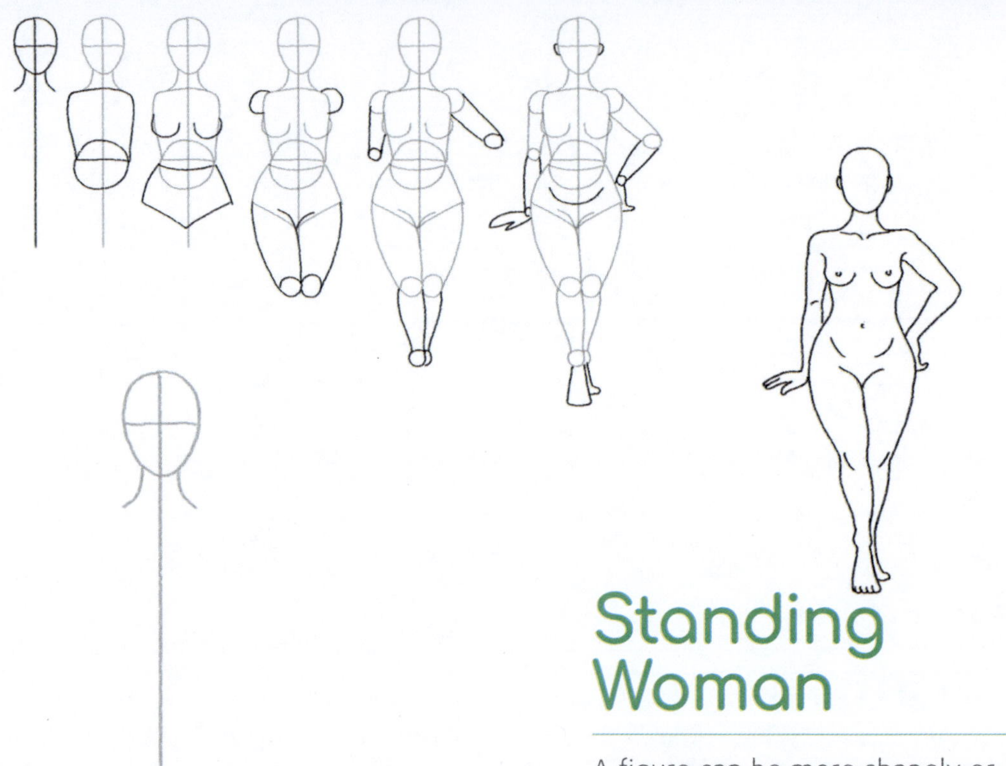

Standing Woman

A figure can be more shapely or less shapely. The upper part of this figure's torso is quite slim in relation to the hips and thighs.

264 th day

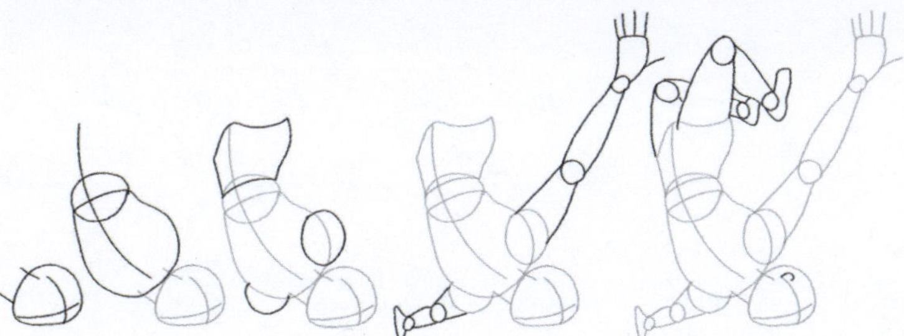

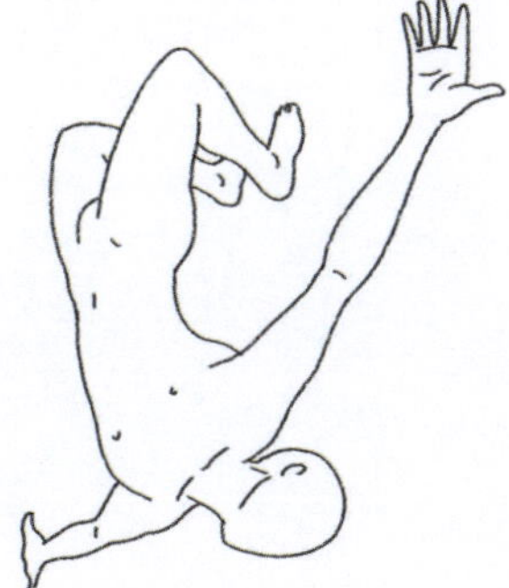

Backflip

This acrobatic figure is shown in perspective. The legs and one arm look much smaller.

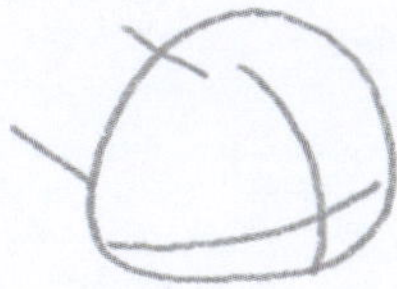

265th day

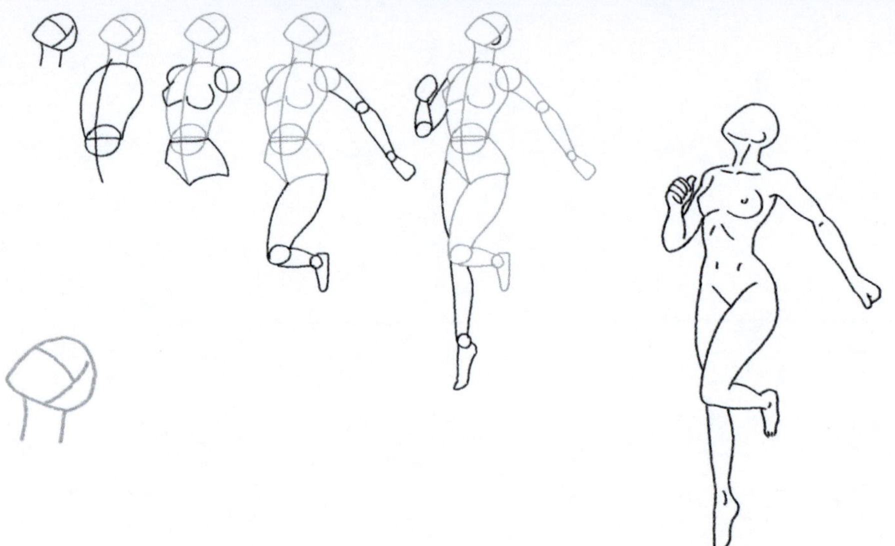

Running
Woman

In this running stance, an opposite arm and leg are bent forward. The other arm is extended backward, and the other leg stretches to the ground.

266 th day

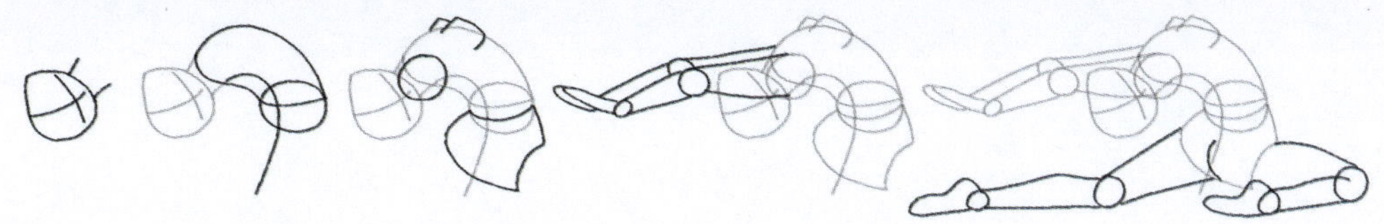

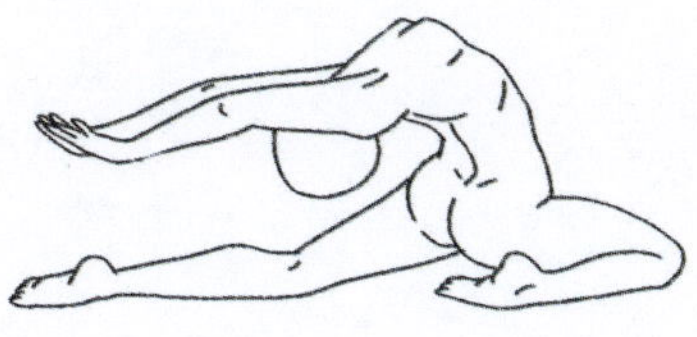

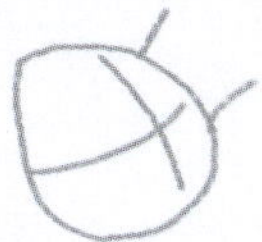

Gymnast

This figure's torso is in a deep
back bend, and the arms and one
leg are extended back, forming a
sideways U shape.

267 th day

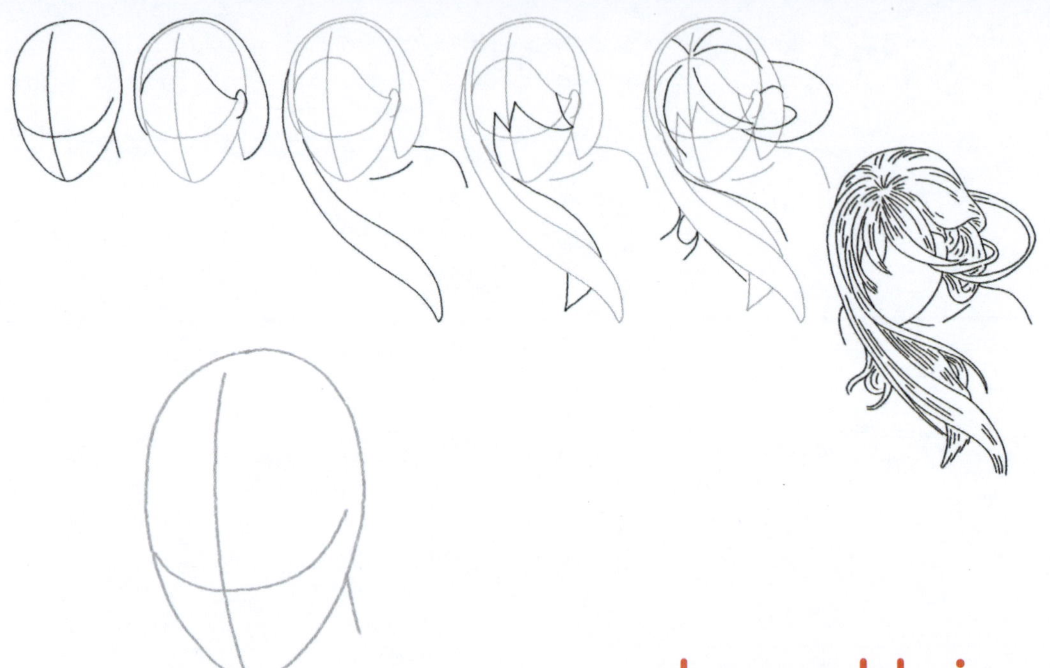

Long Hair

This overhead view shows where the bangs meet the rest of the figure's hair. Long strands wrap around the neck.

268th day

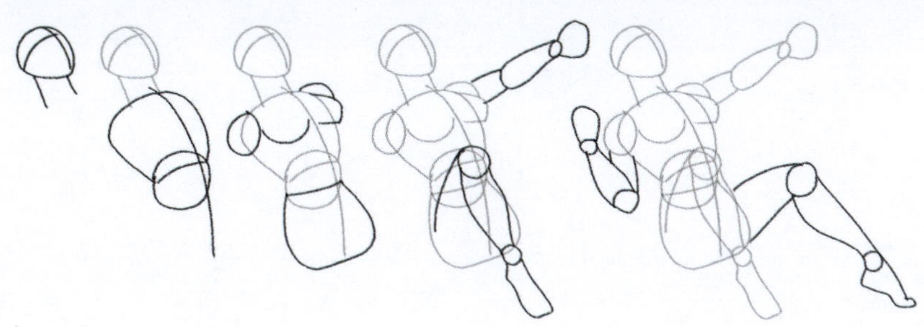

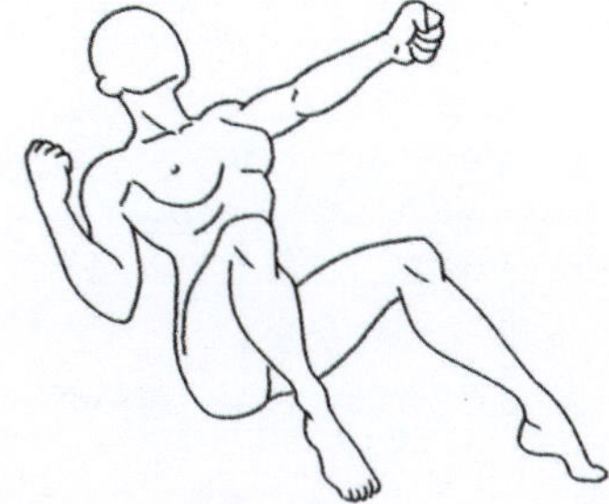

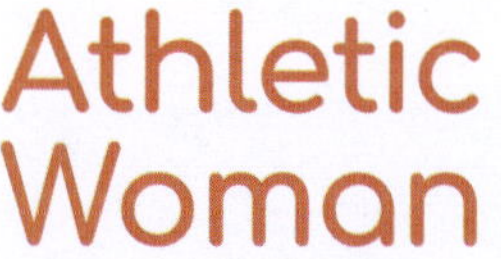

Athletic Woman

In this pose, every part of the
figure's body is tense.

269 th day

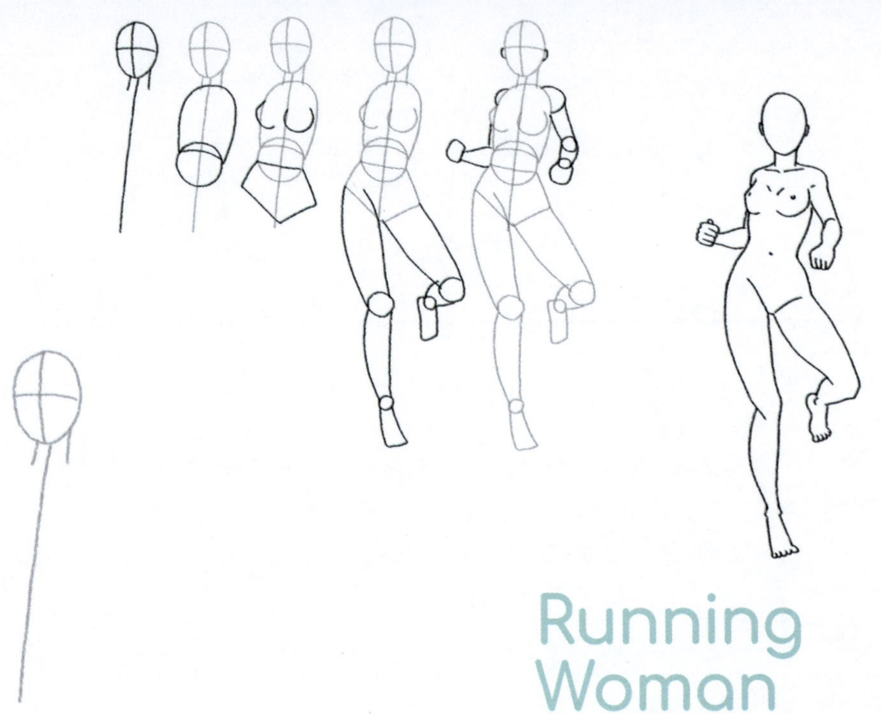

Running
Woman

This forward-running posture twists the torso in the opposite direction to the legs.

270th day

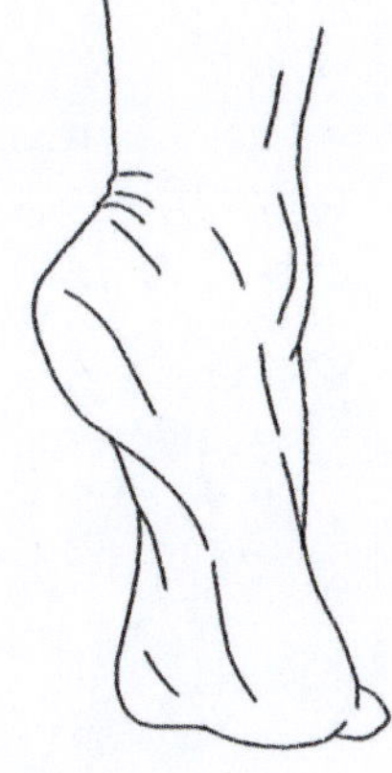

Foot on Tiptoes

In this three-quarter view, the side of the foot hides all but the tip of one toe. The pointed foot creates creases above the heel and along the sole.

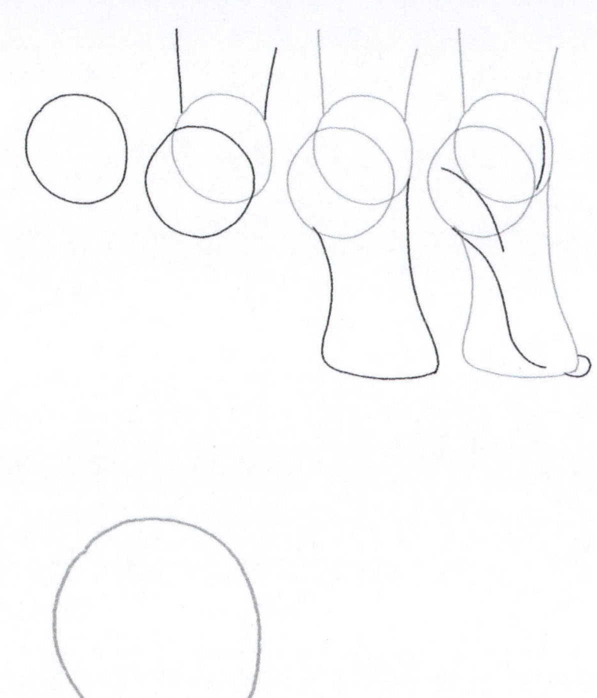

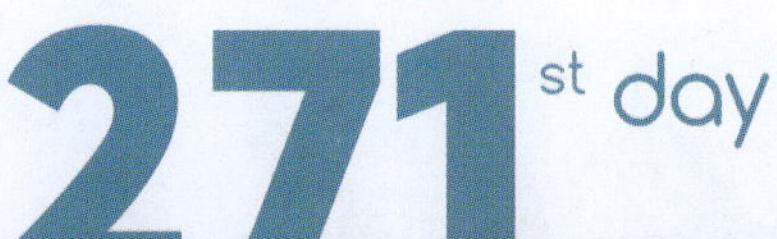

271 st day

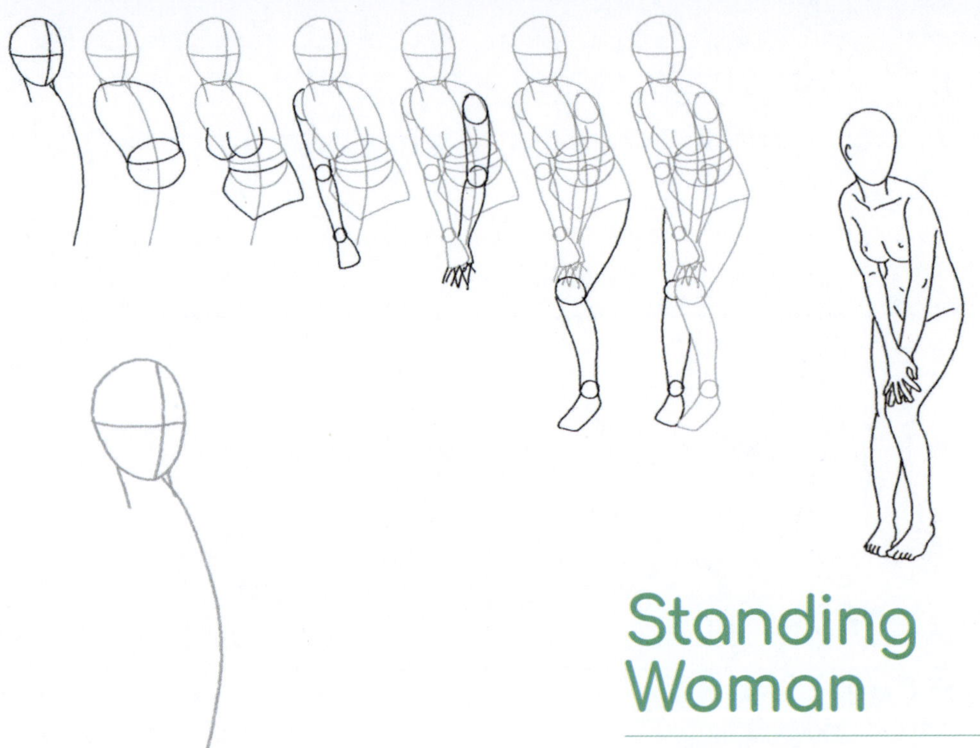

Standing
Woman

When the torso is arched,
the hands sink to the knees
and the shoulders tighten.

272 nd day

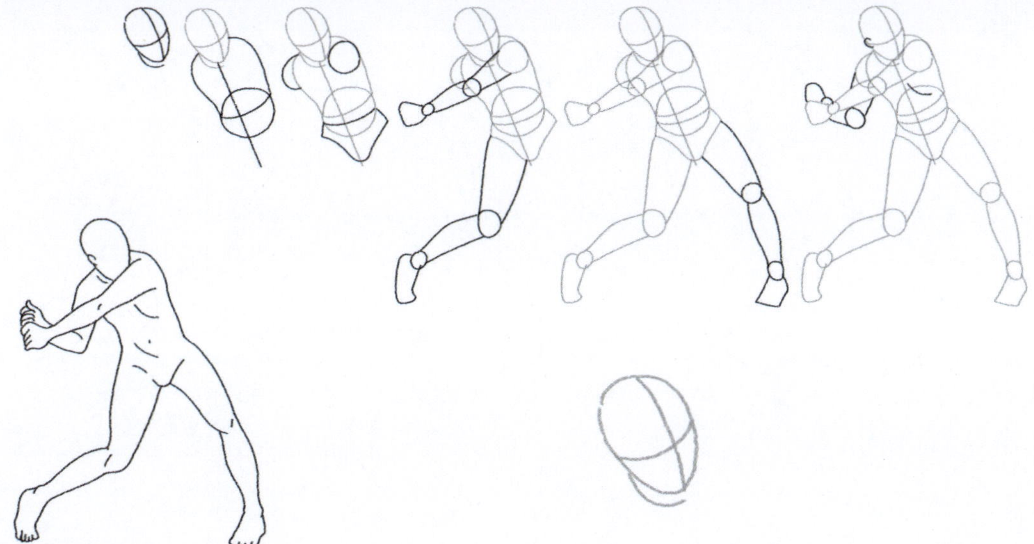

Baseball
Player

This entire pose twists the body on its axis, allowing the player to strike the ball with force.

273rd day

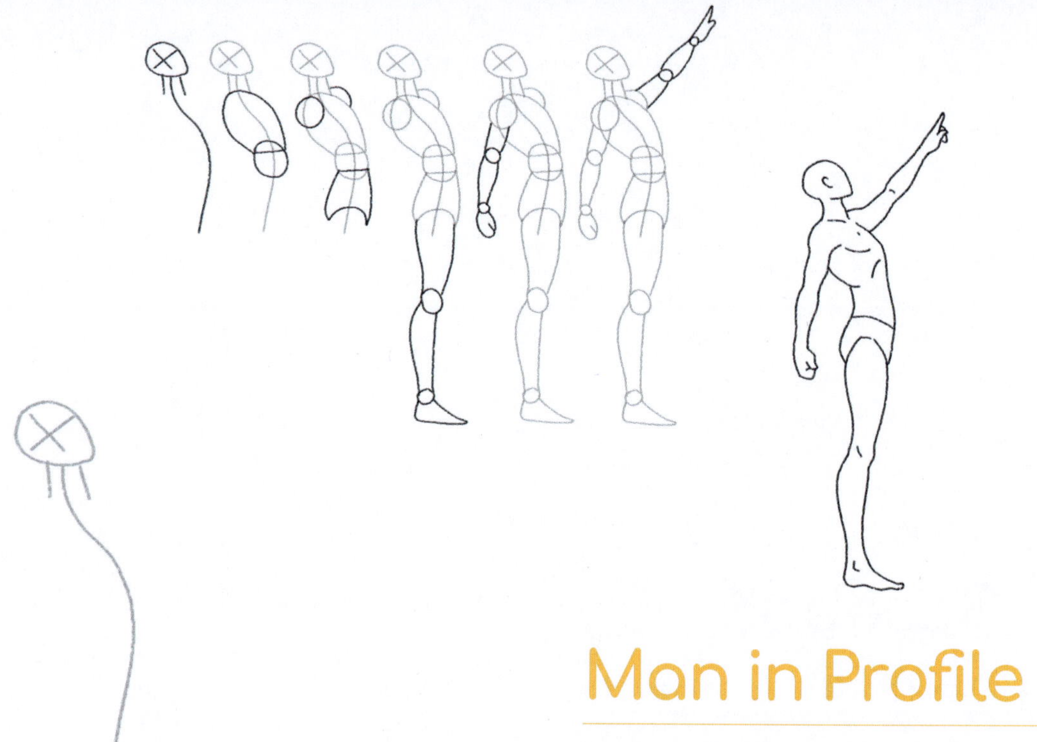

Man in Profile

This figure's raised arm stretches the torso, emphasizes the chest and tapers the stomach.

274th day

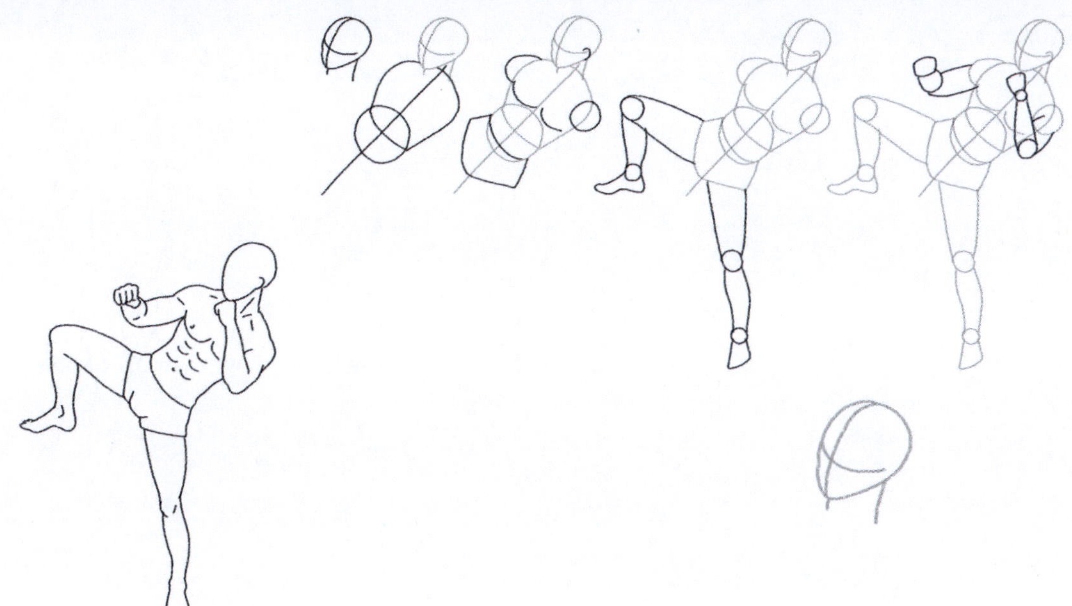

Kickboxer

This figure's weight is resting on his foot on the ground. The rest of the limbs are flexed, ready to extend into a punch or kick.

275th day

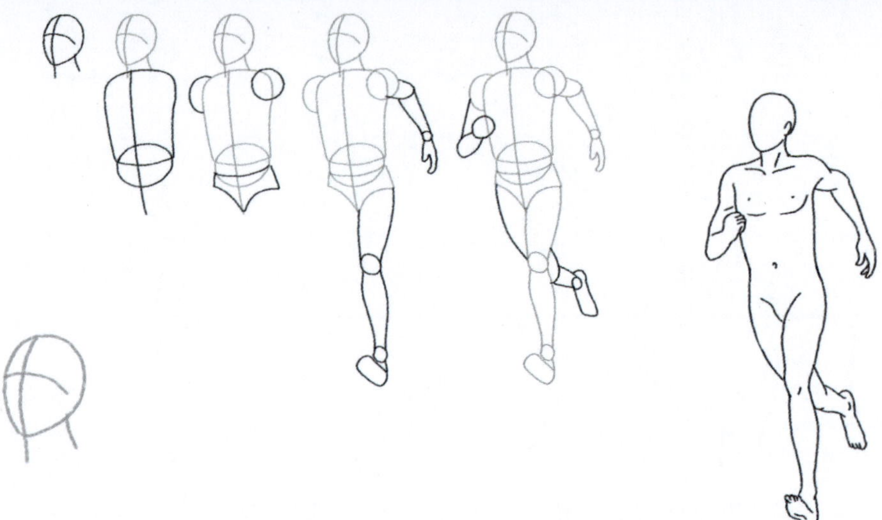

Running Man

When running, the opposite arms and legs move together in the same direction.

276th day

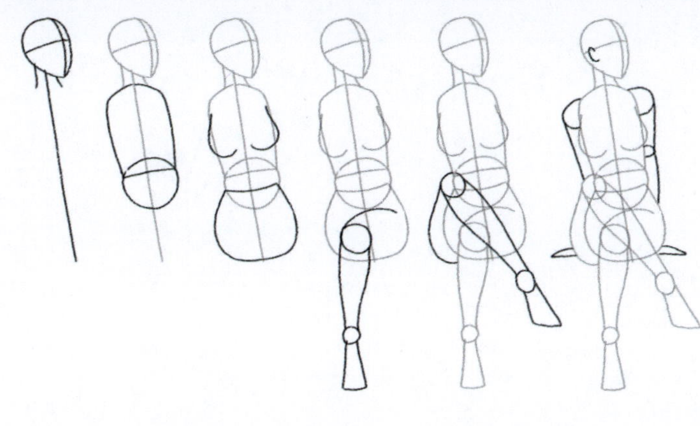

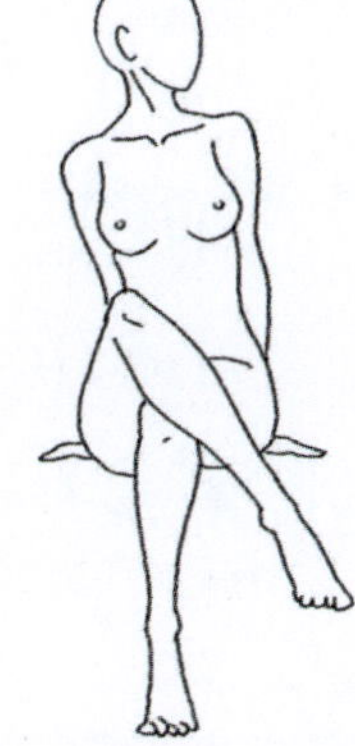

Seated Woman

This seated pose, viewed from the front, dramatically alters the proportions of the thighs. The arms are pressing down behind the torso, tightening the shoulders.

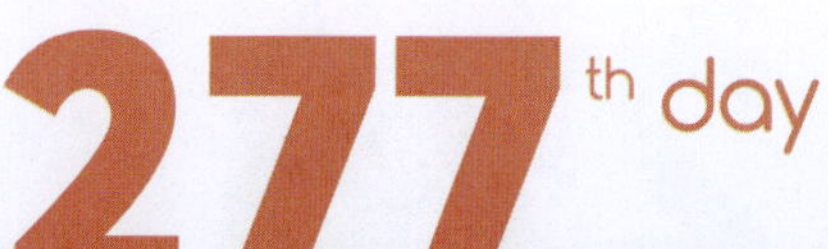

277 th day

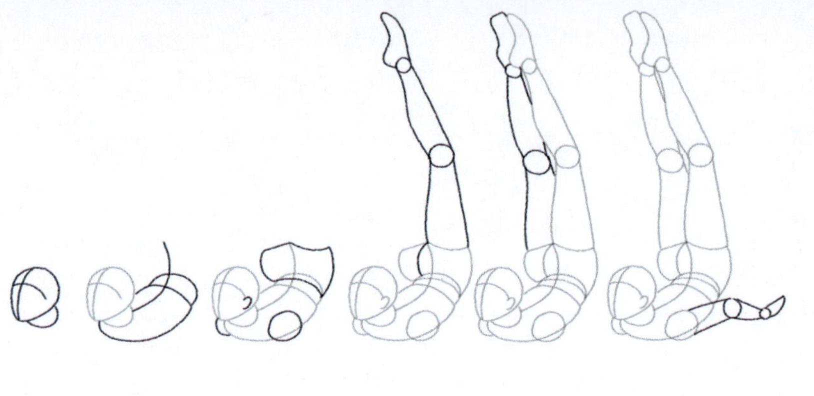

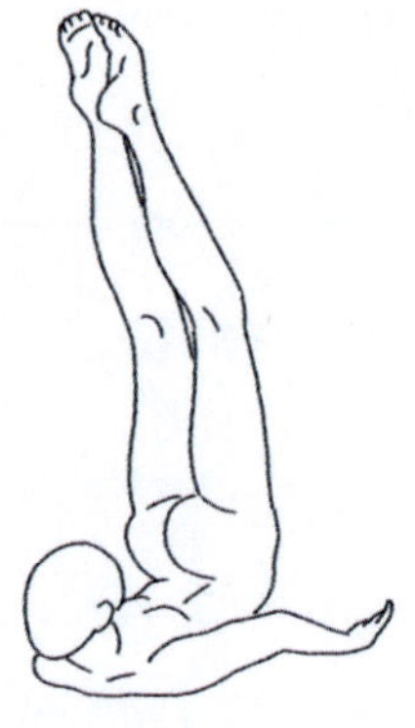

Acrobatic Woman

This figure's torso is oriented toward us along the ground, in perspective. The legs extend high in the air, facing us.

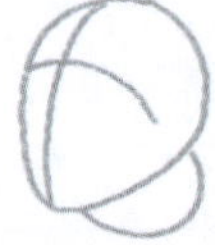

278 th day

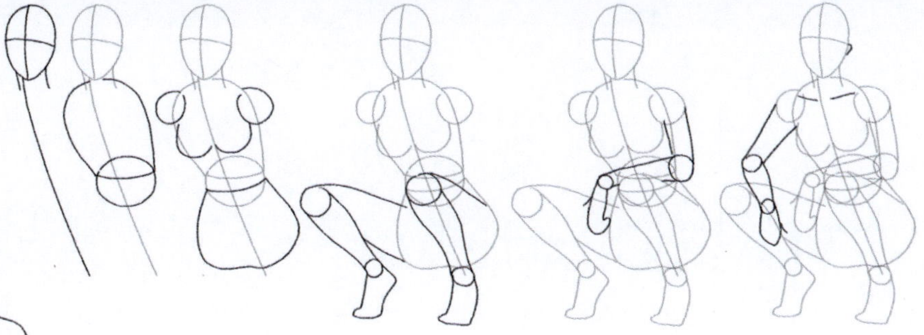

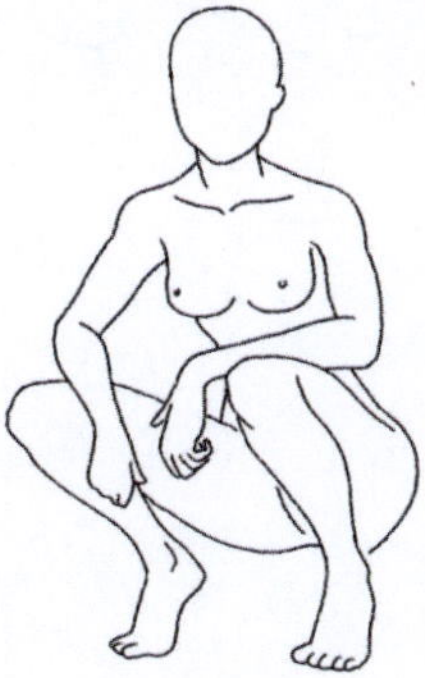

Crouching Woman

This crouched pose puts the figure's thighs in perspective, reducing their length.

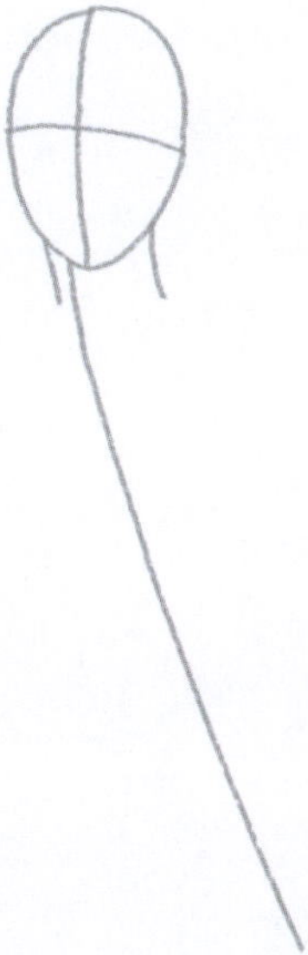

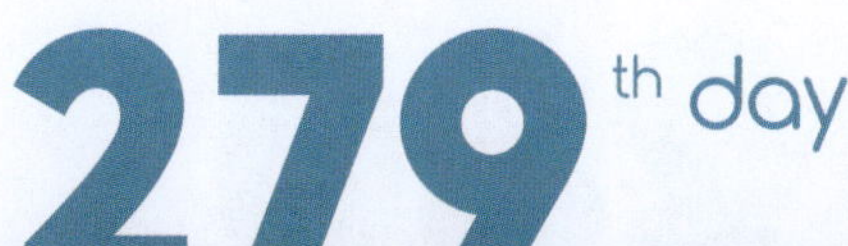

279 th day

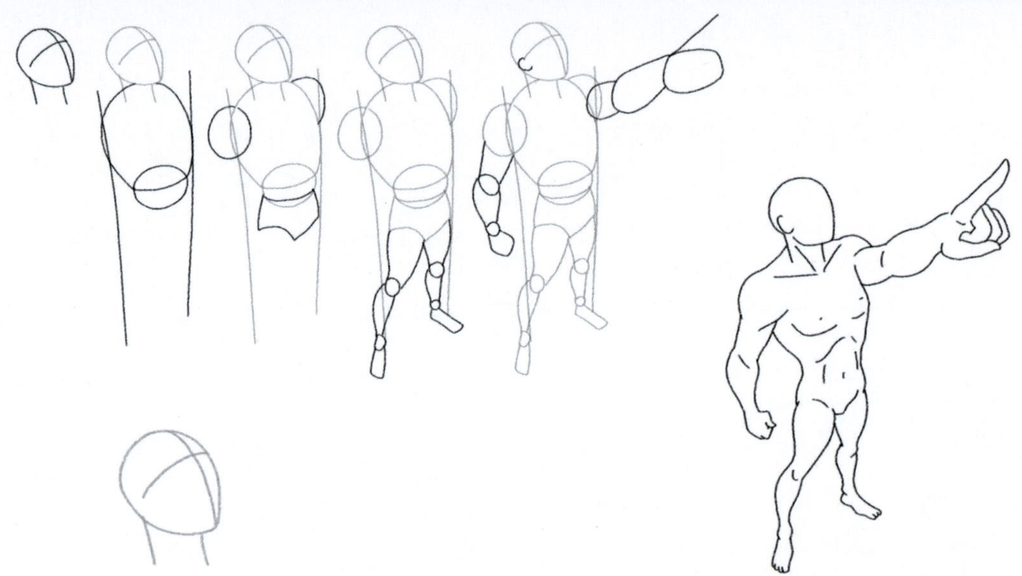

Standing Man

In this overhead view,
the downward flow of the
perspective is impressive
and exaggerated.

280th day

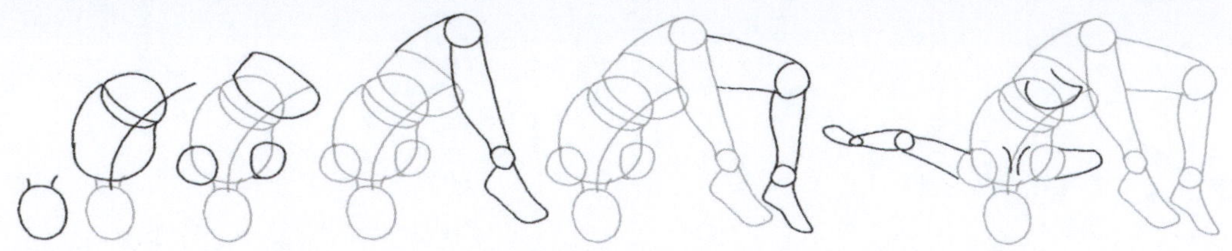

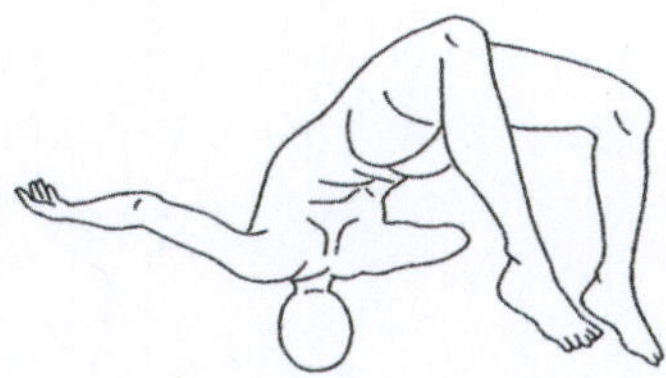

Backflip

This figure performing a backflip is being viewed from behind, so we are looking up at his back. The entire body is rotating on itself.

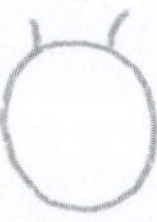

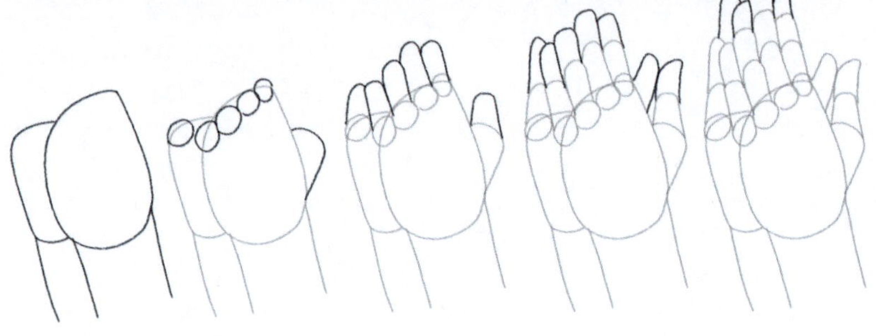

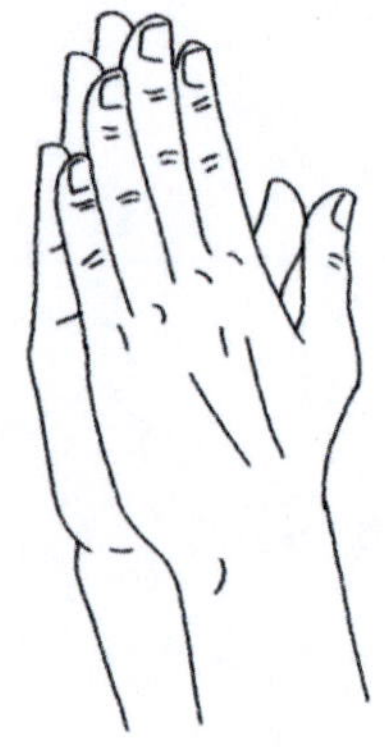

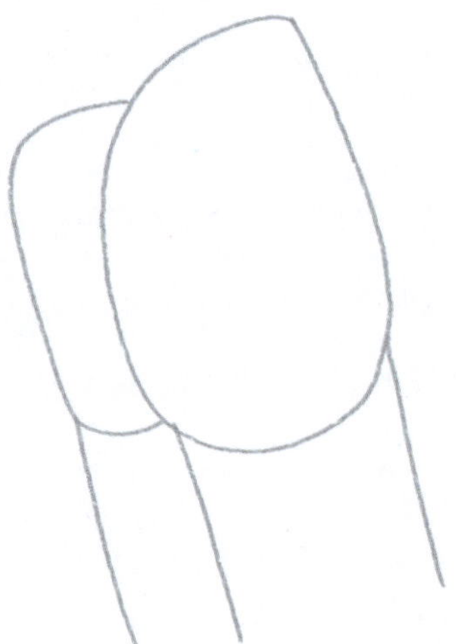

Joined Hands

In this pose, one hand almost completely obscures the other.

282 day

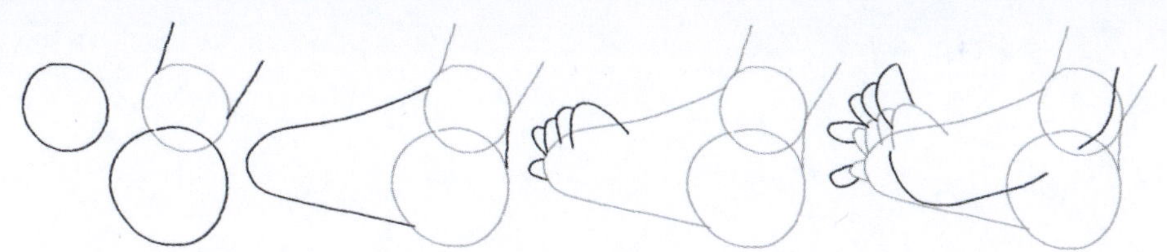

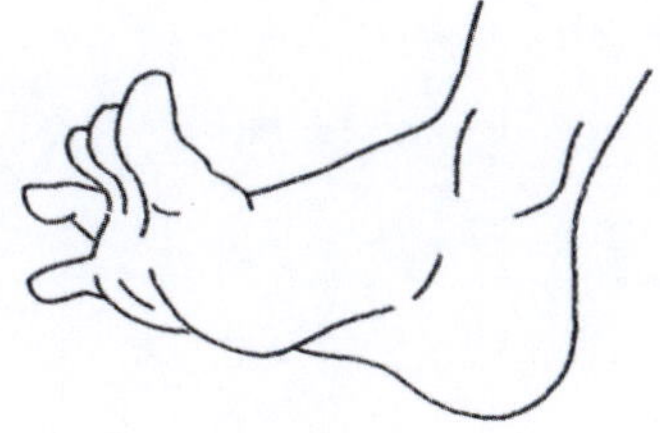

Foot

Each toe can twist in a different direction. When the toes are twisted this way, a bump is visible at the beginning of the arch of the foot.

283rd day

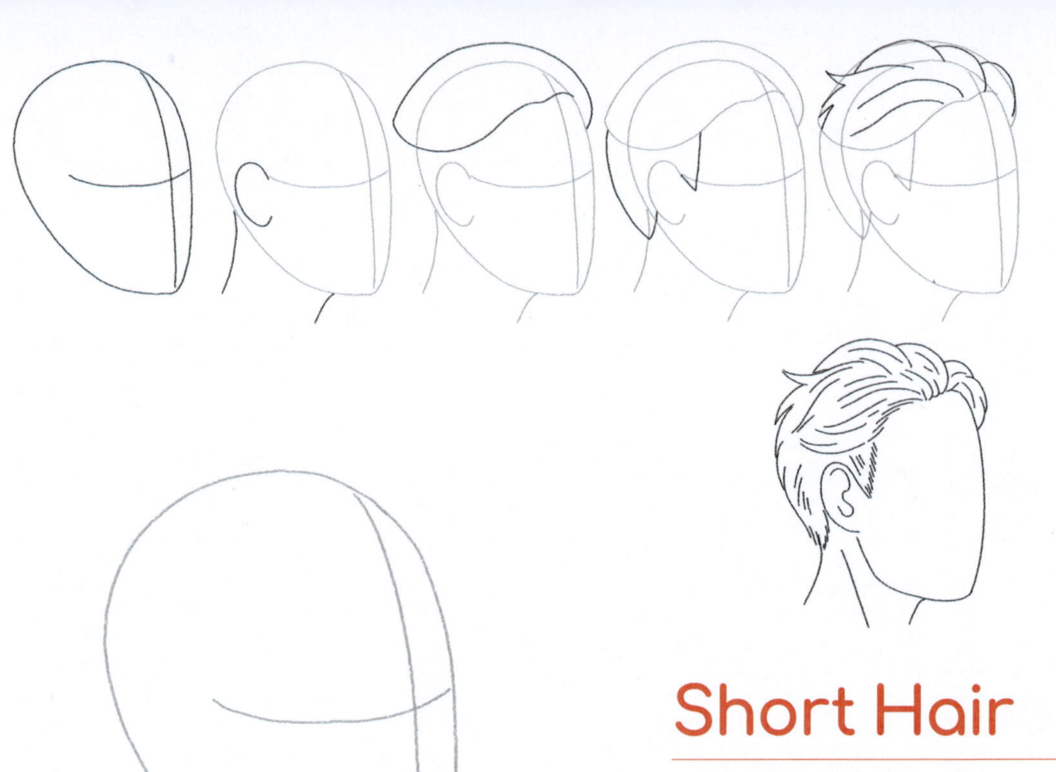

Short Hair

The shortest sections of this
figure's hair are finished with
small strokes. The longer
sections are highlighted with
longer, more flowing lines.

284 th day

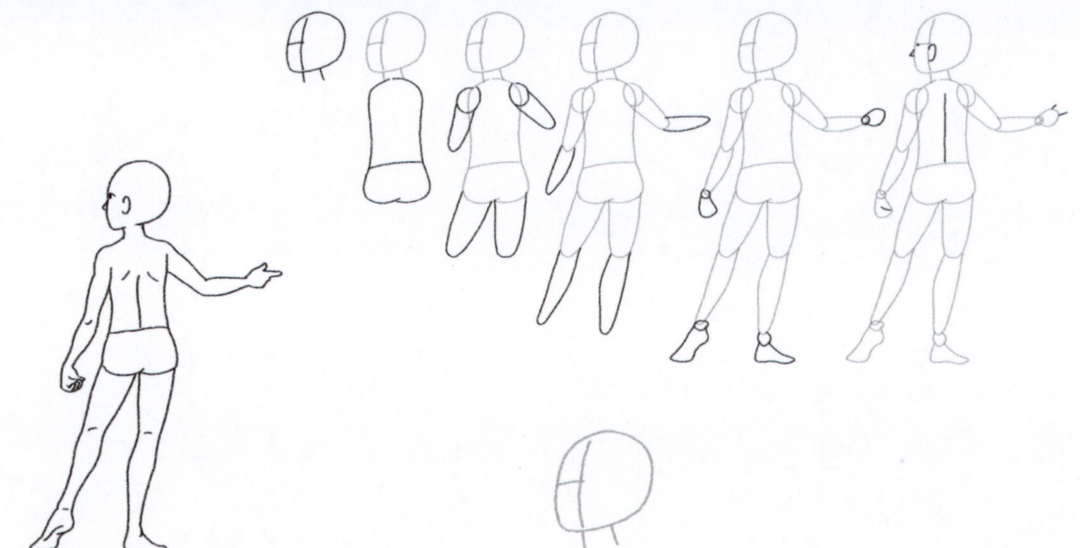

Child from the Back

When viewed from the back, the body of a young child has few distinct forms. Only the head, quite large in relation to the rest of the body, indicates that this figure is a child.

285 th day

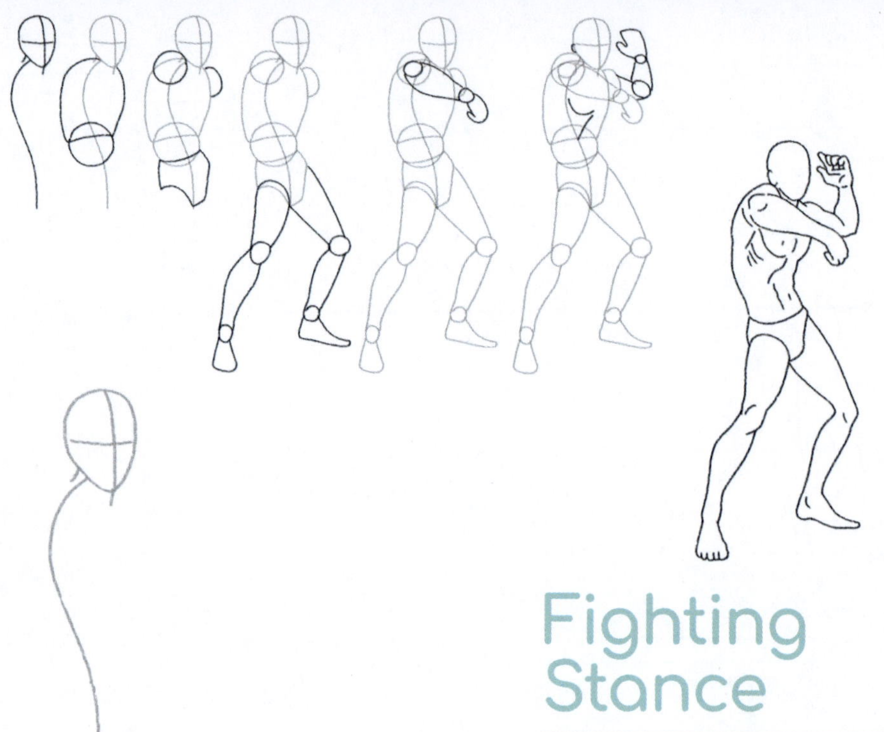

Fighting Stance

In this dynamic pose, the arms are only partially visible and in perspective. One shoulder is raised, and the hips point in the opposite direction.

286th day

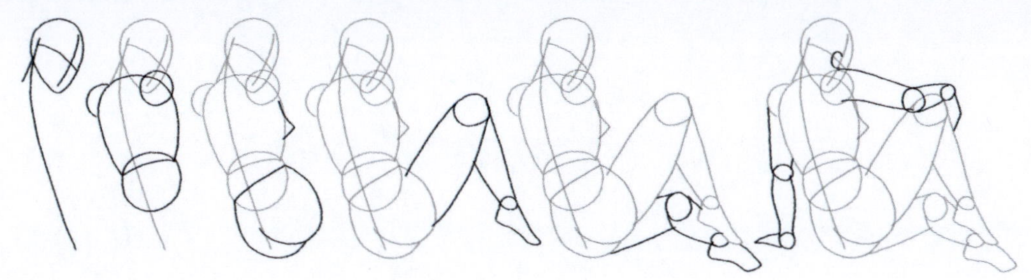

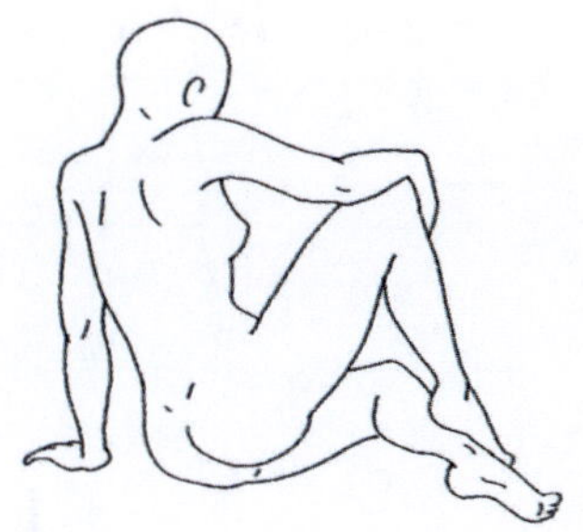

Seated Woman

The perspective drawn here
reduces the proportions of the
leg that is resting on the ground.

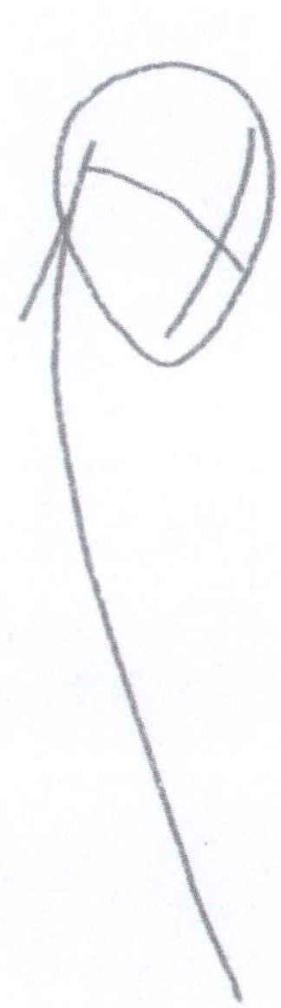

287 th day

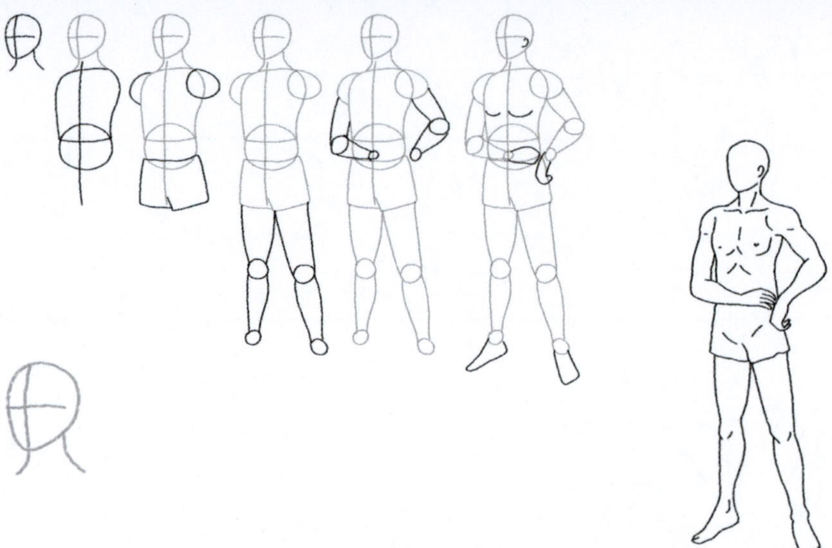

Standing Man

The folded arm highlights the
volume of the muscles.

288 th day

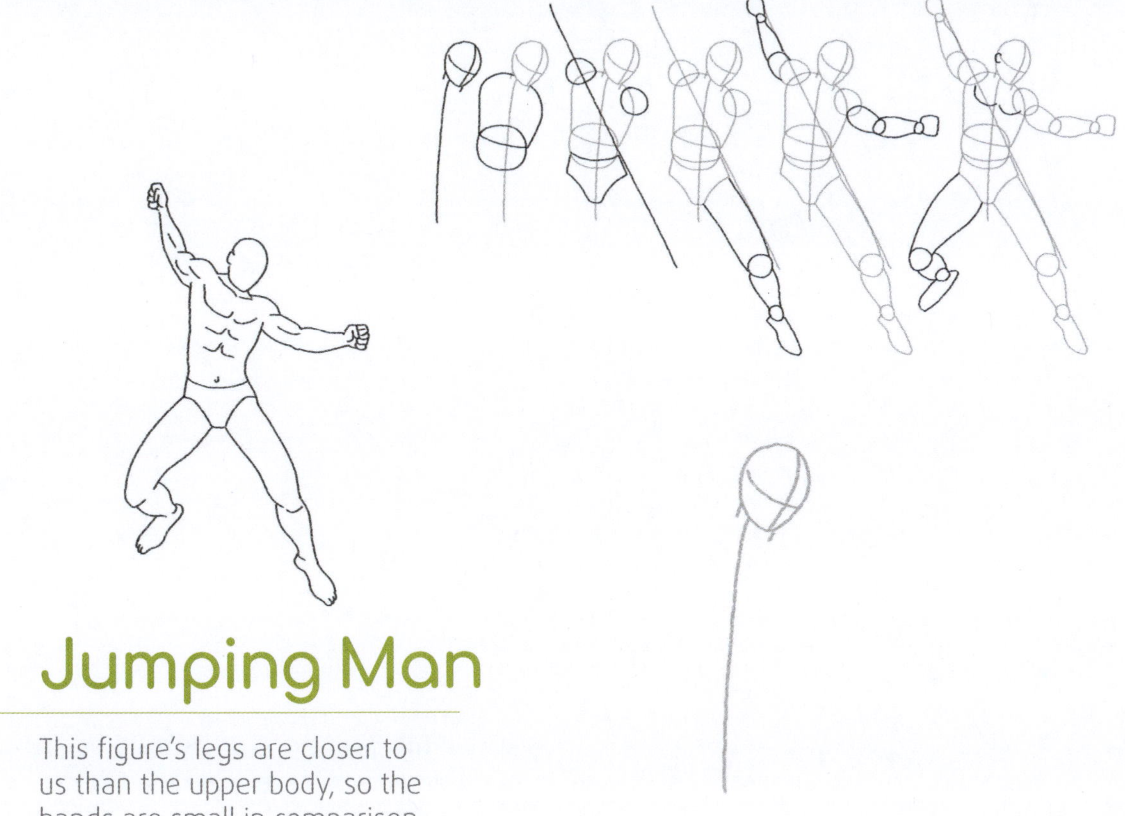

Jumping Man

This figure's legs are closer to us than the upper body, so the hands are small in comparison.

289th **day**

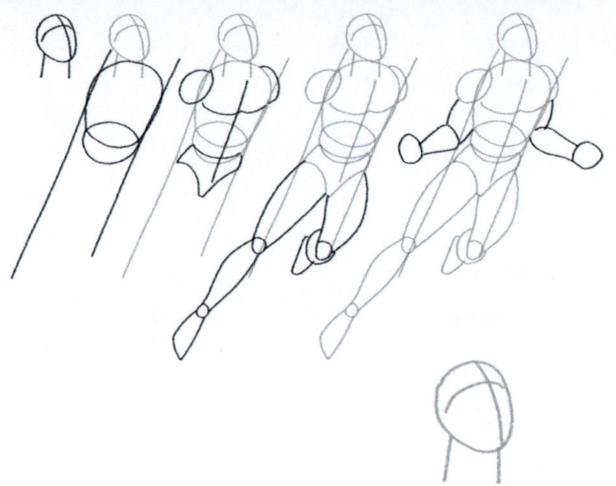

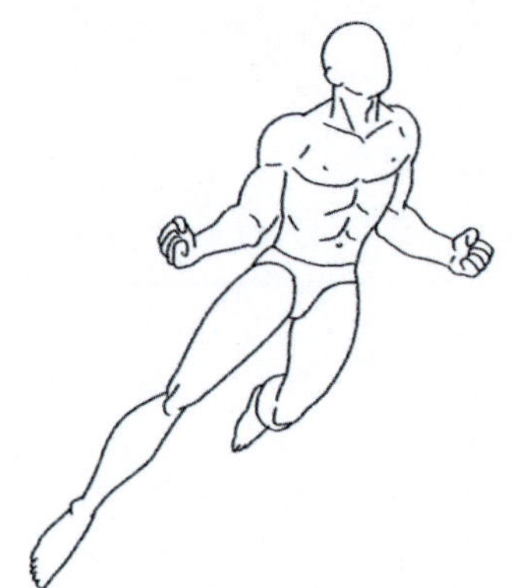

Jumping Man

In this projecting pose, the feet
seem to be far behind the figure
and quite small.

290th day

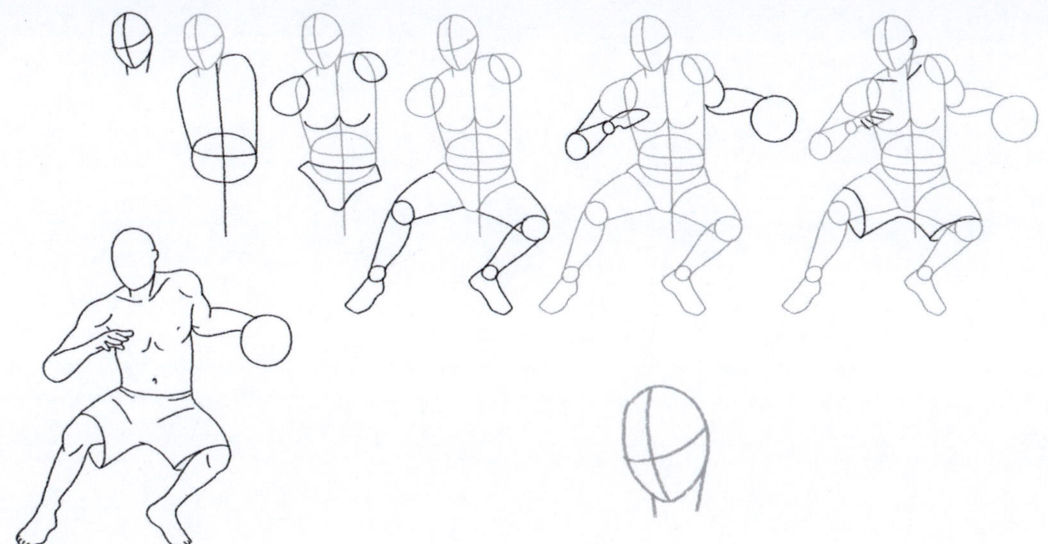

Basketball
Player

This figure is keeping his legs
flexed as he moves. Viewed
from the front, the legs
are in perspective and look
relatively small.

291st day

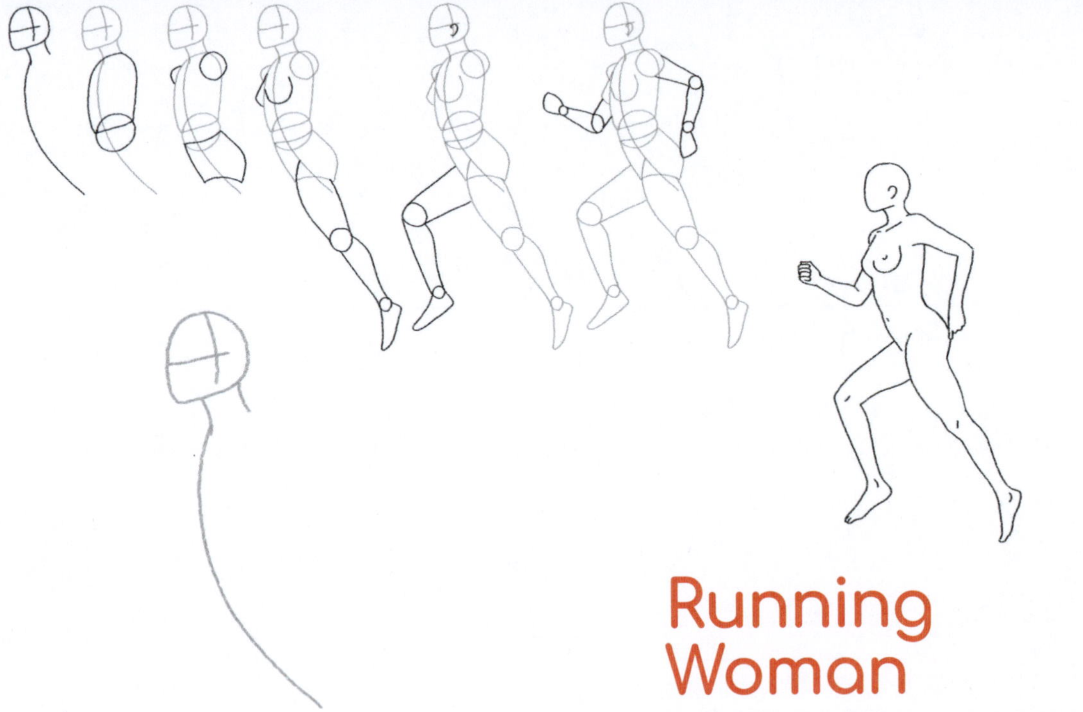

Running
Woman

To project a figure forward, draw one leg straight and the other flexed, with the feet pointed.

292nd day

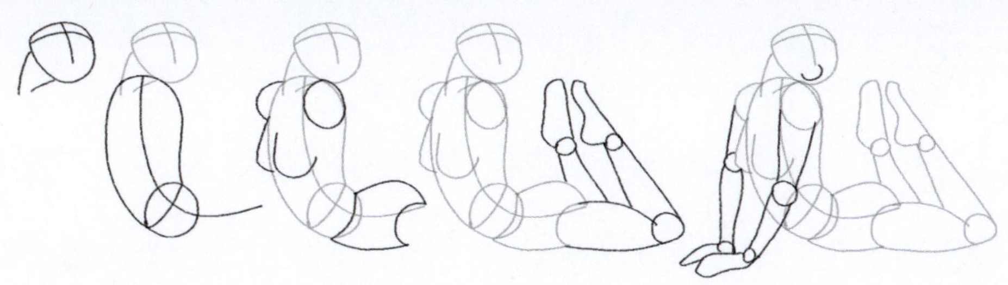

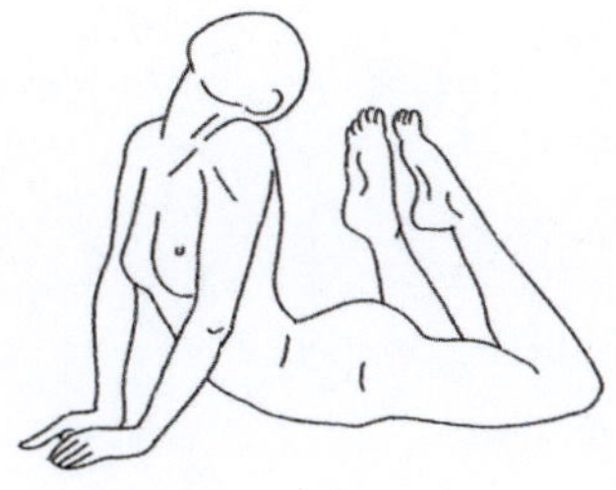

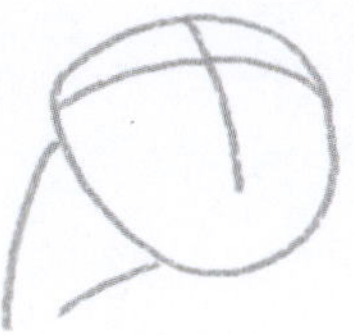

Gymnast

To touch her head with her feet,
this figure is folding her back into
a deep curve.

293rd day

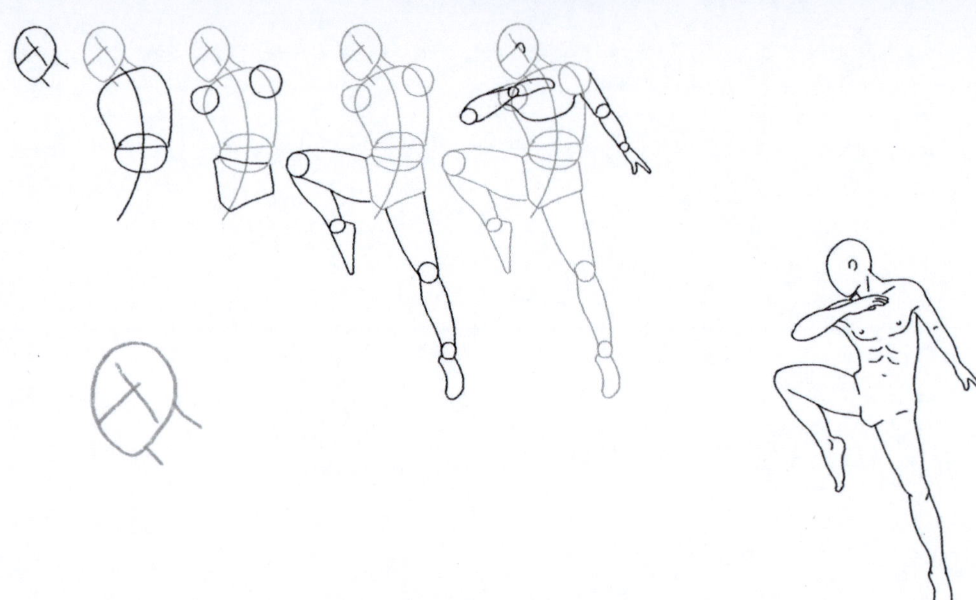

Dancer

This figure is projecting upward while pivoting. One leg serves as an axis point and remains straight.

294th day

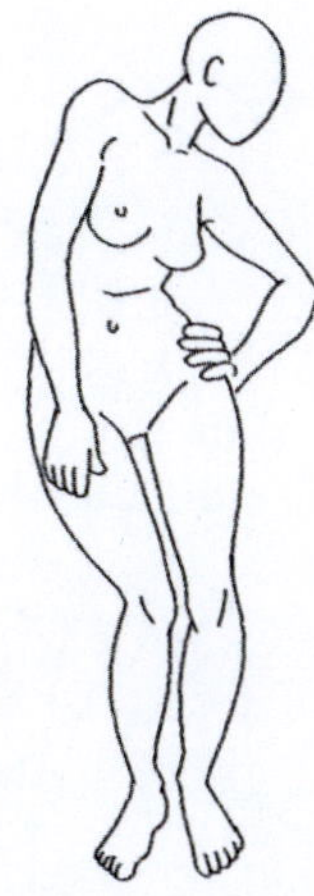

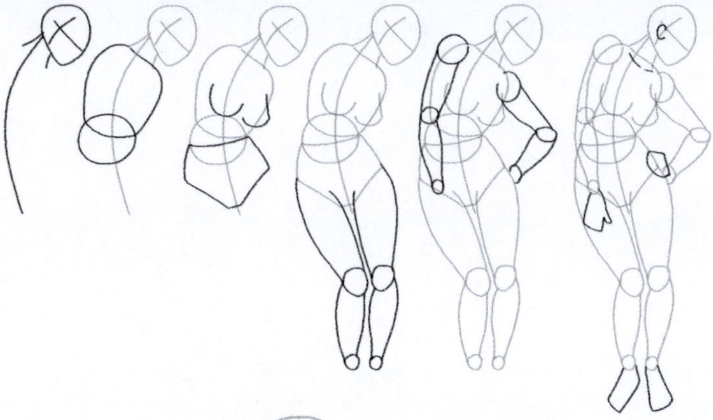

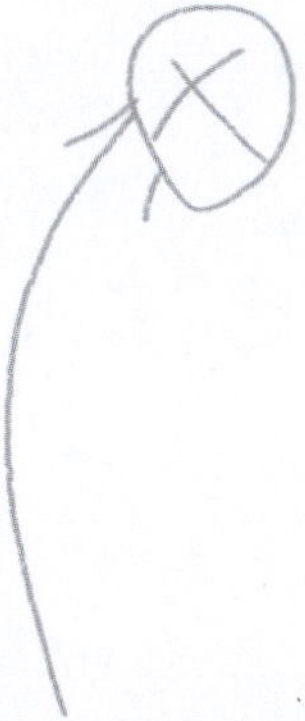

Standing Woman

This figure's entire body is articulated into an S shape. The deep sway of the hips compresses one side of the torso and stretches the other side.

295 th day

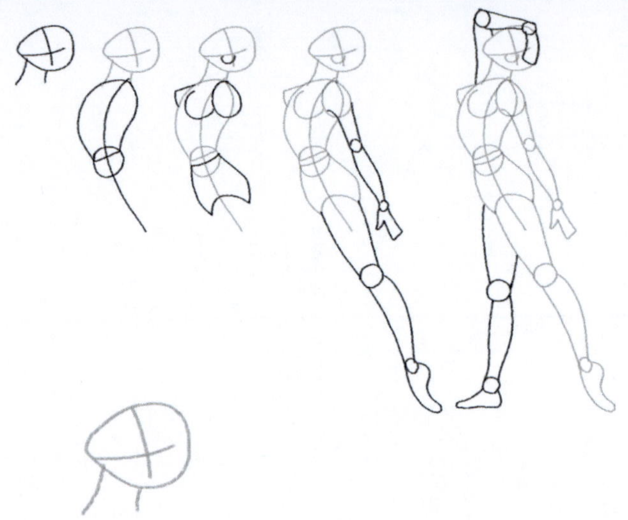

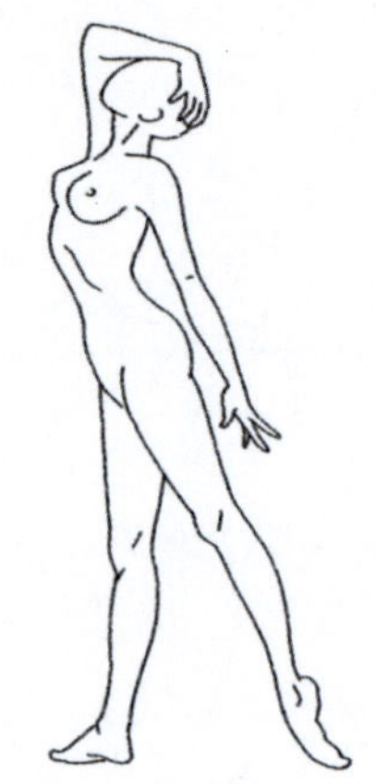

Dancer

The figure's whole body is
stretching upward, with the
torso erect and one arm
folded over the face.

296 th day

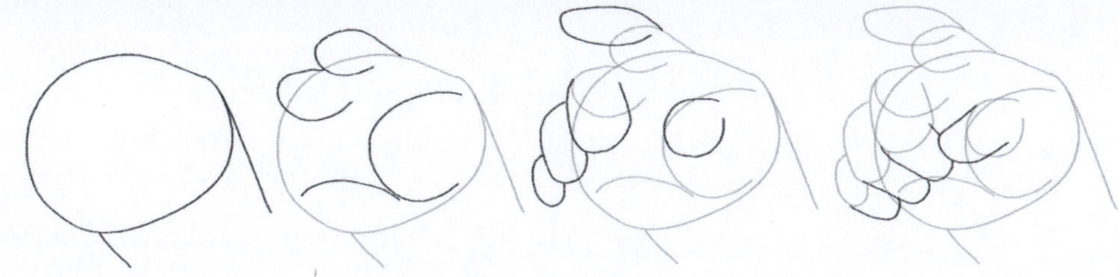

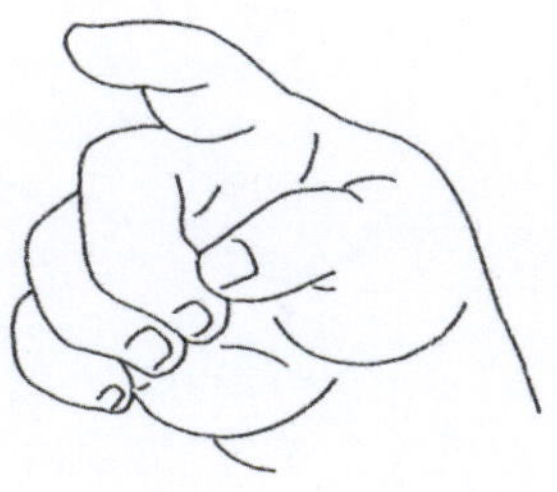

Child's Hand

A child's fingers are so short and chubby that they seem to have fewer bones than that of an adult hand.

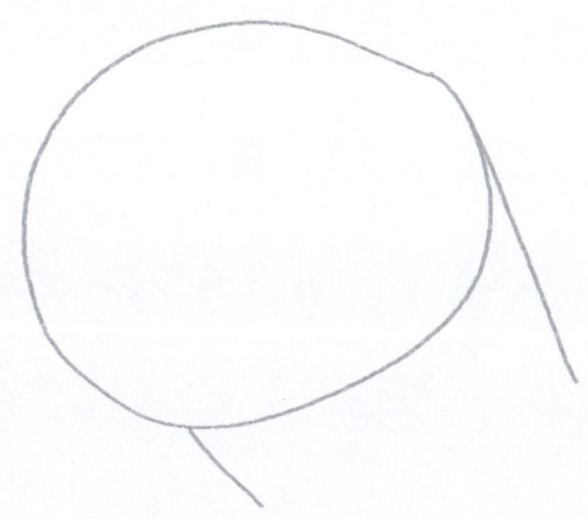

297th day

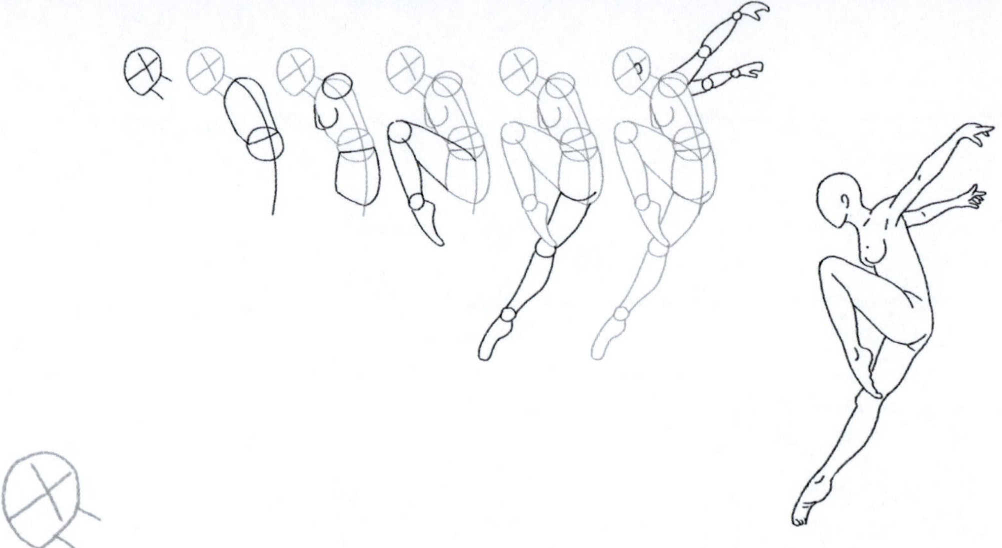

Jumping Woman

This pose points like an arrow toward the foot on the ground. The arms are thrust back, stretching the torso.

298th day

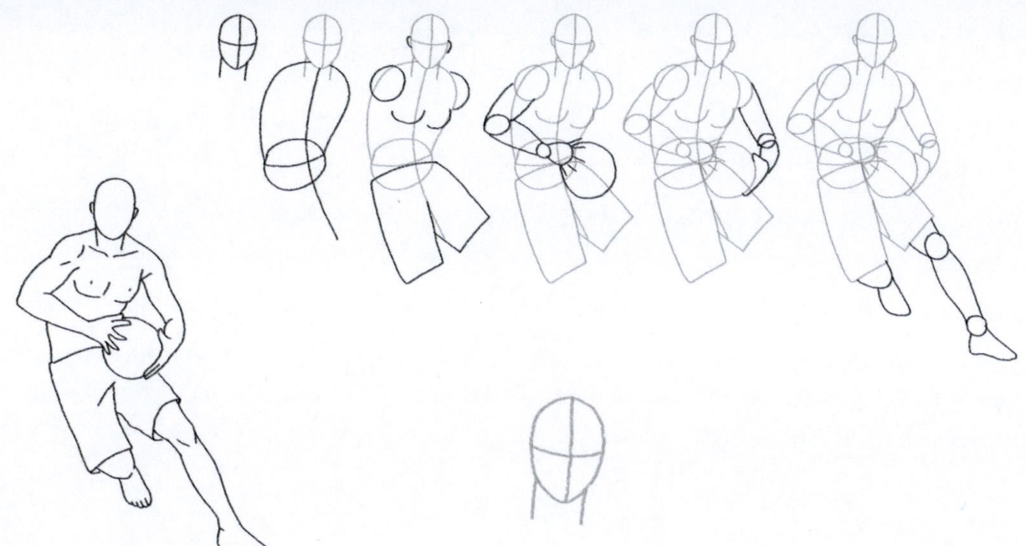

Basketball
Player

In this forward-running pose, the bent leg is in perspective and therefore half hidden.

299

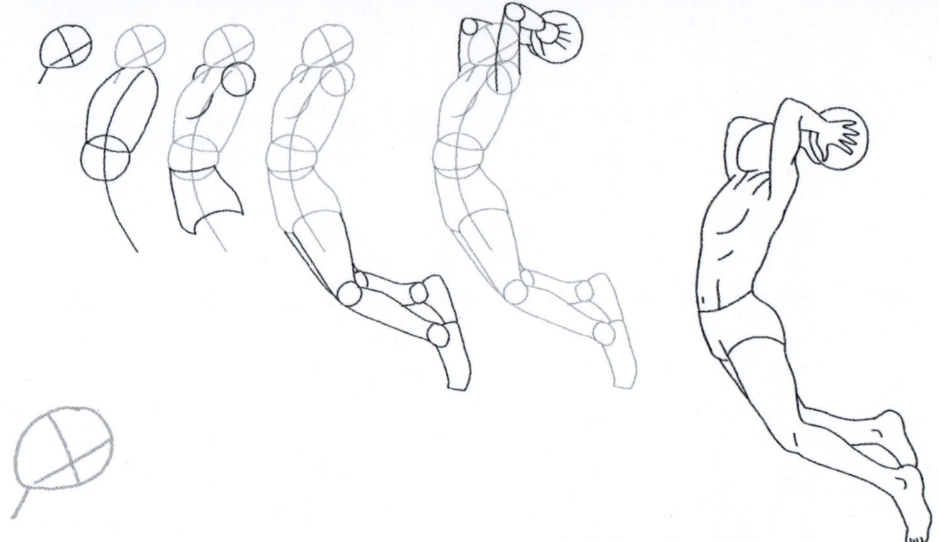

Basketball Player

This figure is projecting his body upward and forward, in an arc, and reaching his arms back to give himself momentum.

300th **day**

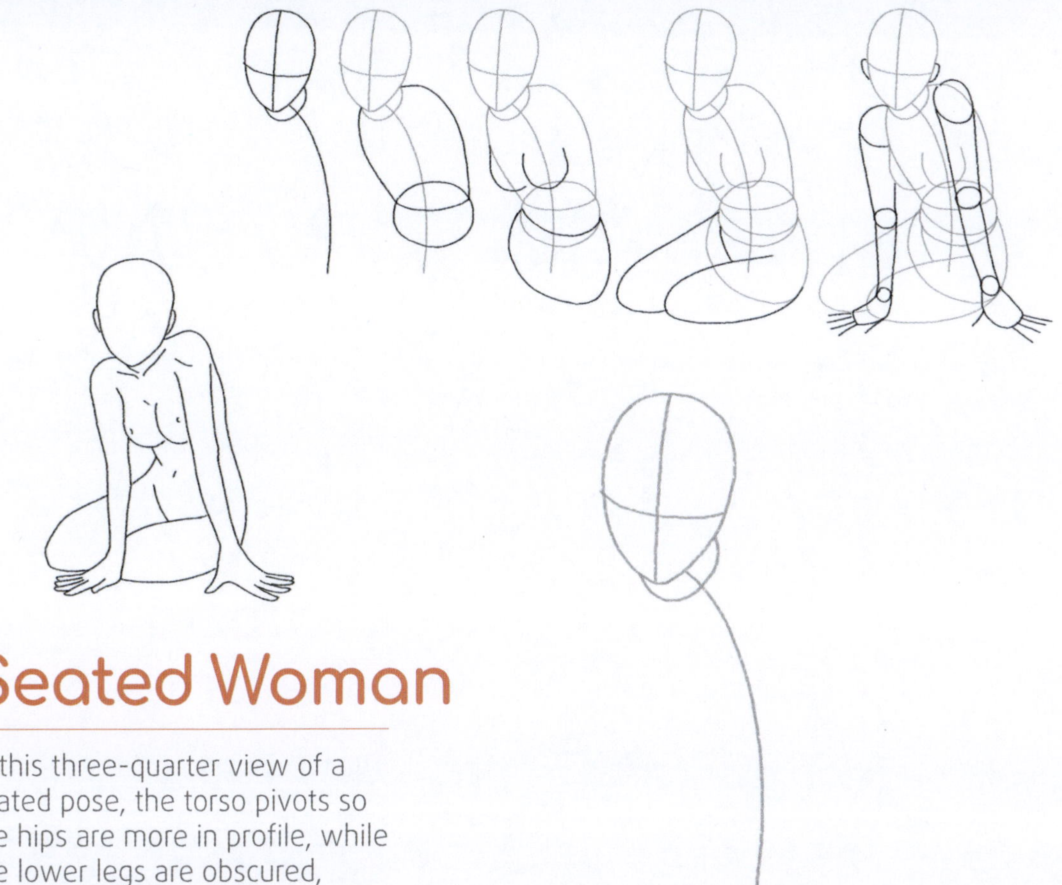

Seated Woman

In this three-quarter view of a
seated pose, the torso pivots so
the hips are more in profile, while
the lower legs are obscured,
tucked behind the thighs.

301st day

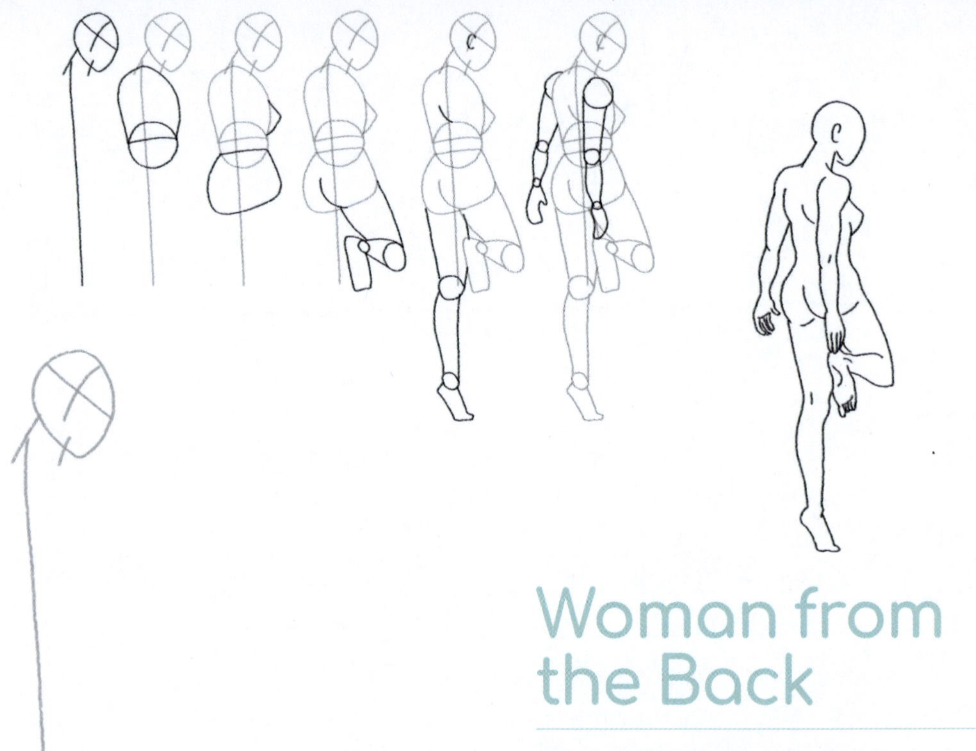

Woman from
the Back

The hand grasping the foot creates a pronounced sway to the hips and twists the torso toward the heel of the foot. The calf of the bent leg is narrowed by the perspective.

302nd day

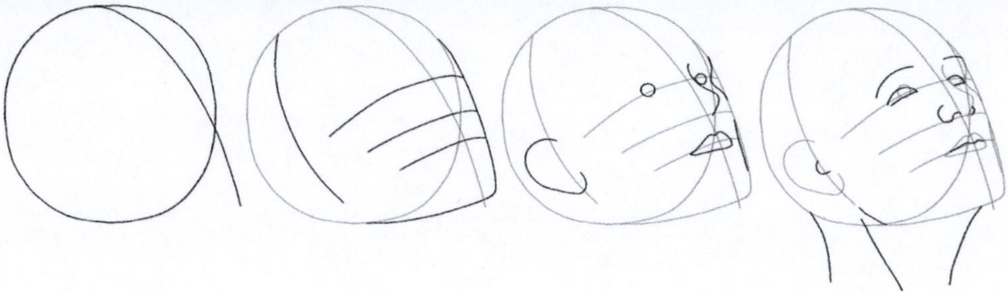

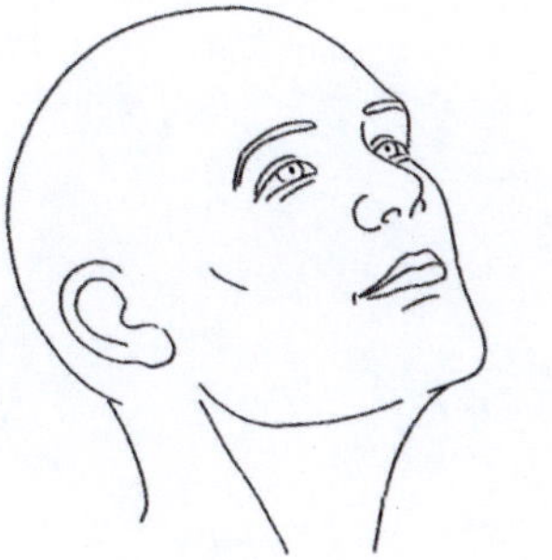

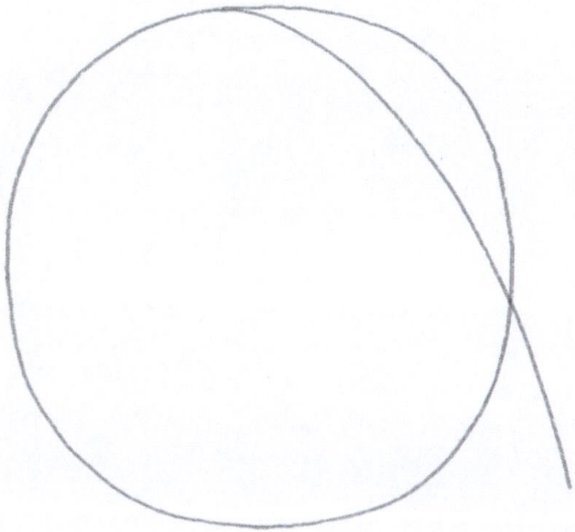

Man's Head

In this three-quarter view of a
head turned upward, the lines
curve upward as well. The
figure's face is sharply cut along
one side.

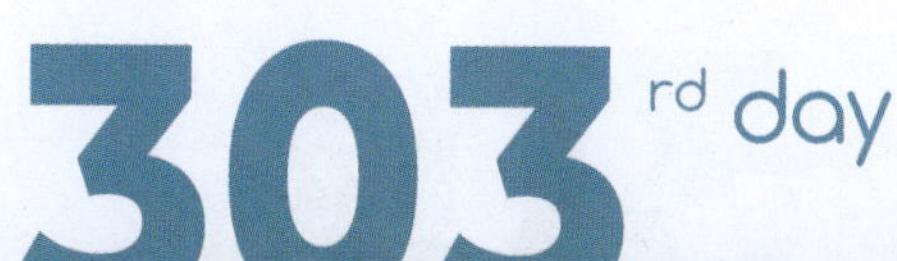

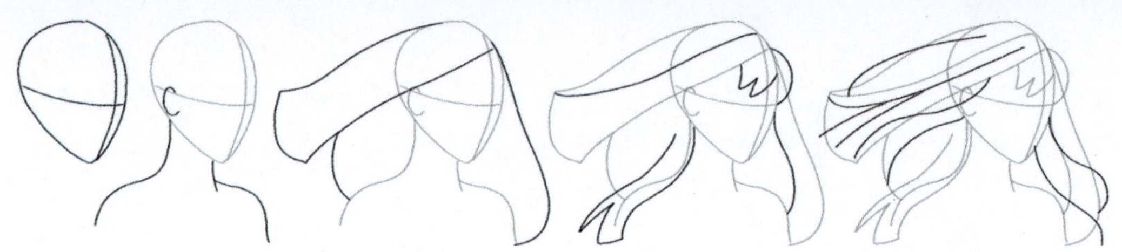

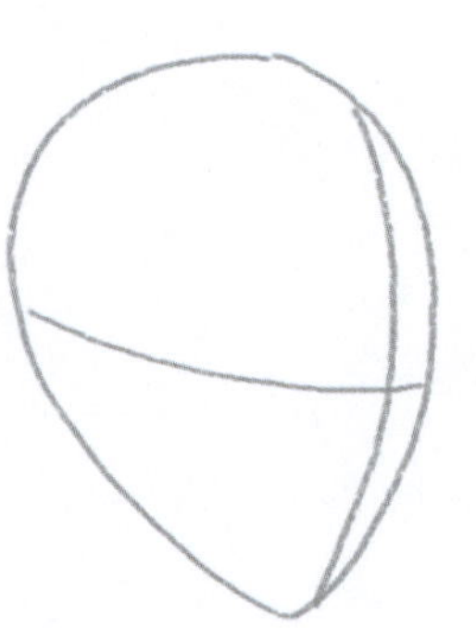

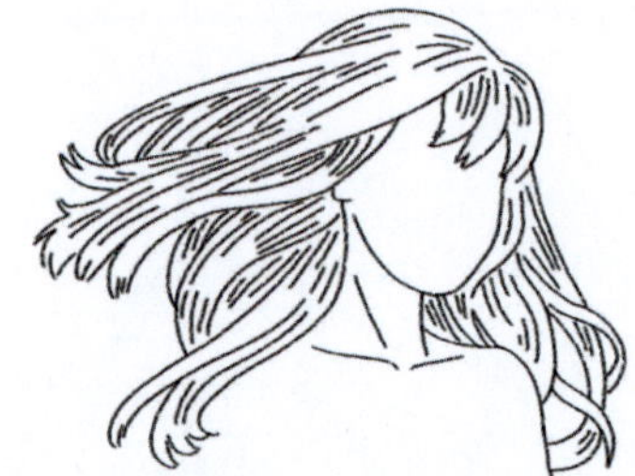

Wind-Blown Hair

Some strands of hair on this figure's head are longer and less defined, while others are shorter and covered with lines. This creates variation in the overall movement of the hair.

304 th day

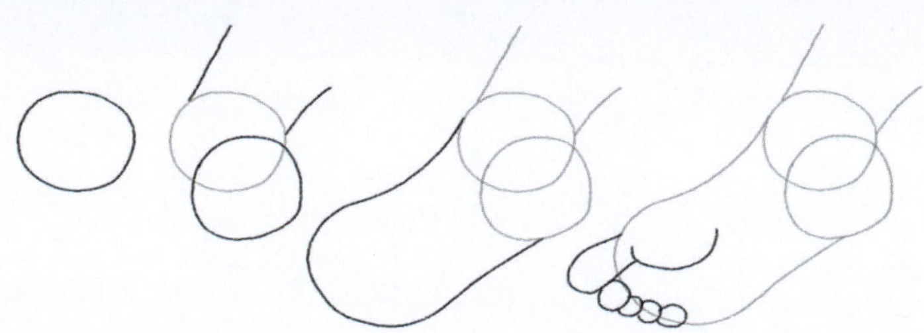

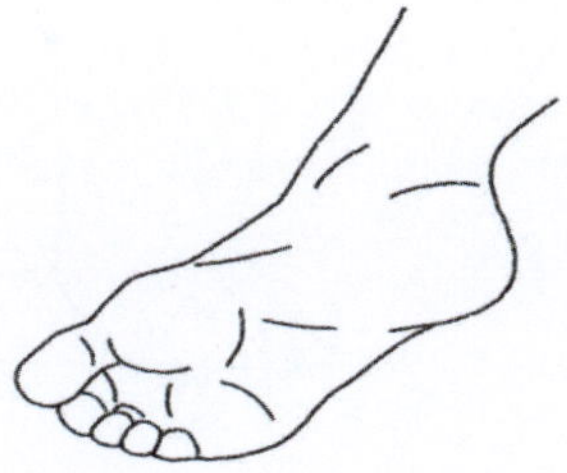

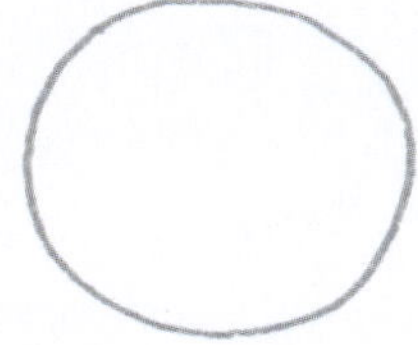

Foot

The fleshy parts of the sole of
the foot can be highlighted with
curved lines.

305 th day

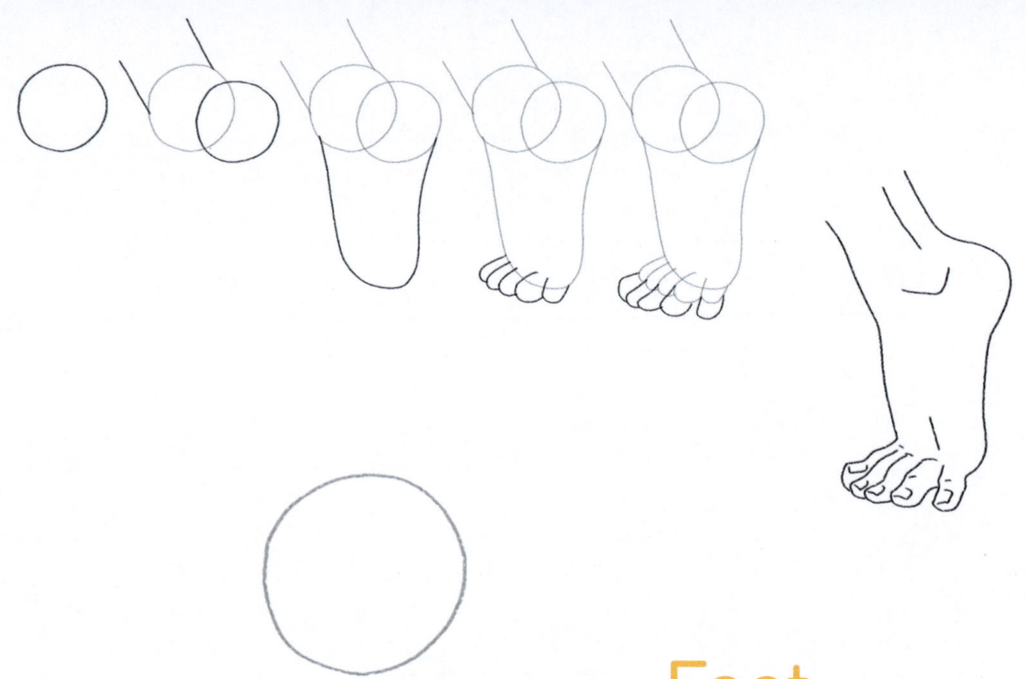

Foot

A foot performing a walking
motion completes the movement
by unrolling the toes.

306th day

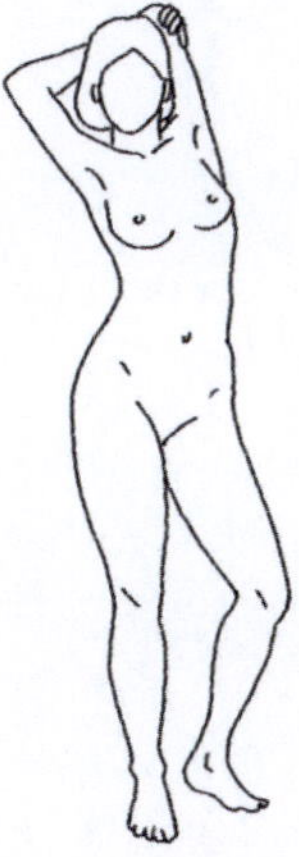

Standing
Woman

By pulling one arm up, this figure
is tilting her shoulders in that
direction. The sway of the hips
points them in the opposite
direction, bending one leg.

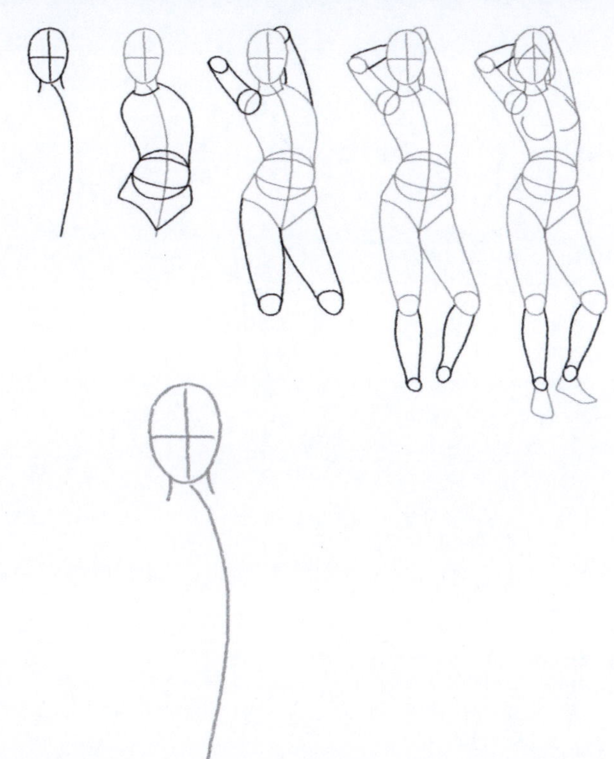

307th day

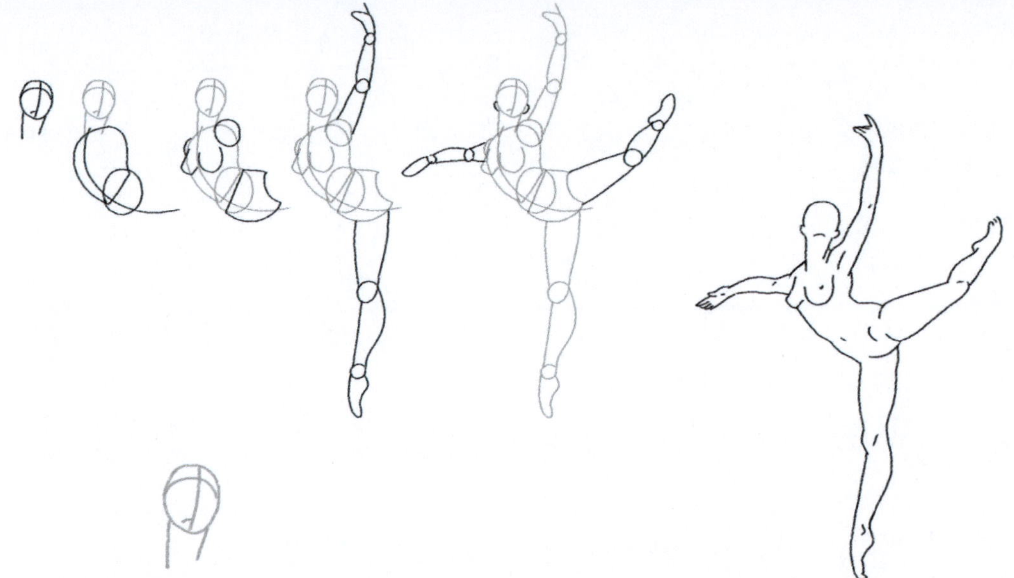

Dancer

The arm and leg that extend
upward are stretching and
arching the torso. The other leg
is extended to the ground, and
the other arm is in perspective,
reaching back.

308 th day

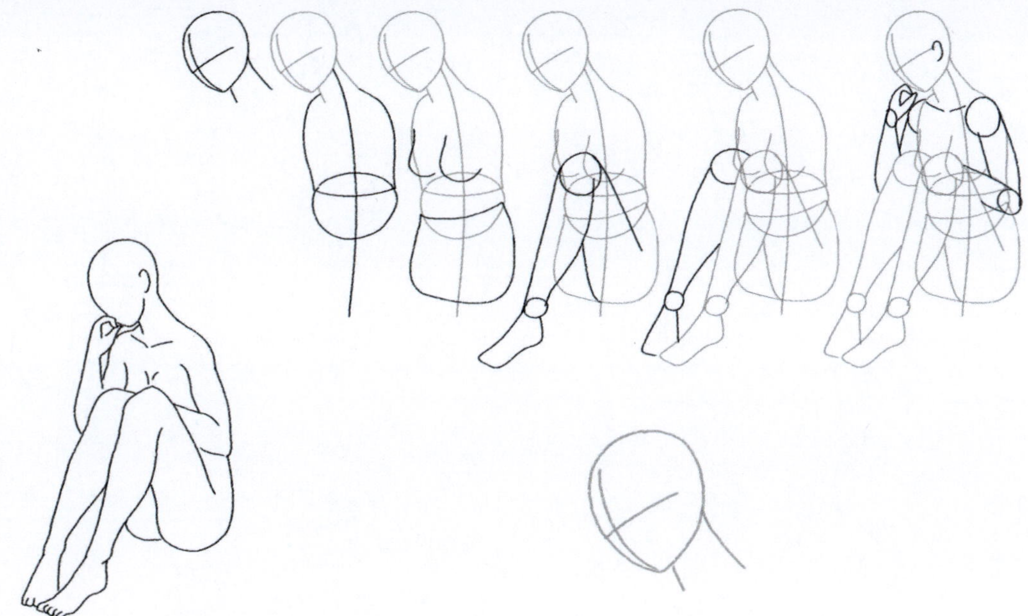

Seated Woman

This very compact pose obscures
much of the arms and torso.

309th day

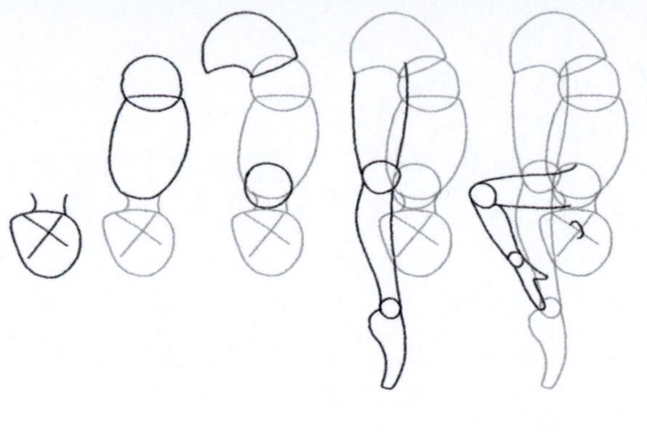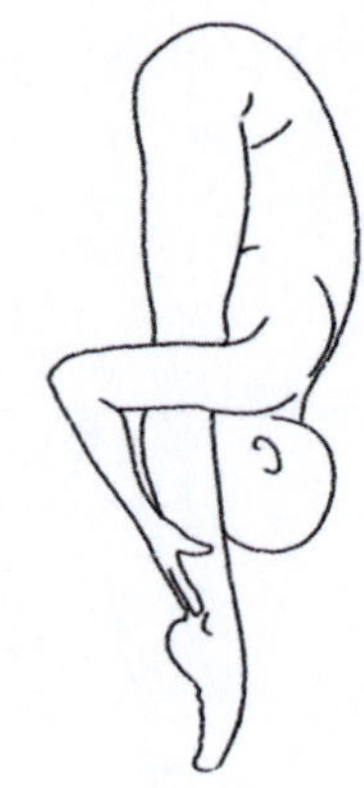

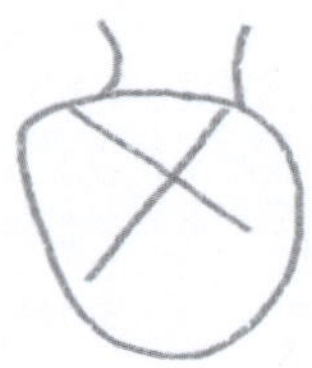

Diver

This figure's body is folded in half and shown in profile. The legs are tense and straight.

310th **day**

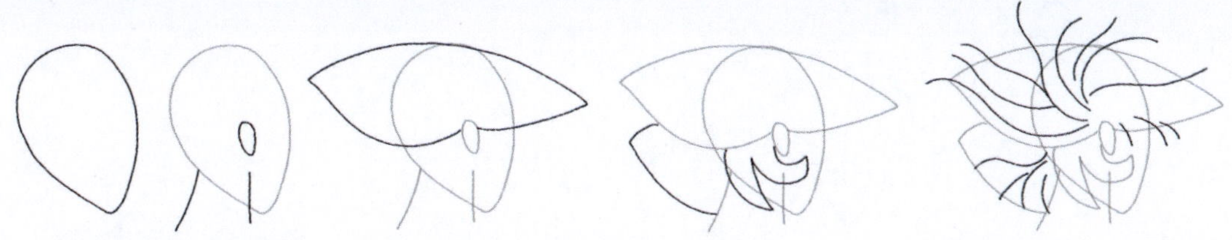

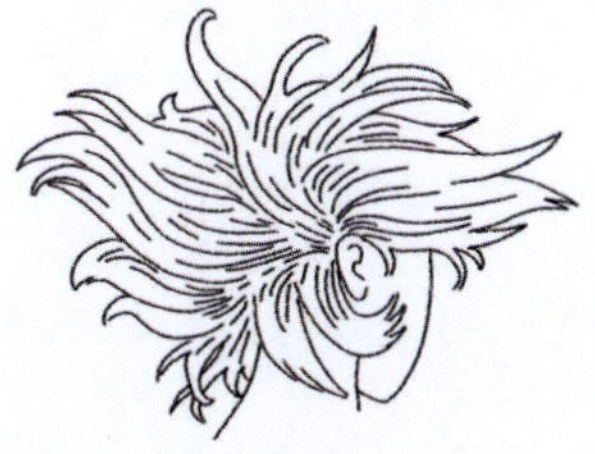

Wind-Blown Hair

A strong gust of wind or very quick movement will separate the hair into a circle around a point.

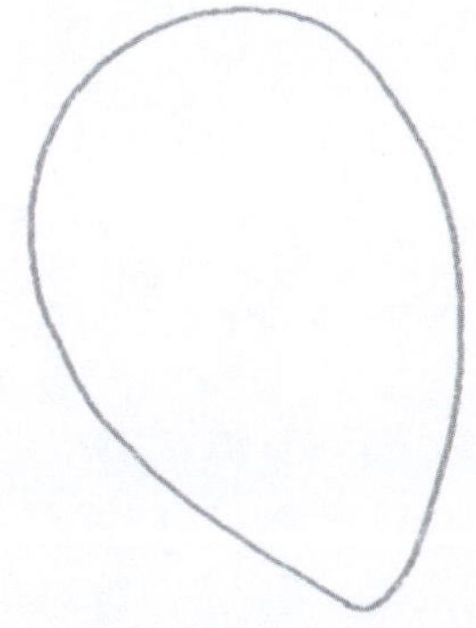

311th day

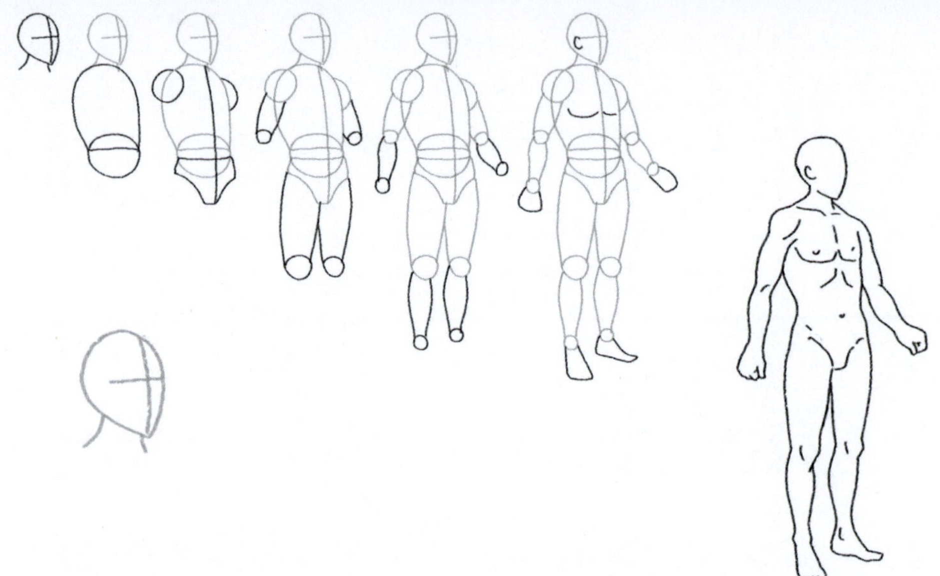

Standing Man

The figure in this three-quarter view is depicted from a fairly low angle, emphasizing the perspective. The distance between the rear shoulder and foot seems shorter than that between the front shoulder and foot.

312th day

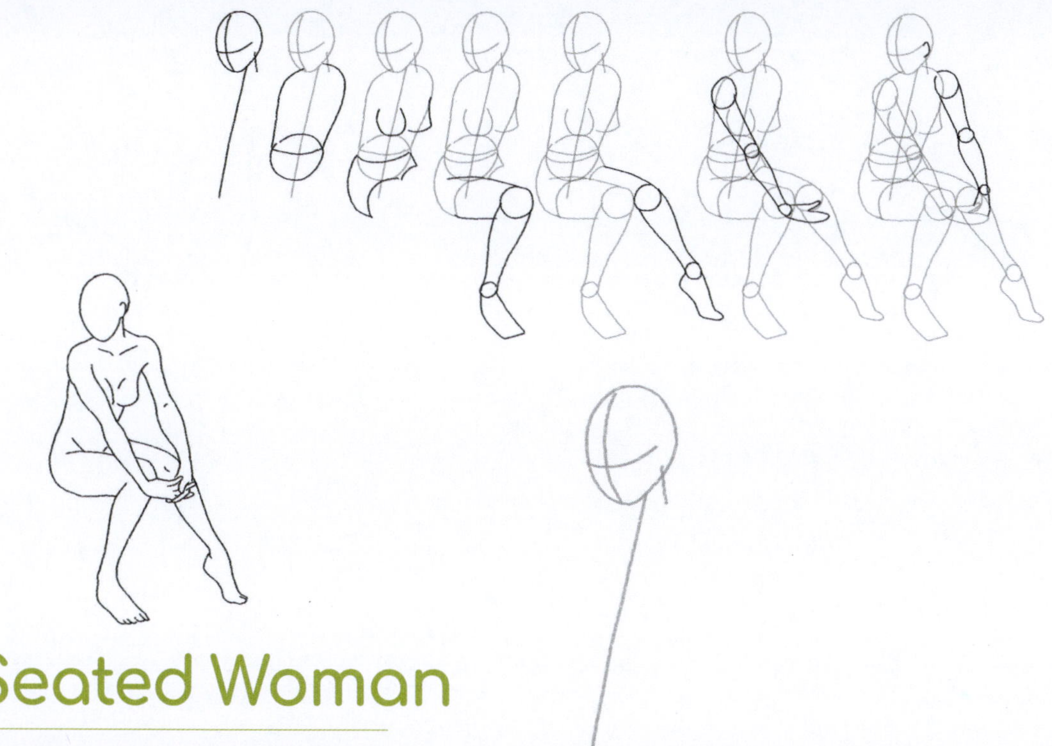

Seated Woman

The three-quarter perspective of this figure partially obscures the length of the thighs.

313th day

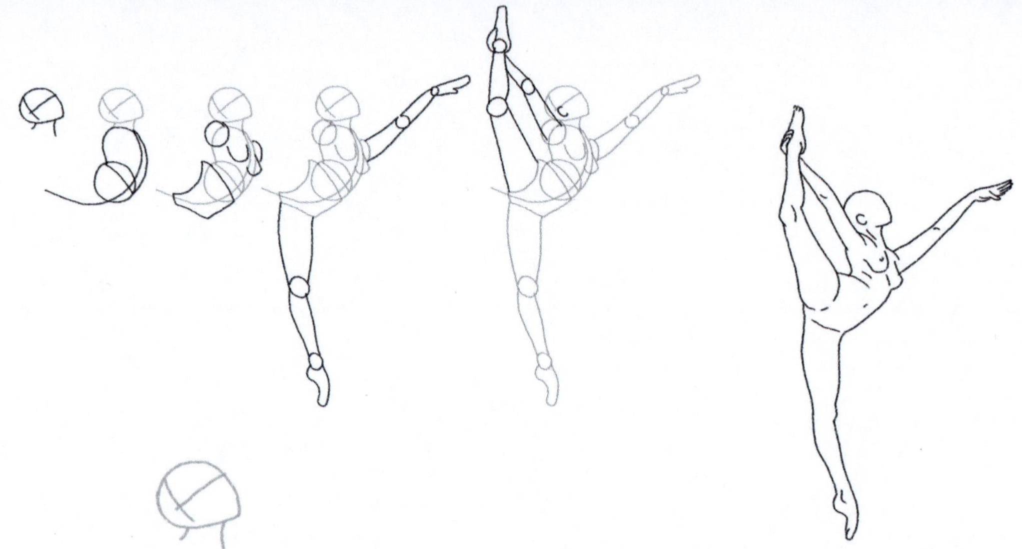

Dancer

This figure's legs are almost entirely vertical, and the back is twisted to achieve this pose.

314th **day**

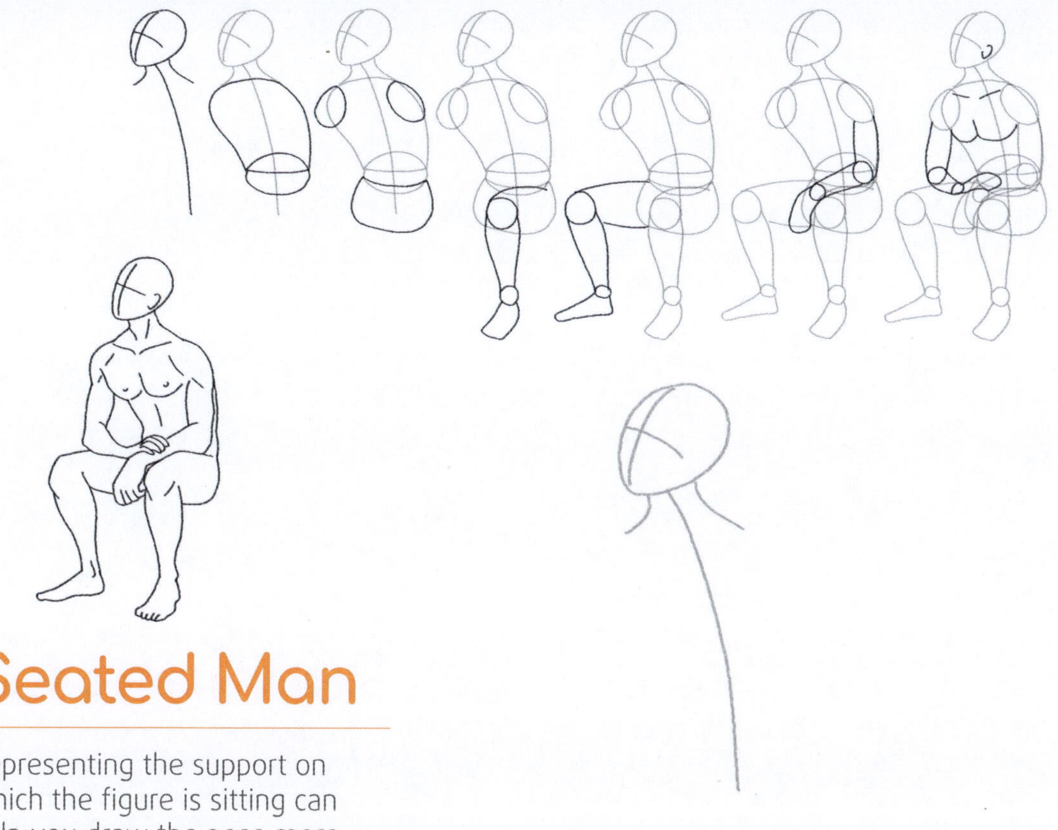

Seated Man

Representing the support on which the figure is sitting can help you draw the pose more accurately. If your drawing is large enough, you can highlight the chest muscles.

315th **day**

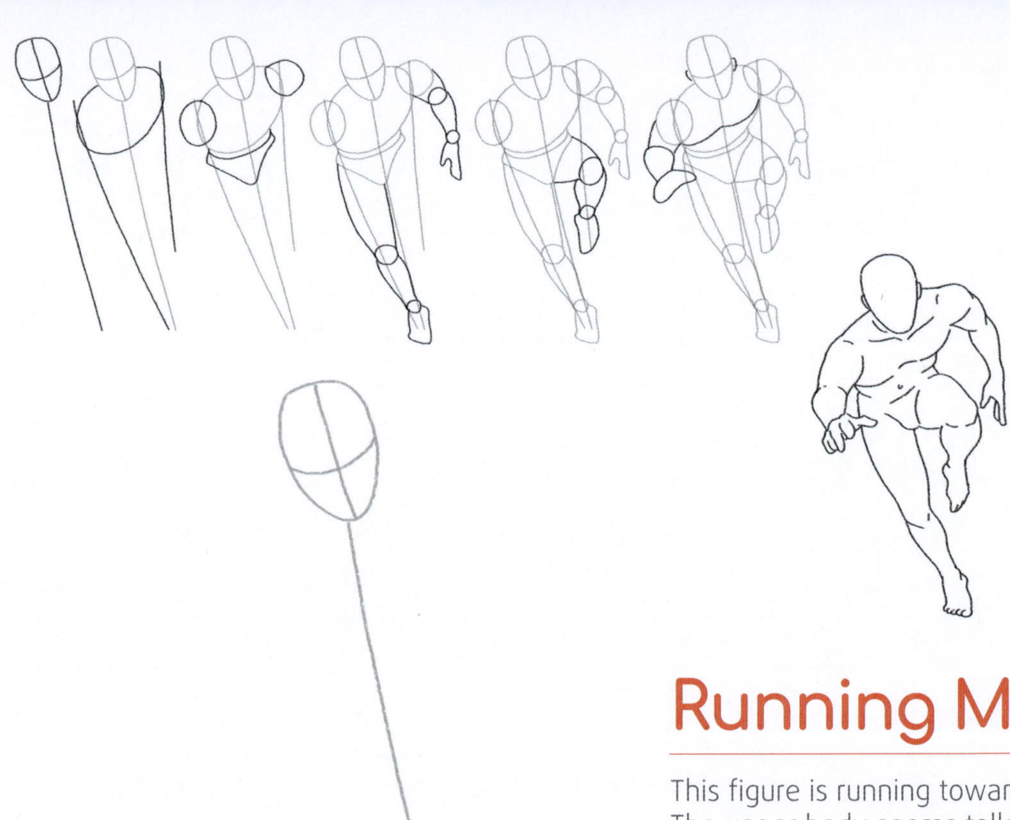

Running Man

This figure is running toward us.
The upper body seems taller,
while the legs and feet stretch
toward the vanishing point.

316th day

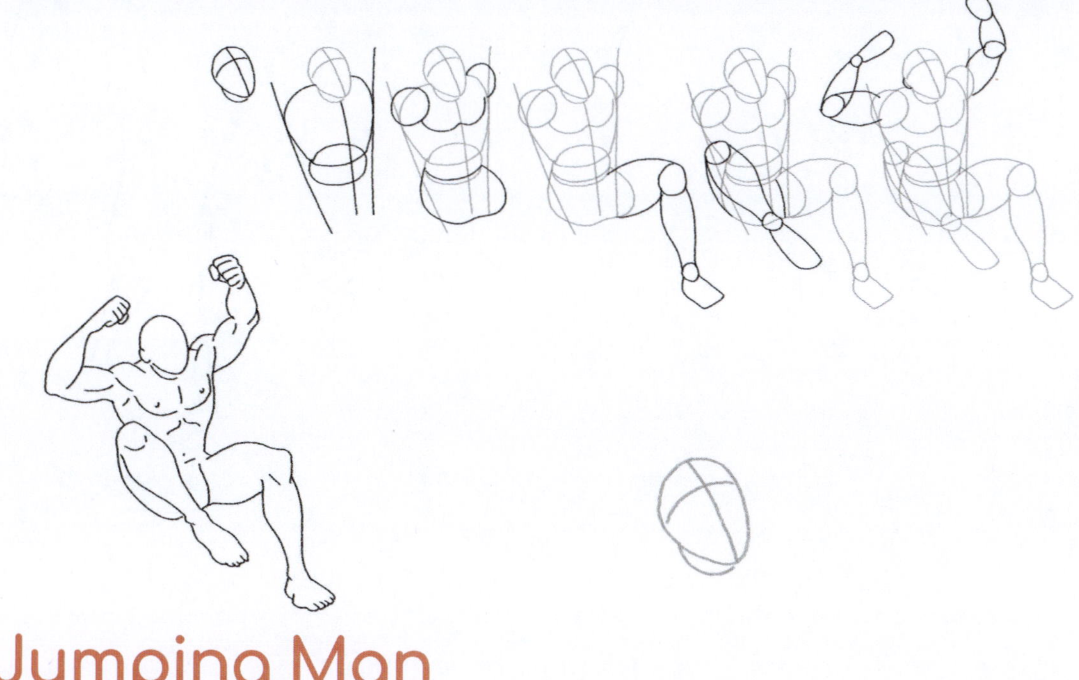

Jumping Man

This pose is fairly compact.
However, the upper body flows
upward, giving it fullness.

317th day

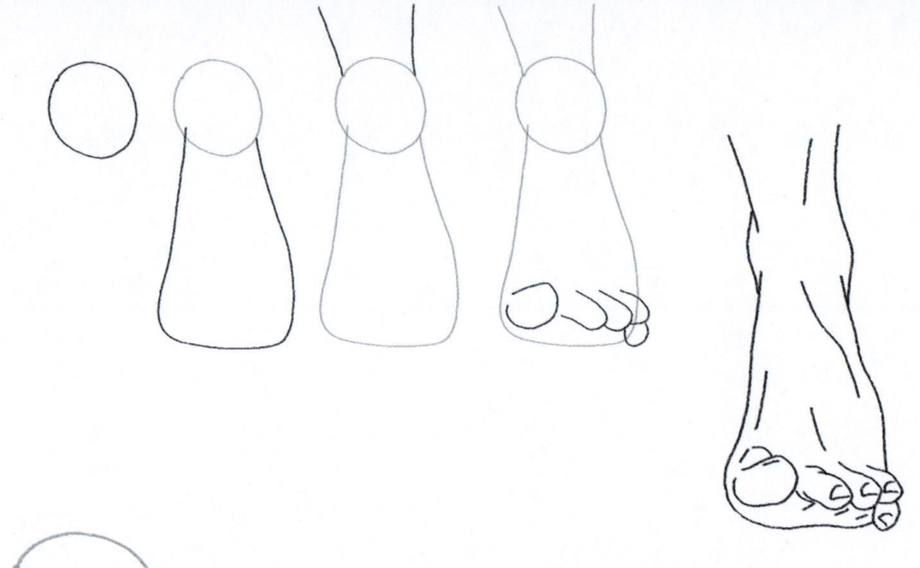

Foot

This head-on view of a foot with straight toes shows the front of the ball of the foot.

318th day

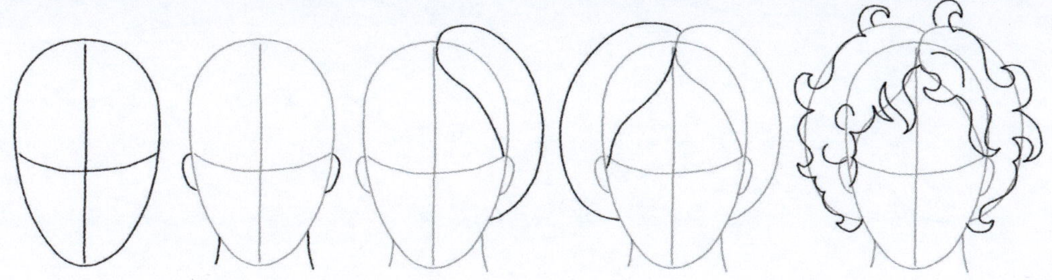

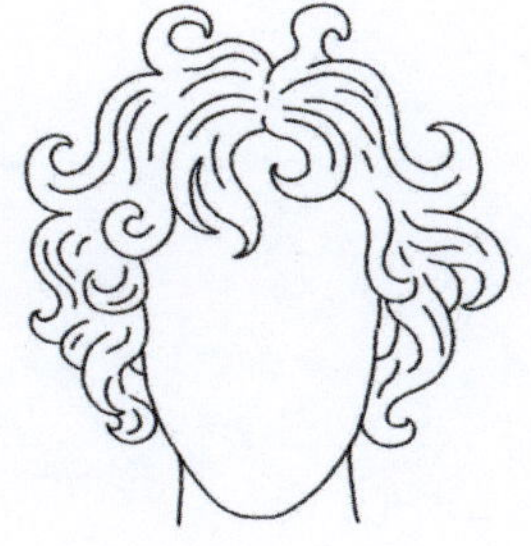

Curly Hair

You only need to add a few strokes to create short, thick curls. Add just enough lines to emphasize the overall movement of the hair and small curls around the ends.

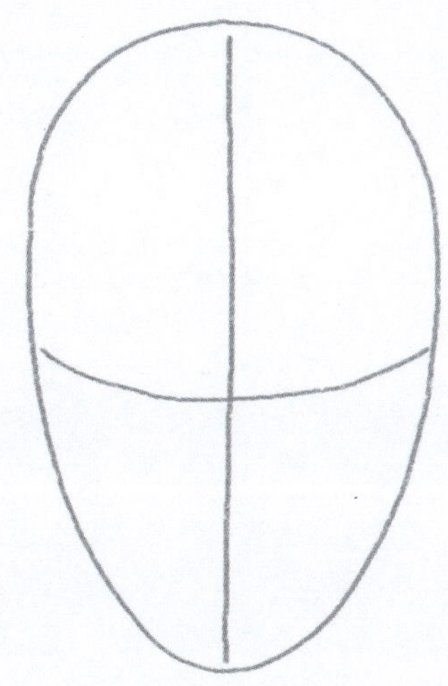

319 th day

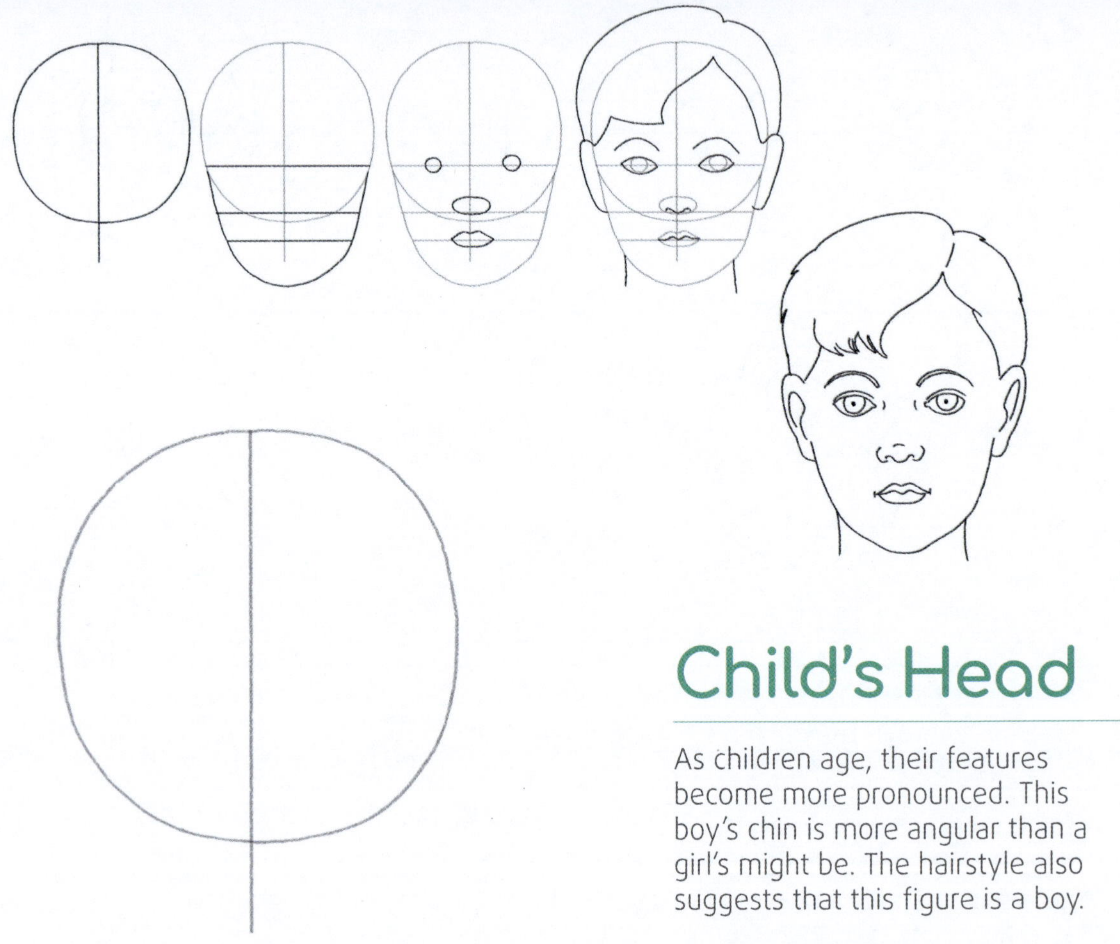

Child's Head

As children age, their features become more pronounced. This boy's chin is more angular than a girl's might be. The hairstyle also suggests that this figure is a boy.

320th day

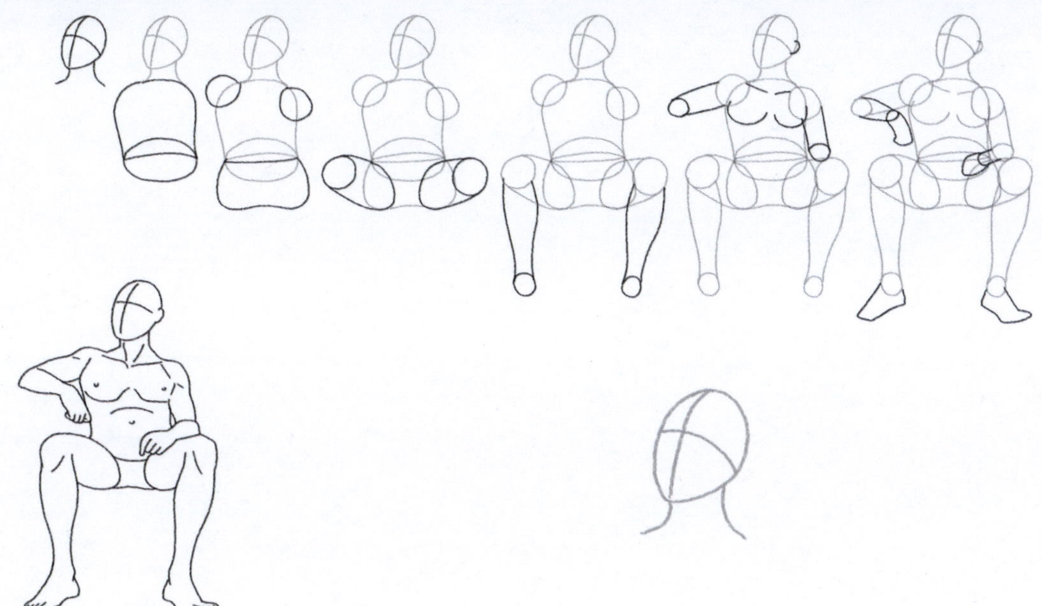

Seated Man

This seated, front-facing pose
with the legs spread wide apart
puts the thighs in perspective,
greatly reducing their length.

321st day

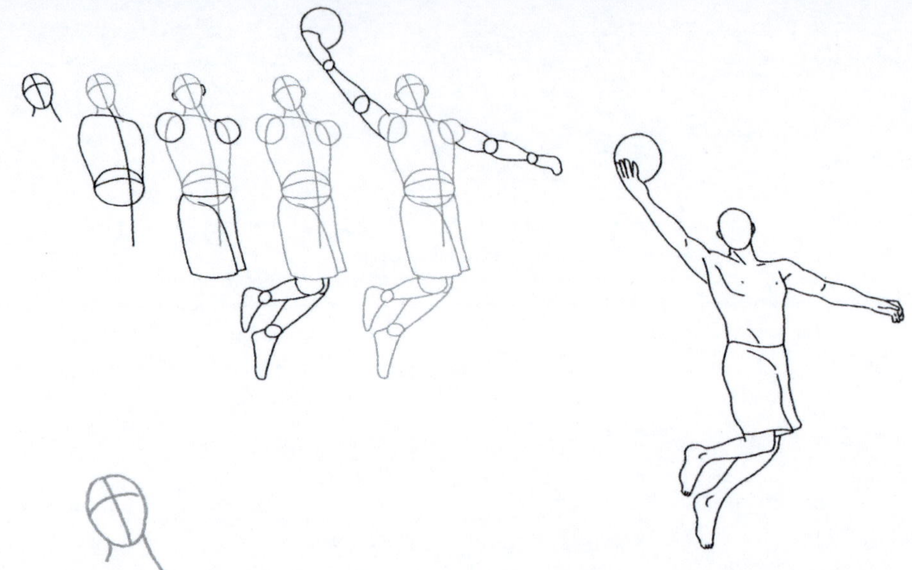

Basketball Player

This whole pose is directed toward the outstretched arm holding the ball. The bent legs project the body upward.

322nd day

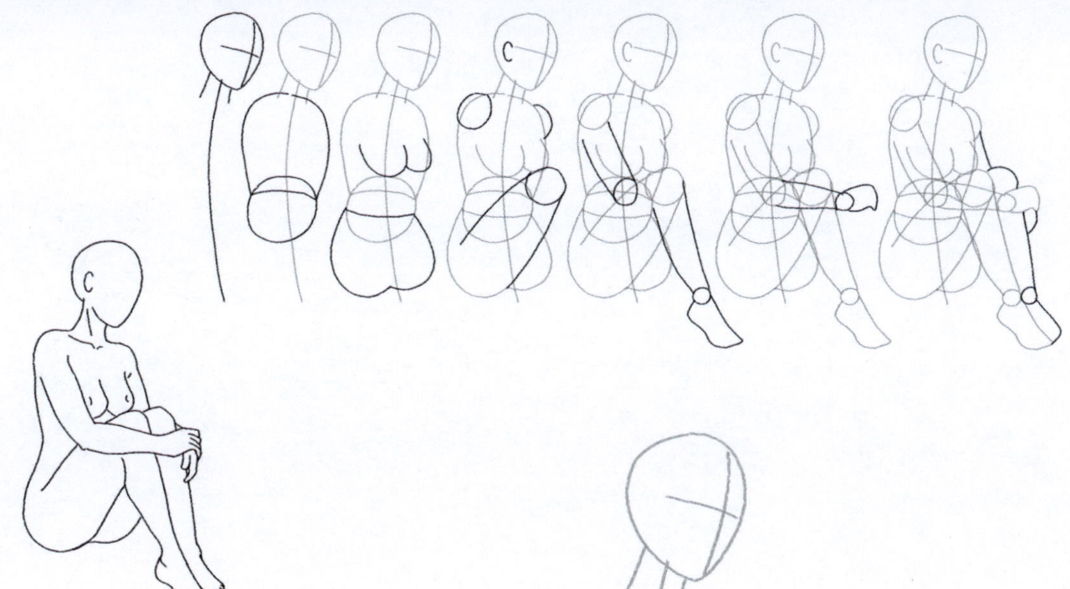

Seated Woman

In this seated pose with bent legs, the spine curves a bit. The parts of the body in the background are obscured.

323rd day

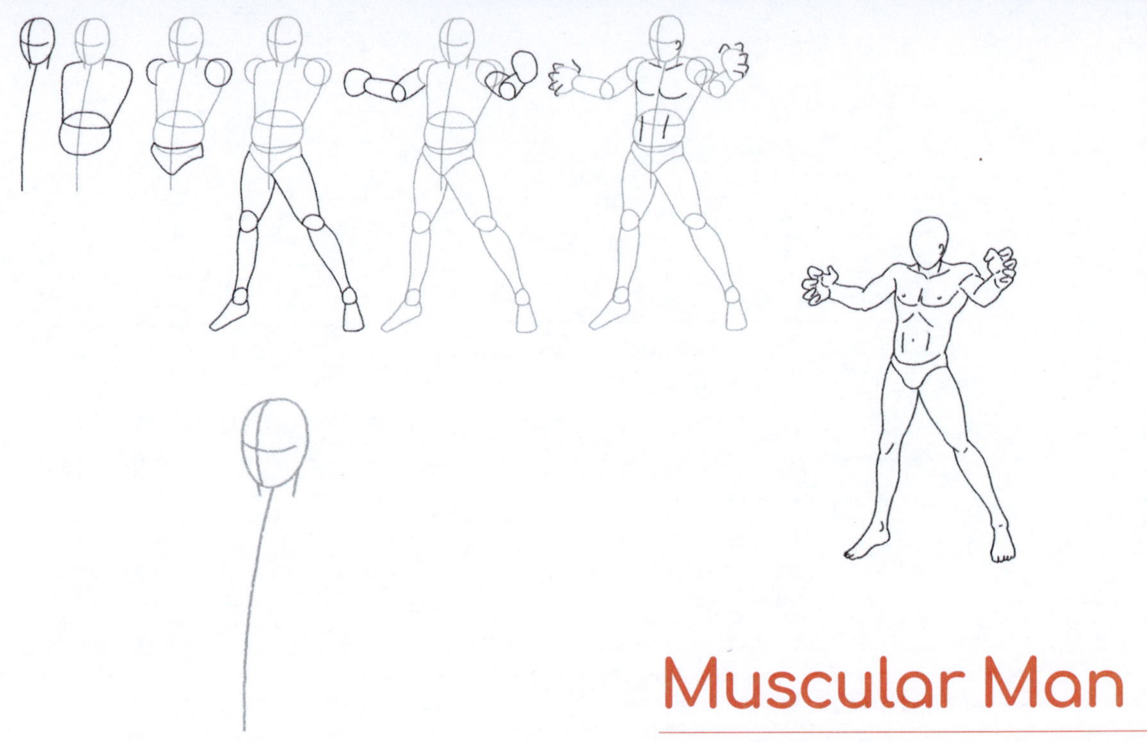

Muscular Man

The effort involved in this pose flexes the arm and chest muscles.

324th day

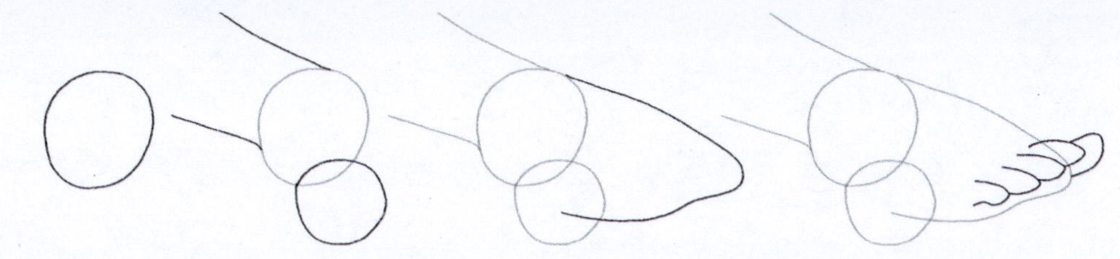

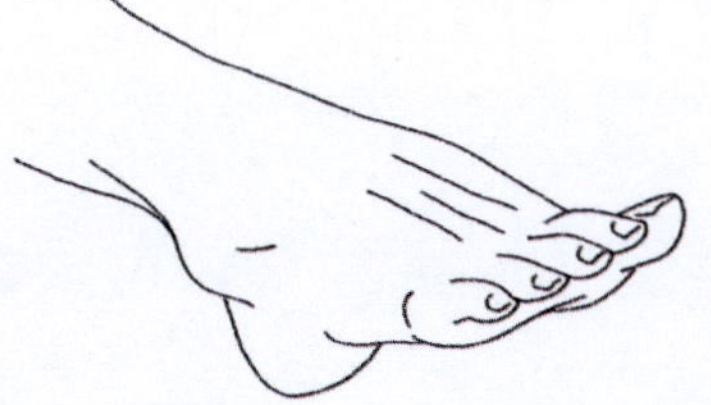

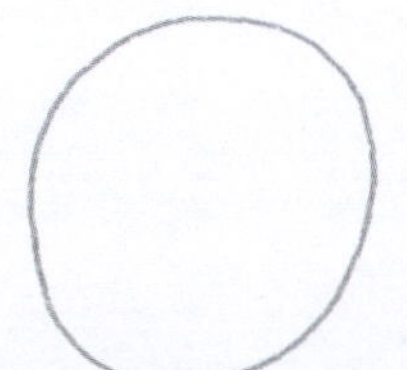

Foot

The more the foot is flattened in perspective, the less of its length can be seen. Here, neither the length of the top nor the length of the bottom of the foot is clearly discernable.

325 th day

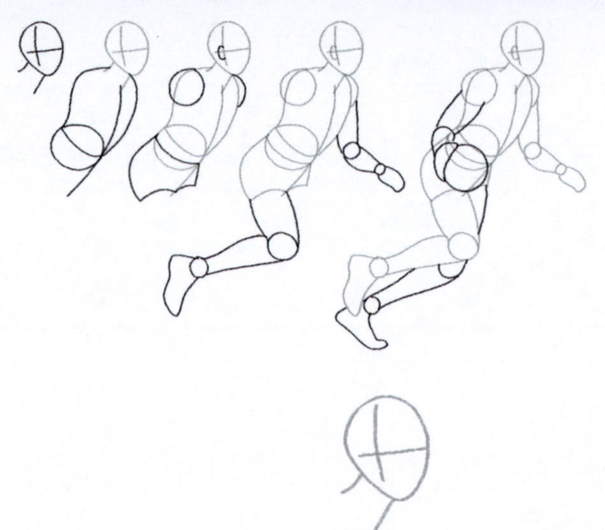

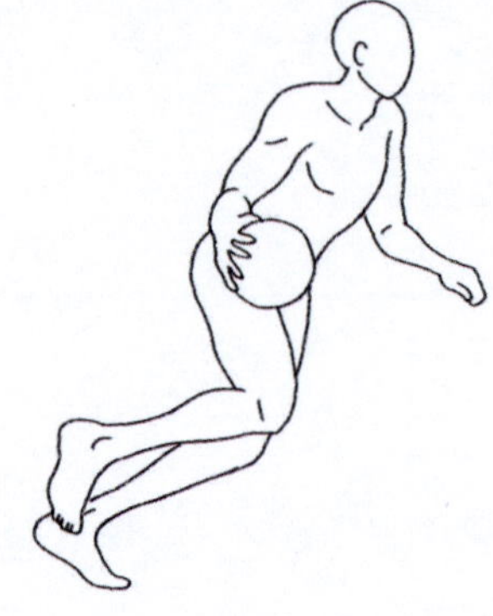

Basketball
Player

This figure is projecting forward, with the whole body bent over and only the tip of one foot on the ground.

326 th day

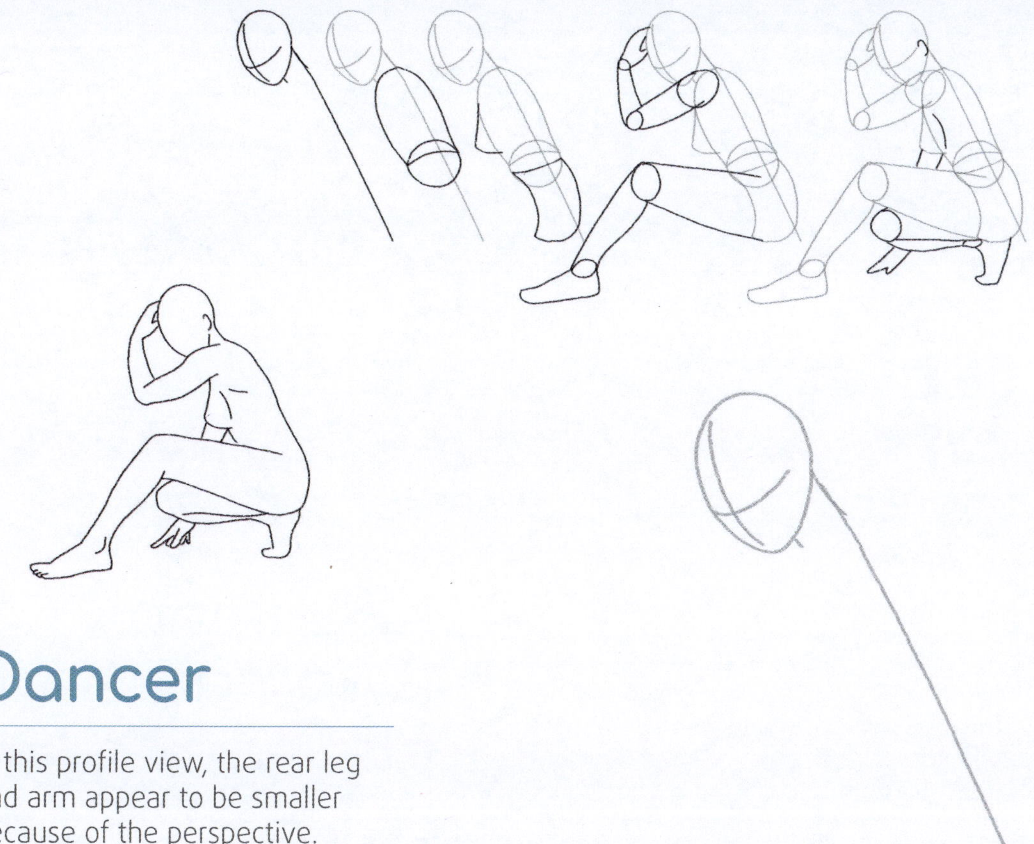

Dancer

In this profile view, the rear leg
and arm appear to be smaller
because of the perspective.

327th day

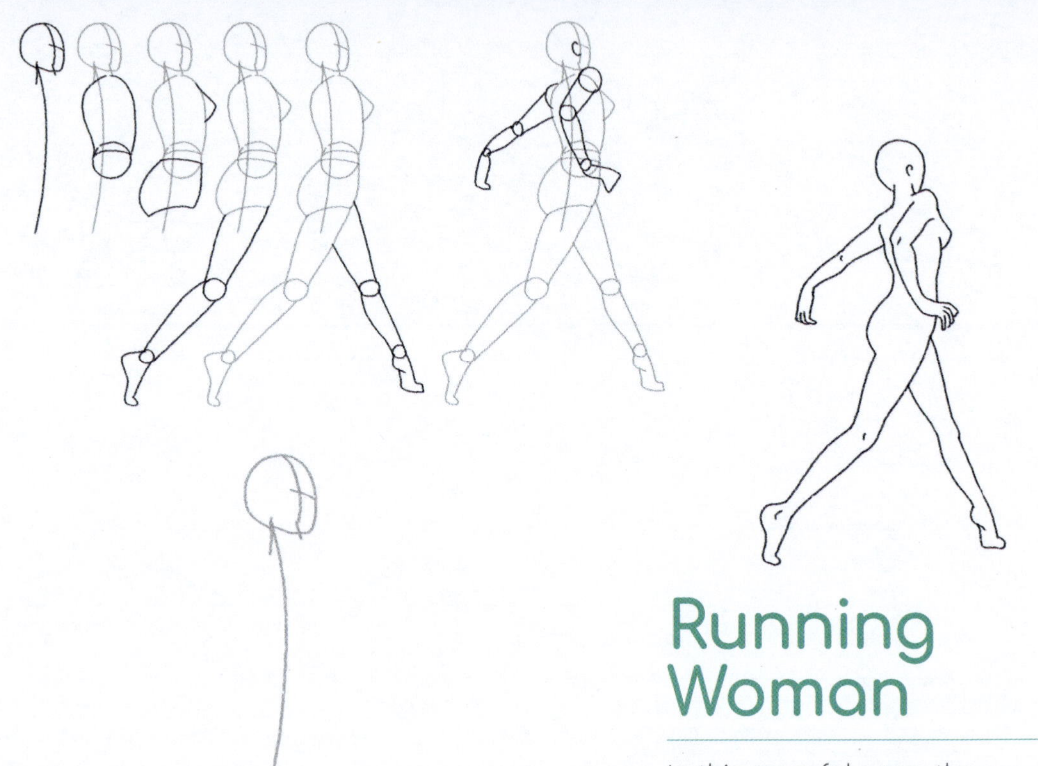

Running
Woman

In this graceful pose, the whole body is twisted and in perspective. The head and rear leg and arm appear to be smaller.

328 th day

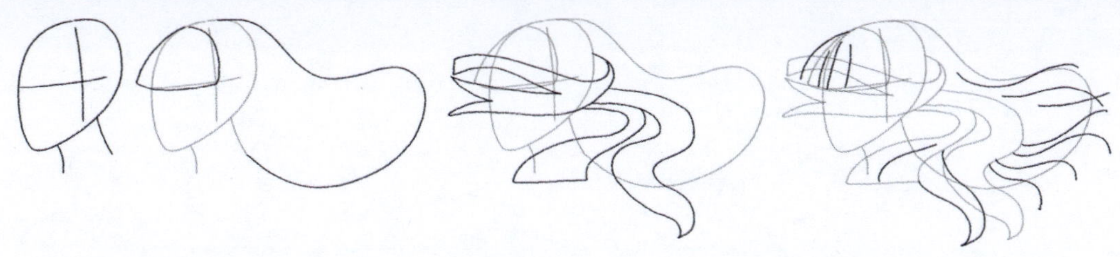

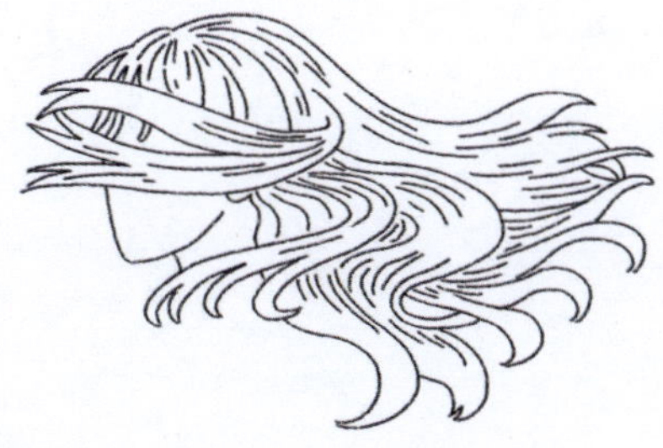

Wind-Blown Hair

To help strands of hair that cover other strands stand out, avoid overworking them.

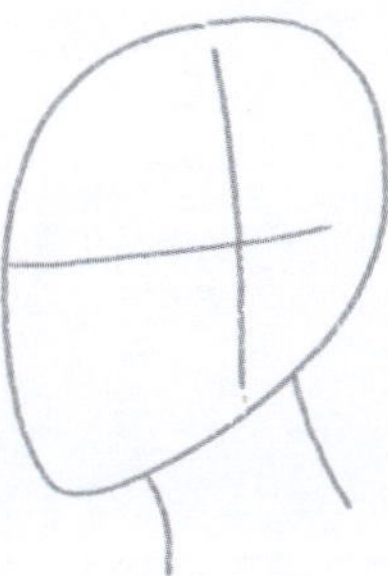

329 th day

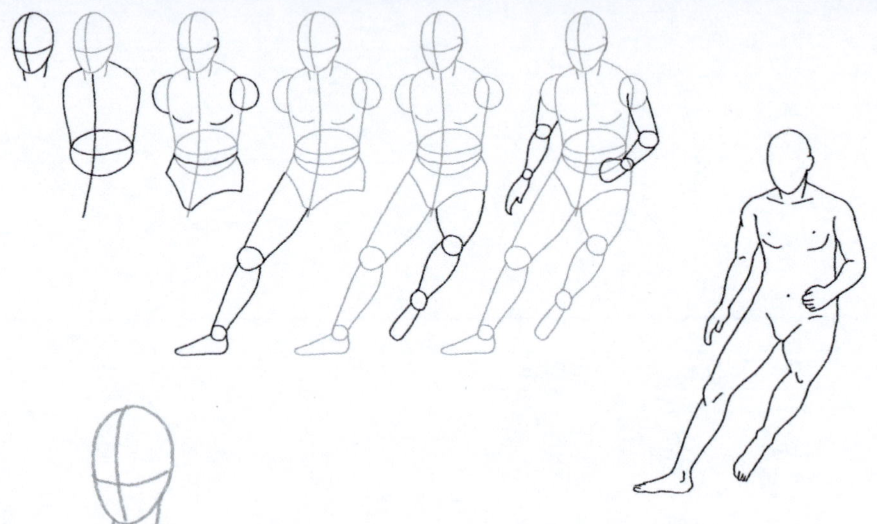

Running Man

The figure's movement is tilting the whole body. The back leg is in perspective, so its proportions are different.

330 th day

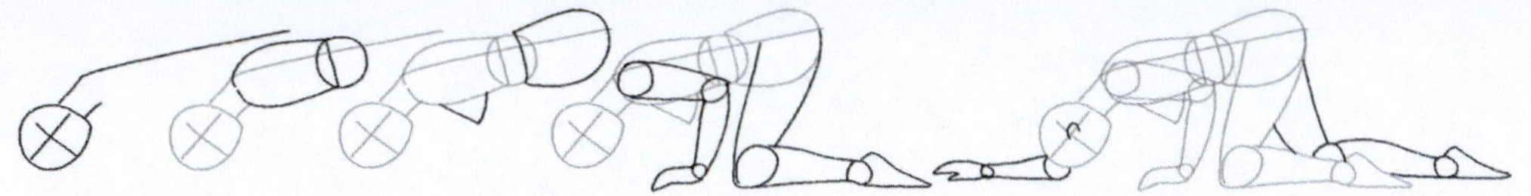

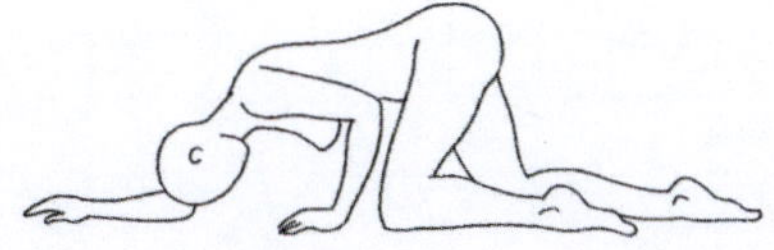

Crawling
Woman

In this profile pose, the back and every other line remain straight. There are no twists, and there is no perspective.

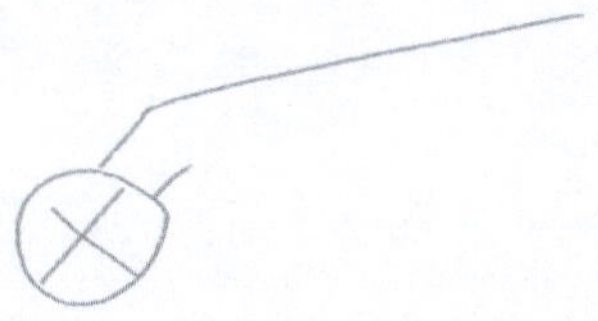

331st day

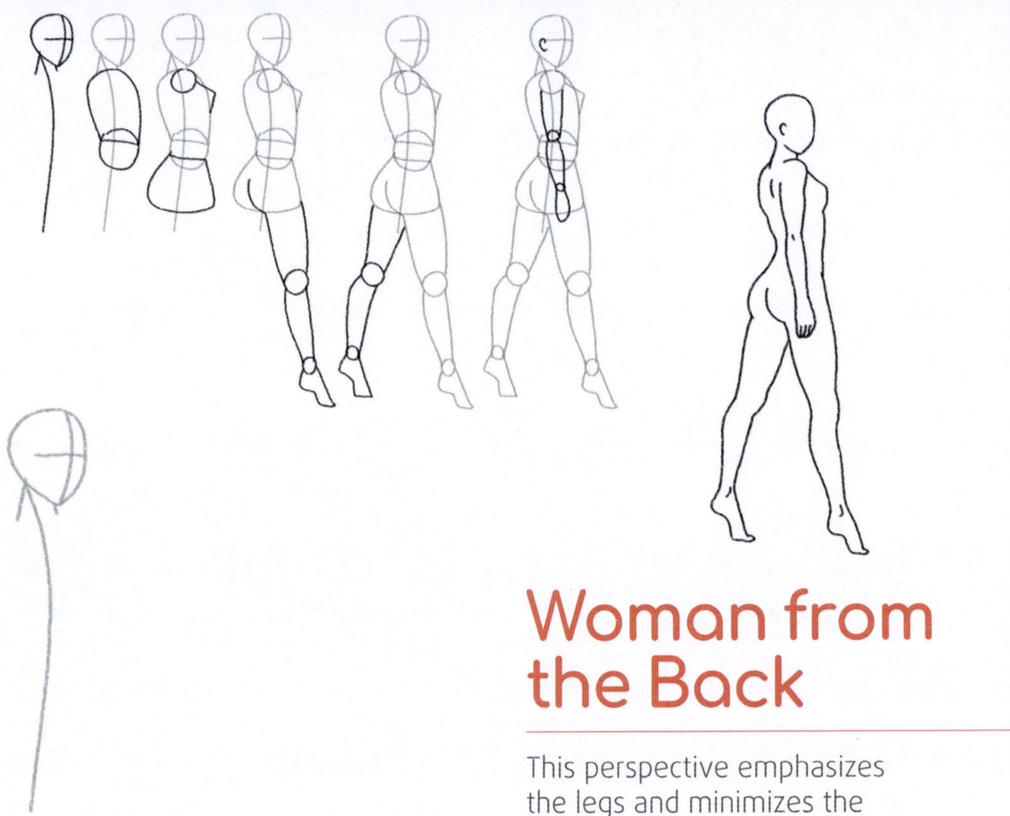

Woman from the Back

This perspective emphasizes the legs and minimizes the upper body.

332nd day

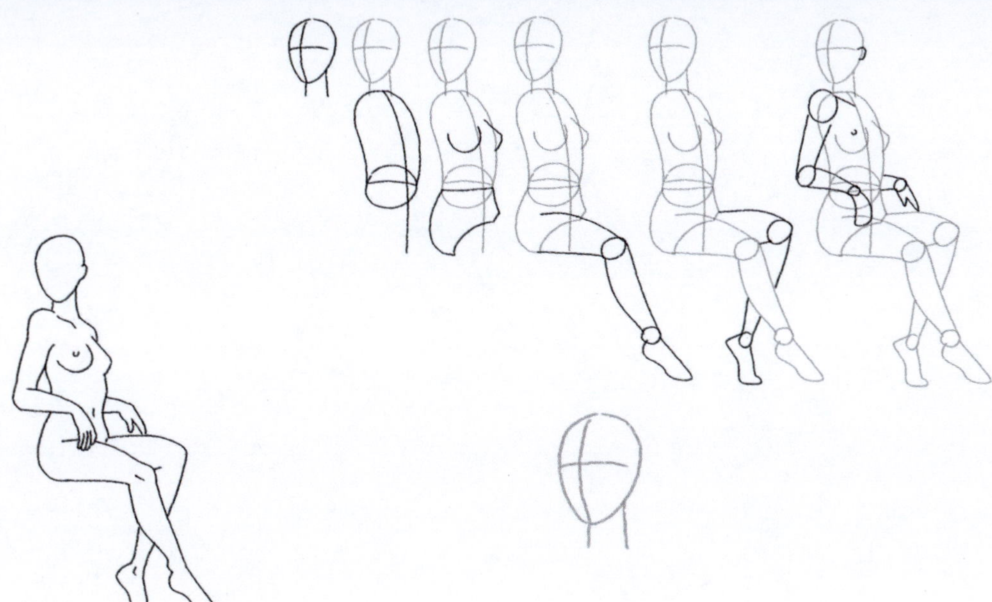

Seated Woman

This figure's torso is slightly arched forward. Drawing the surface on which the figure is sitting can help you capture the pose.

333rd day

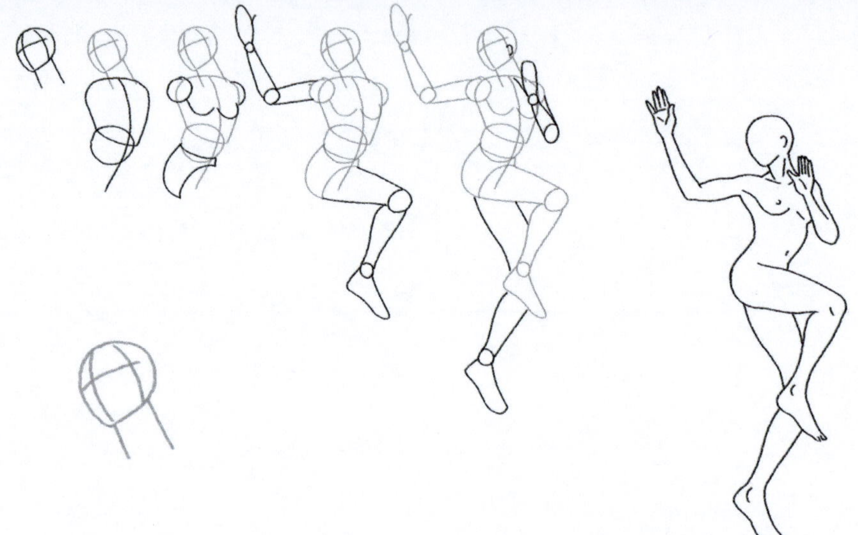

Dancing Woman

This figure's lower body is turned to the side, and the torso and arms are swinging toward us.

334th day

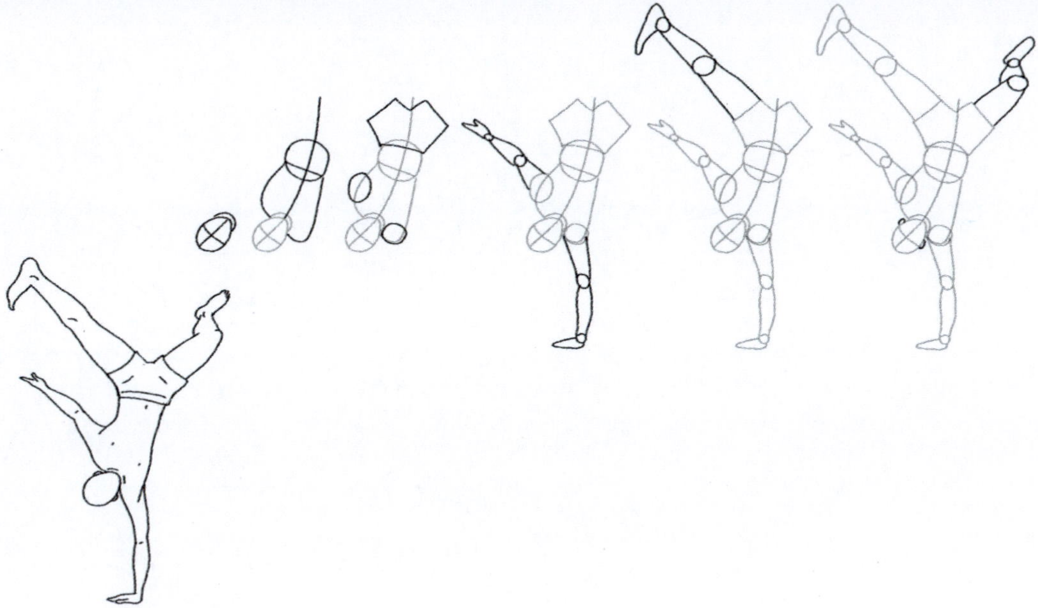

Breakdancer

This figure's whole body is resting on one outstretched arm. He is holding his other limbs in different directions to maintain his balance.

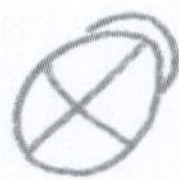

335th day

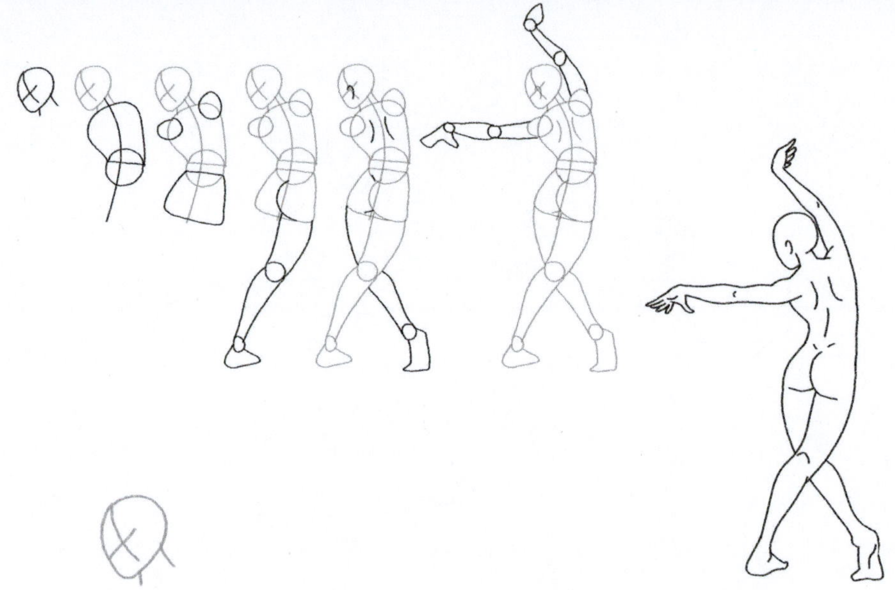

Dancer

This figure's body leans to one side, and the arc the torso creates is extended by a leg and an arm.

336 th day

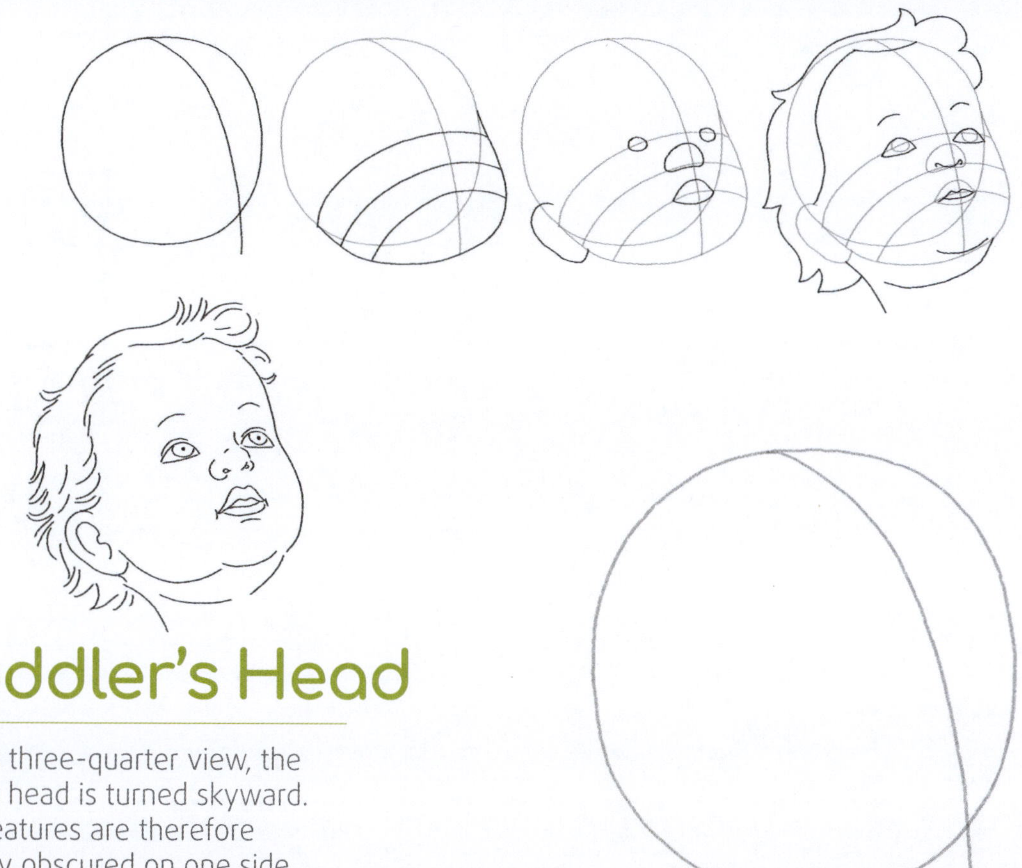

Toddler's Head

In this three-quarter view, the child's head is turned skyward. The features are therefore slightly obscured on one side of the face. The movement of the hair follows the direction of the gaze.

337th day

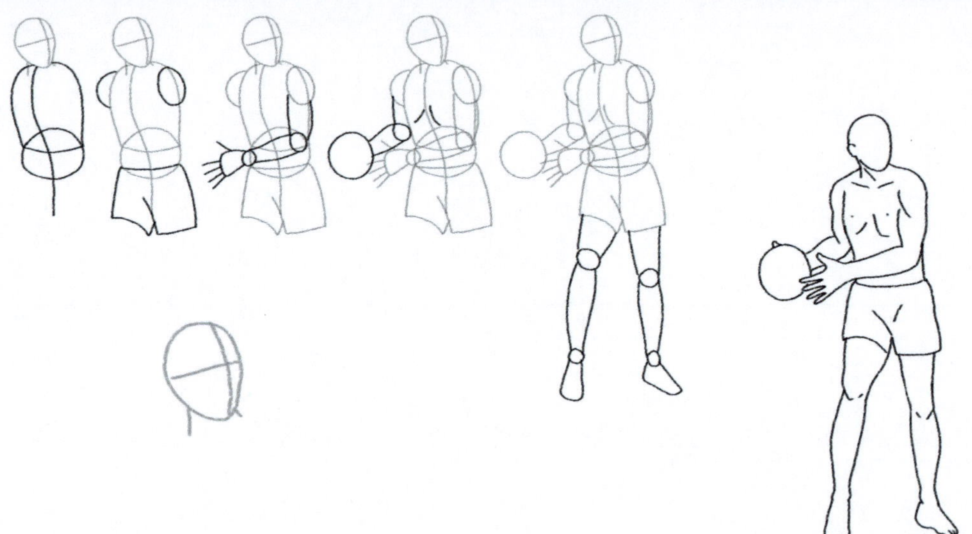

Basketball Player

This figure's lower body is facing the front, while the upper body is turned toward the ball.

338 th day

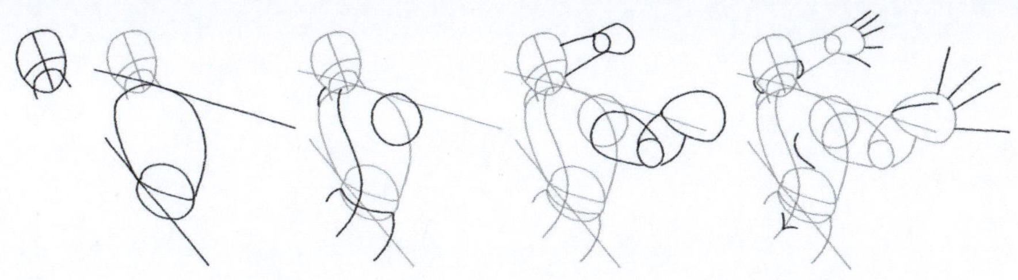

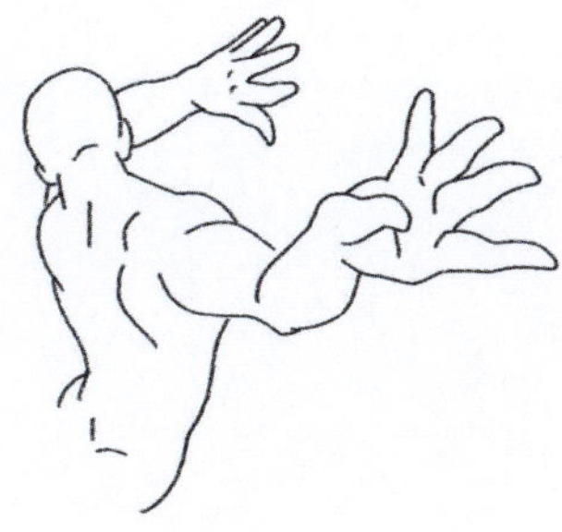

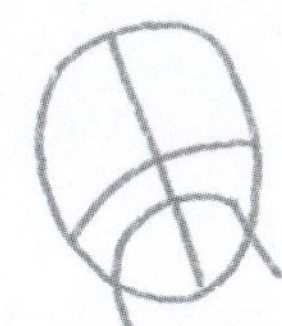

Man's Torso

In this pose, the arm moving toward us exaggerates the size of the hand in the foreground.

339 th day

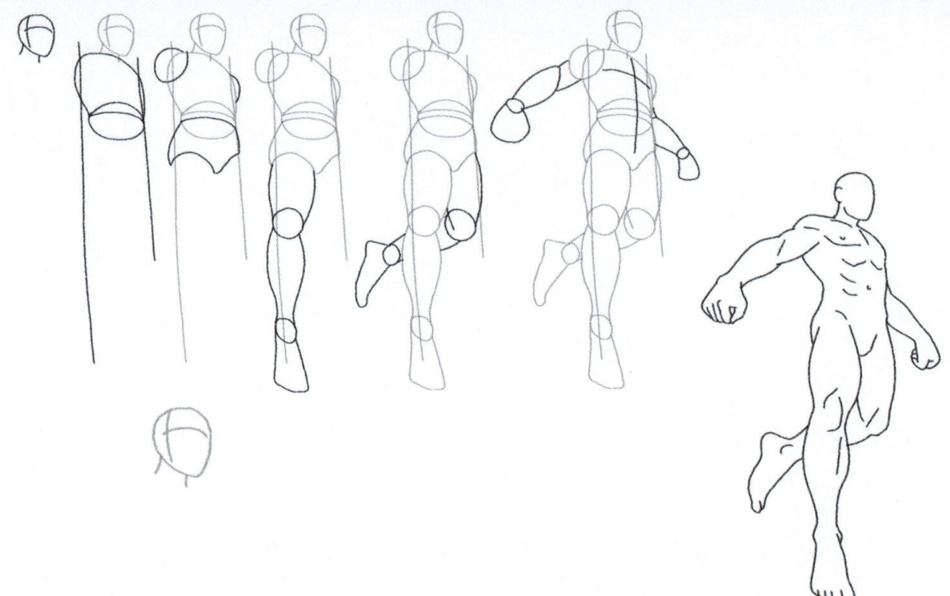

Standing Man

This exaggerated view from below enhances the proportions of the lower body, which appears to be closer to us.

340th day

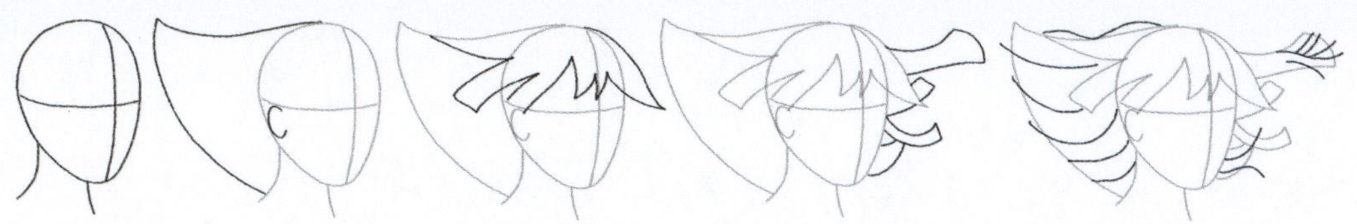

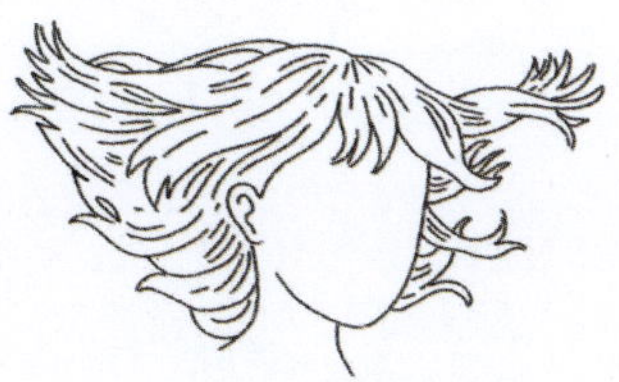

Wind-Blown Hair

If the head turns quickly, the
strands of hair lift near the ends.

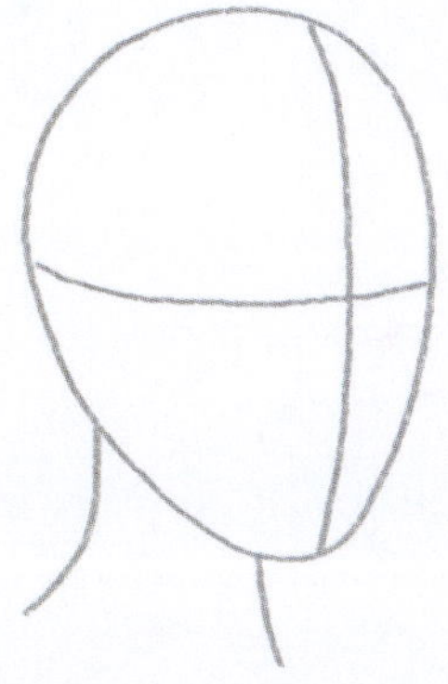

341st day

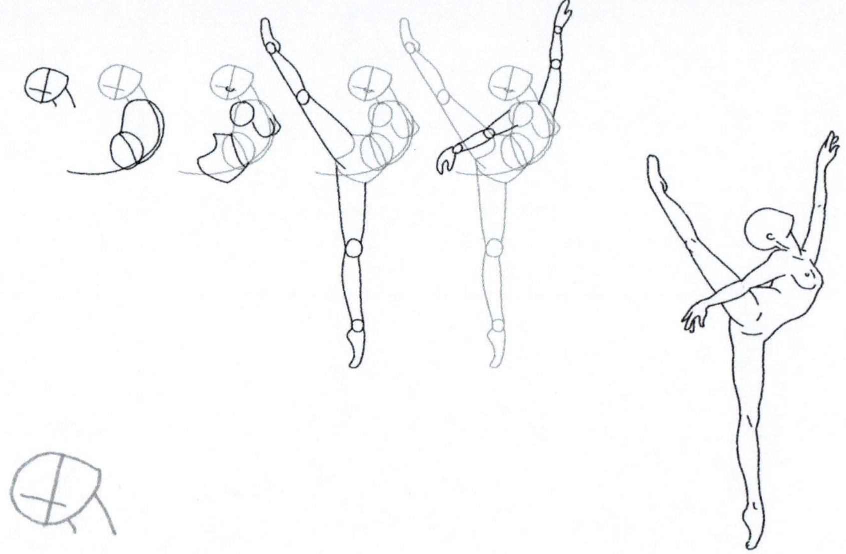

Dancer

This figure's torso is twisted upward to counter the forward tilt, while the raised arm helps to orient her.

342nd day

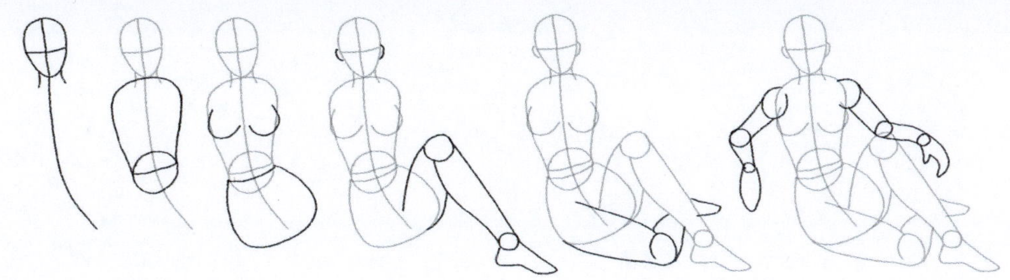

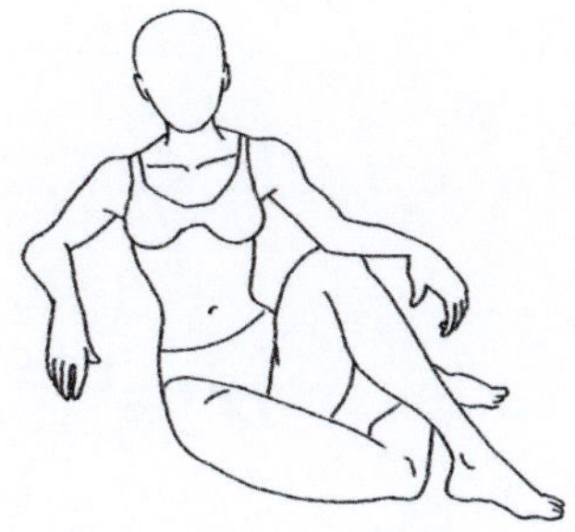

Seated Woman

This figure's torso is facing forward. The calf of the front leg is in perspective, while the thigh of the other leg is shortened.

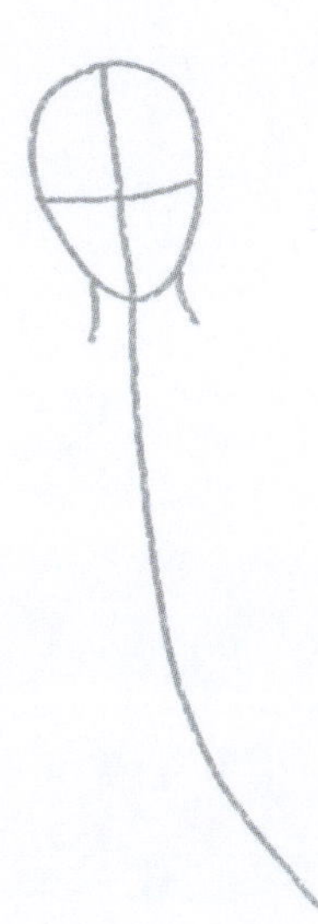

343 rd day

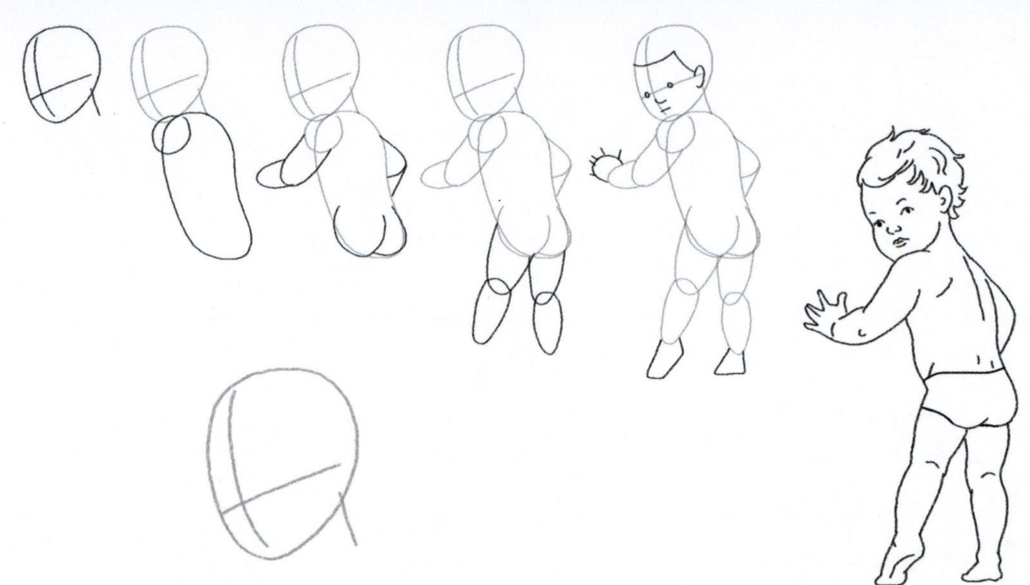

Toddler

A toddler's legs are very slender and small in proportion to the head. In this three-quarter view from the back, the volume of the belly is reduced.

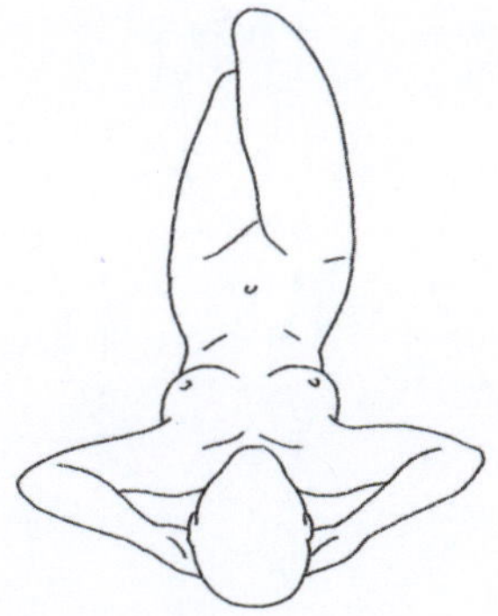

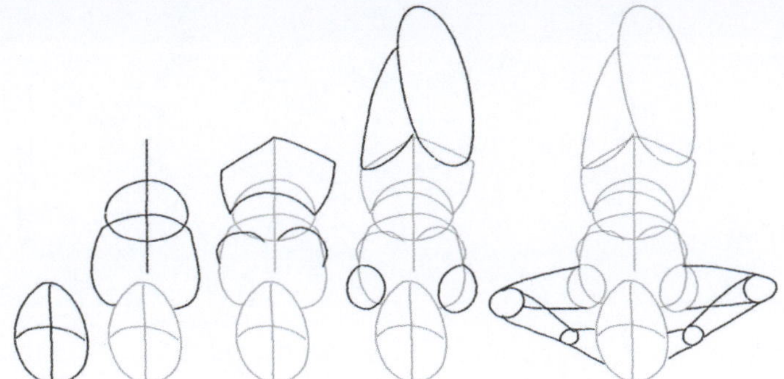

Reclining
Woman

This pose compresses the torso's
volumes, and the perspective
reduces the proportion of the
legs in relation to the upper body.

345th day

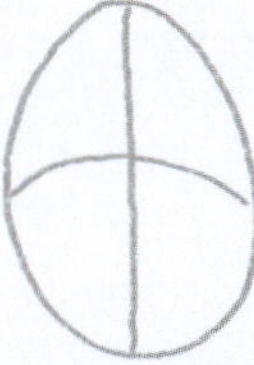

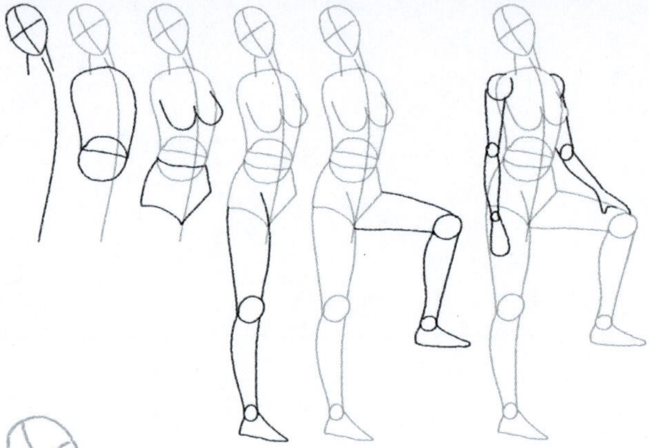

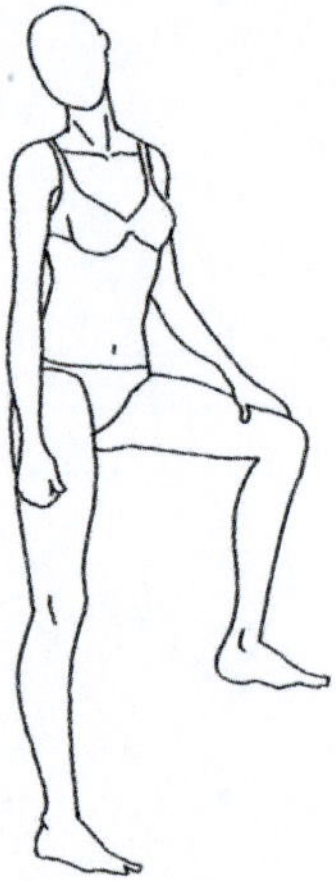

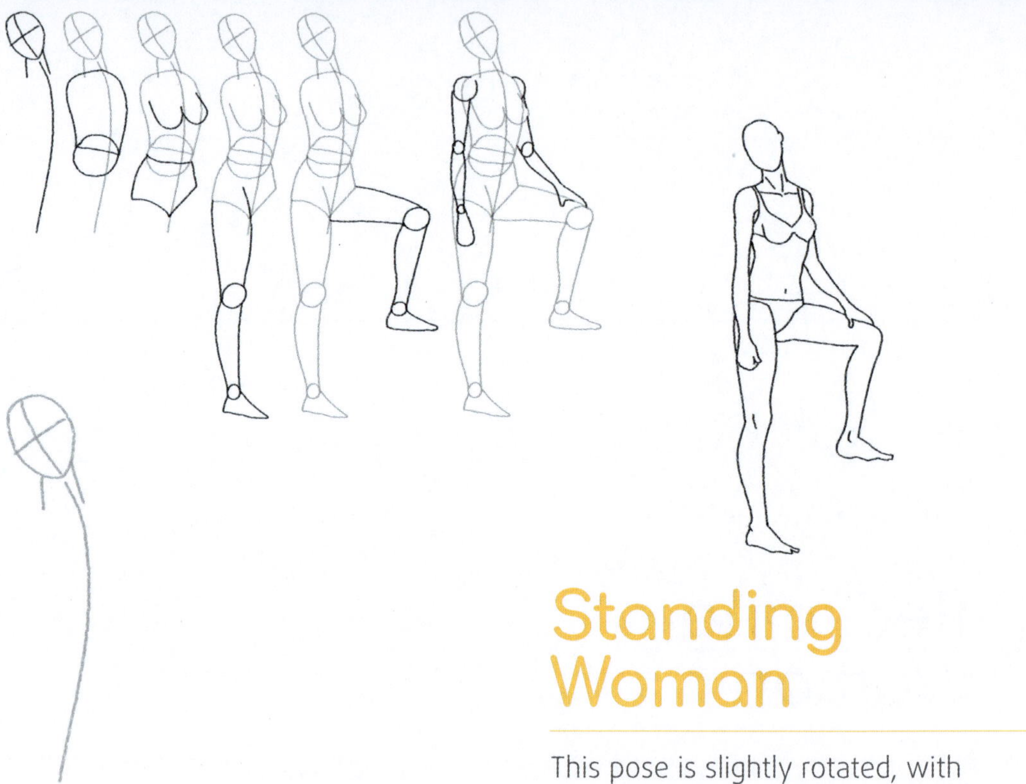

Standing Woman

This pose is slightly rotated, with the torso in perspective.

346th day

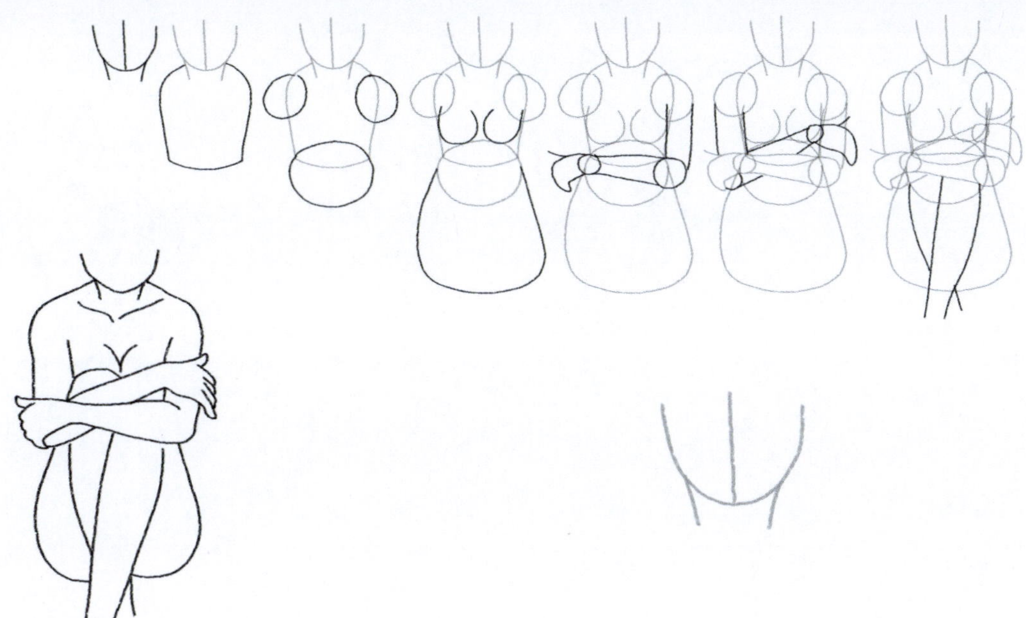

Seated Woman

This seated pose is tight, reducing the width of the torso and creating a crease between the breasts.

347th day

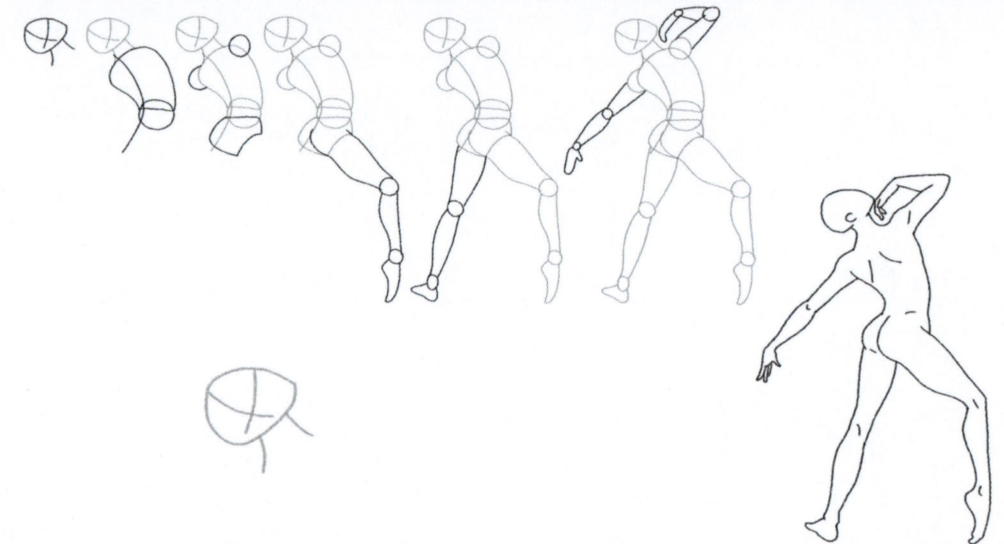

Gymnast

This figure's arching, stretched arms and legs twist the body upward on its axis.

348 th day

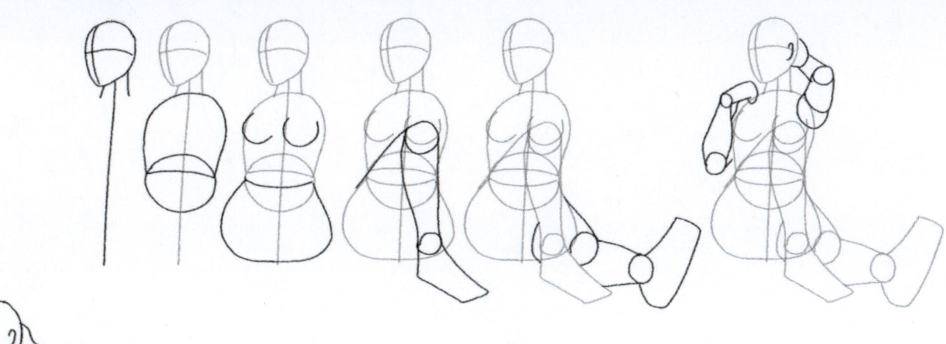

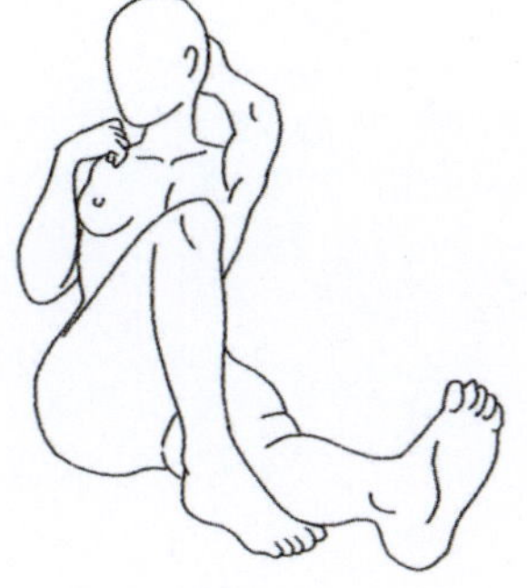

Seated Woman

This perspective highlights the legs and feet, which appear to be very large in proportion to the rest of the body.

349th day

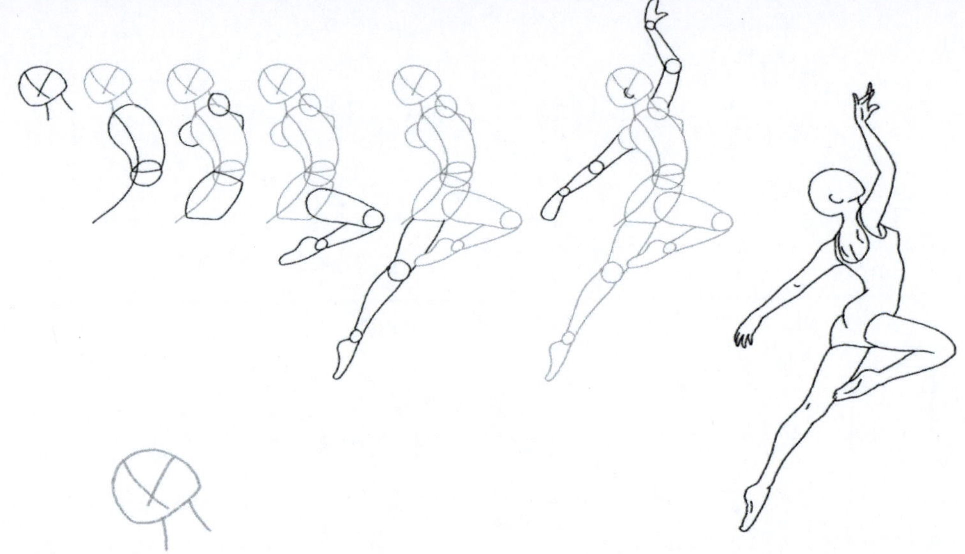

Dancer

This entire pose soars, twists and stretches up. The figure's back is arched, and the arms are graceful.

350th **day**

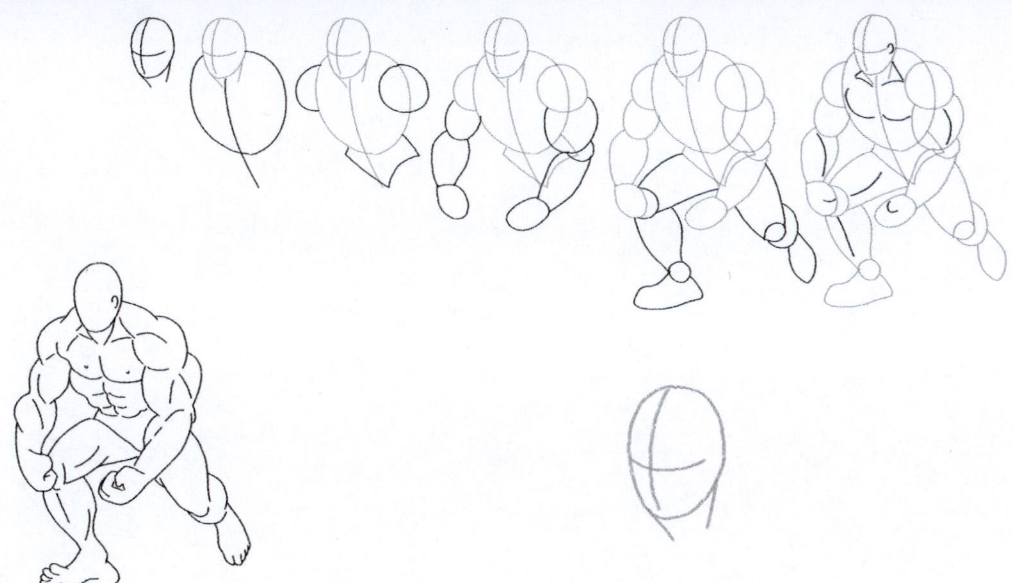

Muscular Man

When drawing a bodybuilder, you can exaggerate the volumes of the various muscles as they flex with the effort of the pose. Here, the back leg is reduced by the perspective.

351st day

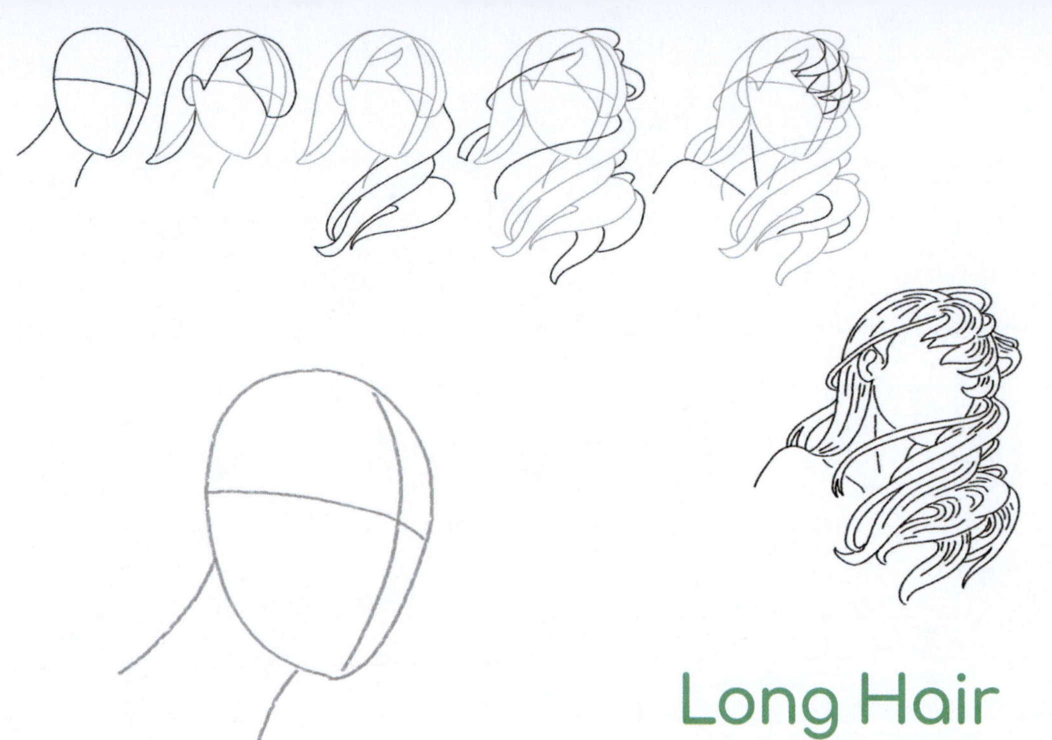

Long Hair

To give hair a fluid yet choppy movement, draw some strands long and stretched and others shorter and more curved.

352nd day

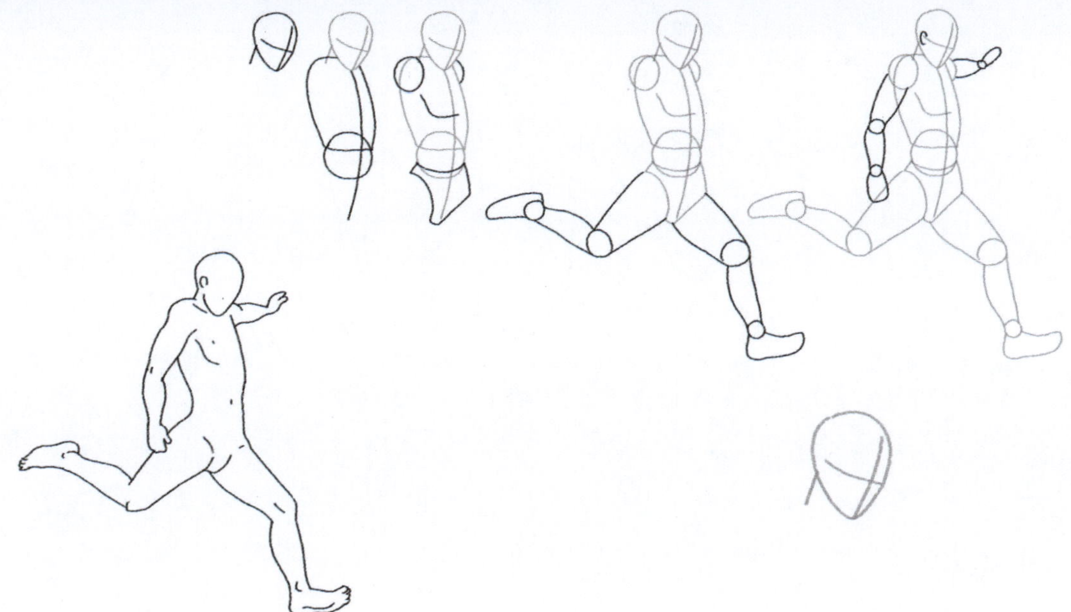

Soccer Player

This figure is projecting his body
to kick a ball. The back foot is
gaining momentum, and the
back arm is in perspective and
looks smaller.

353rd day

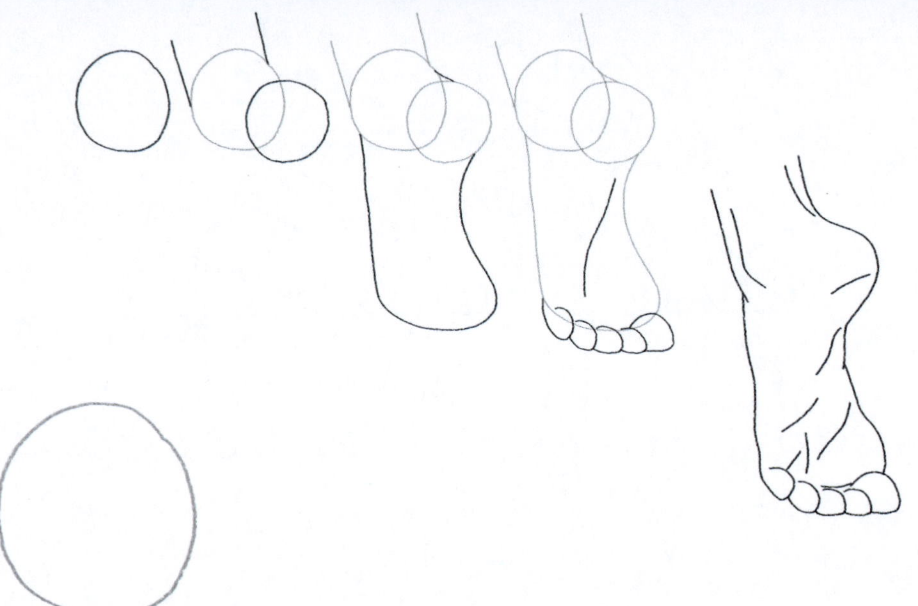

Foot

In this pose, many creases are formed in the curve of the sole of the foot.

354th day

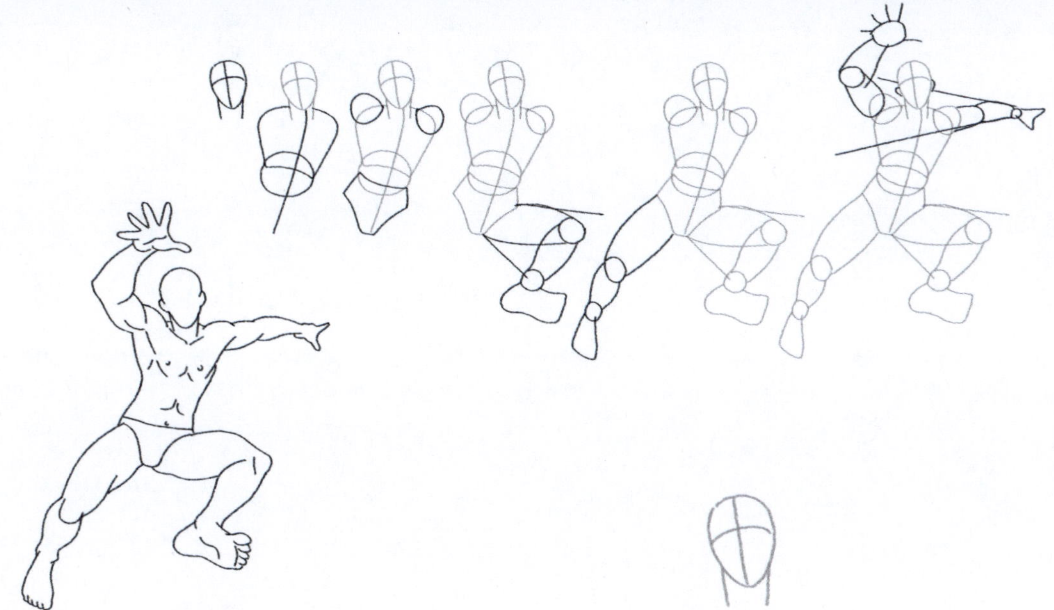

Jumping Man

Drawn in this perspective, the foot and hand that are turned toward us look very large.

355th day

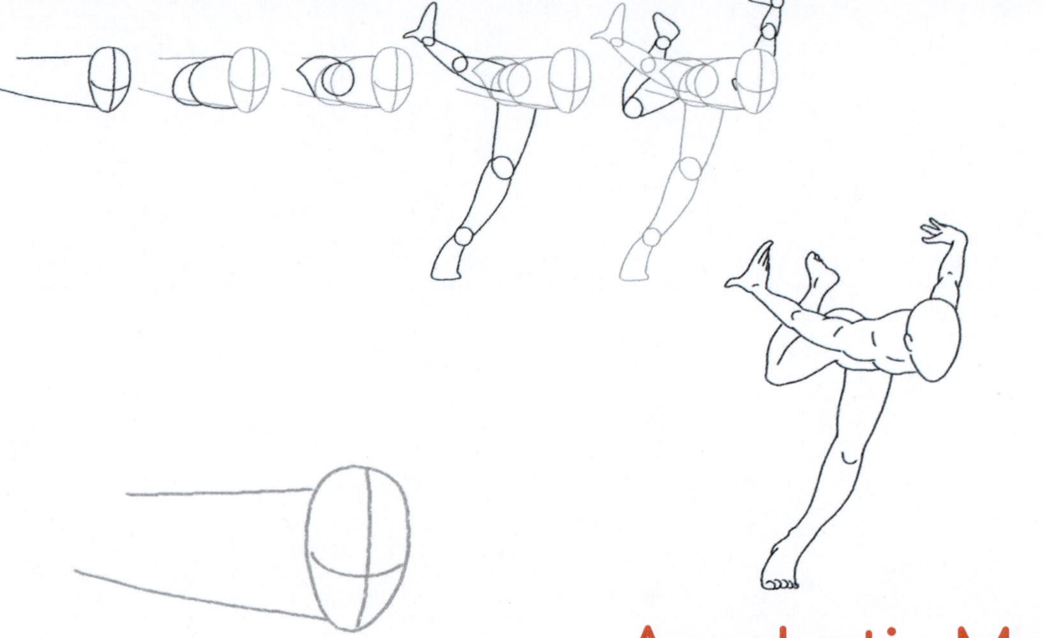

Acrobatic Man

In this projected pose facing
forward, the hands and
bent leg stretch toward the
vanishing point.

356th day

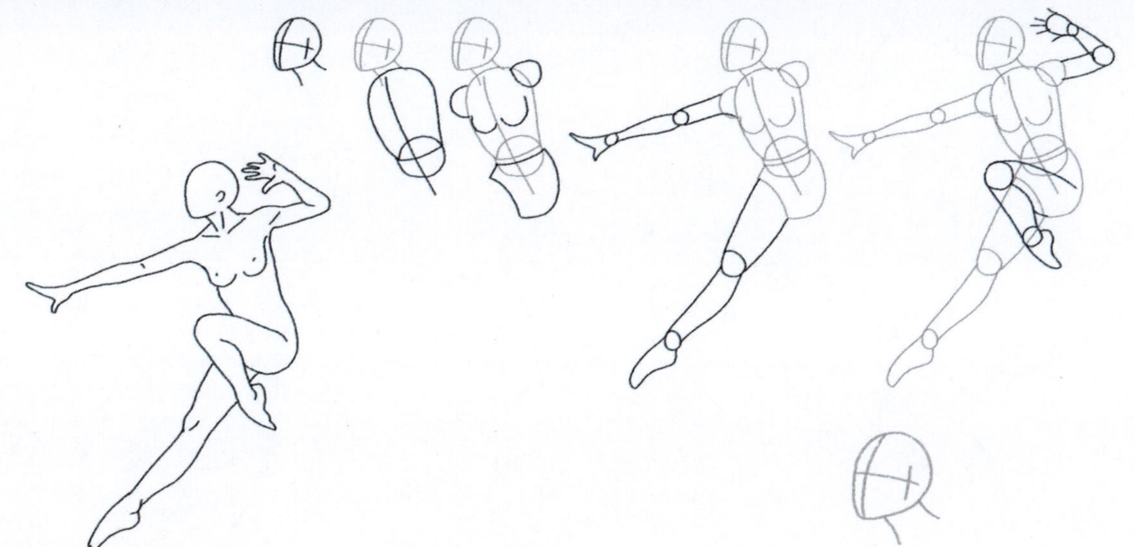

Jumping
Woman

One side of this figure's body is
stretched downward, and the
other side is folded upward.
These movements create a
dynamic, projected pose.

357th day

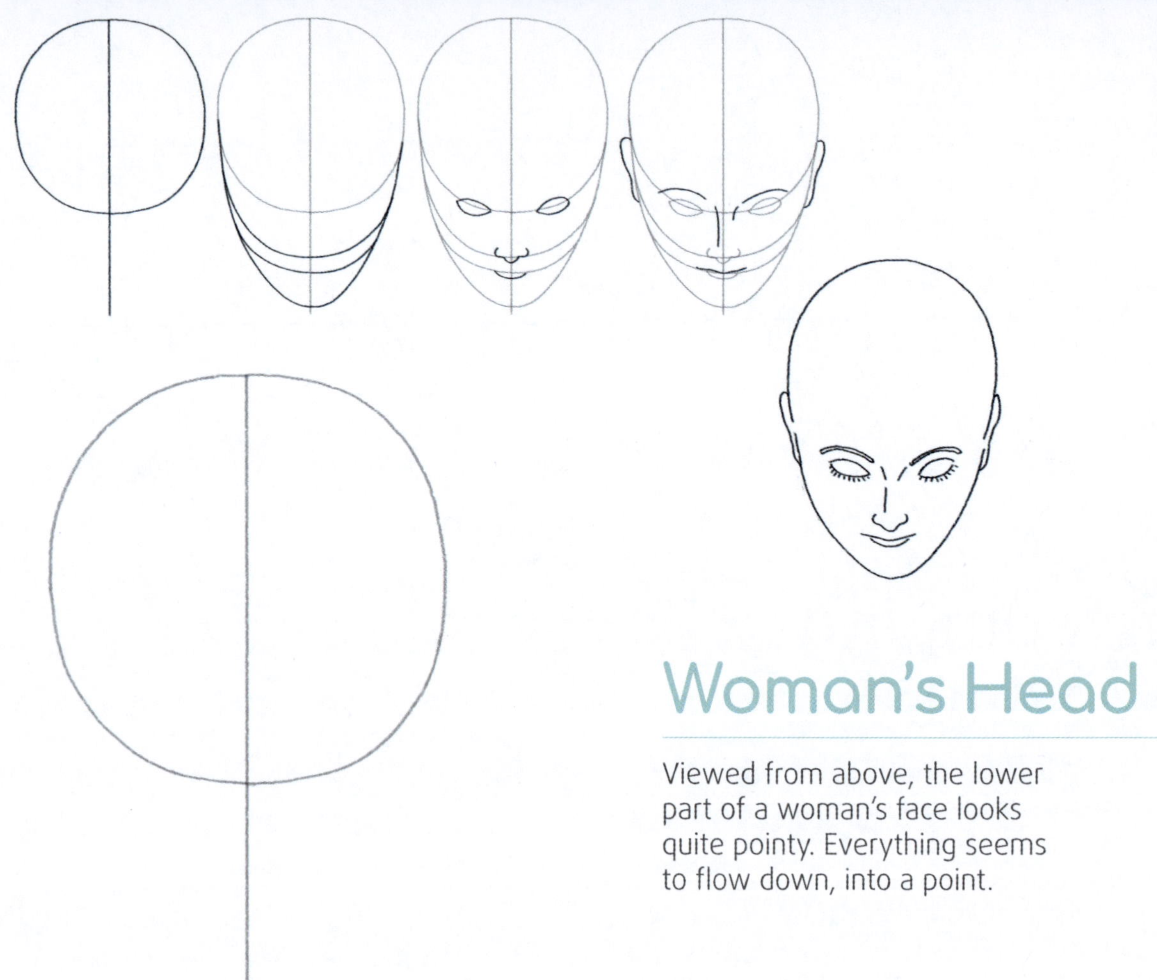

Woman's Head

Viewed from above, the lower
part of a woman's face looks
quite pointy. Everything seems
to flow down, into a point.

358th day

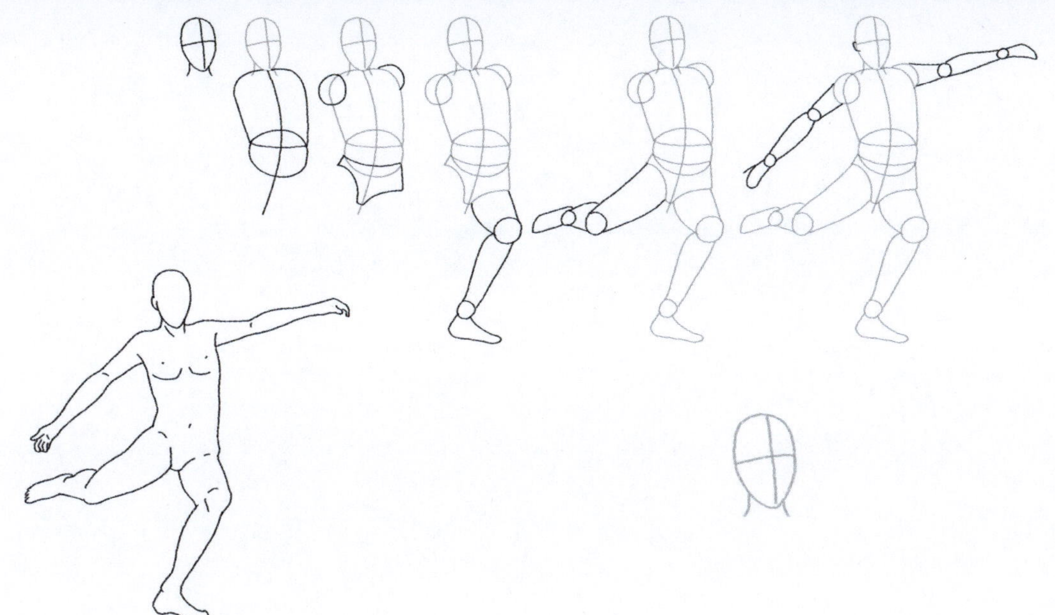

Soccer Player

This figure is swinging
one leg back to kick a ball.
The movement puts the
leg in perspective, so its
proportions change.

359th day

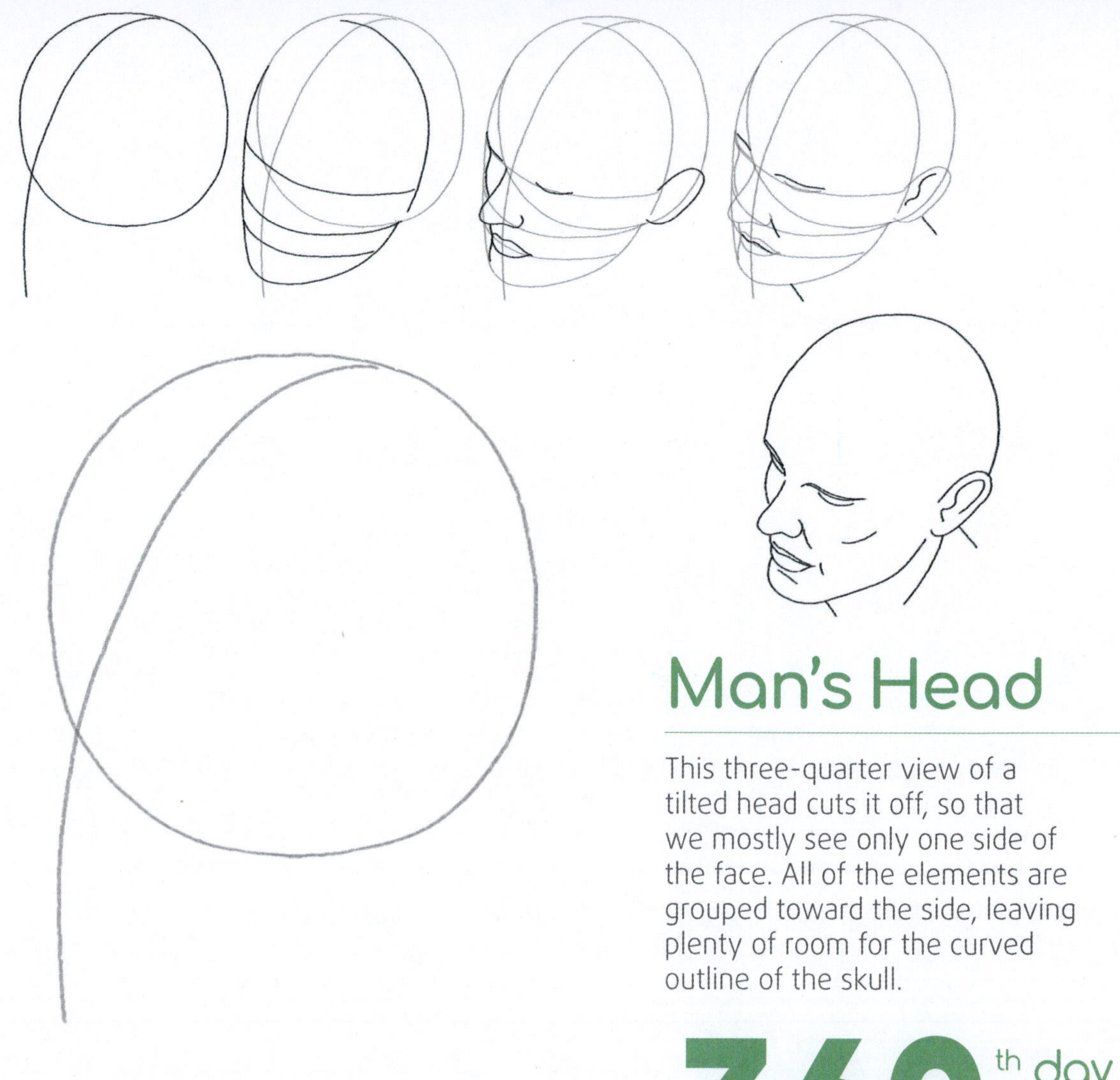

Man's Head

This three-quarter view of a tilted head cuts it off, so that we mostly see only one side of the face. All of the elements are grouped toward the side, leaving plenty of room for the curved outline of the skull.

360 th day

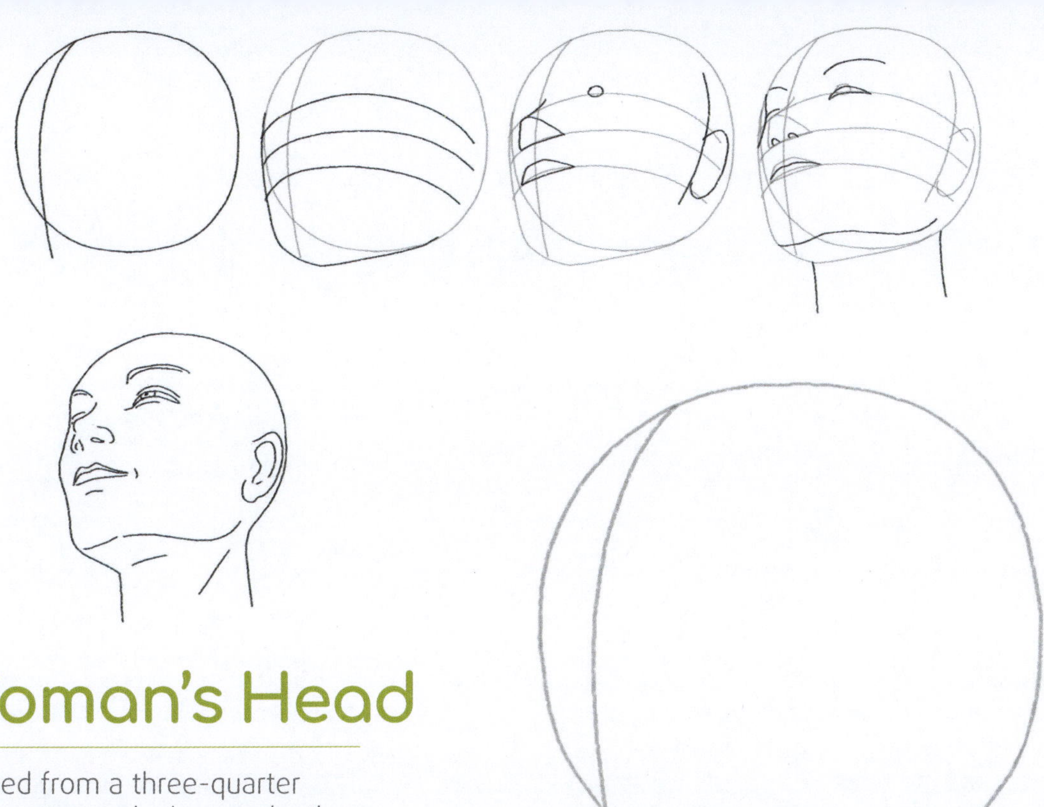

Woman's Head

Viewed from a three-quarter perspective and a low angle, the lines of the face curve sharply, revealing the underside of the chin, nose, eyes and other elements.

361st day

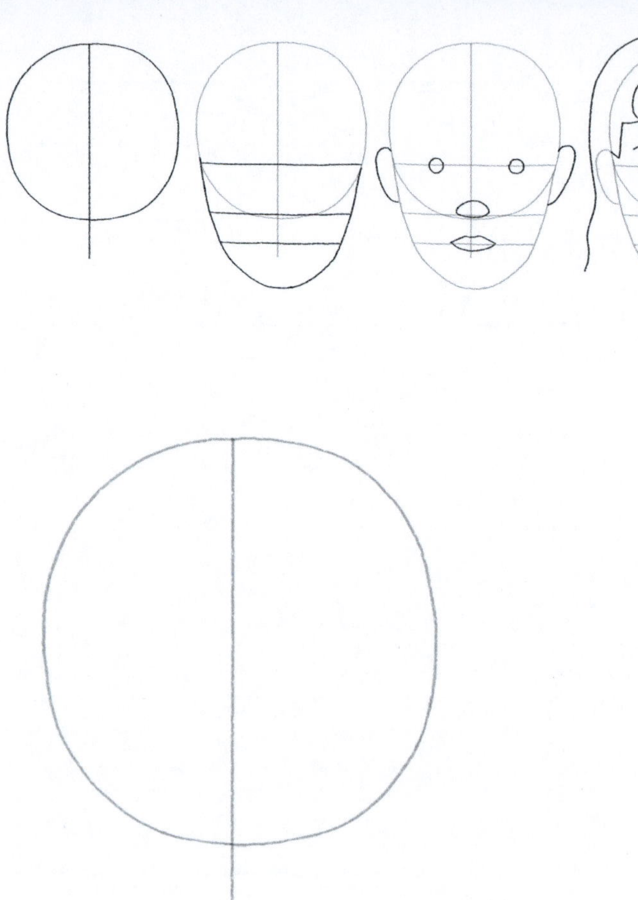

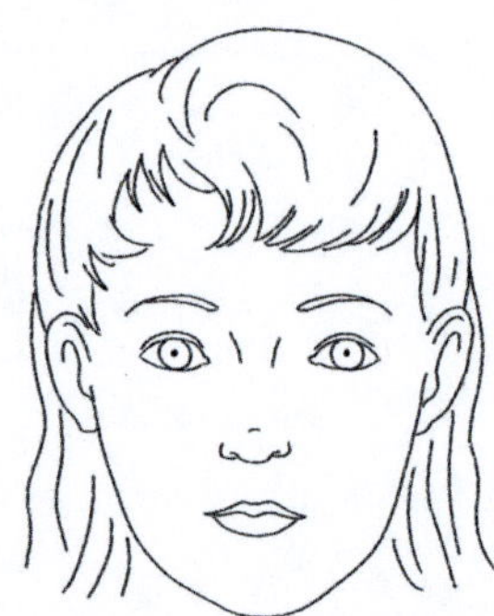

Child's Head

The features of this young girl's face are quite delicate. An invisible line divides the face in half, helping to keep the eyes, eyebrows and nose symmetrical.

362nd day

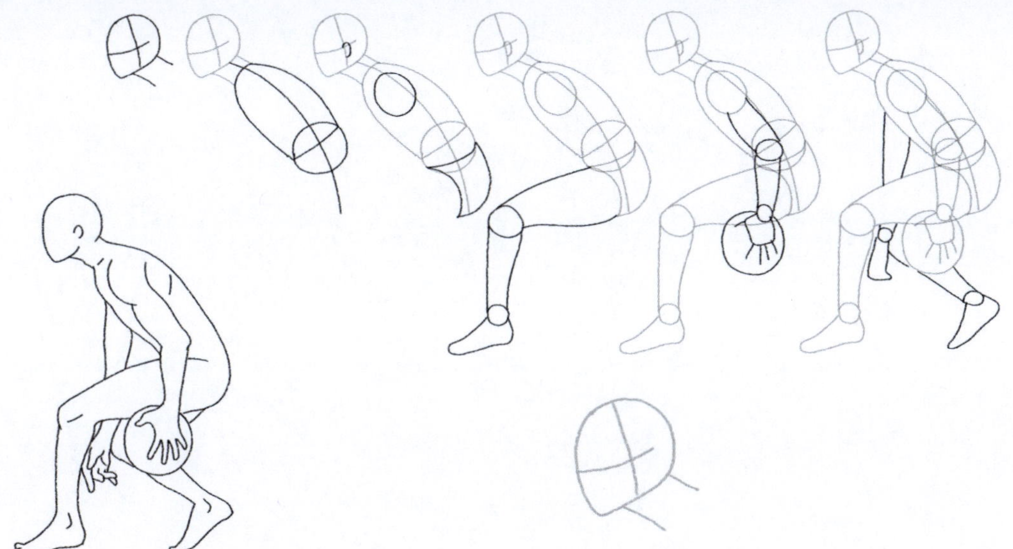

Basketball
Player

This figure is bent over and
moving forward. Even with
this odd gait, one arm and the
opposite leg are moving together
in the same direction.

363rd day

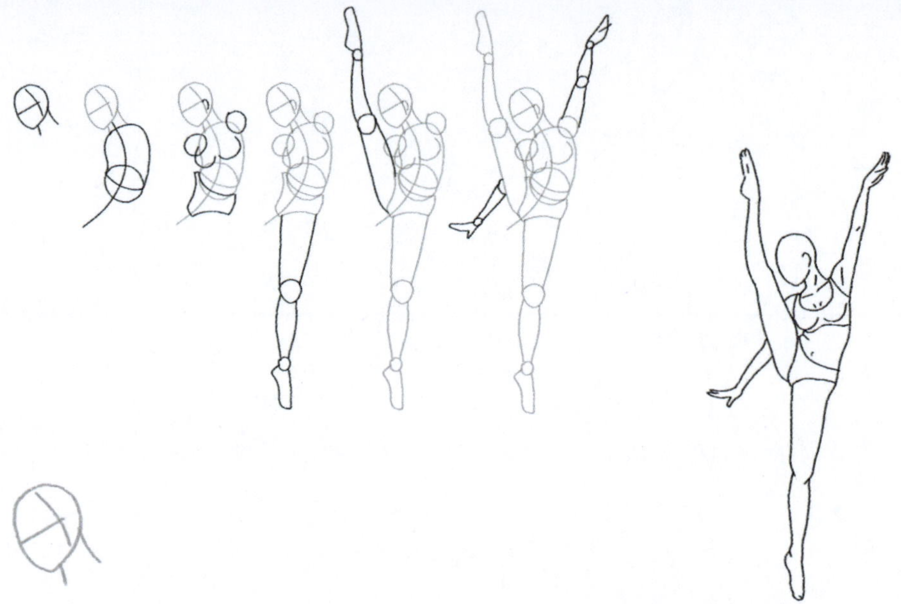

Dancer

One leg and the opposite arm
of this figure point upward.
The other limbs are stretched
downward, and the torso is
twisted to the side.

364th day

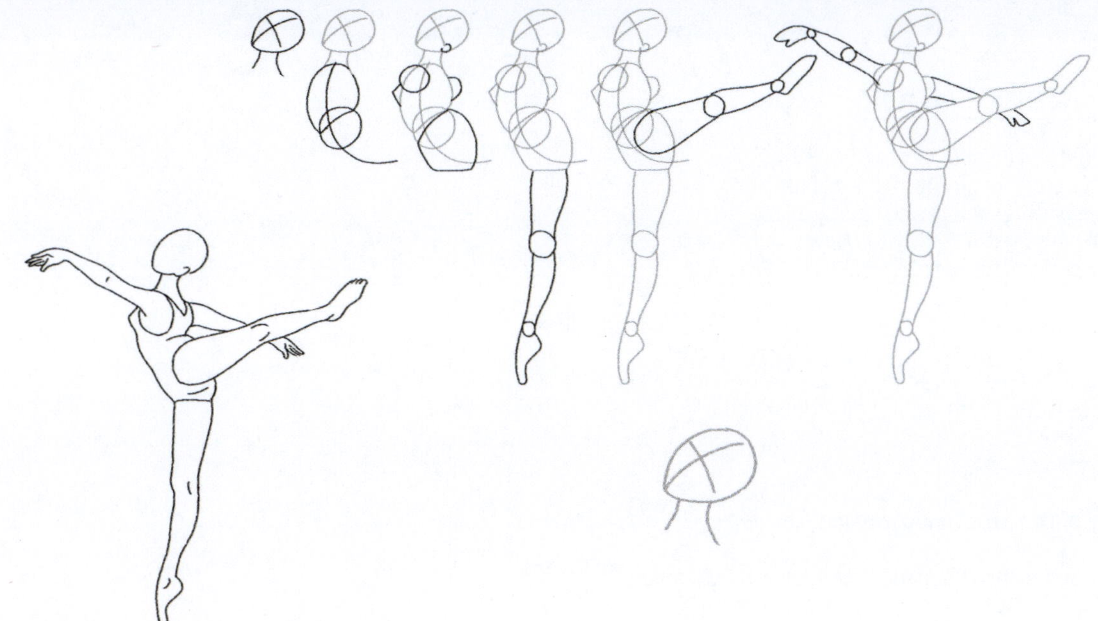

Dancer

This figure is pivoting her body on the leg stretched down to the floor. Every other part of her body is pointing in a different direction.

365th day

A FIREFLY BOOK

Published by Firefly Books Ltd. 2025
English translation © Firefly Books Ltd. 2025
Text and illustrations © Lise Herzog 2023
© First published in French by Mango, Paris, France 2023
as *365 personnages facile* (9782317032929)

First printing

Library of Congress Control Number: 2024949213

Library and Archives Canada Cataloguing in Publication
Title: 365 days of drawing people / Lise Herzog.
Other titles: 365 personnages faciles. English | Three hundred sixty-five
    days of drawing people
Names: Herzog, Lise, author, illustrator
Description: Translation of: 365 personnages faciles.
Identifiers: Canadiana 20240507096 | ISBN 9780228105329 (hardcover)
Subjects: LCSH: Figure drawing—Technique. | LCSH: Human figure in art.
Classification: LCC NC765 .H4713 2025 | DDC 743.4—dc23

Published in the United States by
Firefly Books (U.S.) Inc.
P.O. Box 1338, Ellicott Station
Buffalo, New York 14205

Published in Canada by
Firefly Books Ltd.
50 Staples Avenue, Unit 1
Richmond Hill, Ontario L4B 0A7

Translation: Nancy Foran

Printed in China | E

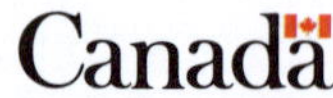

We acknowledge the financial support
of the Government of Canada.